AF600619

ENGAGING ITALY

ENGAGING ITALY

AMERICAN WOMEN'S UTOPIAN VISIONS AND TRANSNATIONAL NETWORKS

ETTA M. MADDEN

Cover: Emily Bliss Gould, engraving by A. H. Ritchie, based on portrait by Lorenzo Suscipj, Rome, from Leonard Woolsey Bacon, *A Life Worth Living*. Courtesy of the New York Public Library. (right)

Anne Hampton Brewster, carte de visite, Fratelli D'Alessandri, Rome, ca. 1874. Courtesy of the Library Company of Philadelphia. (upper left)

Caroline Crane Marsh, ca. 1866, Fratelli Alinari, Florence. Courtesy of Silver Special Collections Library, University Of Vermont. (lower left)

Gould's published "manuscript" letter to Sunday School children, from *Italo-American Schools at Rome* [1874], New-York Historical Society. (center)

Published by State University of New York Press, Albany

Printed in the United States of America

For information, contact State University of New York Press, Albany, NY
www.sunypress.edu

Library of Congress Cataloging-in-Publication Data

Name: Madden, Etta M., 1962– author.
Title: Engaging Italy : American women's utopian visions and transnational networks / Etta M. Madden.
Description: Albany : State University of New York Press, [2022] | Includes bibliographical references and index.
Identifiers: LCCN 2021054853 (print) | LCCN 2021054854 (ebook) | ISBN 9781438488431 (hardcover : alk. paper) | ISBN 9781438488448 (ebook)
Subjects: LCSH: Women—Italy—History—19th century. | Americans—Italy—History—19th century. | Italy—Politics and government—1849–1870.
Classification: LCC HQ1638 .M329 2022 (print) | LCC HQ1638 (ebook) | DDC 305.420945—dc23/eng/20220104
LC record available at https://lccn.loc.gov/2021054853
LC ebook record available at https://lccn.loc.gov/2021054854

10 9 8 7 6 5 4 3 2 1

To all the Italians and Italophiles
who have inspired and sustained this project

Contents

List of Illustrations ix

Acknowledgments xi

Note on the Text xv

Introduction 1

Part I. Portraits of Diversity

Chapter 1 Backstories of Diversity 29

Chapter 2 Vignettes of Diversity 41

Chapter 3 Summer of the Roman Question: A Window on Transnational Networks 59

Part II. Circuits and Networks

Chapter 4 Revising *Daisy Miller*: The Story of "Miss Jones" 73

Chapter 5 "The Daily Ordinary": Language, Lodgings and Hostessing 95

Chapter 6 Circulating People, Circulating Texts: Associational Life 111

Part III. Varieties of Utopian Experiences

Chapter 7 Utopian Visions, Reform, and Religious Beliefs 135

Chapter 8 Emily Bliss Gould: "Works and Wants" 161

Chapter 9 Anne Hampton Brewster: A Catholic Correspondent Negotiates New Rome 195

Chapter 10 Caroline Crane Marsh: "The Power of Doing a Great Service" 229

Coda: Residual Ripples 251

Appendix A: "To ____ ____." 257

Appendix B: "For Queen Anne" 259

List of Abbreviations 261

Notes 263

Bibliography 291

Index 311

List of Illustrations

Figure I.1	Note from Henry Wadsworth Longfellow's daughter, accepting the Thomas Buchanan Read family's invitation for dinner and entertainment.	2
Figure 2.1	George Perkins Marsh in Villa Forini library, Florence.	45
Figure 2.2	Caroline Crane Marsh, seated right, with George Perkins Marsh and sister Lucy Crane, ca. 1849.	51
Figure 2.3	Caroline Crane Marsh, ca. 1866, Fratelli Alinari, Florence.	52
Figure 2.4	Caroline Crane Marsh, ca. 1881, Schemboche Galleries.	53
Figure 2.5	Alexander B. Crane, ca. 1881, Schemboche Galleries.	53
Figure 2.6	Caroline Emma Crane, ca. 1881, Schemboche Galleries.	54
Figure 2.7	Emily Bliss Gould, engraving by A. H. Ritchie, based on portrait by Lorenzo Suscipj, Rome, from Leonard Woolsey Bacon, *A Life Worth Living.*	55
Figure 2.8	Emily Bliss Gould with Venetian Bartoli children, from *Italo-American Schools at Rome* [1874], New-York Historical Society.	55
Figure 2.9	Anne Hampton Brewster, carte de visite, Fratelli D'Alessandri, Rome, ca. 1874.	56
Figure 2.10	Antonio Canova's *Venus Victrix,* ca. 1838, Villa Borghese, Rome.	57

Figure 6.1 Louise Chandler Moulton manuscript poem, "For Queen Anne," Rome, 1876. 116

Figure 6.2 Accademia dell'Arcadia membership certificate. 125

Figure 8.1 Gould's published "manuscript" letter to Sunday School children, from *Italo-American Schools at Rome* [1874], New-York Historical Society. 180

Figure 9.1 Brewster's gift copy of *Ballads*, from author Amelia B. Edwards, "her faithful & attached friend." 226

Figure 10.1 Torn letter from Mario Gigliucci to Caroline Crane Marsh's niece Ellen (addressed as "Elena"). 233

Figure C.1 Announcement of Gould's memorial service, Fourth Avenue Presbyterian Church, with address by Rev. Howard Crosby. 254

Figure C.2 Gould family tombstone, Woodlawn Cemetery, NY, with inscription, "SHE HATH DONE WHAT SHE COULD," from Leonard Woolsey Bacon, *A Life Worth Living*. 255

Acknowledgments

Since this project began eight years ago, the number of people supporting it has mushroomed. Apologies in advance for any oversight of those deserving thanks and recognition. As with most projects, *Engaging Italy* developed through several semesters of teaching, delivering conference presentations, and receiving feedback from colleagues. Additionally, beyond a Fulbright teaching award that initially stimulated my curiosity on the topic in 2009, the financial and emotional support of several fellowships have sustained it. A fellowship from the Library Company of Philadelphia enabled archival work on Anne Hampton Brewster in 2013 and a 2014 Faculty Research Grant from Missouri State University's Graduate College supported bibliographic work on Brewster's extensive library and writings. It also kick started the archival work on Caroline Crane Marsh and Emily Bliss Gould. An MSU sabbatical award in 2015–16 enabled me to give the project full attention. I remain indebted to the Dean of the College of Arts and Letters, the English Department Heads W. D. Blackmon and Linda Moser, and the Graduate College for their ongoing support and belief in the importance of research, even where teaching takes priority. A fellowship from the New York Public Library provided another stepping stone in 2018 along what had become an uncertain path of drafting clear prose.

Initial conversations with several colleagues about women in Italy triggered questions and fostered research. Early in the process, Sirpa Salenius introduced me to Constance Fenimore Woolson's brilliant fiction, shared her scholarship on Americans in Italy, and invited me to write more on little-known Anglo women abroad. She welcomed me to Florence and Tuscany many times with open arms. Briggs Bailey listened to my first thoughts about this project at a tea sponsored jointly by the Margaret Fuller and Catherine Maria Sedgwick societies during a conference of the

Society for the Study of American Women Writers (SSAWW). Members of those organizations and their gatherings have kept me going, but Bailey in particular encouraged me along the way and reminded me by example that books do not simply appear overnight and in a vacuum.

Presentations on panels at conferences of the SSAWW, Communal Studies Association, Society for Utopian Studies, Catherine Maria Sedgwick Society, Constance Fenimore Woolson Society, Margaret Fuller Society, Transatlantic Women II, and the Michel de Montaigne Foundation at Bagni di Lucca garnered feedback on small segments of the work. I owe thanks especially to those who read versions of the manuscript in whole or in part and provided astute suggestions or affirmation later in the process: in addition to Bailey, Elizabeth DeWolfe, David Kertzer, Carol Harrison, Martha Finch, Kate Culkin, Leslie Baynes, and members of the Midwest Nineteenth-Century Americanists writing group led by Melissa Homestead and Laura Mielke: Jill K. Anderson, Jessica DeSpain, Steffi Dippold, Erin Kappeler, Rebecca Bechtold, Timothy Robbins, Matt Cohen, and John Evelev.

Additionally, readers who reviewed articles on Brewster and Marsh that were published elsewhere helped me to see where I had too many details and, likewise, where I didn't have enough. An earlier version of chapter 9 appeared in Roberta Ferrari and Laura Giovannelli's *Questioni di genere: Femminilità e effeminatezza nella cultura vittoriana* and part of chapter 10 appeared in a special collection edited by Stéphanie Durrans for *Transatlantica*, the journal of the French Association for American Studies.[1] Thank you, Stéphanie, for your patience during that process, and Roberta and Laura, for your friendship and collegial support during and since our time together in Pisa and Bagni di Lucca.

Of particular note, an NEH Seminar at the American Academy in Rome in 2013 not only grounded me in the historical period known as the Risorgimento but introduced me to the city and its archives and a host of scholars of all ages. To John Davis and David Kertzer, especially, I owe many thanks for bringing together a diverse set of scholars and bridging interdisciplinary boundaries in a convivial manner. Many of these colleagues—notably, the women of 3D—have continued to encourage me. Carol Harrison, Caterina Pierre, and Morena Corradi—may we maintain the fond memories and mutual support of those short weeks together. Others at the seminar have also provided support—especially Tulio Pagano, who translated a letter when I could not make out the hand, Claire Kovacs, who helped with portraiture, Wendy Pojmann, who continually advises on issues of Italian-English parlance, and Stephen Soper, whose brilliant work on associationalism in Italy gave me a deeper understanding of what these women were and were not doing within their networks. As a result of that seminar, I met Elèna Mortara, whose award-winning scholarship in American Studies, suggested readings, and collegial support have lifted my spirits on several occasions.

And there are those in the archives who pulled photos, folders, and boxes, answered questions about documents and, at times, helped decipher handwriting: Connie King, at the Library Company of Philadelphia, who pointed me to Gould and has remained one of my greatest cheerleaders; Chris Burns in the Silver Special Collections at the University of Vermont; Tal Nadan and her colleagues in the Brooke Russell Astor Reading Room for Rare Books and Manuscripts of the New York Public Library; and staff of the New York Historical Society and the New York University Fales Library and Special Collections. I remain indebted to several in Italy as well: Alyson Price (formerly of the British Institute) in Florence; Gabriella Ballesio and Luca Pilone of the Archivio Tavola Valdese in Torre Pellice; the Valdese archives in Florence; the Biblioteca Nazionale, the American Institute, and the Archivio of the Museo del Risorgimento in Rome.

Several graduate students at Missouri State assisted with bibliographic and editorial details and have since sailed off to brighter futures: Gail Edie, Natalie Whitaker, and Nicole Duncan Rikard, thank you.

I owe thanks as well to friends and family. Fellow Italophile and scholar Saundra Weddle encouraged me through numerous lunches and dinners and also listened tirelessly by the side of the pool on steamy August afternoons in the Ozarks and over *colazione* in Venice. Friends (and friends of friends) with National Avenue Christian Church allowed me to share some of these thoughts with them as we prepared to travel and as we walked through the streets of Rome, Florence, Torre Pellice, Lucca, and Bagni di Lucca. Among those, thanks especially to John White, and to his wife Myrna, for sharing with me their knowledge of Rome, past and present. My Saturday morning cycling buddies, who give the impression of being all ears as they pedal along, must think my interest in women in Italy insufferable. Thanks to them for appearing to listen. And, of course, to Neil Guion, who continues to ride along with almost all my dreams, even after so many years, I owe much more than thanks.

Note on the Text

Nineteenth-century manuscripts—especially letters and diaries—pose a challenge to the researcher translating materials for contemporary readers. How to capture the numerous abbreviations (often singular to the author), the underlining and double-underlining, the superscripts and strikethroughs, the seemingly careless errors in punctuation or spelling? These features often capture the emotions and intensity of the author's inscriptions. At other times, however, the shorthand and errors may be distracting—or even confusing—for contemporary readers. For this project, which relied so heavily on manuscripts, I chose to silently change some spelling, capitalization, and punctuation to conform to contemporary practices. I have kept underlining to highlight the author's emphasis, distinguished from my added emphasis, which is in italics. Similarly, for ease of reading the notes, I have employed abbreviations for frequently used authors' names, books, archives, and archival material.

Introduction

Men of Poetry, Politics, and Power: A Series of Fortunate Events

In December of 1868 Henry Wadsworth Longfellow, lauded for capturing ideals of American individualism, patriotism, and public sentiment in his poetry, arrived in Rome to a series of grand celebrations. Americans and Italians alike admired this fireside poet and esteemed Harvard professor. Children memorized his verses and well-educated adults praised his translation of Dante. This visit, Longfellow's celebrated second sojourn on the peninsula, differed notably from his first—as a little-known young scholar of languages in the late 1820s. Now the events celebrating the poet dotted the international news. One of these accounts was by New Yorker Emily Bliss Gould, then an expatriate in Rome. Gould wrote for Bret Harte's *Overland Monthly*, a California periodical similar to the *Alta California* where Mark Twain's columns on travel—soon to become *Innocents Abroad* (1869)—had begun a year earlier. Gould penned what Harte labeled his "Gossip Abroad" column. Often more political news than commentary on social life, Gould's correspondence that January reported on the affairs surrounding Longfellow's stay in Rome, as well as on events at St. Peter's, preparations for the Vatican Council, battles elsewhere in Europe, and activities of the royal families. Among the winter festivities for the "number of American residents" wintering there, Gould explained, Pennsylvania painter and poet Thomas Buchanan Read had hosted "dinner and . . . evening entertainment" in order "to greet Professor Longfellow."[2]

The "season in Rome" was short that year. The brevity was not because ice briefly glazed Bernini's many fountains, surprising locals and sending them scurrying through the slippery streets rather than sauntering on their

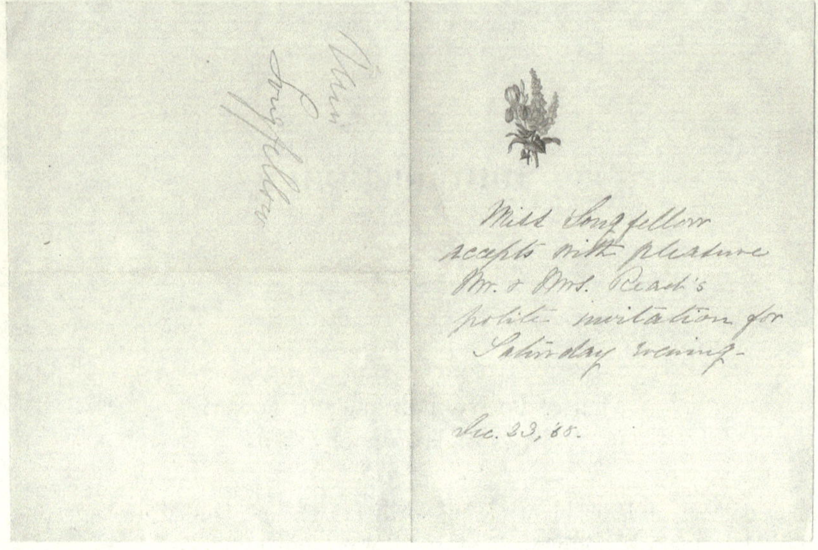
Miss Longfellow
Miss Longfellow
accepts with pleasure
Mr. & Mrs. Read's
polite invitation for
Saturday evening.
Dec. 23, 68.

Figure I.1. Note from Henry Wadsworth Longfellow's daughter, accepting the Thomas Buchanan Read family's invitation for dinner and entertainment. Credit: The Library Company of Philadelphia.

evening strolls. Instead, Lent, marking the end of the festivities, fell early. As a result, expatriates were "almost wild with the engagements that more than fill our days and nights," Gould explained. These affairs no longer bore "the simplicity which [previously] marked the entertainments given at Rome." That simple mode was "vanishing" as the decadent "habits of New York and Boston . . . resumed under the shadow of St. Peter's and the Coliseum." One dinner, for example, included peacock served with "brilliant tail and all."[3] Longfellow's arrival merited such occasions for lavish social performances, according to Gould: "We who have been armed at his hand, and strengthened at his armory for the battle of life, delight to do him what honor we may. Dinners and balls, breakfasts and suppers, receptions and concerts, follow each other in quick succession." His admirers abroad fought to be part of the affairs, she suggested in conclusion: "if to the usual social charm of Roman gatherings is added that of his society, we esteem ourselves happy indeed."[4]

Another Longfellow event that winter, also an elaborate dinner party, was detailed by Gould's neighbor near Rome's Spanish Steps, Anne Hampton Brewster. "The Longfellow receptions and dinners are numerous—many of them brilliant," she wrote. "Mr. and Mrs. Childs entertainment last week was superb." Brewster's introduction to George W. Childs—publisher of Philadelphia's *Public Ledger*—and his wife emerged through the Read family, with whom she had lived since her arrival in Rome in early November. The introduction enabled her to send letters to the *Philadelphia Evening Bulletin* and the *Boston Daily Advertiser*. This publishing agreement began after the evening with Longfellow—for Brewster a fortunate event that fostered her goals as a writer abroad. At the time of the Childs dinner, she had written only one account, of "American Artists in Rome," focused on Read and the sculptor Joseph Mozier. Brewster's detailed notes of the Longfellow dinner, recorded privately in her journal, suggest that she anticipated writing another article for the American press. She wrote of the dinner, "Flowers, lights, table decorations, dinner, every detail was perfect. Monsignor Nardi said he had never seen anything of the kind so beautiful." Brewster's journal entry continued, spilling onto several pages in dialogue form, capturing the lively conversation she conducted with the Monsignor Nardi.[5]

Who was this "Monsignor Nardi," who raved about the dinner décor? And why would Brewster expound at length upon his comments and their conversation? Brewster knew Ernesto Francesco Nardi was a key political figure, controversial in his stature as a leader among the pope's inner circle and in his international relations. During this period of political upheaval, in which questions of papal authority and the future of the Kingdom of Italy abounded, many labeled Nardi *nero*—literally translated black, but also designating evil—and at the time signifying association with nobility who supported the pope. He has been described recently by David Kertzer as "one of the most notorious of the *zelanti*," among the zealous supporters of the pope's continued temporal power who garnered a negative reputation among American Protestants for his secretive politics.[6] But not all saw Nardi as evil—or he certainly would not have been included among the Childses' guests for the Longfellow fête. In fact, Longfellow wrote to family friend Jane Norton that although he "never cared much for his political views, whatever they were," Nardi was not so "nero" as he seemed; rather, he was "an active, energetic, stirring personage" who had been "very kind" to the poet's family.[7]

On this festive evening, the stimulating Nardi escorted Brewster to the table, where the two discussed the controversial Syllabus of Errors, at the center of the Vatican Council's deliberations on papal infallibility. During the dinner conversation, Brewster asked Nardi "as frankly as if it were the program of a concert" for a copy of "an ecclesiastical document meant only for the private use of bishops." Although surprised by her American abruptness, Nardi did not give Brewster the cold shoulder. Instead, their playful tête-à-tête in front of Longfellow that evening triggered correspondence between the two and fueled Brewster's international newspaper work. Her regularly published letters to the Philadelphia and Boston papers provided details of the Vatican Council's meetings, such as insights to the 1870 declaration of papal infallibility, gathered from local informants. She continued reporting on affairs abroad for another twenty years.[8]

But Nardi's behavior with Brewster that January evening was not the same as his decorum with all Americans in Italy that winter—including Gould. The same month as the Longfellow dinner, one US periodical headline announced "An Outrage in Rome," directing attention to Gould's arrest for meeting with Protestants in her home. Soon after the arrest, the news account detailed, the Monsignor interrogated Gould before a Roman tribunal. Especially troubling to the reporter, and contributing to what they saw as a scandalous situation, was that an upstanding and virtuous female American underwent such public torture. Gould was not alone in Rome but accompanied by her husband, a retired US naval physician. As the supposed head of household in which the private worship occurred, Dr. James Gould, rather than his wife, should have been the responsible and interrogated party. But she was the accountable social force. Notably, Gould's arrest and interrogation did not suppress her drive. Instead, they intensified her fervor. Gould's activities evolved into educating young, impoverished Catholics in an industrial school and orphanage she established in 1870. Motivated by her hearing before the tribunal, Gould continued to reach out to other Anglos and Italians who she believed would support the cause of education among these children.[9] For Gould as for Brewster, the encounter with Nardi needled her—contributing to a calling and fostering fruition of her utopian visions while abroad.

The public rendering of Gould's arrest depended on other accounts made popular in the press. Roman Catholics' treatment of those outside the church had garnered increasing attention in American newspapers at least since the forced baptism of Edgardo Mortara, a young Jewish boy in Bologna, in 1858. In 1860 Nathaniel Hawthorne, then as renowned as Longfellow, contributed to public interests in Jesuit operations in the US and abroad with his novel *The Marble Faun*, in which Hilda, a young American in Rome, is kidnapped by church officials. Anti-Catholic sentiment in the US had intensified, as the influx of European immigrants contributed to a growing Roman Catholic population in the US, making it the largest denomination by the mid-1840s. Many parishes were bolstered by leadership and missions of Jesuits in exile after the 1848 European revolutions. The numbers had grown from 3 percent of the US population in 1830, continuing to 18 percent in 1900.[10] This context of anti-Catholic sentiment contributed to support for Gould's work.

Gould's school project depended on many Americans in the US as well as in Italy in the 1860s and '70s. As the Longfellow celebrations illustrated, they were a diverse crowd. Brewster, for example, whose interactions with Nardi had been quite different, was a "Southern sympathizer" during the Civil War and a Roman Catholic. Brewster's and Gould's diverse lives and writings reflect the American interests in what came to be called the Roman Question—in short, a question of the relationship of church and state on the Italian peninsula, and the temporal power of Roman Catholic leadership in what had emerged as the newly unified Kingdom of Italy in 1861. Decisions in Italy, of course, would impact events within the US as well as the nation's relationships with others.

This controversial political situation also influenced the writings of New Englander Caroline Crane Marsh, who interacted in the same networks as Brewster and Gould. In fact, Marsh corresponded in 1867 with a friend who participated in the "Sunday night sings" at Gould's home in Rome, and Gould, while visiting Marsh in Florence the same year, had written to the president of the American and Foreign Christian Union (AFCU) seeking help for their reform work.[11] Marsh, as wife of the first US minister plenipotentiary to Italy, George Perkins Marsh, certainly knew of Nardi's reputation, and Gould's arrest and the troubles among Protestants in Rome intensified her relationship with the Marshes. However, the relationship predated this period. In 1860 a young and unmarried New Yorker, Cornelia Mitchell, had traveled to Europe with the Goulds and, a few years after returning from her Grand Tour, wed Marsh's favorite nephew, Alexander B. Crane.[12] Additionally, linked by their mutual interest in social reform, the two women would communicate more after the move of Italy's capital from Florence to Rome in 1871 and the Marshes' transition to that locale.[13] Marsh, neither an evangelical Protestant like Gould, nor a Roman Catholic like Brewster, wrote of her fascination with Norse and eastern mythology and labeled herself a "Progressivist" after reading Matthew Arnold's *Religion and Dogma: An Essay Towards a Better Understanding of the Bible*.[14] She nonetheless supported the Italian "Free Church" movement, its leaders, such as former political exile Salvatore Ferretti, and its social reform efforts. Distinct from these other women, Marsh was a published translator and wrote poetry.

All three, however, saw their writings in print and wrote voluminously in diaries and private correspondence.

To claim that Marsh, Gould, and Brewster were close friends would exaggerate the nature of their relationships. Rather, their shared citizenship and language linked them through networks of transnational concerns and social obligations that endured for many years. They merit attention in these pages because their diverse lives and writings through these years illuminate the powerful symbiotic and generative relations among people and their texts—especially in explosive moments of political uncertainty. When controversial public figures and institutional powers stimulate speculation on the future, social networks provide a powerful generative force for civic activity and reform—even among those acquaintances who hold differing views. Within these networks and activities, writing provides a record and a reinforcement, as well as an enabler of ideas. The ideas about change, also described here as the utopian visions these three American women held, lie at the center of *Engaging Italy*. Gould, Brewster, and Marsh have remained in the shadow of prominent and powerful men of poetry and politics, such as Longfellow and Nardi. Yet notably a series of fortunate events in Rome on the eve of the peninsula's political unification linked them. These events triggered and fostered their activities for more than a decade. These three women illustrate how they seized opportunities to actualize their utopian visions within a network of Americans abroad, some of whom were engaged with the local and global political climate. The women's writings—specifically, their public and private records—revise stories of women abroad, underscoring that many were more than consumers, artists, or mere spectators.

Gould, who established an industrial school and orphanage in Rome in 1870, generated reports, fundraising pamphlets, and letters to political and religious leaders in Italy to foster its growth and continuation. The Istituto Gould, an educational center in Florence, bears witness today to traces of her past and its ongoing influences.[15] Marsh, too, became a leader of a girls' school and orphanage affiliated with Ferretti in Florence, raising funds for it in the US, organizing events, and overseeing teachers—all while writing regularly and overseeing a complex household of family members, visitors, and staff. In addition to translations, poetry, and encyclopedia entries, Marsh wrote her husband's biography after his death. Brewster sent approximately 750 "letters" to more than a half dozen American newspapers—and was reprinted in at least sixty others—during her twenty-year career in Rome. Regular columns in the *Philadelphia Evening Bulletin* and the *Boston Daily Advertiser* won her a following of readers, who anticipated her weekly news from abroad. *Engaging Italy*'s pages bring all three women's labors—trials, triumphs, and limitations—to light. They, like many other women throughout history, fostered social change in ways that deserve recognition. They followed their callings, sometimes fell in the face of challenges, and yet rose to figure out new ways of moving forward. Through their writing in transnational networks, they continually reconceived their identities and capacities as American women concerned with the world around them.

Armchair Travels and Types of Travelers

> We all know Rome and its famous monuments from pictures we have seen in our childhood. No city is so familiar to us.
>
> —Anne Hampton Brewster, November 1868[16]

> The American in Europe, if a thinking mind, can only become more American.
>
> —Margaret Fuller, *New-York Tribune*, 1848[17]

These women's diverse vocations while abroad were prompted in part by factors predating their arrivals in Italy and by prejudices they brought with them. Even before they arrived in Italy, Europe was nothing new to them. Marsh, for example, first traveled through Europe in 1849 en route to Asia, where her husband would serve as US minister to the Ottoman Empire from 1850 to 1854. This period of life abroad, where she witnessed devout and welcoming Muslims as well as the activities of well-intentioned American missionaries, influenced her experiences later in Italy. Brewster arrived in Europe first in 1857, settling in Vevey, Switzerland, and then Naples for an eighteenth-month sojourn, a full decade before she acted on her calling to move abroad for the final time as a news writer in Rome. Gould set out for Europe first with her husband in 1860, arriving in Rome in February of 1861 after a six-month journey on the typical Grand Tour route from Le Havre overland to Genoa and throughout Italy's Piedmont and Tuscan regions—a decade before she established the industrial school. Both Emily and James had hopes that her feeble health, the publicly stated reason for their journey, would improve. But long before arriving on the peninsula, Brewster's, Gould's, and Marsh's appetites for transnational concerns had been piqued by reading what others had written. These readings not only influenced what they experienced while abroad but motivated them to create their own records—in unpublished diaries and letters as well as in published travel sketches and articles.

This material, largely untouched by scholars, provides rich, multifaceted pictures of their diverse transnational experiences, compiled throughout long periods in which the women lived abroad. This temporal expanse distinguishes them from numerous female travelers who kept diaries in which they sketched what they observed with a "tourist gaze." Studies of travel diaries, initiated more than twenty years ago, have enriched awareness of how women traveled and with whom, the paths of their Grand Tours, and the books that influenced these travelers. These studies also note typical reactions to tourist sites, for example, providing a context for Brewster's, Marsh's, and Gould's responses. Their journal accounts changed over time—much different when the women first arrived than they were later, as they wrote about events that filled and punctuated their daily lives during their decades abroad.[18] These records illuminate how the women visualized themselves in relationship to a historical diorama of Americans and others on the Italian peninsula. Their situations early on would dramatize some typical responses of American exceptionalism but they would also play out with unique and diverse experiences on the world stage. The Roman Catholic news correspondent, the evangelical Protestant reformer, and the more liberal *ambasciatrice* each gained humility as they realized their places within another culture.

Before writing their views, of course, they were enticed to travel by reading, an activity common among Americans of their social class—educated individuals from property-owning families with access to private and circulating libraries. Popular authors such as Hawthorne and Longfellow also wrote of Italy even without having traveled there. Hawthorne set his 1844 story "Rappaccini's Daughter" in Padua, long before he arrived in Italy in 1858. Longfellow's 1824 poem "Italian Scenery" renders his imagined vision of Florence's Arno much differently than his reaction upon arrival in the city in 1828 and his 1874 vision in "The Old Bridge at Florence." Johann Wolfgang von Goethe's *Wilhelm Meisters Wanderjahre* and Germaine de Staël's *Corinne*, both early-nineteenth-century fictional accounts, influenced American readers, providing visions of travelers to Italy who were transformed by the experience. Such works evoked a variety of responses in readers, such as Margaret Fuller, also motivated to travel to Rome by her reading of classical literature and history; Emily Dickinson, stimulated to write of the volcanoes Etna and Vesuvius without ever leaving the US;

and Hawthorne's wife, Sophia Peabody.[19] Brewster, Marsh, and Gould as prospective travelers were not alone in having their imaginations influenced by literary visions of Italy. .

Brewster, born into a long-standing Philadelphia family in 1819, read voraciously, borrowing from the library in Philadelphia and annotating numerous books of European history and literature in her personal collection.[20] Marsh, born in 1816 in Berkley, Massachusetts, read transnational literature and translated, long before going to Constantinople.[21] In her early years she exhibited a gift at learning and helping others learn, an attribute that assisted her as a teacher before her marriage as well as in her years as ambassador's wife. Gould also was a teacher in her youth. Born in New York in 1822 as a child of a physician and leader of the American Sunday School Union (ASSU), her early instruction and teaching was in Sunday schools. As the ASSU was enlarging its missionary activities in this period, Gould would have had access to information on life abroad.[22] And later, while abroad, the women continued their readings about the cultures in which they lived.

One illustrative example from Brewster's library is a volume she heavily annotated, A. H. L. Heeren's *A Manual of the History of the Political System of Europe and Its Colonies* (1857), published just prior to her departure for Italy. It helped prepare her for travels and remained with her as she journeyed across the Atlantic and settled in Rome. She scribbled on the back pages and noted dates and distances from Gibraltar during her voyage. Later, she added her views of 1872 occurrences in Rome and quoted from British political figure Sir Russell Odo's writings. In the section entitled "Political Relations of Europe, 1821," she cited points related to Italy, Napoleon III, France, and Prussia from Archibald Alison's *History of Europe* (1866), a book that appeared just two years before she left for Rome.[23]

Brewster also wrote of the impact of her reading and the numerous "pictures" that formed travelers' ideas of Italy. On her arrival in 1868, she described her tour of Rome by moonlight:

> We all know Rome and its famous monuments from pictures we have seen in our childhood. No city is so familiar to us. So of course I knew that this great mass of brick stone, with trees growing on the summit, this immense ellipse was the Flavian Circus, the Colosseum; this the arch of Titus, and that Constantine's, the hill to the left with its fine front of waving trees the Palatine, the other the famous Capitoline.[24]

Brewster's preparatory reading and armchair traveling, later complemented by her own travels and observations, was not unique to her. It typified many nineteenth-century Americans who traveled to Europe. But what was it they were seeking? Why did these and others cross the Atlantic?

Gould's, Marsh's, and Brewster's desires, activities, and accomplishments abroad shine against the backdrop of comments about travel by their well-known contemporaries, Ralph Waldo Emerson and Margaret Fuller. Fuller advocated the possibilities in one of her first letters from abroad published in Horace Greeley's *New-York Tribune.* Drawing from Emersonian ideals, Fuller described three "species" of American travelers and noted what she believed the superior of the three. While there were those who traveled to "spend" and "indulge" themselves in "fashionable clothes" and "good foreign cookery" in order to show off and gain "importance at home," there was also the "conceited," ignorant and bumbling "Jonathan" type, who asserted "that the frogs in one of our swamps make much finer" music than that of an antique European violin. This second type considered everything at home newer, simpler, and more natural—and therefore better than its counterpart abroad. But the ideal third type opened themselves to learn from their experiences in order to return and improve their own country. This type of traveler—with a "thinking mind"—would be a "Jonathan" nonetheless, an identity he could not shed. However, he would be changed in a positive way by experiencing "thought and culture" abroad, even while also becoming "more American."[25] Such changes in the "thinking American" would occur only with what Emerson idealized in his essay "The American Scholar" as "active reading," in which readers moved from the ideas contained in books, to go beyond the study and into the streets. Such "active reading" suggests engagement with immediate surroundings. Fuller experienced such engagement herself as she wrote about her interactions with people on the Italian peninsula.

Notably, Fuller's friend Emerson differed from her on his idea of travel. He wrote in "Self-Reliance," after his first trip to Europe, of the desires to travel to escape or "lose . . . sadness" as always "a fool's paradise." Noting Italy, England, and Egypt, in particular, as "idols" of travelers, he encouraged American artists not to "follow the Past and the Distant" but to consider what is nearby and within.[26] While Fuller was an advocate of allowing people—especially women—to unfold from within, building from their own inclinations and strengths, she considered insights while abroad essential to personal and social improvement. Her writings, recorded for the *Tribune* readers, distinguished her views from Emerson's in that she considered these international interactions part of a "dialectical and cosmopolitan approach to culture and politics," necessary to deconstruct oppositional and hierarchical boundaries. Chief among her visions emerging from these cross-cultural interactions was a razing of supposed sacrosanct "idols," to which she refused to bow. Fuller's views of "idolatry" emerged in her early writings, prior to her travel to Europe, as she considered her own hero worship of men such as her father and Emerson. Moved by the situations of other women she witnessed in rural Massachusetts and in her urban "conversations" and teaching, she fought against "the incorporation of images of patriarchal power ('male idols') within female psyches." What Fuller saw as women's "melancholic imprisonment in postures of idolatry" she would later apply to the people she observed in Italy—both male and female—as they were depicted by other Americans and Anglos in art and literature. Fuller experienced and wrote of her engagement with Italians, as she had with women in the US, in a way that reconstructed their possibilities and their agency.[27] Her view of the possibilities for travel and the openness it provided through cosmopolitan and cultural exchange provide a point of comparison—and perhaps even influence—for the experiences of other American women abroad.

Gould, Marsh, and Brewster knew of Fuller and likely knew of her writings, as many educated people of the northeastern US did. The Marshes' library contained at least one biography of Fuller, and Gould hosted Fuller's New England Transcendentalist peer, Elizabeth Peabody. Brewster referred specifically to Fuller as she employed the "Jonathan" type in a sketch of Americans in Rome in 1869. In this *Philadelphia Evening Bulletin* letter, Brewster also referred to the Transcendentalist Fuller's time in the failed Fourierest community Brook Farm, where Hawthorne also lived for several months before his marriage.[28] Most importantly, the women's experiences abroad suggest Fuller's concepts of American travelers might be revised and extended to apply to those who remained abroad long enough to be more than tourists.

Three new categories emerging from Fuller's concepts would be, first, those Americans who chose isolation and almost ignored the Italian political landscape; second, those who observed it—as part of the "museum" or "spectacle" Mark Twain and Henry James described when they wrote of Americans abroad—or as a form of entertainment that would reinforce their own concepts of what was good with America; and finally, those such as Marsh, Brewster, and Gould who were open to engage with it more fully and were transformed by these interactions. Fuller advocated that the ideal travelers would bring new insights back to the United States upon their returns. However, Gould, Brewster, and Marsh began to live differently while in Italy.[29] They were open to change while pursuing vocations abroad although they, like Fuller, wrestled with the idols that had been established in their lives as American genteel women. Challenges abounded, though certainly not of the same type they would have faced had they been victims of slavery or of forced exile from scenes of political chaos and war. Some of these challenges emerged due to their American "exceptionalism"—that self-centered perception Fuller described, in which their views were best; other challenges emerged because of their gender and cultural norms about women.

Circumscribed Women and Later Vocations

> I like to think of women as half angels, as we should be.
>
> —Anne Hampton Brewster, *Journal*, 1872[30]

> The woman who has peculiar gifts has a definite line marked out for her, and the call . . . may be as imperative as that which calls the missionary into the moral field or the mother into the family . . .
>
> —Maria Mitchell, 1891[31]

The stories of Marsh, Gould, and Brewster, as they left the northeastern US and sailed abroad, illuminate decisive actions in response to callings, even as they were somewhat circumscribed as women. Their motivations for travel abroad remain relevant among discussions of nineteenth-century female travelers and literary heroines. Why did women such as Brewster, Gould, and Marsh travel? For health or for recreation? For business or pleasure? Did they seek, like so many nineteenth-century Americans taking their Grand Tour of Europe, to be educated and improved, or was the Tour merely a false front for self-indulgence? Did they hope to improve only themselves, or did they wish also to improve the people and places in which they found themselves? The questions suggest simple binaries, of course, and the answers are much more complex. These women imagined nineteenth-century Italy would expose them to centuries of traditions in art, architecture, religion, and culture, leading to self-improvement and, later, improving those with whom they interacted. They imagined life would be less expensive, full of good food and wine, and they might be free from some of society's strictures. They imagined sunnier skies and a warmer climate than that of the northeastern cities they left. These imaginings—their utopian visions—prompted them to act, when at midlife they faced the possibilities of doing otherwise.

The women's visions and accounts of attempts to actualize them within the larger social and cultural contexts exhibit themes of "utopianism" as it has been discussed since Thomas More wrote his 1516 work, *Utopia.* His title captured the impossibilities of achieving *eutopia*, as he punned with the Greek prefixes "ou" and "eu," designating a "good place" that is always "no place." More's vision of a good place impossible to be reached emerged when England was in the throes of economic despair, crime brought about by hunger, and what is now called a "welfare gap." Since then, "utopianism," or "social dreaming" as it has been defined, generally has suggested a civic element, an attempt to improve "the good of the whole" through restructuring of flawed systems.[32] Such "social dreaming," however, often accompanies visions of individual improvement. These personal desires for improvement lie in tension with dreams of making society a better place. The tension sometimes grows too tight, snapping as civic rules stifle individual freedoms, or self-centered desires demonstrate no concern for larger society. Both extremes are dystopian. But the dialectical nature of utopian dreaming dances between the two.

Not only does utopian dreaming shuttle between visions of the present, the past, and a possible future, it often occurs through conversations—or even disagreements—with others. As More's text illustrates, a Platonic dialogue between characters and assumed readers should engage them in thinking about a society or world different from the one they already know and in which they live. Gould, Brewster, and Marsh carried on such dialogues and conversations—with themselves, with others, and with the texts they read. These linguistic activities—including translation—enabled them to dream of lives different from those in which they seemed limited or confined. Nonetheless, as they stepped out on these paths of action, their dreams devolved from a perfect or good place sometimes into quasi-nightmares of its opposite. For the three, these shifts did not generally occur because of their own self-centered desires taking over, but more often as they realized their relative lack of power in the newly unified Kingdom of Italy. Their transformations occurred as they faced their limited positions. As privileged American women endowed with a degree of "exceptionalism," they awakened to the realities of living in a culture that was not their own.

The women's limitations emerged not only from their being outsiders in another culture but also because of gender and their relationships with men, who held much influence over them. Marsh went abroad because of her husband's appointment. Gould traveled with her husband—supposedly for her health, but also as he began a new part of his professional path. Each depended on her husband's finances, to a degree. Brewster, too, relied on some inheritance from her father—although she wrestled with her brother for it. Most notably, though, all three chose behaviors that did not push them to live on the margins of community. Instead, they circulated at the center of networks of Anglos and Americans abroad. And despite any desires they may have had for freedom and independence, they remained within the bounds of behaviors expected of women in the era.

Two statements Brewster wrote illustrate this circumscribed situation. As she wrote to her friend Thomas Davidson, describing her professional and personal struggle with Roman civic leader Rodolfo Lanciani, Brewster confessed and admitted defeat: "I gave in, woman like."[33] She languished in the shadows of Lanciani's limelight, in part because she refused to go beyond the bounds of what was considered appropriate female behavior. Brewster also wrote in her journal in response to the radical behaviors of writer Amelia Edwards, known for her racy romances and lifestyle. When she met Brewster in Rome, the two spent several stimulating evenings together. During the period of their encounters, Edwards began wearing a ring, signaling her marriage to her female traveling companion. Near the end of their short and intense relationship, Brewster wrote of the shock of "women loving women" and confessed, "I like to think of women as half angels, as we should be."[34] Brewster, like Gould and Marsh, chose actions that did not defy her understandings of acceptable womanhood. As a result, these women have fallen into archival crevices.

These privileged women knew of the conversations about questionable behaviors of women in Italy. They knew the stories of the *improvisatrice* Corinne, based on the Roman poet Corilla Olimpica, made famous by Madame de Staël's novel of that title, and how the American Fuller was said to have followed her path. They knew of American artists Louisa Lander and Harriet Hosmer and actress Charlotte Cushman, the "female Romeo," who was scorned for breaking gender boundaries. These women's behaviors, admired by some, helped to circumscribe Brewster, Gould, and Marsh within a compromising vision of "women as half angels." Yet these three older women acted nonetheless. The stories of their visions, engagement, and transformations merit consideration on two accounts: first, for how they reveal the women's decisions to take action, fostered largely by the networks in which they interacted; and second, for how writing significantly developed, sustained, and recorded those deliberative actions. This book intertwines their literary activities and the voluminous pages each generated with the women's decisive behaviors in their public and private lives, noting at the same time the difficulty of distinguishing between public and private realms as they wrote for themselves, family, friends, and the larger world. These transnational networks in which they lived and wrote expand our understanding of women's lives and influences. Finally, these pages illustrate their changing utopian visions, as they recognized the problems of American exceptionalism and their own limitations. They did what they could, as women following their later vocations in Italy.

Of course, these women were not the only American women, writers, and artists who traveled to and lived in Italy, with attention to the political and social upheaval surrounding them. Marsh's husband had noted in an official dispatch of 1868 that "many Americans . . . for long terms of years . . . spent considerable periods in this country for reasons of health, economy, society and culture." He wrote of his opposition to impending trade taxes that he feared would doom the long-standing relationships between the two countries, explaining that Americans had never paid taxes to Italy. The potential imposition of taxes on Italians in the US might lead to reciprocity on those living abroad. In fact, temporary visitors as well as those who chose longer sojourns had "pursued different branches of art, industry, and commerce" and had increased dramatically in the Jacksonian and antebellum years.[35] Many of these Americans were women. The Grand Tour expected of elite men early in the century as part of their education, somewhat typical of privileged newly married couples on their honeymoons, and occasionally experienced by single women traveling with families, changed as the century progressed. The numbers exploded and began to include women traveling with other women or alone in the Gilded Age.[36] The stories of several of these travelers, especially visual artists, have been told.

Perhaps best known among these, news correspondent Fuller—the "Mythic Margaret"—looms large in the study of Americans in Italy. Fuller's tragic death by drowning just prior to reaching New York on her return home to the States in 1850 undoubtedly has contributed to her mythic stature. Her relationship with Emerson and her "foreign correspondence" for Greeley's politically progressive *New-York Tribune* had gained her quite an audience before she, her young son, and his father, Giovanni Ossoli, fled the political upheavals on the Italian peninsula following the Roman revolution of 1848 and the short-lived Republic in the Eternal City. In addition to Fuller, many other women not as "mythic" engaged in social and political activism. English-born Jessie White Mario, for example, also witnessed military battles and wrote of them for American (as well as British) newspapers. Frances Power Cobbe wrote from Florence for the British press, and Eliza Lynn Linton also wrote of the social needs of impoverished children in Florence rather than romanticizing tourist sites. Hosmer and Edmonia Lewis responded to political controversy in the US and around them through their sculptures. And reformer Sarah Parker Remond—neither a visual artist nor a widely published author—contributed to abolition and equal rights movements through her European lecture circuit, medical studies, and a career in Italy.[37]

In light of these numerous American and British women traveling to and living in Italy, and the numerous men who were traveling as well, two questions often asked about this project are "Why women?" and "Why *these* women?" The answers—at least to the first question—seem obvious to anyone familiar with women's history and the pages that have been printed since the 1970s, when recovering stories of women's lives long left languishing began to flourish within and outside of the academy. As the field of history emerged in the nineteenth century, decisions about genre and style impacted content as well, eliminating many works by intelligent, observant women writers such as Staël, whose histories did not fit the boundary-delineating definitions. Their works, what came to be referred to inappropriately as "amateur writing," became distinct from "a more transcendent, professionalized, male realm of history writing." By contrast, "women who made their living by writing for the marketplace" fell into a different category, although they combed libraries, newspapers, and artifacts for their sources, and at the same time "wrote endlessly, managed childbirths, families, and political catastrophe while doing so." They "tried to make this material vibrant in travel books and historical novels," even while they "haggled with publishers for terms."[38] These smart, insightful works they left behind enlarge our views of culture and its strata, the numerous layers factoring in to social forces which lead to change.

Through their writings, the answer to the second question, "Why *these* women," begins to emerge. The women in this study wrote genres that even today might not be deemed "serious" works—newspaper correspondence, fundraising reports, translations of poetry, and original verses, encyclopedia entries, and biography—yet they contributed to American and international history in the process. Additionally, their experiences enlarge arguments about domesticity and "woman's sphere," especially in recent decades interested in globalization and mobility.[39] These women not only pushed the traditionally conceived boundaries of the "home" but also labored outside the "domestic" US space while they engaged with global affairs as they followed their "vocations" in Italy. I employ the term "vocations" to distinguish Brewster, Gould, and Marsh from what others have written about American women's transformative experiences abroad. Helen Barolini, for example, describes Italy's "lure" that enabled "personal metamorphoses," and Sirpa Salenius has described the reasons for travel to Italy and its outcomes as "acculturation" and "self-fulfillment" where "Americans could concretize their potential."[40]

Records illustrating the successes of such female "professionals" abound—from the sculptors Hosmer and Lewis to the widely published American authors Catharine Maria Sedgwick, Harriet Beecher Stowe, and Constance Fenimore Woolson. While these studies provide valid explanations of their female subjects, Gould's, Brewster's, and Marsh's experiences stray from prior patterns. Although all three women were transformed, *Engaging Italy* adds attention to each woman's response to a calling, or "later vocation," not initially anticipated. Each vocation centered on a "utopian vision" that arose from reflections on and negotiations with their past lives, present social situations, and uncertain futures. These negotiations, as laid bare here, distinguish these women's stories.

Bergland's description of Maria Mitchell's life, travels, and writing are helpful in making this point. Mitchell, late in her life, reflected on women with a "call from God," a phrase that aptly depicts Brewster's, Gould's, and Marsh's activities in Italy. Mitchell expounded in 1891, reflecting on earlier years and their contemporaries:

> The woman who has peculiar gifts has a definite line marked out for her, and the call from God to do his work in the field of scientific investigation may be as imperative as that which calls the missionary into the moral field or the mother into the family: as missionary, or as scientist, as sister or as mother, no woman has the right to lose her individuality.

Mitchell went on to comment on the impact of specific nineteenth-century women whose exemplary "callings" had an influence on her own professional trajectory, in a sense recognizing what I call a "sisterhood of support" even as she emphasized "the right to . . . individuality": "We cannot overrate the consequences of such lives, whether it be Mrs. Somerville translating

LaPlace, Harriet Hosmer modeling her statues, Mrs. Browning writing her poems or Caroline Herschel spending nights under the open canopy; in all *it is devotion to idea, the loyalty to duty* which reaches to all ages."[41] This "devotion to an idea" and "loyalty to duty" by a translator, a visual artist, a poet, and an astronomer indicate what I label "vocations." The term "vocation," used interchangeably with "profession" in its secular sense, notes a movement to a particular type of work, or "special function," toward which a person seems to have a "natural tendency . . . or fitness." However, the primary definition of "vocation" includes also a spiritual or "divine influence" that "directs" or guide a person.[42] This definition of "vocation" evokes the "devotion" and "duty" Mitchell describes and the sense of calling that reverberates in the writings of Brewster, Marsh, and Gould. It also suggests the use of "engaging" in this book's title.

Engagement in the realm of courtship and marriage sometimes connotes an ethereal or ineffable bond that links people privately, yet it also indicates a bond that has public manifestations, and it suggests commitment to duty and responsibility. Sometimes the scientific metaphor of "chemistry" describes such an engagement, as though a rational, mathematic equation might explain a link otherwise considered inexplicable. So, too, whether considered divinely inspired or rationally explained, Brewster, Marsh, and Gould became engaged by the environment of Italy, called to "special functions" while abroad. For Brewster, it was relaying to the US information about the Vatican and the politics of new Rome, the latest excavations, and social and cultural events she deemed important to them. For Gould, it was raising funds for and directing the Roman schools that she believed would save spiritually and economically impoverished Italians. For Marsh, it was literary translation and writing, leading committee work for the Florentine orphanage and school, supervising young nieces, and assisting her husband's work as they both interacted in the new Italy's cosmopolitan and political circles.

Noting how these women responded to their callings—neither sent abroad as Christian missionaries nor following husbands who went for evangelical reasons—increases the already numerous facets of how women traveled and lived in cultures not originally their own. Of course, their experiences contrast greatly with those of women who came into the US in the nineteenth century, fleeing Europe and Asia for political, religious, and economic reasons. And they differ markedly as well from those who were brought as slaves, subject to the brutalities of the economic system. And there were those who became US citizens without moving, as the nation annexed colonies on the same continent or within the same hemisphere. This story of privileged white women, whose paths reversed the traditional migration direction as they followed their callings abroad, is not meant to minimize other accounts of pain and struggle—including American expatriate visual artists and writers who went abroad as "exiles," such as Constance Fenimore Woolson.[43] All deserve attention, yet all cannot be told within a single volume. Rather, this volume zooms in on how these three women to illustrate the networks in which they engaged and chose to act.

These privileged positions often emerge poignantly for readers today and are an important part of the story. The stereotypes about Others on the peninsula come through. Whether discussing the aristocratic, as Marsh often did when she critiqued their arranged marriages, or with references to impoverished laborers, as Gould did, or to the intermarriages of privileged, literate Anglo-Americans with less educated Romans, as Brewster did, the women's words and actions resonate for readers now. The women's successes and their failures as they took steps toward their utopian dreams speak loudly of human strengths and weaknesses. They learned about others and about themselves in the process, and their education in the face of these facts provides a redemptive quality—perhaps at least in the eyes of readers. While later learning does not excuse previous bad behavior, it may push readers to consider their own actions driven by ignorance.

Similarly, the stories of these women's strengths and weaknesses, triumphs, and trials are not meant to minimize the roles of "the men in their lives"—to use a rather worn phrase. Their decisions of how to act and their abilities to do so often depended upon these men. Men, then, are not absent from this story. One way to visualize them is through Fuller's vision of male–female relations as she matured as a writer and thinker. Fuller began to see the problem of hero worship, and the necessity of breaking the idealized "statues" as she matured and wrote her reflective "Autobiographical Romance." She had idolized her father and Emerson as well as the heroes of Greek, Roman, German, and English literature and history, only eventually learning how these figures and her admiration of them reinforced the imbalanced and gendered roles of adoration that surrounded her in nineteenth-century culture. The everyday realities she faced moved her to action. Women she encountered in rural New England and in Boston, if they were to become more capable of achieving what we now call agency, needed to be taught to look within rather than to look to external sources for their truths and value. They should allow the "natural unfolding" from within themselves, stimulated by friends they considered their equals rather than by men they idolized.[44] Men in Brewster's, Gould's, and Marsh's lives should be seen similarly in their supporting roles. This view is almost impossible, given the way in which men controlled so much of civic and cultural life. Unfortunately for Brewster, Gould, and Marsh, glimpses of hero worship emerge in their writings, sometimes conflicting with and limiting their visions of activism and engagement while abroad. Nonetheless, even with such social circumscriptions and dependency, Brewster, Gould, and Marsh responded to their callings, doing what they could to help those around them and to sustain themselves.

Italy as "Museum" and "Spectacle": Actors and Agents

Marsh, Gould, and Brewster were among many Americans abroad who witnessed firsthand the physical turmoil of political changes affiliated with global networks. But Gould's, Brewster's, and Marsh's actions help to revise the perspectives of James and Twain that Italy in this period was for Americans abroad a "museum" or a "mere spectacle."[45] The women became engaged with the volatile political situation around them as actors and agents of change rather than as spectators or merely self-centered performers. During this time of Italian "Unification," controversies about national unity, the pope's temporal power, and monarchial authority abounded, following not long after the Risorgimento Fuller had witnessed at midcentury. "Unification" and "Risorgimento" are fraught terms that embody complex, ongoing processes of negotiation and uncertainty; both labels designate periods whose boundaries blur. Some historians mark Unification as occurring in 1861, when the first capital and parliament of the Kingdom of Italy were established at Turin (the point at which the US President appointed Marsh to serve there). In 1861, however, the Papal States (from Rome in the west and extending to the Adriatic in the east) remained separate, in effect dividing the peninsula into northern and southern regions. Other scholars mark Unification as the moment when Rome was taken by the Italian soldiers of the new Kingdom of Italy, with their entry on September 20, 1870. But even after the breach of the Roman walls at Porta Pia, the uncertainties of leadership and diversity, of dialects, languages, and regions—which had been a part of Italian history for centuries—continued.[46]

Earlier in the century, for example, Napoleon had ushered in changes with his revolutionary leadership and rise to power, even overthrowing two popes. After the fall of his system in 1814, the papacy and Papal States had regained their position, maintained through Pope Pius IX's reign until the Risorgimento led to a briefly lived new Roman Republic in 1849, about which Fuller had written for readers of the *Tribune*. But Pius IX had resumed temporal power over Rome soon after, as France sent forces to support the papacy. In the decade that followed, Americans continued to "watch" from across the Atlantic, as ongoing battles to the north (in Piedmont, Lombardy, and Veneto) and the south (the Kingdom of Two Sicilies, including what are now known as Naples and Sicily) continued. The accounts often were presented as attempts to throw off the rule and authority of external powers and empires—French and Austrian, in particular. In this period the military leader Giuseppe Garibaldi, seen as heroic by many Americans, and the Piedmont monarch Victor Emmanuel emerged as leaders of the initial unification of the Kingdom of Italy in 1861, established in opposition to the Roman Catholic temporal authority and its seat in Rome.

For those on the peninsula in the 1860s and in the 1870s, and for those elsewhere who were observing, Italy's future and development of a unified kingdom or nation were uncertain.[47] Mixed attitudes toward the powers of the Roman Catholic Church and the new Kingdom of Italy remained as well. Prejudices of northerners toward southerners were staunch, and southerners were not happy about the influx of northerners affiliated with the new government to southern regions, including Rome. In the US during the same period, north–south differences also remained intense. A contributing factor to the political climate building toward secession and the Civil War had been an increasing number of Roman Catholic immigrants from Europe in the 1840s and 1850s and the Roman Catholic Church's Declarations of the Immaculate Conception in 1854 under Pius IX. US citizens wrestled first with ideas of abolition, then with the realities of the Civil War and, finally, with the aftermath of emancipation. In Italy, near the end of the US Civil War, the Syllabus of Errors rendered in the spring of 1864 added to American concerns with what might emerge from Rome next. How would any further declarations impact the already unstable civic foundation in the US, which political and religious leaders were attempting to rebuild? During these decades of political upheaval, Americans employed utopian ideas of "Italy" to foster sentiments about civic engagement and social progress.[48]

That is, as they turned their eyes abroad, their beliefs in republican government and self-rule, rather than control by foreign powers, and struggles with church and state relations, contributed to a sense of "cultural mutuality" that caused Italy, more so than other European entities, to become a magnet of American attention as well as a destination for tourists and artists, male and female.[49] Many saw "how profoundly Italy's experience paralleled America's."[50] This magnet appeal of church-state relations in Italy, known as "the Roman Question," combined in the US with increasing possibilities for travel and for reading travel literature, supported by new technologies such as the steam engine and press improvements. Not surprisingly, American interests became intertwined with the Italian scene to varying degrees. This backdrop of continual and uncertain change sets the stage for Brewster's, Marsh's, and Gould's roles that unfolded in this theatrical spectacle of "Italy" Americans read about and experienced firsthand. However, these women became actresses and agents of change rather than mere observers.

Their responses in writing not only document what they observed but also present their engagement with enacting change. Despite of their idealism about Italy, they and other Americans differed in their views of what it offered and how "progress" and improvements might be implemented.[51] Influenced by the optimism of Italian Unification in the American Reconstruction years, the women's expressive writing in newspaper publications, letters, journals, poems, and reports, primarily during the years 1868–78, captures the hope central to utopianism. Yet this optimism is juxtaposed with moments of hopelessness and frustration; language of certainty transitions into expressions of anxiety and failure. Their utopian visions and actions to realize them, their writings reveal, were neither uniform nor singular. These diverse reflections in Gould's, Brewster's, and Marsh's public and private writings expand our language, and cultures were new to them and often differed from their own. Yet even with their moments of despair, these stories of hope and civic engagement speak to readers today. Specifically, they illuminate how expressive writing and social networking, as reciprocal activities, evoke new ideas and transform individuals, their circles, and, at times, the larger world.

Accounts of these women contribute to studies of nineteenth-century Italian–American and global relations, gender, religion, and, especially, discussions of American "exceptionalism" and utopianism. The latter underscores that ideals are never realized, even while pointing to the necessary dialectical relation between both hopeful and despairing visions when considering social change. Without these utopian visions, change would not occur. Equally significant, one person's utopian vison may be another's view of dystopia, as Margaret Atwood has written.[52]

Engaging Italy presents the challenges of these individual women actualizing these visions while living abroad, following the pattern of Elèna Mortara's study of the writings by and about American-born Victor Séjour, who wrote for the European stage. Mortara's analysis of newspaper accounts, letters, and published scripts circulating in Europe and the US examines social and political exchange and transformation through writing. Her work asks readers to rethink stories of American "exceptionalism" as it illuminates how people move beyond their initial expectations of other cultures; this book aims to do likewise. "Finding connections" with others even while seeing differences, these women expressed through writing their changing visions, which "shed new light on the intercourse of cultures." In doing so, they contribute to the "transnational turn" in American studies that celebrates plurality of citizens as well as relationships that break the barriers of American isolationist and "exceptionalist" thinking, even while recognizing its pervasive existence.[53] Additionally, this analysis draws from recent studies of the circulation of texts, such as Mathew C. Cohen's *The Social Lives of Poems in Nineteenth-Century America*, which examine the multiple pathways in which texts and people influence each other. Cohen demonstrates "the ways poems were meaningful outside of a model based on literary analysis" as he asserts that they "facilitated actions" in "complex webs" that were at times "political."[54] Similarly, *Engaging Italy*, rather than focusing on a single author, genre, or literary movement, illustrates how the multiple genres in which these women wrote provide windows into networks of liberating expression—both its provocations and its reiterations.

This study of multiple authors and genres within their transnational networks could be even more extensive than it is. To set limitations, *Engaging Italy* primarily zooms in on the decade 1868–78, encompassing the period in which all three were abroad. However, it is impossible to consider that decade without remembering its wider frame. Their larger stories—their backstories and their afterlives—span what historian Marcella Sutcliffe refers to as "the *longue durée*."[55] As Sutcliffe notes, this period is framed at one end by the exiled revolutionary leader Giuseppe Mazzini's arrival in London in 1837 and at the other end, 1890, by the death of Mazzini's long-dedicated follower Aurelio Saffi.[56] The life spans of these political leaders, figuring only in the background of the women's lives, overlap with them historically and thus highlight the longer span of their lives and ongoing change. Brewster, for example, was born the same year as Saffi, and they died within two years of each other. When Gould died in 1875, political and religious life in Italy continued to change. In fact, historians employ the term *trasformismo* to refer to the ongoing changes within the Italian culture following Unification, specifically "the national political strategy . . . of overcoming . . . division."[57]

To capture the women's utopian visions and vocations within this political context, this book does not follow a straight chronological arrangement but instead is divided into three parts. The first, "Portraits of Diversity," depicts the women's backstories, representative vignettes of their time in Italy, and a contextualization of the historical moment of the summer of 1870, when Italian soldiers marched into Rome and the pope abdicated his official rule over the city. Part II, "Circuits and Networks," focuses on the contexts for their international travel, circulating texts that idealized and fostered life abroad, and this complex webs of relations—both supportive and debilitating—in which these literary women were engaged. This section differs from what precedes and follows it in that it shifts from more narrative accounts to descriptive literary analysis. For example, the chapter "Revising *Daisy Miller*: The Story of 'Miss Jones' " focuses on an 1875 tale in a memorial volume dedicated to Gould and issued by the Italo-American School's press. Both the venue and the tale create the context for social reform abroad. The fictional "Miss Jones" demonstrates how some women did not meet the ends of Americans visualized by Hawthorne in his notebooks and James in his novels, although fears of such outcomes prevailed. The story also introduces details of everyday life for those traveling and living abroad, from languages and lodgings to clothing, companions, and salon culture—the subjects of the next chapter. "Receptions" such as those hosted by Brewster and Marsh contributed to social fabric that kept many women emotionally and intellectually afloat. This nexus of exchange blurred boundaries between people and texts, the chapter "Circulating People, Circulating Texts" explains. Homage poetry, letters of introduction and invitation, and a single issue of a Roman newspaper illustrate the challenges of distinguishing between events intended overtly to reform (that flourished in the years of Italian Unification) and receptions of salon culture that illustrate the needs of socializing and entertainment—all part of the myths of agency and independence.[58]

The book's third part, "Varieties of Utopian Experiences," returns to a narrative style with accounts of each woman's visions and transformations, especially with attention to their religious affiliations and writings. An inscribed gift copy of Sherwood Bonner's popular sarcastic poem "The Radical Club," in Brewster's library, raises questions about the relevance of reform associations alongside theological debates and religious life.[59] Attention to miracles and saints' lives in Roman Catholicism, a larger interest in Spiritism and the spirit world, resistance to liberalism, and approaches to education set the stage for understanding Gould's, Brewster's, and Marsh's works.[60]

"Emily Bliss Gould: 'Works and Wants'" captures both the urgency and the sense of agency infiltrating her later writings. Tracing this developing sense from Gould's early travel writings through her later reform efforts, the chapter notes the rhetorical stances of her private correspondence and published fundraising reports. These exude what Susan K. Harris and Theresa Strouth Gaul, respectively, refer to as "epistolary negotiations" and "political meanings" of private letters.[61] Letters between Gould and prominent males—Ambassador Marsh and Waldensian (non–Roman Catholic) leader Matteo Prochet—reveal her strength of vision and behaviors that led others to respond financially to her works. At the same time, she crafted a public image of motherhood, as a portrait with the Venetian orphans demonstrates. This work advances and refines studies on national identity, "domestic" roles, and missionary literature and culture by Karen Sánchez-Eppler and Sarah Robbins, among others.[62] Gould resisted cultural norms for gender, encouraged by Italian leaders for her reform efforts to fight for what she wanted and believed others needed.

Although she sustained herself and negotiated religious, political, and literary circles through her colorful, chameleon behavior, the chapter "Anne Hampton Brewster: A Catholic Correspondent Negotiates New Rome" demonstrates Brewster's anxieties and missteps as well. It asserts that she has been forgotten due to ways in which she differed from more famous female reporters such as Fuller, Jessie White Mario, and "Nellie Bly."[63] Although Brewster's letters were published and republished widely across the US—from New England to California, in the deep South and in the Midwest, in more densely Catholic areas as well as in staunchly Protestant towns—Brewster did not take risks with her body or her writing style, as other reporters did. These risks included the possibilities of intimate relations with both women and men. Rather, her metaphorical marriage to her work contributed to Brewster's distance from intimate relationships that might have stabilized and buoyed her. Constantly wrestling with her own faith, fearing intimacy, and lacking the radicalism for social reform, Brewster and her voluminous pages fell to the shadows.

Marsh's utopian visions and her multifaceted views of herself emerge in "Caroline Crane Marsh: 'The Power of Doing a Great Service.'" The chapter asserts the complementary roles of her literary work and her activism, all within the confines of being a dutiful wife. She saw herself as social activist, teacher, and surrogate mother to stepson, nieces, nephews, orphans, and an adopted child (several of whom lived with her in Italy). Marsh dedicated one of her first published poems to her husband, who inspired, supported, and sometimes collaborated in her literary labors. She devoted herself to literary endeavors not only as a translator but also as an aspiring author—fiction, poetry and, later, George's biography complement her frequent letter and journal writing. All these positions, documented in the manuscripts she left behind, shifted as did Marsh's changing ideas of Italy. Rather than merely escapist "utopianism" or transcendent Romanticism, these readings and writings illuminate her evolving ideas about the cultural and religious differences which surrounded her. They underscore how Marsh, like Brewster and Gould, found and fulfilled her vocation abroad through networks that in turn caused her to negotiate her own shifting position as a woman living transnationally.

Beyond these chapters, the book's coda, "Residual Ripples," refers to the women's lives and works beyond 1878. Their verbal expressions—circulated first during their lives—speak from the archives for further dialectical engagement today. They reveal the diverse ways in which writing about transnational experiences of engagement with others *do* lead to transformations, although they are not always fulfillments of the utopian visions that initially prompted them.

PART I

PORTRAITS OF DIVERSITY

Chapter 1

Backstories of Diversity

Accounts of Marsh, Gould, and Brewster and their diverse utopian visions and experiences in transnational networks begin neither with the dinners celebrating Longfellow in 1869 nor with the women's first encounters with each other. The three had arrived on the peninsula at different moments, and they had experienced transnational travel long before. Brewster, the most recently arrived, had been in Rome since November of 1868.[1] Gould, who usually summered in the Alps, had arrived with her husband, James, in Italy seven years earlier, in 1861.[2] Marsh had come to Italy that same year, when her husband became the first US minister plenipotentiary to the newly formed Kingdom of Italy. Even prior to their experiences in Italy, highlights of their backstories—including time in Europe—illuminate the callings they followed abroad.

Caroline Crane Marsh: Literary Activist and *Ambasciatrice*

Marsh traveled abroad first in 1849 a few months after George was appointed American minister to the Ottoman Empire, but she had exhibited much earlier her love of learning, of books, and of travel. The three went together throughout her life. Travels, building on what she had read, widened her horizons. At twelve years Marsh went from rural Massachusetts to live with her brother Silas Crane in Providence, Rhode Island, where she began her formal education, and then at sixteen she traveled with him to Vermont, where he began a new position as minister and she began teaching in the school he had established. Next she traveled to New York to teach in Martha

Mitchell's school. Before she left for New York, she had met in 1838 the widowed attorney George, who expressed that he was stimulated "by her intellect and personal charm," a reason to see her often. Their marriage soon followed, along with additional years in Burlington. By 1843 she was with him in Washington, where he was serving as a member of congress, alongside the well-known Daniel Webster, John C. Calhoun, Henry Clay, and John Adams. Although chronic illness affected her ability to stand, to walk, and to see, she continued to cultivate her love of books, languages, and translating with the help of family and friends, who often read to and wrote for her. While she was living in Washington, summer visits to Providence, Boston, and Burlington kept Marsh in close contact with additional family and friends. Letters among these and others capture her anticipations of and reflections on travel and life abroad.[3]

Marsh's first travel through Europe, while en route to Turkey, occurred not only with her husband but also with her sister Lucy and members of George's prior family—now her own: his son George Ozias and his sister-in-law's daughter. While Marsh recorded impressions in letters sent to family and friends, she also included details of her physical condition as an "invalid," providing a picture of the challenges for some traveling abroad. In Paris, for example, her husband carried her up and down stairs in the Louvre and rolled her in a wheelchair through the galleries. Marsh described the rigor of getting from Paris to Marseille: "a little bed was prepared for me and put into the carriage, and in this way I found I could travel in ease and comfort."[4] In Constantinople, her health was "certainly better than when they left America." However, her physical condition did not improve greatly during the years in Turkey. She had been near death with fever in 1851, although a winter in Egypt had provided some relief.[5]

While Marsh had her own discomforts, they paled in comparison to the extreme poverty she saw on her first journey in Italy, en route to Turkey. Like many Americans, she was shocked and moved by what she witnessed, after passing through the Alps to Genoa and into Tuscany. As she wrote, "It would be vain to try to convey . . . the want and discomfort we witnessed during this journey. Whole towns might be seen without a pane of glass or chimney, and it was lamentable to see half naked and half starved inhabitants gathering as night drew on under the lightless roof, which seemed for them and their beasts a shelter."[6] Later the same month, she expressed despair, as her family traveled south of Rome toward Naples, "through an incredible amount of idleness, poverty and beggary." She noted that they "often had twenty or thirty persons" chasing their carriage, "assuring us they were starving and entreating us for a copper." Of Naples, known for its extremes of beauty and poverty, she continued, "These beggars are less numerous in the city, but still one cannot go out without being surrounded by them."[7] While Marsh did not make overt connections between the "beggars" she witnessed and American slaves (as Fuller had in her *Tribune* dispatches), she saw the problem of poverty as endemic to the system of government and the culture it cultivated. The theme would emerge full force after she arrived in Italy in 1861 and interacted with political leaders, nobility, house servants, and gardeners.

After she left Naples and sailed to Constantinople, Marsh's reflections changed. She began to write and to study eastern and non-Christian cultures. Her insights to human needs and foibles would later factor into her deepening understandings of Roman Catholicism in Italy and Protestant Americans' sometimes simplistic views of the problems. For example, while she took comfort in the circle of ambassadors surrounding her in Constantinople, writing that "the foreign Ministers and their families" were also likable, Marsh felt differences with them. Acknowledging that they were "very nice people," she and her husband differed from them in their beliefs and interactions with the local culture. She became "much interested in St. Augustine," reflecting a venture into theological traditions, and was "nibbling at Turkish, being moved thereto by a desire to talk with the Turkish women." During the fall and winter of 1851, she also "became much interested in the political refugees gathered there." These included the Hungarian statesman Louis Kossuth and, from what is now the northern region of Italy, the Princess Cristina Trivulzio di Belgiojoso.[8] She sought to understand the social controversies that led to political exile. Marsh's reflections during this first year abroad capture an openness to the world around her, her attempts to engage with it, and her desires to do what she could to improve people's conditions. These characteristics would continue during her later years in Italy.

In fact, Marsh's interactions with political refugees may have contributed to her strong reactions to meeting expatriate English poets Elizabeth Barrett and Robert Browning at their home, Casa Guidi, in Florence in the winter of 1853 while visiting friend Hiram Powers there. Before the meeting, Marsh knew Elizabeth's poetry, although she did not know Robert's.[9] The famous female poet likely influenced Marsh's work as both writer and social activist. Elizabeth's "The Cry of the Children," affiliated with child labor reform, had been published a decade earlier in *Blackwood's Magazine*, and *Casa Guidi Windows*, about the revolutionaries in Florence, appeared just two years before. The Marsh and Browning meeting stimulated later correspondence and invitations for further visits.[10] The Marshes stopped in Italy again late in 1854, en route home after George's term ended, before they sailed for the US.

Marsh passed the phase following this international political appointment primarily with her husband in Burlington, Boston, and New York, where George lectured on the English language. In response to their financial strains, she scrimped as much as possible on household expenses so that he might have his books. But likely this prioritizing of the literary was of personal interest to her as well. As Marsh's early family biographer wrote of her challenging balance between familial duty and internal desires, "she had the rare combination of practical good sense and brilliant intellectual gifts"; "each moment that she could snatch from these household cares, was spent by her in literary work."[11]

Chief among Marsh's literary work of this period in the US were two volumes of translation that reflect her transnational interests: *The Hallig, or the Sheepfold in the Waters: A Tale of Humble Life on the Coast of Schleswig* (1856) and *Wolfe of the Knoll, and other Poems* (1860).[12] As translations these books reflect her cross-cultural linguistic skills. However, they also demonstrate two additional notable features. While *The Hallig* demonstrates fewer translating demands because, as prose, it did not necessitate that Marsh wrestle with rhyme and meter, it includes a preface in which she delineates her views of theology, literature, and their relationship to a culture—an important revelation. The views emerged from her time as a Protestant US citizen who had lived and traveled in Muslim cultures and had traveled through Roman Catholic ones as well. She explained, for example, "The religion of a people is . . . influential in the formation of . . . national character . . . and if we would rightly estimate their social, moral, and intellectual condition, we must become acquainted with their faith . . . their government and the spirit of their laws."[13] Marsh carried this attitude toward religious and political practices, languages, and tales passed on orally with her into Italy.

Reflecting Marsh's ongoing balance of both familial duty and literary calling, the second translated volume's significance emerges within one of her first published poems—a poem of adoration for George (Appendix A). In this ode to her "Beloved," she wrote of her husband as her "teacher," who introduced her to a world larger than what she would have known. The lines explain that his "beloved voice," sharing "many a sage's, many a nation's lore," had "charmed" her "ear" and given her "culture." When her "eyes could look no more" upon "page sublime," his teaching lifted her soul "above each selfish care."[14]

Indeed, Marsh's lengthy time in Italy was instigated by George's appointment, and both hoped that her health would be improved by it. They both also were optimistic about the financial sustenance the position would provide.[15] While living first at Turin, Marsh began extensive journaling, which complements scenes described in letters to family. Seventeen notebooks, comprising approximately one thousand manuscript pages, record the period of 1861 to 1865. The journal pages provide glimpses of her concerns for the impoverished and their lack of education, about the attitudes of both Roman Catholics and non-Catholic religious reformers, and with the behaviors of aristocracy, who gave little attention to their marriage vows.[16] While these concerns are not surprising for a nineteenth-century Protestant American abroad, Marsh's private writings also give glimpses of how she changed through her experiences and interactions, pulled by her callings as social activist and expressive author.

Following Turin, Marsh moved with George as the Kingdom of Italy's capital moved to Florence and then to Rome. She remained abroad until just after her husband's death in 1882. During these two decades, she not only fulfilled the role of ambassador's wife, greeting and entertaining visitors from throughout Europe and the US, but also served as surrogate mother to nieces and nephews and Italian adopted children. She engaged with activism through the Italian war efforts and establishment of Salvatore Ferretti's "orphan asylum" in Florence and supported English philanthropy with Turkish immigrants to London. Throughout these years, then, she found her vocation not only as *ambasciatrice* assisting her husband but as an activist and author herself, engaged with writing and translating as well as social reform.

Emily Bliss Gould: Glimpsing Garibaldi's Redshirts, Remembering Sunday Schools

Like Marsh, Gould went abroad in 1860 accompanied by her husband and hoping a change in health would be brought about by Italy's sunny clime. In the two decades that followed her marriage in 1853, Gould rose from what might be seen as the feeble or "invalid" spouse of a physician to a forceful woman with her own utopian visions of social improvements and specific paths for achieving them. Gould prepared for social activism in her youth. One biographer, Leonard Woolsey Bacon, described Gould in her early years as "distinguished in New York society" by "youthful beauty and grace" and having "fine feminine wit and address . . . such as to fit her for an easy and unenvied leadership in whatever social circle she might enter." He continued that "to these attractive qualities were added a true dignity of Christian discipleship, and an 'enthusiasm of humanity,' which had endeared her to a multitude, not only of the high, but of the lowly."[17] Another sketch described her as having taught a Sunday School class of forty "when herself little more than a child."[18] And an autobiographical evangelistic sketch Gould wrote for the American Tract Society's *Little Pilgrims* (1866) tells the story of a young girl, the title's "Little Caroline," who becomes a Sunday School teacher among the urban impoverished.[19] "Little Caroline" drew from Gould's early experiences in New York but more importantly signals the memories and dreams Gould carried abroad with her, which reemerged as she observed Italian children she deemed in need of education. Filling out the six years before the tale appeared, Gould's venture across the Atlantic and her initial reactions to Europe add to her backstory.

After a nine-month journey across the Atlantic and continental Europe, Gould arrived in Rome in February 1861. Like most traveling, literate women, she recorded extensively in her journal many vivid responses to what she saw upon her arrival in Europe, contributing to her developing writing career and later published sketches. The entries follow the typical Grand Tour route, moving overland from Le Havre, France, and crossing the Alps into the Italian peninsula. Once in Italy, Gould moved from Turin to Milan, to Verona and to Venice on the Adriatic, and then back across the peninsula to Genoa, Leghorn (Livorno), and finally Rome on the west coast.[20] Gould arrived at a significant moment: the first unification of the numerous Italian kingdoms under the military and political leadership, respectively, of Giuseppe Garibaldi and King Victor Emmanuel of Piedmont. Another nineteenth-century biographer explained: "Just as she landed in Havre, at the end of May, 1860, the tidings reached her that Garibaldi, with his red shirts had entered Palermo in triumph, and by the 8th of September, with uplifted fore-finger, the symbol of '*Italia Una*,' he had entered Naples and announced that the peninsula of Italy was to be a united and free country." In addition to Garibaldi's leadership of a successful populist army, the reigning king from the Piedmont region "had entered the States of the Church and annexed the two Sicilies, and the Marches and Umbria to the crown of Italy."[21] This historical context for Gould's arrival helps to explain why her journal comments were at times predictable for an Anglo-American Protestant traveling abroad.

These predictable views exuded hope while presenting Italian people in need of direction and uplift. In many observations by American and Anglo viewers, Bailey has explained, "the absence of purposeful activity" among Italian peasants fed fraught images. These people, "outside of time," might be seen as directionless waste, trapped in what viewers saw as a simpler past, or they might be seen as full of fecund possibility, just waiting to be cultivated.[22] Little different in her ambivalent views, Gould wrote of the people in Genoa, for example, "Such slow, poky, good-natured, noisy, gesticulating, gaping, thoroughly lazy people I never saw as those we see in the streets. They are out of doors all the time. They are moving about, but such motion. The hour-hand of a clock is faster."[23] Her negative, stereotypical comments, however, were juxtaposed with utopian optimism, as she wrote of two generations of young, red-shirted "Garibaldini"—soldiers following Garibaldi—who had fought for unification:

> They wore the Garibaldi red shirt and necktie, blue pants, and broad, blue belt. Checked lilac-and-white undershirt. They were beautiful, bright, beardless boys, evidently full of life and hope, and gentle and modest as women. Of such stuff as this—this father and these children—is Garibaldi's army constituted. Such lovely boys as these lie stiff and stark under their own native sky, after every battle with the hated foreigner. And their mothers, their poor mothers, send them and watch and wait and pray for their return.

The passage continued, reverberating with language Walt Whitman, the "poet of Democracy," had used in his 1850 poem about the revolutions in Europe and would use in describing young men during the Civil War.[24] In a scene that parallels historically those in which young Civil War soldiers—especially "beautiful, bright, beardless boys"—back in the States soon would "lie stiff and stark . . . after every battle," Gould described details of wounds and the numbers who fought. Here, though, the enemy was "the hated foreigner" rather than slavery.[25] Gould tapped into American sentiments against the idea of foreign control rather than self-rule, but as she described the scene by the sea in Genoa, she avoided mention of the controversial slavery that divided the nation across the Atlantic. It would be less than a year before

Confederate soldiers would fire on Union troops at Fort Sumter and Marsh would sail abroad.

Indeed, Gould and her husband arrived in Rome in February of 1861, two months before the April battle known as the start of the Civil War. Before their arrival, however, they stopped for two months in Florence, a common recovery point in the Grand Tour. The city provided "religious comfort" for Gould "in the worship and fellowship of the Italian Protestant Church." Here she also gained insights to the local culture in which, as Bacon described, "some of Mrs. Gould's best charitable labors" occurred. During the summers that followed, Gould often would return to Florence and the Tuscan hills around it, travel to the Alps in the north of Italy, where she would be moved by the schools established by Waldenisan leaders in the Valais region, or escape Rome's heat in the hills nearby. The ideas she gleaned from these travels—to Tuscany and Piedmont, especially—fed what she imagined might occur in Rome with the urban poor. She wrote of these experiences in her journal as well as in later published travel sketches.[26]

Gould's published sketches began to appear in 1866, the same year as "Little Caroline." Entitled "Rambles among the Italian Hills," and found in Scribner's *Hours at Home*, they continued through 1867 and primarily provided views of rural tourist sites for American readers. In the process, they reveal Gould's attitudes toward the Italian rural poor as beautiful within their "natural," simple environments. They had become oppressed by "pagan" and Roman Catholic civilizations, which had petrified them, like geological layers through the centuries. The view was not unusual for American Protestants. Most notably, however, Gould's writing developed and her engagement increased within this environment. As she wrote of monasteries at Vallombrosa and Subiaco, for example, she interjected not only details of the children and priests but also herself. Observing what she considered poorly managed situations, she took charge to change them. When a monastery's kitchen needed organizational aid, for example, she stepped in, and she wrote of it for her American readers.[27]

In addition to these sketches for Scribner's, Gould began to send "news" from Rome to Bret Harte, published in the "Gossip Abroad" section of some 1869 issues of his *Overland Monthly*. Harte wrote to Gould that her "correspondence satisfies" and he would "be glad to have [her] services." The only condition he included was, "as long as I shall continue the . . . department as a feature of the magazine."[28] Whether Harte discontinued the department or Gould was swept away by her social activism before he did so remains unclear. Gould's newsletters notably did *not* contain merely gossip about

Americans abroad but rather described the political climate in Italy and elsewhere in Europe. Only occasionally, as with references to the Longfellow affairs, did they lapse into social events in Rome, comments on the weather, or events such as Mount Vesuvius's eruptions.

What becomes clear in these early publications is that they chart a movement in Gould's understanding of audience and vocation. Her early journals and letters provided practice, stepping stones in a trajectory of development. Gould moved from writing personal reflections on the natural world and Italian human landscape to commenting on the political climate. Both types of writing, meant to entice readers at home, were not unusual for women writers of the era, of course. The well-known Sedgwick and Fuller already had recorded their visions of people, places, and politics as they traveled abroad, and the lesser-known Grace Greenwood (Sara Jane Lippincott) and Elizabeth Stoddard had written travel accounts for children as well as for adults when Gould's began to appear. Many other women followed suit during the next three decades, sending not only travel writings but also fiction based on time on the Italian peninsula: Brewster, Woolson, Helen Hunt Jackson, and Harriet Beecher Stowe are only a few.[29] But Gould's travel and "gossip" writing eventually became overshadowed by her work with schools in Piedmont, Florence, and Rome. Her writing transitioned to private letters to leaders, published reports, and appeals for funds related to this work.

Also of note, Gould's position in Italy differed significantly from Marsh's. Although Gould's debility due to "hay fever" was not as hampering as Marsh's struggles, her husband was not an ambassador. She had no easy path into politics. Nor were she and her husband among the *literati*. They left no traces that have contributed to the stuff of romantic mythos that surrounds the Brownings, Fuller and Ossoli, or even Mary and Percy Bysshe Shelley earlier in the century. Nonetheless, like these other women, Gould, nearly forty years old upon her arrival in Rome, soon became swept up in the social and educational reforms surrounding her in the politically uncertain peninsula.[30] Gould's writings on behalf of education reform in Italy appeared in American newspapers, such as the New York *Observer*, Hartford *Commercial*, Hartford *Churchman*, Chicago *Advance*, and New York *Evening Post*. This "voluminous correspondence . . . with several different American journals at once," along with her private correspondence and ongoing work with children, "broke down her health" and led to her death, according to Bacon.[31] Her literary endeavors—both published and unpublished—trace her transition and transformation from seemingly invalid spouse to reform leader. As many have asked of Fuller, what might Gould have accomplished, had she not died so prematurely in 1875, little more than fifty years old?

Anne Hampton Brewster: Escaping Family, Chasing Charlotte

Brewster's reasons for travel to Europe were more complicated than simply traveling for health or accompanying a husband. As such, they illuminate the diversity of reasons American women traveled abroad and the ways in which they did so. Like Gould and Marsh, she desired improved health, but she sought emotional more than physical well-being. As a single woman, she had neither the facility of following a husband nor the support of a concerned spouse. Rather, she was more like Fuller, who strategically planned her travels. She had first traveled abroad on a steamer in 1857, accompanied by her "maid" Lina and her dog Beauty. When they had to share a room, and the bedding was uncomfortable, Brewster wrote in her journal of how it cramped her style as well as her body. For security and peace of mind, anticipating arrival in crowded cities and new cultures, she carried a letter of introduction from Robert Dale Owen, then US minister to the Kingdom of Two Sicilies. She depended upon this paper document and the kindness of strangers when negotiating her path from the busy port of Le Havre, France, to Vevey, Switzerland. The crowded trains, the bustling rail stations, the uncertain banking, and the sometimes less-than-pleasant hotels often left her unsettled. Living alone in Switzerland was not as nice as she had imagined, when autumn leaves fell and winter's alpine winds blew. An invitation to Naples in the sunny south, where she joined the Owens in February, provided comfort and a change of heart.

When Brewster first planned what became almost a two-year sojourn in Switzerland and Naples, she had hoped to generate a book manuscript. She had already written and published approximately forty short stories, sketches, and poems, primarily in *Graham's American Monthly Magazine*, as well as a novella of conversion, *Spirit Sculpture*.[32] Brewster differed from the other two women, then, in that she traveled abroad the first time as a well-published author. However, up to this point, she had published all her works under the pseudonym Enna Duval, perhaps indicating that she lacked faith in the value of her calling or the public place of women writers.

Brewster's plans did not go as smoothly as she had hoped in Europe on this first trip abroad. A publisher rejected a manuscript (her hope for ongoing financial independence), she suffered loneliness and illness near death in Switzerland, and she had to return to the US in 1858 to deal with a family financial crisis. Nonetheless, her tastes of Italy, in particular, motivated her to spend much of the decade that followed dreaming about and planning a second trip.[33]

This second trip, Brewster imagined, would be an escape from what she sensed as her brother's fiscal and emotional control of her life. She had attempted such an escape on her first departure. In fact, the family crisis that precipitated her early return from Naples was a wrangling over the estate left to her brother after her mother's death. Brewster's conflict with this brother, Benjamin, a successful Philadelphia attorney who later became US attorney general, emerged as a lawsuit in 1856 and continued through 1859. Yet other factors also prompted and secured Brewster's second sojourn abroad. She knew that the actress Charlotte Cushman, "the female Romeo," had flourished there. Brewster and Cushman had developed a close relationship in the 1840s, when Cushman was in Philadelphia, but Benjamin had squelched it, due to what he saw as its "unnaturalness." Brewster wrote of their past relationship in June of 1847, "the only being I ever truly loved or shall ever love. . . . Oh father above is such love wrong? Can a feeling which seemed to elevate and refine my nature as did that love for her be wicked? . . . I feel assured though separated in this life, in another world we shall meet & never know the wretchedness of separation!"[34]

Memories of this relationship, added to her first Italian experiences, and a letter from Cushman and two other women in July 1867 stating that Brewster could live inexpensively in Rome and inviting her to join them, contributed to Brewster's plans to move to the politically divided city. At this point, more than two decades later, Cushman was surrounded by a circle of women. Nonetheless, Brewster's journal entries suggest she followed Cushman at least as a model, if not with hopes for a continued friendship. She saw Cushman in Maine just before departing for Europe in August of 1868 and then again in Rome in December, only four months later. Soon after Brewster's arrival in November that same year, she visited Cushman's brother several times, and then she "welcomed" the actress to Rome the next month, just after Christmas.[35] Brewster sent positive accounts of Cushman's activities in Rome back to the *Philadelphia Evening Bulletin*, but she wrote privately that she was disappointed in Cushman's behavior. Both types of accounts, in spite of their disparate tones, reveal that throughout Brewster's time abroad, she savored memories of what their relationship once had been. These poignant feelings emerged again in the memorial sketches she wrote for *Blackwood's Magazine* and the *Boston Daily Advertiser* after Cushman's death in 1878.[36]

To make her dream of departure for Rome a reality, Brewster labored intensively during the decade after her return from Naples in 1858. Soon after arriving in Philadelphia, where her brother lived, Brewster moved to family property in Bridgeton, New Jersey, where she continued the professional writing career begun in the 1840s. Her time, however, was also devoted to teaching French and music to supplement the income garnered from both her writing and interest on family property that her brother continued to manage. Brewster's publications in the period drew largely from her first trip abroad. For example, two autobiographical novels, *Compensation; or, Always a Future* (1860) and *St. Martin's Summer* (1866), each focus on an unmarried and highly musical heroine who lives in Europe. The heroines grow through their experiences abroad, especially due to the support and influence of female circles. Brewster's shorter works of the period similarly drew from transnational experiences and appeared in *Harper's Magazine*, *Lippincott's Magazine*, *The Atlantic Monthly*, and *Peterson's*.[37]

Close examination of these works and Brewster's journals and personal library indicate that her writing during the decade also was fueled by reading. The reading, like the writing, allowed her to live on memories and fed her dreams and desires to travel again. That is, in typical utopian fashion, she was looking at the past and present as well as forward in time. For example, Brewster's annotations in Heinrich Heine's *Lutèce; or the Future belongs to the Communists*, a popular volume for those interested in the European revolutions, and references to Heine's book in *St. Martin's Summer* demonstrate her ongoing reading and reflections about European politics. That is, although characters in her novel refer to Heine's book while they travel in Europe, Brewster's inscriptions dated 1859 and 1860 indicate she was reading it *after* her trip rather than during it.[38]

Brewster's publications in this decade helped her to secure an agreement with George W. Childs of the Philadelphia *Public Ledger* to provide correspondence from Italy; other agreements followed. These gave her some financial security and confidence that allowed her to go abroad indefinitely.[39] Nonetheless, because Brewster was concerned about the indeterminate end date and her limited finances, she left the US this time not on an elegant steamer but on a freighter, accompanying the captain, his wife, and their young children. Rather than sailing with a ship full of the types of comfortable Americans who would be enticed by her writings from abroad, Brewster traveled only with a handful of humans very unlike herself. This challenging social situation—a feeling of being alone and different—would become par for her course for the next quarter century.

Chapter 2

Vignettes of Diversity

Emily Bliss Gould: A Bold Beggar

We beg you to come over and help us.

—Emily Bliss Gould to Dr. Thompson, President, American and Foreign Christian Union, 1867[1]

Late in 1867, as the sun set earlier and earlier each evening over the Arno River in Florence, and the damp chill set into the city's stone buildings, Emily Bliss Gould sat in the warm and lit dining room of the Villa Forini, Caroline Marsh's home. With pen in hand, a determined mind, and the moral support of the US ambassador' wife, Gould composed a letter to Dr. Thompson, then president of the American Foreign and Christian Union.[2] She opened the lengthy letter with careful choices in wording, demonstrating her keen awareness of rhetorical arts. Gould noted that she, Caroline, *and* George sat "sealed in their dining room . . . in solemn enclave," as though they were deliberating on a new pope. Gould included the ambassador—the local man of power—in the conversation. And she chose the plural pronoun "we," rather than "I," not only to include the Marshes, but also as a "royal we." She wrote with a voice that spoke on behalf of the Anglo community in Florence, much as the bishops in Rome wrote about their papal decisions.

> *We* finally decided that *we* must apply to our good friends at home in aid of the country where our lot has been cast. Our own purses are emptied, while our hearts are brimming full.

> Florence as you know is now open to religious and intellectual Improvement. And in Italy as elsewhere, *we* find that *we* must begin at the foundation. *We* must educate future regeneration of the land.[3]

"The land" served as synecdoche, standing in for the Italian people, rather than a literal reference to agricultural teaching about replenishing the peninsula's depleted soil. The rhetorical flourish, common to Gould's writings, supported her cause. She wrote to the most powerful aid organization in the US for funding Protestant work abroad—the AFCU. She sought help for the Florence Evangelical School, "a school of some 200 or 300 children," she explained. The institution was not new. "Established some years [ago] in the city," she continued, it complemented one established by the Waldensians, which was "full of children of their own congregation and others." But in a city "of 200,000 souls," more support was needed. Gould continued with specifics of the institution, reminding Thompson that "Mr. and Mrs. Marsh spoke to you of it when you were here last year" and that it "has derived its support from the Wesleyans of England." Unfortunately, the Wesleyans had "determined to cut off their supplies for its care," as they "concentrate[d] their efforts in other parts of Italy." Providentially, Gould explained, she and Marsh had learned of the cause from Madame De Sanctis—likely the wife of Francesco De Sanctis, revolutionary political leader, literateur, and minister of public instruction under the newly formed government.

Gould and the Anglo community, like many people today, often first provided aid at the winter holiday season, when the cold, dark, and short days prompted awareness and sympathy. For a second winter the beneficent Anglo community had decided to provide a Christmas tree and gifts. "The little fingers of our American children have been busy for some weeks," Gould wrote, "in preparing activities for their comfort and pleasure." But the "numbers [had] greatly enlarged during the year," with "many poor little children much in need of comfortable clothing." Nonetheless, Gould's group had arranged "to clothe a large number who have been almost freezing during the very cold weather."

Following this statement of the beneficent Anglos and the idealized busy "little fingers" of the American children, Gould's most important request appears: "But now comes a burden which we cannot bear. The school requires for the support of its 8 or 10 teachers, heat and other expenses some 10,000 Francs per year. This sum we Italian residents cannot pay." Gould next cleverly inserted a biblical allusion, echoing a phrase attributed to Paul in his missionary journeys to further Christianity—"we beg you at home to come over and help us." Rather than a literal plea that Americans come abroad, she invited them to support "foreign missions" through their funds. To thicken her argument, Gould turned to a description of the school day and the primarily Roman Catholic students in "the little 'Evangelical School.'" The day began "with reading the scriptures and prayer," and, not surprisingly, she explained, "the children are taught to sing such hymns as our little ones sing at home, and to the dear old Sunday Schools tunes of America." A new addition to educational programs was "an evening school . . . largely attended by children and young people who are learning trades during the day." The day school teachers work at night as well, illustrating their devotedness. Finally, she explained the urgency of her request. "One after another, the cities of Italy are being thrown open to Christian [i.e., Anglo] influences. Its capital particularly needs such influences."

Florence, the new monarchy's capital at this time, drew Gould's attention more than Rome, which remained under the pope's power. She continued her explanation, "As long as our hands are tied in Rome, we unite to do what we can here for this most interesting people. They are so greatly in need of sympathy and aid from America. We want to have the seed well sown here in the capital of Italy, and trust to the fruit of the tree we shall one day gather in Rome." Returning to the agricultural metaphor with which she had opened the letter, Gould explained how the community labored toward their goal. Americans abroad had spent themselves emotionally and literally "drain[ed]" their "purses," Gould argued. "One American church [in Florence] is supported entirely by donations and subscriptions from the residents here and those passing through the city in their travels." She blamed American institutions, which had not followed through on their commitments: "We were promised . . . help in a certain quarter, and have been disappointed." As a result, she continued, "we therefore find ourselves suddenly obliged to consider whether this school must be abandoned, and these children now under the best religious moral and intellectual instruction be returned to the care of the priests who so long have enslaved the hearts and minds of Italy, or whether we shall appeal to our country people at home for aid." One result of their consideration was Gould's picking up the pen and composing the letter to Thompson, the powerful man in charge, in which she pleaded, "We cannot hesitate, and we do most earnestly beg you *dear sir* to make known to those able and willing to help in this most pressing need."[4]

Gould concluded her letter with apologies for what she had not included: "something about our situation in Rome." With a sense of urgency, and "anxious to take advantage of the next mail," she chose to forgo that step. Instead, she added briefly that she would "return to Rome, and to my husband as soon as our Christmas tree for the school is over." But above all, she hoped "you have not forgotten us in Rome or in Florence." In standard closing lines, she noted that "Mr. & Mrs. Marsh join[ed]" her "in warm regards to yourself & Mrs. & Miss Thompson," and added her "wish" that her absent husband were at hand so that "his might go also." Within a year, she would be brought before the Roman tribunal—without her husband—for her church work there.

Caroline Crane Marsh: Library Lover and Activist

> What do you say then to our having the catalogue finished as you desire . . . ?
>
> —Caroline Crane Marsh to husband George, August 1869[5]

In the spring of 1869, eight years into her sojourn in Italy, Marsh left Florence for the US, where she would spend six months without George. Her goals were threefold. She would visit family—in New York, in New England, and scattered throughout the then-western states of Indiana and Missouri. Because she and George had been on the peninsula since his appointment to Turin as US minister plenipotentiary in 1861, seeing family after a full seven years abroad was an important complement to her frequent letter writing, which was never the same as face-to-face communication. Marsh was also charged with overseeing the packing and shipment of selected volumes from the Marshes' expansive library—eventually consisting of about 12,000 volumes, including many "rich and choice works"—which they had been without since they left their home in Burlington, Vermont.[6] The library was a significant part of her identity. The chosen books would be shipped back with her to the library in the Villa Forini, while others would be sold to meet the Marshes' financial needs. And a third challenge Marsh would take up was fundraising for the newly established Florentine school and orphanage for girls.

These three goals of Marsh's six-month sojourn in the US emerge in the letters she wrote to George. Marsh's letters written in August 1869 from Burlington, where she was arranging for the sale of many of their books, the packing of others, and the dispersal of belongings that made the house a home, demonstrate not only the trust George had in her to fulfill her duties but also her self-assertions and differences with him.[7] She wrote of having "spent a part of two mornings in the Library," where she found "everything [was] in as good condition as could possibly be expected after so many years." It had been almost a decade since they had departed. Bittersweet memories accentuated the slight chaos Marsh discovered when she reentered the property left untended and in someone else's care. The dampness of melting winter snows in spring, followed by humid summers in a structure with poor insulation and without air conditioning or dehumidifiers, might have created an unpleasant odor and a damaging mess. Marsh wrote to her husband that with attempts "to keep the books from mildew, and the frequent removal of them from the shelves in order to dry them,"

Figure 2.1. George Perkins Marsh in Villa Forini library, Florence. Credit: Manuscripts and Archives Division, the New York Public Library.

there had been "much misplacing." She explained one cause—"the replacing of them by those who could not well read their titles." Nonetheless, Marsh believed that most of the volumes George had requested would "be found sooner or later." Likely to fill "at least six large cases," she would use her own literary judgement to add to his list of requests: "I shall doubtless find some others that I think will be acceptable to us in Florence."[8]

Marsh asserted her thoughts in a fashion typical of many women—masked behind the opinions of men with authority. George's brother Charles and the congressman George F. Edmunds, the nephew who had helped to secure George's position in Italy, joined Caroline in this library work.[9] Drawing from their authority, Marsh wrote to her husband, "On looking over the pile selected for the college, Charles suggests, and Mr. Edmunds concurs, that even these books might be sold for a sum that would be worth considering by us, and they propose that they should not be handed over until I have asked you whether you will not reconsider." Then she blended into the argument of monetary value her masked desires that the library not be "scatter[ed]": "Charles is also desirous to rerent the Library for himself, if this can be done, and he thinks this an additional argument why you should not . . . scatter your books more than is necessary just at present."[10]

Marsh extended her desire and the argument by inserting the views of additional family and friends in Vermont: she wrote, "I find also that *everybody*—I mean all our friends—would prefer that all the little knick-knacks be left in the Library [and] should still remain our property rather than become theirs" (author's emphasis). Recognizing the emotional needs of family and friends, and perhaps wanting to hide her own difficulties in letting go of the house and their possessions, she began to negotiate with George some alternatives to dispersal of the contents. As she explained, "So long as we have something here, there is still a feeling that we may be with *them* again at some future day, and even if this hope is never realized, I see that it gives *them* more pleasure than the possession of any of our little treasures could possibly do."[11]

Marsh initiated these negotiations with a question directed toward George. She asked his opinion, but she clearly directed him as well: "What do you say then to our having the catalogue finished as you desire and sent to you for your direction as to the disposition to be made of the books?" Although she acknowledged his "desire" of "having the catalogue finished" and his "direction as to the disposition of the books," she also proposed, "only sending to you the books already directed . . . leaving all others in the Library for the present except such as I see would be useful to our young people here and elsewhere." The dutiful wife shifted to suggest "only sending" him those she believed "useful" and retaining "all others." The movement between her thoughts, his desires, and her wishes reveals Marsh's subtle assertions and delicate negotiations, which continued as she explained that these books distributed "to our young people here and elsewhere" would be "with the understanding . . . that they are loans and not gifts." Lending rather than giving, Marsh explained, would make her "much happier." Finally, she concluded, "but of course it is for you to decide, and we shall none of us raise objections farther than to express our own personal feeling."[12]

Marsh reassured her husband a few days later, adding to the yet-unsent letter, "You may be sure I will try to do nothing that does not seem to me clearly a duty, and for all my duties I have confident hopes that my strength will be sufficient."[13] Yet Marsh's persuasive strategies for dealing with the books and other possessions must have carried some weight. The library did stay intact. After George's death, railroad magnate Frederick Billings purchased it, combining the volumes in Florence with the volumes that had been left in Burlington. He donated all to the University of Vermont, along with funds to build what became the Billings Library, which stands as a reminder—illuminated by these letters—of Marsh's identity.[14]

The events in the late spring and summer of 1869 stand as representative of the complex layers of her identity as a dutiful wife, mother figure, socially minded teacher, translator, and literary aspirant. The impressive library afforded her both volumes and comfortable spaces for literary work with which she was accustomed most of her life. Marsh's experiences of overseeing the library's move, along with her literary activities or translating and writing letters, journals, short fiction, and poetry illuminate how the writing process—more than published products—contributed to her transformations. The library accordingly serves as an important symbol of Marsh herself, the tree from which roots and branches drew nourishment and produced fruit.[15] Although it risked being split and scattered in 1869, it remains today as a complexly layered record of her life as it intertwined with others. Within the library, volumes of poetry by Elizabeth Barrett Browning and Matthew Arnold's writings in English, for example, influenced Marsh, as did Italian children's tales and other non-Anglo texts. Alongside these textual influences, however, were her experiences as an activist, wife, mother, and *ambasciatrice*. All these views of herself, documented in the manuscripts she left behind, shifted as did Marsh's changing utopian visions of Italy. These visions manifest how she was transformed by poignant experiences abroad as she engaged with the local culture and with her literary processes. Self-proclaimed—and labeled by others as—"invalid," Marsh remained always a teacher, focused on family close at hand as well as on those she met within other cultures. While she recognized her limitations outside the US, she would continue to believe in the power of literary endeavors in the learning process.

Anne Hampton Brewster: Mr. Kate Cromo

> If she had been a man, she would have been a lawyer. . . . And if she were a man and a lawyer, and I needed some one . . . I would instantly retain Mr. Kate Cromo.
>
> —Mary Agnes Tincker, *By the Tiber* (1881)

More than a decade into following her calling in Rome, Brewster found herself brutalized by her one-time friend, Mary Agnes Tincker. Fellow author and adult convert to Roman Catholicism, Tincker poked fun at Brewster in her popular novel *By the Tiber* (1881) by creating the character Kate Cromo—pushy, assertive, and manipulative—viewed as less than ideal by several characters.[16] Certainly, however, as much as it may have dismayed Brewster, the appearance of Cromo in *By the Tiber* also spoke to her prominence in Rome at the time as a female correspondent. Brewster attracted attention and comments by both men and women, who noted her rhetorical and social power. Yet Brewster's dedication to her writing also caused her to alienate many people.

Cromo's character in Tincker's novel illustrates the tensions with which Brewster lived as a female correspondent in Rome. Although several characters considered Cromo less than ideal, some described her otherwise. One saw her as "very clever . . . and very amusing," because "she can caricature a person perfectly."[17] These skills would even "make you laugh at your best friend." And another character, writer Clive Willis, explained that "the key-note" to understanding Cromo "is a capital I." In spite of these egotistical and self-centered behaviors, Cromo persuaded many that her concern was for them. In fact, Willis continued,

> If she had been a man, she would have been a lawyer. . . . And if she were a man and a lawyer, and I needed some one to prove that I never existed, and that all who imagined to have seen me were suffering from an optical illusion, and that my own notion

> that I existed was an hallucination, and, since a person who never existed cannot have an hallucination, that I never even fancied that I existed; and then, this having been all satisfactorily proved to the world, if I needed that my counsel should turn about the next day, and prove to all the world that he never said any such thing,—I would instantly retain Mr. Kate Cromo for any fee which he should choose to name.[18]

Willis explained and justified that Cromo's arguments were not "fibs" but rather "grafted truths," what he called "Cromatics." While these Cromatics gesture toward concerns now with "fake news" and truth-telling, Tincker's fictionalized rendering of Brewster through Cromo and Willis speaks even more loudly of gendered expectations then for acceptable behavior. Cromo crossed gender boundaries somewhat successfully; by contrast, Brewster's behaviors stayed within the confines of expected behavior. As she wrote to her friend Thomas Davidson in 1876, she "gave in, woman like" when another friend and informant, Rodolfo Lanciani, was lauded for achievements that had caused a breach between the two of them.

Brewster's career path ended in the shadows, illuminating her situation as a female reporter. The commentary on Cromo as "Mr. Kate" presents this vexed circumstance, resembling in some ways Henry James's caricatured news writer Henrietta Stackpole, who appeared in his *Portrait of a Lady* the same year as Tincker's novel. This fictional "foreign correspondent" has been associated with a number of potential sources—Constance Fenimore Woolson, Kate Fields, and Mary Marcy McClellan among them—but never Brewster.[19] Aggressive and patriotic, Stackpole asserts the goodness of all things American and gains iconic power, in some readers' eyes, as representing and writing for the masses. At the same time, she is a "monster"—without family money and "brash" among the more cosmopolitan characters, especially a "foil, moral touchstone and comic relief" for the tragic figure Isabel Archer. As Jean Marie Lutes has explained, Stackpole represents newspaper women in the era of a changing industry, who created anxieties among male writers, especially because of the audiences they drew. They were "both standard-bearers and scapegoats"—"agent(s) and object(s) of the news."[20] Lutes's comments about the increasing mechanization and loss of sensuality and "sexual attributes" among newspaper women provide a backdrop for considering Brewster's transformations throughout her career as well as her dogged determination to remain independent and "free" from any "Beloved"—words she would employ later, as she channeled Ralph Waldo Emerson to describe her path.[21]

Several points illuminate Brewster's situation. First, Lutes associates fictional "foreign correspondents" with their sources in reality. Second, she points to changes in the American newspaper industry that were associated with women, their professional lives, and their writing styles. And finally, Lutes brings up gendered distinctions in behavior that caused anxiety among some men in the field as well as women who encountered female news writers, leading often to condemnation. As Lutes has noted, "existing scholarship on journalism and literature [after the Civil War] dismisses women as deviants from a culture that tied newspaper work to male identity."[22] Similarly, Sari Edelstein, writing of the earlier Civil War reporting by women such as Alcott, has underscored that women writers who attempted objectivity and lack of personal references were condemned for being without feelings.[23] These ideas not only render the richness of Tincker's character, Cromo, but also Brewster's situation as an initially successful reporter in Rome. Tincker's and James's depictions provide powerful lenses for understanding the ways in which Brewster negotiated the complex circles of new Rome, what she had envisioned as her utopian New World. Complementing these fictional lenses, Brewster's writing clarifies what might be otherwise blurred.

Brewster's journal entries and private correspondence alongside her published "letters" from Rome reveal how she went to great lengths to gather information that those in the US would find interesting and informative. She went about Rome—whether to tourist sites, artists' studios, concerts, receptions, political events, or religious services—with an eye and ear for her writing. She interacted with others—some of whom she did not care to engage—to generate stories for the presses. Less than a century earlier, renowned Philadelphia leaders such as Benjamin Franklin and Benjamin Rush had deemed all social interactions important keys to professional success, and they passed this message on to their readers.[24] Of course, they likely imagined males rather than females heeding their advice. Even two decades after nineteenth-century strides in advocacy for women's rights (such as the convention at Seneca Falls, New York, in 1848), Brewster, a female opportunist in the era of US Reconstruction and Italian Unification, was judged harshly.

Diversity in Self-Presentation: A Summary View

Portraits Brewster, Marsh, and Gould left behind, like the vignettes above, capture their activities during the larger expanse of their time abroad. Self-presentation in portraiture—similar to today's "selfie" choices—often was created intentionally and in collaboration with the portrait artist.[25] These visuals provide introductions for readers today to women whose words present other views. An early portrait of Marsh, for example, with her husband and sister depicts her seated within a family, as she saw herself throughout her life. Their physically connected bodies—with Caroline's hand on her husband's wrist, and Lucy's hands on George's shoulder—reflect the web of relations within Marsh's marital family as well as her extensive biological family of origin. Caroline's other hand holds a leaf of paper, perhaps a letter to family, or perhaps reflecting her literary interests, as George, too, holds a leaf. In a later portrait, taken in Florence by the Fratelli Alinari (ca. 1866) when Caroline was about fifty, she sits alone at a desk. The portrait presents her

Figure 2.2. Caroline Crane Marsh, seated right, with George Perkins Marsh and sister Lucy Crane, ca. 1849. Credit: Library of Congress, DAG no. 231.

more overtly as a genteel woman of letters—perhaps even more accustomed to being distant from her husband and developing a more independent view of herself, although she remained connected to them and others by correspondence throughout her life. A final portrait, from the Schemboche galleries (ca. 1881), in which she also appears alone, is deceptive—since the photo was one among a set taken by others in her family of origin: her nephew Alexander and one of his daughters, Caroline, or "Lina." These, too, illustrate how Marsh remained connected to them, even after her husband George died in 1882, with these family members present. She would live near or with "Alick," as she affectionately referred to her nephew, and his family in Scarsdale, New York, up to the time of her death.

Gould's portrait, in the opening pages of the biography *A Life Worth Living* (1879), which Leonard Woolsey Bacon composed, presents and preserves the romanticized image of a genteel American woman abroad.

Figure 2.3. Caroline Crane Marsh, ca. 1866, Fratelli Alinari, Florence. Credit: Silver Special Collections Library, University of Vermont.

Figure 2.4. Caroline Crane Marsh, ca. 1881, Schemboche Galleries. Credit: Manuscripts and Archives Division, the New York Public Library.

Figure 2.5. Alexander B. Crane, ca. 1881, Schemboche Galleries. Credit: Manuscripts and Archives Division, the New York Public Library.

Figure 2.6. Caroline Emma Crane, ca. 1881, Schemboche Galleries. Credit: Manuscripts and Archives Division, the New York Public Library.

The engraving by A. H. Ritchie, based on a portrait by Lorenzo Suscipj, suggests Gould's social background. Suscipj, a daguerrotype artist whose status in Rome was similar to that of the Fratelli D'Alessandri in Rome or Alinari in Florence, created portraits of members of the royal family and other prominent patrons. Gould's portrait is not unique in its backdrop, posture, and garb: well-dressed in black with a lace head-covering and surrounded by columns and arches of Roman architecture, she stands alone rather than with her husband. Additionally notable, however, the choices and arrangement of accoutrements speak to viewers. A fan—seen often in other portraits—in this case neither hides nor cools the face. Not in hand, the fan rests on a nearby pillar. Instead, Gould extends a book, appearing as a woman with intellectual concerns rather than those of physical comfort or social games. Later, in the report of the Italo-American Schools published just before her death, she presented herself as a mother figure, posing with two Venetian children whom her school had taken in.

In contrast to Gould's upright position, Brewster's portrait in a *carte de visite* created by the Alessandri brothers around 1874 presents her in the

Figure 2.7. Emily Bliss Gould, engraving by A. H. Ritchie, based on portrait by Lorenzo Suscipj, Rome, from Leonard Woolsey Bacon, *A Life Worth Living*. Credit: General Research Division, the New York Public Library.

Figure 2.8. Emily Bliss Gould with Venetian Bartoli children, from *Italo-American Schools at Rome* [1874], New-York Historical Society. Credit: Photography ©New-York Historical Society.

striking reclining Roman pose. Rather than reclining nude, like the famous Antonio Canova sculpture of the infamous Pauline Bonaparte as Venus Victrix (1805–08), Brewster is clothed—in the black velvet and simple jewels she most often chose for public occasions. Bonaparte's reputation for self-centeredness and sexual looseness ran through popular literary culture, noted in Leonora Sansay's *Secret History; or, the Horrors of San Domingo* (1808) and Catharine Maria Sedgwick's *Clarence* (1830).[26] In light of Bonaparte's behaviors and the Canova sculpture, most intriguing about Brewster's portrait choice are her age and her posture. A woman in her fifties, Brewster selected a pose of leisure and sensuality rather than the upright posture of Gould's, which suggests moral activism. The portrait illustrates one utopian vision of life abroad—she would escape the confines of her brother's control and engage in literary work, as would the other two women, but as she wrote about Roman life and culture, she would also focus on the sensual and less overtly "improving" and practical topics of art and music. Although she was neither amoral nor unethical, Brewster's vision was not undergirded as much by a Protestant work ethic and restraint as the other women's.

Figure 2.9. Anne Hampton Brewster, Carte de Visite, Fratelli D'Alessandri, Rome, ca. 1874. Credit: The Library Company of Philadelphia.

Figure 2.10. Antonio Canova's *Venus Victrix*, 1805–08, Villa Borghese, Rome. Credit: Daderot on Wikimedia Commons, 14 April 2019.

As their portraits suggest their varying postures and actions, the later vocations these women pursued resist any monolithic idea of Italy, magnifying the diversity of sexual, religious, and political views of it. The diversity also emerges through the window of the tumultuous summer of 1870—the period in which "the Roman Question" peaked, as many in the western world watched and waited to see whether and when Italian soldiers would march into the Eternal City and how the pope would respond.

Chapter 3

Summer of the Roman Question

A Window on Transnational Networks

> How wonderful it is! Italy and France both set free from the influence and authority of the two worst men in Europe and the continent itself from the first dread evil of the serpent which has so long coiled itself about the liberty and morality of the people. I do hope the vile old Vaticaner will run away.
>
> —Emily Bliss Gould to Caroline Crane Marsh, September 1870[1]

In July of 1870, Anne Hampton Brewster wrote from a desk at 107 Via del Babuino in Rome, just off the Piazza di Spagna. Known for the density of Anglo authors who lived there in the nineteenth century, the area's streets housed Elizabeth Barrett Browning and her husband Robert, Mary Wollstonecraft Shelley and her husband Percy Bysshe, Nathaniel Hawthorne and his wife Sophia, and John Keats, among others.[2] While these expatriates sought Rome's sunny skies in the winter, most escaped the lower-lying streets near the Tiber River for reasons of health during the summer heat, when "Roman Fever"—malaria—erupted. Despite the dangers of the summer season in Rome, however, Brewster wrote happily of her surroundings. She was "snugly settled" with "a maid to wait on" her, and she had her friends from Philadelphia, the Thomas Buchanan Read family, to dine with. The painter Read, his wife, and his daughter "Hattie," especially, provided Brewster company. She had been "miserable all winter" in the "wretched . . . rooms" of her lodgings in 71 Via della Croce, just a few steps away. From those "wretched . . . rooms," however, Brewster had written almost obsessively—not only in her journal but also letters that were being published weekly in the *Philadelphia Evening Bulletin*. And occasionally she sent letters to the *Boston Daily Advertiser*. But in July Brewster reflected in her journal on the improvement of her work space, thanks to "Mrs. Gould," who "kindly" invited Brewster into "her fine airy apartment . . . during her absence."[3]

The Goulds' "airy apartment" in Via del Babuino, just around the corner from her winter lodgings in Via della Croce, brought Brewster back to the palazzo she had first inhabited upon her arrival in Rome, in November of 1868. Now a floor below where she had lived for several months with the Reads, the rooms were likely of the *piano nobile*, the palazzo's main floor, with loftier ceilings, more light, and ventilation—all important to the regular writing that occupied much of her days. Upon her arrival in Rome she had begun sending "letters" to Gibson Peacock's daily paper, whose front page claimed it was news for and of "the world." Having written for Peacock's *Evening Bulletin* for more than a year, and with her letters sometimes appearing twice weekly on the front page throughout the spring of 1870, Brewster was compelled to stay in Rome that summer in order to report on the Vatican Council's ongoing discussions of papal infallibility. She had a calling to write, and she had a following of readers.

In fact, the *Boston Daily Advertiser* editor, Delano A. Goddard, had written to her in May, paying her eight pounds sterling—the equivalent of about UK£950 or US$1150 in 2019—for her previous letters, which had been well received "everywhere."[4] He also expressed disappointment that she would not be staying in Rome to write of the political events.[5] Goddard's supportive correspondence apparently influenced Brewster. Earlier that year, in January, she had written of plans to travel north in summer to Dresden, the Tyrol, Salzburg, Venice, and Florence, but as the months rolled by, she took only brief trips closer to her Roman home: to Naples, Sorrento, and Capri. In fact, in March she noted in her journal how busy she was and how much money she had made. Having written sixty-four "letters" since November, she had earned six hundred dollars. In fewer than four months, she had earned the equivalent of about US$11,700 today, and was "well in advance of" her expenses.[6]

Chief among her activities during the winter and spring was keeping up with both the Vatican discussions and responses to them. In March she participated in the pope's visit to the American College for "Mass, the Beatification of a Bishop, a collation and a reception." The American College was a relatively new venture, established after American bishops attended the pope's proclamation of the new dogma of Immaculate Conception in 1854. Key supporters were Archbishop Hughes of New York, Archbishop Kenrick of Baltimore, Bishop Michael O'Connor of Pittsburgh, Bishop Neumann of Philadelphia, and Dr. Lynch, Administrator of Charleston. The college had officially opened in 1859.[7] Following the event at the American College, the group migrated to an evening gathering at a Mrs. Whelan's home. There Brewster "met a lot of Bishops and a number of the disagreeable American Catholics." Despite her conversion to Roman Catholicism, Brewster vented in her journal, "A more snobbish set of people surely were never gathered together than the American petticoat fringe of the American Bishops."[8] Brewster's motivations for her own snobbishness toward this group remain unclear. Were they due to her not being married and not having an escort for the social events? She was an "old maid" of 52 years. Given her numerous social engagements, this reason seems unlikely. Perhaps her attitude emerged from her not being a cradle Catholic? Her first communion had been at age 29, and she was confirmed again in Rome late in 1869. But there were other adult converts in Rome, her journal acknowledged. Or was it her financial status? Although a descendant of New England Puritans and having a brother who was financially successful, she constantly worried about being short of funds as she labored for money. Or was Brewster merely too independent to want to be a part of "the American petticoat fringe" who were trailing the American bishops?

The answer likely is some combination of these. She always saw herself as an outsider, different from the others, yet at the same time she longed to be a part of the elegant social class and often wrote about marriage and sexual relationships. Brewster's ambivalence resulted in a clear divide—anxieties and spite erupt in her private journal writings, but not in the pages that poured from the press for the public. Whatever the reasons for such vitriolic comments as she recorded privately that spring, Brewster's public reports continued regularly in Boston and Philadelphia papers, sharing the divided attitudes toward papal infallibility. Brewster sent back two letters to Boston, as well as approximately thirty accounts to other papers that reported on the changing scene. The letters captured the stances of American bishops, about which she wrote bald comments in her journal. She found Rochester's Bishop Bernard John McQuaid "shrewd and clever"; she considered Father Isaac Thomas Hecker "coarse"; and Father McNeiring, Archbishop of Halifax, was "a very jolly Irishman." She heard sermons delivered by Archbishop Martin John Spalding and Monsignor Thomas John Capel at the church of Saint Andrea della Valle and commented on both their delivery and their arguments. The former she found "straight forward . . . not eloquent but powerful—earnest, practical & strong." Capel had "an entirely different style" but had gained "considerable notoriety" for converting the Marquis of Bute.

The brash comments of Brewster's journal rarely appeared in her news stories, likely ensuring that her engagements with multiple papers would continue. Indeed, that year McQuaid had arranged for her to contribute to a Rochester publication, and Brewster also noted agreements with papers in St. Louis and New Orleans. In March of 1870, as American interest in the Roman Question increased, Brewster contributed to the *Cincinnati Commercial* and the *Boston Daily Advertiser* as well. All these agreements were for publications in cities with large Roman Catholic populations. By October, she had sent them nine lengthy front- or second-page stories (more than one per month), each different from the twenty she had sent to Philadelphia from June through October. Other newspapers scattered from Charleston and Columbia, South Carolina, to Winchester and Memphis, Tennessee, and as far west as Honolulu, Hawaii, picked up and reprinted from Brewster's letters without her awareness. This reprinting, typical of the era, depended on agreements between the publishers, not with the authors.[9]

To gather news, Brewster not only read papers in French and Italian from throughout the peninsula, but also talked with her Roman and French informants. And, of course, she ventured about the city and its environs. Usually, she referred openly to these sources—both people and print—and placed herself within the stories. She valued eyewitness observation, which had emerged as important during the Civil War years, and in which writers such as Louisa May Alcott rose to recognition for their works.[10] Beginning in mid-August, for example, her journal pages were packed with details she observed from her windows above the Piazza di Spagna and from roaming about outside. As many Anglos left Rome at the time surrounding the Italian soldiers' entry, she poked about with her sculptor friend Harriet Hosmer and another writer, Englishman Augustus John Cuthbert Hare. She, Hosmer, and Hare attended vespers at St. Peter's to witness the pope and other church leaders. They circled the city to see the earthworks being constructed at several ancient entrances to the city: Porta Pia, Porta Salera, and Porta del Popolo. Brewster explained how Americans prepared for the entry. "Mr. Read has put out the American flag" due to his "fear of soldiers in the city." He hoped the sign would save him from harm.

Continuing through late September, Brewster captured in her journal the anticipation, excitement, and confusion of a political world turned upside down. She wrote of the French soldiers' departure, the pope's plans to abdicate, the declarations at Paris, and the impact on the people: "The fear now is of a Revolution and proclamation of a Republic in Italy. If so there will be terrible scenes in Rome. The people are disappointed. Yesterday there was the greatest gayety: today complete discouragement." Brewster referred to her local informants, such as the young Roman Rodolfo Lanciani: "Lanciani was in this evening and spoke as if all hope was at an end." After Brewster's young friend left, another young Roman "in utter despair" appeared "and mourned as one without hope." As Brewster exclaimed, "These poor young men! They ought to live in a country like America where there is room for advancement. In Europe all places are filled and young talent has no chance."[11] Brewster, like other Americans, wrestled with the view of these Italians as "waste," stifled and unable to grow from their "natural" inborn desires, because their environment did not consist of the proper, nutritive civil soil of republican government.[12]

Such journal entries reveal that Brewster's key informants, young Roman men, and her background as an American influenced her feelings and perspective, just as young revolutionaries Giuseppe Mazzini and Giovanni Ossoli had influenced the American correspondent Fuller two decades earlier. Brewster poured onto the pages her emotional responses to what she witnessed: "What a crowd of events since . . . 18 July when the dogma of Papal Infallibility was proclaimed and how fast they have hurried on! The war between France & Prussia, downfall of Napoleon, French republic and now these approaching troubles in Italy! And one week, one day may show us still more startling events."[13] Yet Brewster also revealed dismay, emerging from her position as a Roman Catholic: church property, such as convents and monasteries, as well as beautiful churches such as St. Martin's, were being wrested by the secular state.

Brewster exuded her anxieties in these entries: "In the distance I can hear the tramp of men marching; then comes the sound of a swiftly galloping horse then all falls back into night stillness; then rise up sounds of voices which seem out of place. . . . I cannot sleep nor read nor do any thing but go to the window and admire the sky and notice the warlike preparations." Brewster tried to calm herself through focused study and mental occupation. As she explained, "I come back to my reading. [But] I am not able to read anything interesting, so I am translating an Italian life of Canova which is a little task and can be dropped at the least notice or sound." In these days and nights of sleepless anticipation, Brewster lost track of dates, correcting her journal entries, "10'oc Wednesday no Thursday morning 15 Sept" and

"4"oc (same night) Thursday morning. 15 Sept: 70." She recorded with disappointment in the early morning hours: "All night I have watched. This is the dawn of the day on which the famous Convention between Napoleon 3 & Victor Emanuel ends. We fully expected something would take place this night but nothing has. Still as death the town has been."

Circuits to visit the earthworks surrounding the city punctuated Brewster's restless nights. She traveled up the Janiculum hill to the church of San Pietro in Montorio and the Pauline Fountain, a favorite elevated viewing point from the west. "Crowds of persons were assembled on these points," she explained, "striving to see the Italian camp near Monte Mario" to the northwest of Rome. The previous day they had witnessed a blindfolded "*parlamentaire*" coming from the Italians, asking the city to surrender—but contrary to her expectations, the response was "no." Brewster had heard the day before from her informant friend Lanciani that Prince Altieri had told him "that . . . he & the Senator of Rome called on his Holiness [and] asked the Pope what course had been concluded upon." Pius IX's response was, "If the people of Rome obey me there will be nothing done beyond a protest." Such rumors flew, but the people did not bow to the pope's wish, and Rome fell from his power. After the "flag of truce" appeared over the Vatican and the "storming" of the city, Brewster went about with her friends Hosmer, American sculptor Albert Harnisch, and the Anglo-Italian poet and artist Dante Gabriel Rossetti, before returning home to write of witnessing the French Zouave soldiers "scampering" away. She observed "all from the top of Rossetti's house," near the Porta Pinceana.[14]

Many of these privately recorded observations made their way into Brewster's published correspondence. Since the new technology of the transatlantic cable rapidly sent war and political news from Europe to the US, a fact Brewster acknowledged on the printed page, how did her later-arriving accounts maintain a readership? With the approximate two-week delay between writing and publication, why did Brewster's observations of the excitement on the ground in Rome find a following in the US? Distinguishing them from the more quickly dispatched articles, Brewster's voice provided personal details and insights.[15] Like today's feature stories of the weekend and Sunday press, Brewster's longer letters provided a different style than the daily coverage. Their prominent position on the first or second page, often in the Thursday or Sunday issues, attest to how her writing style and presence on the ground in Rome contributed to her appeal.

~

During the summer of 1870, Brewster's gracious hostess in Via Babuino, "Mrs. Gould," was among those escaping Rome's heat and fevers. She and her husband, a physician to Americans abroad, habitually headed to the mountains further north. This year they had traveled through the Alps to Switzerland, where they enjoyed the mountain air of Pontresina, just a few kilometers from the well-known resort of St. Moritz. Emily sought the area's mineral springs, known for healing. From Pontresina, Emily and James would travel on to Le Prese on Lake Poschiavo and then to Milan to see their friends the Waylands. James would remain behind to consult on Mrs. Wayland's health, while Emily would continue to Lake Como, Turin, La Tour, and the Valais, the Swiss canton closest to France. The mountainous region was full of villages with Waldensians, members of a non-Catholic Christian group whose history pre-dates what is considered the beginning of the Protestant Reformation in 1520, Martin Luther's excommunication. Emily's first meetings with Waldensians on her overland trip to Rome in 1860 and glimpses of their schools in La Tour in 1861 had inspired her interest in securing financial support for them and employing their models elsewhere on the peninsula.

Gould had already been brought before a Roman tribunal for her involvement with Anglo Protestants who were meeting privately in 1868. But the event had not slowed her fervor in maintaining her faith and reaching out to children she believed would benefit from education. Like many Protestants, she believed the Roman Catholic Church repressed education. Because religious freedom had been proclaimed in the Piedmont region in 1848, a result of the revolutions in Europe, and she had witnessed the results of Waldensian education in the mountain villages around Turin upon her first arrival in Italy, she had contributed to the push for broader education in Tuscany. She had cast her efforts upon new works in Florence, where the former political exile Salvatore Ferretti had returned from London and established in 1862 the Casa per Orfane, an orphanage and school for poor Italian children. The institution linked him with the Italian "Free Church" and Alessandro Galvazzi, who had made highly publicized, anti-Catholic lecture tours in the US. Like Galvazzi, Ferretti was a former Roman Catholic who had advocated changes while abroad, and he established schools for poor Italian children in London.[16] These works influenced Gould, so that when news arrived of the Vatican Council's ruling of papal infallibility in the summer of 1870 and the potential political fallout, she envisioned future freedom of religion in the Papal States and anticipated its arrival in Rome. Should papal temporal power be abolished, the opportunities to teach Roman children now under the authority of the pope would be limitless.

In fact, Gould's motivation for time in the Valais in 1870 was, she wrote, "to do my duty to my poor babes in the Alps."[17] She commented on these travels in letters written to the Marshes throughout the period. Gould expressed her excitement about European political activities and the increasing speculations about the Italian soldiers' movements. Just before the Italian army's triumphal march into Rome in September of 1870, for example, she wrote to Caroline Marsh from Pontresina:

> We have been so bewildered by the late news that we have not known what to do or where to go. That those two bad men [Napoleon III and Pope Pius IX] should fall in one little week; how wonderful it is! Italy and France both set free from the influence and authority of the two worst men in Europe and the continent itself from the first dread evil of the serpent which has so long coiled itself about the liberty and morality of the people. I do hope the vile old Vaticaner will run away. There is nobody to bring him back, and while he remains in Rome, he can plot more to the purpose than when he is not of it.[18]

Although Gould's vehemently anti-Catholic language of "The vile old Vaticaner" and the "serpent which has so long coiled itself about . . . the people" differed greatly from Brewster's of the same season, it included the same jittery anticipation of dramatic changes.

Like Brewster, Gould wrote specifically of her sources and the circuits of these letters and newspapers: "I received a letter yesterday written on the fifth." It provided the stances of Prussia, England, and the Pope's chief adviser Giacomo Antonelli, who "entreated" him "to be reconciled with Italy." She saw Antonelli's behaviors as overly dramatic, especially in his threats of martyrdom. She wrote of his stubbornness, "He says he will never give up, wishes his army to retreat step by step before the Italians until they reach the Vatican; there to be slain, and he will die with them. Beautiful, is it not, but not quite original." She concluded with her contrasting view: "I think he will run away."[19]

Gould's writing here, as in articles of the *Overland Monthly*, demonstrates her literary acumen. Metaphors and punning spark her commentary, making her self-presentation as important as news of unfolding events. For example, in another letter she wrote to Marsh, she mused, "They say that the Immaculate Conception has its chapel in charming order, but [it] is not altogether sea-worthy. So perhaps the Pope will prefer to say his masses in a vessel which will not necessitate his having wet feet." She turns from images of the pope in a sinking ship to her analogies of the first and third Napoleons' behaviors as voracious, victimizing leaders of France: "How like the old tiger has the young one proved himself!" Then Gould commented on the news at hand, broadcast through the European press, revealing her impatience: "The Doctor [Gould] has just returned from St. Möritz with papers e[tc] and we see that the actual march upon Rome is delayed for the sake of attending to the necessary preceding formalities. I wish they would give these 2 camps down there no more time for preparation."[20]

Not long after, Gould wrote from Lake Como and posted from Turin a letter to "Mr. Marsh" that revealed more of her agitation, her calling to work with "poor babes" in the Valais, and her excitement about the Italian King Victor Emmanuel's entrance to Rome. Additionally, the letter expressed her sense of power through wealth and connections as well as her affection for the US Ambassador. She wrote, "I want to do my duty to my poor babes in the Alps, but I do also want to be in Rome when the king goes in." She wanted to arrive in Rome "two or three days beforehand" just so that she could receive George as a guest. She explained, "We have a big house now, and I know I can make you more comfortable than you could be at a hotel and we want you and have waited for you so long that now we will not be denied. . . . We have rooms also for your servants at the top of our same house; having taken them for store rooms, servants rooms, or whatever, and they are as yet empty." Although she employed "you," which might refer to both Mr. and Mrs. Marsh, she addressed the letter only to George, and the prior letter she had addressed only to Caroline.

Before mailing the letter, Gould set it aside, only to pick it up a few days later, continuing the political gossip and revelation of her growing relationship with George: "I hear that the entry of the king is to be on the 18th. If you have any means of knowing, will you kindly drop me a line. I wanted a fortnight for the Valais, but of course if this is true, shall give but a week and then come directly down, stopping in Florence just long enough to see you, and then direct to Rome." She added, "I will cover the flag of my country with disgrace if you do not come to us." George had written to her with "gibes against" the Goulds' "healthy residence and . . . profession"—likely a reference to the posh lakes region and financial status of a physician's family—but she did not respond to those comments, due to her "haste." Gould playfully noted that she would "leave them to rankle for the moment," before signing, "With best love & hopes."[21] She could have addressed the letter to "Mrs. Marsh," but Gould's choice was George—and such was her choice for most of the Gould–Marsh correspondence. This playful letter and affectionate closing reinforce the complexities of the networks in Rome—including some crossing of expected gender boundaries—in which Gould, Brewster, and Marsh interacted as they followed their vocations. The three women depended on men and fulfilled traditional gendered expectations, but they also occasionally pushed the boundaries in the midst of this politically charged climate.

In mid-August of 1870 Caroline Marsh was in Paris, one of the reasons that Gould wrote only to George. She had traveled there for medical treatment, since the ill health that often debilitated her had recurred. In the summers just prior to 1870, Marsh had taken sea baths near Livorno and mineral baths at Bagni di Lucca, both in Tuscany, and had traveled to Switzerland and to Paris, seeking medical help. In March of 1870, while Brewster was writing of the American "petticoat fringe" in Rome, George had confidentially requested a two-month leave from his post, explaining by letter what would separate the married couple for part of the summer: "The health of Mrs. Marsh will probably require her to resort to Paris for medical aid in the course of the approaching spring or summer, and I desire to spend a few weeks at a watering place in Germany for similar reasons."[22]

The spring and early summer months had added to Caroline's stresses and concerns. Her favorite nephew, Alexander, New York attorney and businessman, had written about his own stress-induced ill health in the winter, including studying for cases and the manifesting symptom of a "carbuncle," or cold sore, on his lip. "Alick" had been a successful and decorated Union Colonel from Terre Haute, Indiana, during the Civil War. But at this time, when he wrote to his aunt of his burdens, he was fewer than five years into his marriage and a business partnership with his father-in-law, attorney John W. Mitchell. Alick's letter also referred to books that were being packed and shipped to the Marshes, the task that Caroline had helped to oversee in her trip back to the US the previous summer and fall. These concerns remained heavy on her mind. In the spring, a letter from Caroline's sister Lucy Wislizenus, who lived near St. Louis, included confidential information about debts. Closer at hand in Florence, Caroline was busy responding to requests by interested supporters for visits to the school for girls, or "Asylum."

While arranging potential supporters' visits occupied her, concerns about the institution's debts and teachers equally weighed her down. The school's organizers had been hanging on to paper "bills" during the political upheavals, "hoping that they will be worth more [in the future] than they are now," rather than pay the debts with deflated currency. Gould wrote to Marsh that summer, advising "that if the Orphan House or School are living on credit, you should at once draw the money. It was sent for them." Gould's letter also touched upon another of Marsh's preoccupations—the ongoing ill health of her niece Ellen, whose "cough" was not to be "soften[ed]" by the Florentine air nor cured by the cod liver oil Gould advised.[23] In sum, Caroline's concerns for her niece, her nephew, her calling with the school, the Marsh library, and her position as *ambasciatrice* captured her attention and energies, even as she gave attention to the political changes surrounding her and struggled with her own physical limitations.

Certainly, all of these had an impact on Marsh's health, a situation that she humbly believed was perhaps worse for "Mrs. Gould," who also wrestled with ill health. Marsh wrote in November 1869, "Mrs. Gould has been with us some days, and left Sunday evening to join her husband, just arrived in Rome. She is not well, but loses nothing of her old course and does enough for half a dozen." Just prior to writing this letter, Marsh had been "brought lower than [she had] been for many years" and was even "forbidden to write on account of the bad effect" it had on her "nerves."[24] So in the summer of 1870, when news of the increasing turmoil and potential for war in Paris reached Marsh's husband, who was in France at Aix-les-Bains, where he had been taking water treatment for his sciatica, he responded immediately. As he explained in a confidential letter to his superior, although he had left Caroline and Ellen "both in inferior health" in Paris three weeks earlier, "the alarming state of things" there "induced" him "to return to Paris." His goal, he wrote, was "accompanying [his] family to Florence in the course of the present month." Prompted by fear for his family as well as duties to his position in Italy, George retrieved Caroline and their niece and returned immediately with them to his post in Florence.[25]

Whether or not the Marshes accepted Gould's invitation to be in Rome in her ample lodgings with household servants, or whether Gould covered the US flag and hung her head "in disgrace" because the Marshes did not visit, remains unknown. What is clear from the women's writings, however, is that the event in Rome was expected to be a momentous one. Gould had written frantically that she wanted to be in Rome to witness the king's entry, and she wanted the ambassador and his wife to be her guests. But as the stories spread, many fears were allayed and optimism abounded. Brewster wrote for US papers of sitting in her "balcony window, which overlooks the Piazza di Spagna and Babuino," of seeing "cavalry, cannon, soldiers and sand bags go up to the Pincian gardens," and of "the poor inhabitants" at first fleeing—but then returning, as they realized the preparations "meant business and not war." By September 19 and 20, she wrote of being "at the Campidoglio when the flag went up to the summit, and when the Papal arms were taken down." She saw "the entry of the Generals and troops" and she witnessed a grand "ovation" in their honor. She remarked that "the city is illuminated every night" and concluded that "in all this confusion: the people are behaving well!"[26]

While Brewster's activities of the summer of 1870 marked a flurry of professional developments and excitement about a new high point in her life, Gould's activities of the same period were marked by her devotion to the schools' projects and her own ability to move about Europe, writing to and entertaining her friend the ambassador and his wife. Meanwhile, by contrast, the *ambasciatrice*'s activities exuded her burden of family responsibilities, of which these other two women were free. The three women would continue these diverse reactions to their experiences abroad, with this historical moment later providing only one of many bookmarks in their stories. The moment illuminates, however, how transnational networks fostered their writings and engagement with the political situation surrounding them, even as each followed her utopian vision and later vocation in a unique way. Like many other women of their day and social backgrounds, these three generated voluminous pages of letters and journals, which reveal their intertwined experiences. Unfortunately, Gould's extensive journals, which would enhance greatly an understanding of her labors, have not been located. Branching out from the personal roots of journal pages, however, the story of "Miss Jones," in a volume dedicated to Gould, provides another path to understanding her calling in Rome. Unlike Marsh's poetry or Brewster's autobiographical fiction, this tale appears *not* as a self-rendered autobiographical piece but rather as a fictional exhortation drawn from a few elements of Gould's life as depicted by others. This story by the pseudonymous author "Aunt Friendly"—the center of the next chapter—and the volume in which it appears attest further to the transnational networking environment in which these women lived and wrote.[27]

PART II

CIRCUITS AND NETWORKS

Chapter 4

Revising *Daisy Miller*

The Story of "Miss Jones"

> Miss Jones was not traveling alone. She was far too proper for that.
>
> —Aunt Friendly, 1875[1]

> Traveling without "maid or man" is no pleasant business for me.
>
> —Anne Hampton Brewster, 1873[2]

> He is devoted to her as son, friend, or lover—according as one is malicious or not in viewing the connection.
>
> —Caroline Carson, 1873 on Albert Harnisch and Anne Hampton Brewster[3]

When Henry James's now famous fiction of the young Daisy Miller appeared in the *Atlantic Monthly* in 1878, the tragic tale of a young American in Rome "created an uproar" in the American presses—both popular and elite. They had devoted much attention to "the 'American Girl' " abroad.[4] Since Madame de Staël's 1807 novel *Corinne* had depicted a traveling Englishman seduced by an Italian woman on the peninsula, various versions of single Anglo men and women in Italy had sallied forth in print. In all of these, Italy itself became a culprit—its culture and its people could seduce unsuspecting travelers. Women—considered weaker and more vulnerable—especially were susceptible to its dangers. Catharine Maria Sedgwick's *Letters from Abroad to Kindred at Home* (1841), Margaret Fuller's *New-York Tribune* dispatches followed by her *Memoirs* (1852), and Grace Greenwood's humorous sketches collected in *Stories and Sights of France and Italy* (1867), for example, all provided pictures of American women in Italy. Such fictional accounts, autobiographical travel narratives, and letters contributed to the milieu that ripened American audiences, preparing them for James's "sensational publication" that became an instant success and soon rose in the canon of American literature.[5] What the novella *Daisy Miller* makes clear is that the young woman's demise was due to her being "unrestrained," without a chaperone or mother, "oblivious" to the "voices of respectable society" and "ignorant of European customs," as she flirted with a servant and chose to visit the Colosseum by night with an Italian man—alone. Yet not so clear, and what readers past and present have debated, is the verisimilitude of James's depiction, described from the perspective of a male narrator, and whether Daisy is "a virtuous (i.e. innocent) or simply an amoral flirt."[6] More important than resolving this concern, however, is understanding its place in the print culture of the time, which churned around the theme of American women's behaviors in Italy.

Another fictional account—not discussed in American literary or cultural studies—provides an enriching and equally problematic depiction, although for different reasons. "Miss Jones," written by "Aunt Friendly" (most likely Sarah Schoonmaker Baker, who wrote didactic and moralistic works for children with this pseudonym), appeared three years earlier than James's *Daisy Miller* and deserves attention for how it revives and revises discussions of his tale.[7] Because the account's publication predates the publication of James's story of the tragic Daisy by three years, "Aunt Friendly" actually did not aim to "revise" the narrative, as this chapter's title suggests. The images James's work amplified, popularized and reified were already part of the public imagination. Instead, this consideration of "Miss Jones" revises *Daisy Miller* in two other ways. First, it points to the rekindled interest in images of American women in Italy—an interest recent scholarship has enflamed. Second, it highlights another female character's behaviors with local citizens, clothing, meals, lodging, languages, and sightseeing—all conscious choices she made about daily life that shaped her time abroad and differed significantly from Daisy's. These choices culminate in another decisive action: Miss Jones's response to a calling or "vocation." As a result of her choices, this American woman saw a different end than Daisy. As the tale transpires differently, it enlarges contemporary visions of the print public sphere with which American women abroad were engaged and in which they were often, for better or worse, implicated. As it does so, it illuminates the arena of social activism into which Gould, Brewster, and Marsh arrived and engaged themselves.

Set as well as published in Rome, "Miss Jones" sports an entitled heroine who undergoes a dramatic change. Entitled not only in name but also financially, Miss Jones sets aside her initial interest in absorbing the sites of the "Eternal City's" glorious ancient past. Instead, this young unmarried American turns her attention away from the past to the present, and from herself toward the needs of impoverished, illiterate Roman youths she sees around her. Indeed, a conversion, or new mindset, and "resurrection" to a new life in Rome occur through her influence upon another human. Miss Jones contributes to the recovery and revival of an ill child, her "servant" Vittorio. Through Vittorio's new life, Miss Jones herself gains a new life, and the potential for reviving many more lives comes before the eyes of American and British readers of the hopeful and didactic sentimental tale.

The fictional account of Miss Jones appeared in a collection published in 1875 by the Italo-American School that Gould had established in Rome.[8] Entitled *In Memoriam: A Wreath of Stray Leaves to the Memory of Emily Bliss Gould*, the collection was edited by English author Thomas Adolphus Trollope, with a preface by the well-known English poet Mary Howitt and an array of other contributors known in Anglo-American literary and political circles. The collection—its initial conception, its contributors, and its publication—illustrates the networks at the center of this study (discussed in a later chapter) and the ways in which Gould in her life in Rome and the fictional Miss Jones differed significantly from Daisy. Of course, Gould was older than both Miss Jones and Daisy, and she was married. Most significantly, as the tale addresses the pervasive concern with American women abroad at the time of Italian Unification, it adds a concern for Italian children's plight in a system that seemed to have doomed them to illiteracy and poverty from birth. Through this concern "Miss Jones" provides images that attempt also to revise popular stereotypes.

As the tale illustrates choices women travelers made, it points to many acute concerns, fears, and emotional tensions that several authors, both male and female, expressed about life abroad. The emphasis on women's choices and optimistic hopes, however, places them in the subject position, objectifying and depending on the young, impoverished Romans to stay afloat and maintain their sense of an upright status. Gould's industrial school and its exemplary memorial volume collectively embody the fraught subject–object relationship in which she and other contributors were complicit as they contributed to social reform. While Miss Jones and the collection's editors do not recognize the problematic power dynamics of this complicit relationship, Gould and other American reformers abroad, as *Engaging Italy* demonstrates, often did begin to realize these positions as their labors progressed. Consider first, though, the very real fears that instigated James's tale and others, and then the ways in which "Miss Jones" attempted to revise such fears through utopian optimism and patterns for life abroad. The constant awareness of the dangers and dilemmas of living in another culture for extended periods lay alongside the promises of liberty, freedom, rebirth, and utopian renewal.

Abroad Alone: Myths and Realities of Independence

While American women such as Fuller and the fictional Daisy were accused of being independent and becoming increasingly and dangerously more so as they spent time in Italy, very few, if any, would become completely independent of relationships and connections. Few people went it alone. Sedgwick traveled with her brother and his family. Fuller at first traveled with the Spring family, serving as a tutor to the children. Woolson traveled abroad with her sister Clara and niece Clare to France, then met the unmarried Emily Clark in Switzerland before the two of them and Emily's "maid" headed to Italy.[9] Even later in the nineteenth century, the Boston-based Women's Rest Tour Association provided a means of liberation and an alternative for women who did not choose to travel with family.[10] It linked up single women and female friends who wished to see Europe, even as it marketed itineraries and lodgings abroad. Often women would act differently once they adjusted to life on the continent. Fuller and Woolson, for example, both later lived alone—but this status did not mean they were isolated from interactions with household help or without connections to other people. Correspondence and journaling also were essential.

Earlier in the century, the single Brewster had carefully planned her two trips abroad—almost alone. Her first, in 1857–58, was with her "maid" and her dog. Nonetheless, she was overwhelmed by the crowds when she landed at Le Havre and relieved only slightly by the letter of introduction from US Minister Owen. Even so, she expressed in her journal thankfulness for the goodness of a young man who assisted them at a train station in France, as they journeyed to Switzerland. Her fears in France were perhaps prompted by a man on shipboard during the first Atlantic crossing, who crossed boundaries of propriety in suggestive conversations with her. Such fears emerged in her fictional account of this time abroad, *St. Martin's Summer*. Her second trip, a decade later, was on a freighter with a family of five—the Captain Percy, his wife, and three children ranging from five years to twenty-two months. Although on this long journey Brewster despised the crying children, she never expressed fears of being preyed upon. Her only desperation was expressed forty-nine days into the crossing—longing for a bath as they approached the port of Messina on the Sicilian coast after seven weeks at sea.[11]

More than the mature Brewster, a younger, single woman would be at risk of danger traveling alone, so she usually journeyed with family or friends. To them she could be both a help and a hindrance, providing both freedom and obligation. Marsh's nieces, for example, provided company when they traveled and lived with their aunt. But such young, single women posed dangers for the responsible parties as well. The young Cornelia Mitchell, who traveled with the Goulds, wrote in her journal of being called upon and approached by men—some significantly older—in hotels and train stations. Married and widowed women also met challenges. If they did not face physical threats, they may have endured the rumors and gossip bandied about, potentially harmful to their reputations. Caroline Carson, for example, wrote of Eleanor Fearing Strong of North Carolina living in Europe without her husband. She noted that Strong had an Irish female traveling companion as well as a handsome Italian young man, who seemed too familiar. Carson wrote similarly of her neighbor Brewster and the American sculptor Albert Harnisch, speculating on their relationship: "She is a bright little woman coquettish at 54 and has attached to her service a young sculptor Harnisch whom she pushed on, and in return he is devoted to her as son, friend, or lover—according as one is malicious or not in viewing the connection."[12]

Brewster wrote quite differently of her relationship with Harnisch and with several younger women, noting their importance to her as other than lovers. Harnisch provided assistance to her on several levels. First, he helped with her expenses. Their shared housing was a mutually beneficial arrangement. Second, he provided her respectful accompaniment. She wrote in the winter of 1873 when he first began lodging with her, "Harnisch has a room . . . which is a great comfort to me—He is a gentlemanly, kind, good youth, very faithful to me. His presence is a protection to me as well as a companionship. He and I have turned into good steady study. We refuse all gay invitations and have set ourselves straight down to work. He rises early & goes to his studio." Then that summer, when traveling outside Rome to the Tuscan resort region of Bagni di Lucca, he provided her "a sense of safety and assistance." As she wrote later in her journal, "traveling without 'maid or man' is no pleasant business for me."[13]

Later journal entries about Harnisch clearly show Brewster's frustration with him, not only for his late nights out but also for his romantic involvement with and marriage to her servant or "maid." Not merely what Brewster deemed inappropriate behavior rankled her—the older woman was hurt by the loss of attention she suffered. Jealousy triumphed from time to time. In fact, attention Brewster enjoyed from several women reinforces this relational need. Hosmer, Louise Chandler Moulton, Helen Hunt Jackson and, most notably, Amelia Edwards provided Brewster social sustenance. However, younger women in particular, such as Anna Vernon and Grace Bristed, whom Brewster wrote of as "friends," provided the older single woman traveling companions while they also enabled her to feel in control and needed. Nonetheless, they, like Harnisch, did not "need" her as she needed them, she recognized in her journal.[14] As an older, single woman abroad, Brewster reveals in her private writings that these relationships ironically gave her a false feeling of power and independence. These examples of older and younger women in Italy speak to the necessities of relationships in their daily lives, underscoring the networks inevitable to both tourist travelers and expatriate residents.[15] Depending on perspective, such dependencies and myths of independence may be judged negatively or positively, but they clarify the importance of relationships while abroad and provide the context in which James's *Daisy Miller* and Aunt Friendly's "Miss Jones" appeared.

Articulated Fears: The Malinconia

> Roman fever. It seizes you when you arrive. It does not trouble you much while you stay, except to make you gloriously happy—but when you leave, it burns into your vitals and makes you miserable all the rest of your life unless you come back.
>
> —Anne Hampton Brewster to Thomas Davidson, 1878[16]

Two decades earlier than these fictions, in May of 1858, following a "farewell walk in the Pincian gardens" in Rome with his daughter Una, Nathaniel Hawthorne recorded his concerns about the culture's impact on her. Writing in his journal, he noted his hopes that the fourteen-year-old's life would not "be a dream of this 'city of the soul,' and an unsatisfied yearning to come back." Undoubtedly, Hawthorne's desire—manifest as fearful concern—was motivated by his interactions with some American women residing in Rome. He had written pointedly of them in his notebooks. Visual artists Louisa Lander and Hosmer, for example, piqued his meditations. Lander had interacted frequently with the family, gaining Una's friendship and admiration, and Hawthorne had frequented her studio, as he sat for the bust she sculpted. But after she became the subject of questions of sexual looseness, he severed his and the family's ties to her.[17] As he described Lander following a February encounter, she was "a young woman, living in almost perfect independence, thousands of miles from her New England home, going fearlessly about," living a "peculiar mode of life . . . [with] freedom from the enthrallments of society." Hosmer also reflected the results of such "freedom" from American social constraints, according to Hawthorne. Her sculpture of "the beautiful needy Venus," in his eyes, manifested a "lascivious warmth of hue" and "something fascinating and delectable," such that it caused "one [to] feel ashamed to look at the naked limbs in the company of women."[18] Even more direct than these pointed comments about female visual artists and his own sensuality are those Hawthorne recorded about the intellectual Fuller in the same entry as that on visiting Hosmer. Together they suggest these American women in Italy likely prompted Hawthorne to note his fears for his daughter. Una's dynamic personality, the poignant period of her life—"at the turning tide" of womanhood—and her illness likely also influenced his concerns.[19]

Even when Hawthorne wrote his notebook entry, about eight years after Fuller's death, the news correspondent's story was available in print. Emerson, James Freeman Clarke, and William Henry Channing, for example, had hastily edited and published her memoirs in 1852.[20] Not only did Fuller heartily and openly embrace the attempts of the revolutionary group known as La Giovine Italia to establish a new Republic and a unified peninsula in 1848, but she also embraced quite literally one of the young revolutionaries, the impoverished and Catholic-by-birth Marquis Giovanni Ossoli, with whom she conceived and parented a child. Whether the two were legally married or not has been debated, because of their religious differences and Fuller's much-delayed and emotional letter to her mother revealing the child's existence. Usually Fuller's story is told with attention to the dramatic changes that occurred in her life and career as a writer after she set sail from New York in 1846. The Spring family provided the appropriate companionship expected for a single female—even one almost forty years old, as Fuller was. She met Italian revolutionaries, such as Giuseppe Mazzini, in London and Paris, and arrived in Italy in March 1847. Settling eventually but briefly in Rome (after deciding to part with the Springs) and witnessing the revolutions of 1848, she gave birth to her child in the nearby mountain village of Rieti, and then fled Italy in 1850 after a brief stay in Florence. There she visited the poets Elizabeth Barrett and Robert Browning, before she, Giovanni, and their son, Angelo, made their ill-fated departure for the US that summer.

Hawthorne wrote passionately of an evening conversation about Fuller less than two months prior to the notebook entry expressing his concern for Una. A visit with a former New York businessman turned sculptor, Joseph Mozier, had turned to Mozier's impressions of Fuller in Rome. As Hawthorne recorded it, Mozier moved from his pejorative descriptions of Ossoli and his family, wondering "what attraction [Fuller] found in this boor," to what he saw as the deterioration of "all power of literary production" and "a total collapse in poor Margaret, morally and intellectually." Although neither Mozier nor Hawthorne explicitly blamed what they saw as a "purely sensual" relationship between Ossoli and Fuller for the woman's "collapse," the strong suggestion emerges in Hawthorne's wording. He wrote, "Margaret has not left, in the hearts and minds of those who knew her, any deep witness for her integrity and purity." By contrast, his entry continues, her time in Italy brought out her desire "to fill up her experience in all directions" and "to try all things." This desire for a wider range of experiences contributed to the "tragic . . . catastrophe" that was "her whole story." Because Hawthorne's record does not include quotation marks, it is impossible to distinguish Mozier's comments on Fuller from Hawthorne's glossing of Mozier's account.[21] Hawthorne's entry concludes, "Providence was, after all, kind in putting her, and her clownish husband, and their child, on board that fated ship." Hawthorne's journal entry on April 3, 1858, includes both the visit with Mozier and the visit to Hosmer's studio, suggesting that he intertwined the women in his thoughts.

These negative comments about Fuller, Hosmer, and Lander predate by twenty years James's depictions of Daisy. James's naïve character appeared in 1878, a full thirty years after the single Fuller arrived in Europe. Soon after James created the young Daisy, whose headstrong attitude and interest in an Italian male led to her demise, he depicted a similarly tragic heroine, Isabelle Archer of *Portrait of a Lady* (1881), another American in Italy. In the same novel, alongside of Archer, James placed American newspaper correspondent Henrietta Stackpole. All three females suffered under James's pen. As he depicted these women, the Italian culture influenced them to make poor choices, acting beyond the bounds of appropriate female behavior. These characterizations and James's reference to the circle of females surrounding the sculptor Hosmer in Rome as a "marmorean flock" create an almost mythic negative image of American women in Italy.[22]

James's and Hawthorne's negative depictions, however, are only one facet of a sparkling gem illuminating women's global networks. Among James's and Hawthorne's peers, New Englander Charles Eliot Norton also wrote of the peninsula's transformative power in his popular *Notes of Study and Travel in Italy* (1859). Best known for his contributions to the *Nation* and lectures on art history at Harvard, Norton also left behind powerful descriptions of female transformation in accounts of his wife, the former Susan Sedgwick. Debilitated physically but, like many other women of her New England family, a social activist, Susan changed dramatically for the better during what Charles described as the couple's Edenic time in Siena, Florence, and Venice.[23] Susan gained strength following the birth of their fifth child and before the conception of their sixth.

A haunting nightmare of Italy emerged for Norton—but one neither of artistic and independent American women abroad, nor of concern that his wife or daughters might slide down a slippery slope of self-centered immorality if they were to "try all things" as Fuller had. He did not express concern that they would grow discontented about their distance from the sunny clime when back in New England. Rather, Norton was haunted by memories of his and Susan's Edenic time together. Susan died after giving birth to the sixth child in Dresden in 1872. Norton journeyed home alone and returned to Italy afterward only in his imagination and through his lectures. He—rather than his wife or daughters—began to live what he described to his friend James as a "ghost life."[24]

Susan Sedgwick Norton's transformation and death, then, provides one revision of James's Daisy, underscoring the varied experiences of American women abroad, both married and single. Her transformation also points to diverse responses by men. Indeed, even Hawthorne and James saw Italy as promising greater understandings of life through the rich history and art it presented, as well as freedom from some of the more stultifying elements of American culture. Hawthorne, for example, included in his notebook entry regarding fears for Una that "nothing elevating and refining can be really injurious; and so I hope she will always be the better for Rome, even if her life should be spent where there are no pictures, no statues, nothing but the dryness and meagerness of a New England village." He appreciated the way in which the Italian experience transformed women—when it was through "elevation." James, too, waffled between spite and admiration, or repulsion and fascination. He met his inspirational muse, for example, author Constance Fenimore Woolson—a single woman dedicated to her verbal artistry—after her arrival in Italy. She drew strength and creativity from her time on the peninsula, as well as from her exchanges with James and their relationship during her fifteen years in Europe.[25]

Benefits of life in Italy, juxtaposed with concerns of life abroad, did not lie solely with men who wrote about women. Women as well as men, single as well as married, expressed these concerns, which crossed gender boundaries. Even before Fuller's arrival in 1848, Susan Sedgwick Norton's cousin, the popular New England author Catharine Maria Sedgwick, also provided pictures of concern. In her 1841 *Letters from Abroad to Kindred at Home,* Sedgwick recorded the delights and fascinations of her journey over the Alps and into the plains of Piedmont, swept away by the geography, the people, and the history. Sedgwick's responses were prompted by her family's political engagement with the revolutions earlier in the century, as they supported political exiles such as J.-C.-L. Simonde de Sismondi.[26] Yet in her writing from Turin and Milan in the north to Rome and Naples further south, negative judgmental comments about poverty and Roman Catholicism emerge, intertwined with her fears of those sharply different from herself. These pages remind readers of the unsettling nature of some cross-cultural contacts. Sedgwick wrote, for example, of walking alone in a rural area, when a farmer dressed in animal skins—typical for him and his region—unintentionally frightened her.[27]

And Sedgwick's fictional sketch, "An Incident in Rome," depicts dangers for a young, well-bred Englishman who chose traveling to Italy to study rather than remaining in the technical (and therefore practical) university in London. His metaphorical descent into a dark hole of Otherness occurs during his literal excavations for Etruscan artifacts. He is soon lost to his family and indistinguishable from local beggars receiving alms. Sedgwick's story—written after her time abroad—marks her concern with Anglos who risked losing themselves on the peninsula. Women or men might become like impoverished Italians in their behaviors, while striving to learn about an idealized past civilization or to be free from their own cultural constraints.[28] She concluded the tale with the young man's salvation (by a mother who went looking for him) and return home to marry an English woman, a cousin, initially intended as his bride. The narrator describes her as "a more fitting mistress than Italy," who has "taken possession of the young man's imagination." Sedgwick taps into and reinforces the dangerous allure of the feminized seductress Italy to the vulnerable Anglo imagination. Pointedly, the tale's last lines, including an excerpt from William Wordsworth's poetry, reinforce the safety of such an imaginative vision from afar: the couple "could look back with tranquil minds, to that 'beautiful region' where 'A spirit hangs o'er towns and farms, Statues and temples, and memorial tombs.' "[29] That "spirit," exerting evil influence when near, would only serve as a safe soporific from a distance.

Later in the century, some women's tales such as Woolson's became much darker than Sedgwick's, as they presented harsh realities of expatriate life for both men and women. "Miss Grief," "The Front Yard," and "A Transplanted Boy" demonstrate diverse challenges Americans faced. In the first, an unmarried American woman writer in Rome dies almost alone, with most of her manuscripts "unread," while the male narrator, a famous and successful author to whom she looked for support, acknowledges that "she, with the greater power, failed." In "The Front Yard" a New England woman in Tuscany chooses not to return to the US after a charming Italian peasant farmer proposes marriage. Yet married rural life in the hills living with his family turns out to be more harsh and confining than she had imagined. As she daily casts her gaze over the stinking pigpen before her, the housewife consoles herself by daydreaming of transforming it into a front yard with lilacs and a picket fence, a memorable image of her American past. Even more painful is "A Transplanted Boy," in which an expatriate boy attempts to survive during and after his mother's illness and death. Mother and son have become impoverished both financially and culturally, we learn, as the twelve-year-old who has lived most of his life in Italy arrives at the US Embassy in Leghorn (Livorno) on July 4 to ask for assistance. Not recognized as American because he does not realize the important holiday, he is sent on his way, with longing and hunger that only increase as hours and days pass. Such despairing and seemingly unvarnished stories emerged from Woolson's keen eye, attention to craft, and her own poignant experiences living abroad. Contributing to contemporary receptions of these moving tales is Woolson's own death, following a fall from a window in her lodgings in Venice. Her death has been interpreted variously—as suicide caused by ongoing bouts of depression, a failed romantic relationship with James, and a fall due to dizziness and confusion during illness.[30]

A less well-known example, Mary Agnes Tincker's autobiographical novel, *By the Tiber* (1881), presents another frightening version of travel to Rome, quite different from Woolson's, Sedgwick's, James's, or Fuller's.

In it a young American woman, although not traveling alone, becomes ill and ends up in a convent for what she believes will be treatment of her physical health. However, she soon learns she has been confined for mental instability. Tincker, a Roman Catholic convert in Maine who later traveled to Italy, may have been attacking the church during a brief period of a lapse in faith.[31] Most important, however, is the novel's focus on lack of female agency, the power of others' judgments of women, and the dangers of dissociating from social networks. This tragic gothic romance predates by a decade Charlotte Perkins Gilman's well-known "The Yellow Wallpaper" (1892), while it similarly illustrates problems of forced isolation.

Enhancing the poignant veracity of Tincker's autobiographical fiction, Brewster wrote of Tincker's increasing illness and mental instability. The two had met in September of 1874 and become friends. By the spring of 1877, Brewster wrote of Tincker's ill health and in November of 1878 concluded, "Poor Miss Tincker who has been in a very uncertain state of health and mind for over a year is now positively insane and will have to be put in the Malinconia"—a name she used for an asylum for the mentally unwell.[32] Brewster was so troubled by the situation that she expounded on it in letters to her friend Tom Davidson:

> I am very anxious and unhappy about my poor friend Miss Tincker. . . . She is a handsome charming woman and is known among Catholics as the authoress of the "House of Yorke" and also "Six sunny months in Italy." Hard work, poverty, anxiety about money, weather, debt—all those dreadful troubles have made her not only very ill but have shattered her reason. She is positively insane and we all stand frightened not knowing what to do. She is growing worse every day. I cannot go near her, as she has taken an aversion to me, but I do all I can for her without her knowledge. I have been suspecting something was wrong with her mind for a year past, and she told me such unlikely tales of mysterious persons watching and following her to do her some unknown evil. It is a most sad case. She has no kindred near—no intimates even—for she has persisted in leading a most solitary life and has always repelled all advances that went beyond the simplest acquaintanceship. She has been fonder of me than anyone else, but sometimes she would even refuse to come to me for several weeks. I fancy this mental trouble has had a clutch on her longer than we can know of,

> and now we are all unable to decide on what might be done. [Dr.] Taussig says she must be put in the insane asylum. But who is to take the responsibility of doing it? Is it not a sad affair? Don't say anything about it, for if they succeed in putting her in the Malinconia, she may be cured and then it would be a mortification to her to have it known.

Brewster wrote later to Davidson that Tincker remained in the "Malinconia" three months, thanks to "Miss Jane Sedgwick's generosity," which "made her most comfortable."[33]

Brewster reinforced the realities of such dangerous situations as she wrote in two other journal accounts. One depicted Hawthorne's daughter Una, who had "gone mad," according to her aunt, the well-known New England reformer and Transcendentalist Elizabeth Peabody, Sophia Hawthorne's sister. Elizabeth was visiting Rome in 1872, when she shared Una's "very sad story" with Gould, who passed it along to Brewster, illustrating the expatriate network of exchange.[34] Brewster's journal entry of the account extends for eight pages on the "orphaned" Hawthorne children (Nathaniel had died in 1864 and Sophia in 1871), especially focusing on Una's instability after her mother's death. Una's ill health has been interpreted variously, reaching back to her brother Julian. Biographers have pointed not only to her mother's death but to her strong personality, repressed as she entered adolescence and wrestled with nineteenth-century expectations of womanhood and, later, with two broken engagements. Accounts also have linked her illness with malaria in Rome and the treatments of the Italian homeopathic physician Dr. Franco. His house calls and passionate and sexually aggressive interactions with the Hawthornes' tutor, Ada Shepard, barely older than Una, may have been shared with her. At least, Una likely sensed them. Even Sophia was influenced by Franco's charm and regular presence in their home, during a time when her husband was himself preoccupied with the sculptor Lander.[35] But rather than determining the cause of Una's illness, most important here is Brewster's almost obsessive retelling of it.

Brewster explained in her presumably private journal that Una, in her "morbid" condition, had isolated herself and her sister Rose from social contact, and had become "an extreme Ritualist," as far as religion was concerned. Brewster noted, "so far had her aberration gone that she imagined herself the Bride of Christ." While visiting friends who were concerned about her condition, she "wandered off in a half clad condition without shoes only in stockings . . . searching for her Lord—for her dear Spiritual

Bride groom—who would give her peace!" Through her wanderings she was brought into "a house of ill fame" where Una delivered a surprising "sort of sermon." Una's message "persuaded the whole covey of young feminine reprobates" to attend St. Barnabas church near London with her. The friends, who were at St. Barnabas, reconnected with Una and were able to place her into an asylum and contact her aunt. As Peabody arranged for Una's care, Sophia Hawthorne's estate, and travel to Rome, Una "drew back" in fear. She "retained of Rome only the sad and disagreeable memories of the dangerous illness she had had . . . in 1858." Brewster concluded that this "strange, weird romance" was a result of Una's father—not because he took his daughter to Rome, but because he was "impractical, moody" and "filled with all manner of unhealthy imaginings, occupied in every mode of morbid analytical examination of human emotions."[36] While the account allowed Brewster to vent about what she disliked about the famous American author who had been in Italy less than a decade before she arrived, it likely reminded her—as the accounts of Tincker did—of the fragility of the stability and identity of an American living abroad without sufficient support, structure, and guidance.

Less than a month later, Brewster wrote of another—this time a young male, the English author and activist Caroline Norton's son. As with the story of Una, the tale circulated orally, again underscoring how people and their tales became public discourse in the exchange networks abroad. William Wetmore Story and his wife shared this account with Brewster when the three had attended the theater together.[37] Brewster wrote that Norton's son "took up with an uneducated woman from Capri" and had two children with her. Suggesting excessive indulgences in Italian wine, Brewster wrote of Norton in the context of "intemperances" she had witnessed with her brother Ben in the US, and more recently with her host Read. The young Norton's children, playing with the Story children, had asked how *their* father behaved when drunk, as though being drunk were a normal situation for a father, Brewster wrote with dismay. Brewster returned to the story three years later, writing of Norton's "artist son who 'went to the bad' " and his marriage to the "savage" of Capri. In both instances she noted "Mrs." Norton's willingness to raise her son's children and to embrace and educate the young mother. Such educating was difficult work, Brewster wrote, because the young, ignorant woman had no interest in history.[38] Brewster's final comment reiterates a theme that both Hawthorne and Sedgwick had touched upon. If Americans abroad could keep the right balance of attention to history and appreciation for the present moment, then their time in Italy might be safe. Yet too much attention to the past, with its art, or indulgence in the present, with its beautiful, passionate men and women and inexpensive wine, might lead to destruction.

Brewster's comments on the woman from Capri also resonate with racist stereotypes, even while they capture details of sexual and marital relations that cross ethnic and class boundaries. Other journal entries would show these attitudes as well, as Brewster wrote of desires to have "a safe peep" at such lifestyles, which fascinated her. For example, only a month earlier she had written of encountering California writer Joaquin Miller.[39] Known for "his contributions to the mythos of the West," Miller had taken on the name Joaquin and the figure "of a colorful Mexican desperado," although born in Indiana and raised in Oregon, where he became a miner and lawyer before turning to authorship.[40] Brewster wrote of talking with Miller at one of her receptions about a "Modoc girl" he claimed to be "educating" and a woman named Anna who was with him. She concluded, "When I am listening to him it is like taking a safe peep into a wild Indian camp. He shows to me a class of semi-barbaric existence that I am most curious to know of."

Brewster added comments that marginalize by religion and sexual practices as well as by race, ethnicity, and class. Joseph Smith, Latter-day Saints visionary, prophet, founder, and supposed polygamist, had a daughter with "a Spanish woman," Brewster noted. (No record exists of such a daughter to Joseph Smith, who died in Missouri in 1844, or of his son, Joseph Smith III, who opposed polygamy.) Brewster, who had chosen Roman Catholicism with its teachings about sexuality as a sin and newly confirmed declaration of the Virgin Mary's Immaculate Conception, also noted the daughter's ability to choose her own path. Anna not only had left "Mormonism," she detested it and had chosen "a proper life." This tension between the "proper life" and what Italy the "seductress" might offer to Anglos abroad remained at the forefront of Brewster's mind throughout her time in Rome.

Brewster's extensive journal records and others by Anglos about their non-Anglo encounters demonstrate both the power of social networks in Italy and their potential damage. Sharing stories orally and reinforcing them through writing could be devastating to a person's social situation, but the stories also provided warnings. They reminded those sharing them about their own mental health and the importance of supportive social connections while living abroad. Brewster's journals, punctuated by such passages about others, also refer to her own dark periods and troubles—including female–female relationships and their potential for sexual intimacy. Brewster's frequent negative reflections about others likely emerged from her own struggles. Likewise, although married, Marsh wrote in her journals and letters of concerns about her nieces, for whom she was guardian while they were abroad. For example, just before Marsh returned to the US in the summer of 1869, leaving her niece Ellen under her husband George's supervision, Ellen received a love letter from Mario Gigliucci, the son of a cross-cultural marriage between the English opera soprano Clara Novello and Count Gigliucci, Governor of Fermo. (Gigliucci fell in love with the opera diva while she was imprisoned and under his charge. The children seemed poorly supervised.) Caroline wrote to George, begging that he not let Ellen go stay with the Gigliucci family but rather keep her with him or "leave her in some nice family in France or Switzerland."[41] Through such accounts we garner glimpses of struggles these women faced in Italy while they worked to maintain their initial utopian visions. Against this backdrop the tale of Aunt Friendly's "Miss Jones" and its symbolic message emerge.

She "Must Do Something": Miss Jones as Activist

In the early pages of the short tale, before Vittorio's and Miss Jones's dramatic encounter and conjoined "resurrections," "Miss Jones" provides glimpses of practical practices for a young American woman abroad. The story opens, for example, with a description of Miss Jones "traveling unencumbered," with only "one trunk" and without "her gala-dresses, her flounces and her furbelows." She wears practical clothing—"the thickest of thick cloth garments." Yet these also indicate that "She was emancipated; even her scruples and her fastidiousness and almost her conscience she had left behind her." Miss Jones had grown increasingly independent while abroad, learning a "perfect freedom, a rest from the conventional shackles against which she had inwardly chafed at home." This "mannish deportment," a type she might have despised when back in the US, "was making a shade deeper the portrait of her country-women, too often accepted in Italian cities, and criticized with scorching severity." From these opening descriptions, the tale builds from numerous stereotypes of Italy's power to transform women's gendered behaviors into "mannish" ones.[42]

While these images evoke the independent American woman abroad, another important feature of Aunt Friendly's story contradicts them. In its early pages the tale also underscores that "Miss Jones was *not* traveling alone," for "She was far too proper for that."[43] The narrator explains, "She was duly escorted and accompanied by a select party of congenial souls," among whom she became the leader, in spite of being "the youngest." Employing military imagery, the narrator describes Miss Jones as the one who "planned the campaigns, and let the van, Baedecker in one hand, and a white *en-tout-cas* [parasol/umbrella] in the other."[44] Although she had the capacity to be their tour guide, these "judicious tourists" with whom she traveled often "went their way, and let her go hers." Miss Jones and the group often had similar sightseeing goals, with "paths . . . in the same direction," but the American woman's "self-reliant" nature allowed her to move about as she wished, while her traveling companions provided a false front of group safety.

Not simply her personality directed her. Miss Jones's language skills fed her leadership and independence. They contributed at least to her self-confidence, if not to flawless communication, as the somewhat ironic narrative commentary suggests. Miss Jones was able to "argue with a cabman" regarding the fare and to "call for what she wanted in a crowded restaurant, in bad French or worse Italian, without a blush," even when with large groups. Her language skills also impacted their lodgings: "With the aid of her inestimable knowledge of the modern languages," the narrator explains, "they had secured a sunny suite of rooms, looking out upon a cheerful piazza." The lodgings provided a comfortable, safe spot for reading on "history and art" and journal writing. Fortified and prepared in the quiet rooms of the palazzo, she "sallied out, with a sense of perfect freedom, a rest from the conventional shackles against which she had inwardly chafed at home."[45] Most importantly, Miss Jones's ability to communicate in Italian with her little servant Vittorio provided a human connection beyond nonverbal signs. She spoke with him about her fire—which he daily laid, lit, and kept burning—and her books—which he retrieved from and returned to a library. She also spoke with Vittorio's mother, Assunta, about his illness. Even if Miss Jones's imperfect language skills at times fed her pride and a false sense of security, they also enabled her literally and emotionally—two actions critical to the story's climax and resolution. When Vittorio's mother called Miss Jones from the grand, bright palazzo in which she and other privileged tourists lodged, to the Italian family's dark, damp hovel—"A sunless, chilly, damp, sepulchral world"—in the alley behind and under the palazzo, the American became witness to Vittorio's life and his deathbed. There, Miss Jones was moved to "loving sympathetic tears."[46]

With boyish bravery Vittorio voiced from his deathbed his desires "to be a soldier and fight for Italy" under Garibaldi's leadership. Notably, his name not only means "victory" but also echoes that of the newly unified

Italy's first king, Victor Emmanuel. Vittorio's patriotic fervor, unrealistic considering his inability even to raise himself from the bed, awakened Miss Jones's heart, which had been "dormant through long months of traveling." It evoked poignant memories of her own brother, who had died of a similar illness in the US. Consequent to this heart-softening, Miss Jones determined that she "must do something." Significantly, her "deportment" enabled her to act. Because "she must have action," she moved quickly to retrieve Dr. G.—likely readers imagined Dr. Gould, Emily's husband, a physician well known for his capable services to "strangers in Rome." Almost miraculously, Vittorio revived. Even more notable is that while Vittorio's "was but physical recovery," the narrator tells us, Miss Jones "had passed through a better resurrection." She had learned "that this was not a mere world in which to see sights, write journals, and go to bed."[47]

Miss Jones had not been transformed to "preach and distribute tracts right and left," however, but to devote "herself heart and soul, hand and purse, to the children of the land of her pilgrimage."[48] Social activism driven by human connection and need trumped any sectarian desires of explicit conversion to a creed. She did not "preach" the steps of salvation listed on published "tracts." Rather, through this face-to-face, personal encounter abroad—the humanizing of a "servant" in his home—Miss Jones became a better person, determined to improve the world by reaching out to children in need. She would do so with heart and hands moved by emotion rather than a mind driven by reason.

While the story begins with seemingly negative aspects of Miss Jones's independence and freedom in clothing and deportment, it also highlights how her practical dress, without "flounces and . . . furbelows," and her linguistic skills enabled effective action across cultures and class.[49] The tale minimizes—even eradicates—any self-centered socializing that would demand impractical dress on Miss Jones's part. Readers learn that in spite of her independence, Miss Jones's "mannish deportment" had not gone so far as to smother "her conscience," which she had not "left behind." Miss Jones remains sensitive as the story's dramatic tension builds to its triumphant conclusion.

The story ends not simply with Miss Jones's conversion but also with an indirect appeal to readers that they imitate her behavior. Miss Jones went home "not merely with the so-called polish of foreign travel, a superficial knowledge of many things, but with a deep, earnest purpose," which was to be a "loving, active, [and] useful, Christian woman." The narrator/author Aunt Friendly explains, "The money that would have been spent in cameos and mosaics, coral and shell-work, she devoted to the Christian education of black-eyed boys and girls."[50] The pseudonymous author, "Aunt Friendly," by name suggests a well-meaning, kind and gentle, older woman—neither scolding shrew nor patronizing preacher. The name evokes her imagined youthful audience, for whom Aunt Friendly employs a teaching voice and taps into recognizable imagery of nineteenth-century deathbed conversions and to the benevolence imagery of popular reform literature written by women. Her tale prompts youth at home who may be dreaming of trips abroad. They might be anticipating sightseeing adventures and acquisitions of jewelry and art, and they might be looking for advice or guidance in the planning process. The tale, however, provides them visions of other possible paths.

Through its conclusion, the tale's larger arc revises negative imagery associated with American women abroad, even as it reinforces some stereotypes, such as the emancipation from both convention and consciousness. "Miss Jones" renders the revision not simply by stating that the stereotypes are wrong, but by presenting an American female who chooses to act otherwise. Miss Jones breaks the type through her choices. In stark contrast to James's Daisy, who loses her flower-fresh innocence and dies without any such conversion—in part because of her self-centered, childlike interests—Miss Jones is changed in how she will live and act. This dramatic conversion, central to the story's plot, climax, and conclusion, captures the complex responses of Americans to the peninsula and its cultures during Unification. Miss Jones, like Daisy, is one among many women before and after 1875 with such dramatic yet varied life-changing experiences in Italy.

At the same time, the tale's narrative movement, with the literal contiguity of Miss Jones's and Vittorio's living spaces, also reinforces the dependence of the Anglo elite upon the impoverished laboring classes. Likewise, the prejudicial and racist commentary on "black-eyed girls and boys" represented for many readers in the US and England how they might maintain a sense of superiority by supporting Gould's mission and those of others like her. The complex and problematic element of this racist and class-based codependency emerges in the stories of Gould, Brewster, and Marsh as they lived abroad and as they wrote of their interactions with the people around them. By responding to what they saw and came to understand while living in Italy, as well as by reading about politics and history, the sojourns of these woman abroad were marked by engagement with their "servants," with other Anglo travelers, and with local political leaders in the present rather than merely with tourist sites and with romantic renditions of the past or artistic escape.

The goals of most Americans abroad, "Miss Jones" points out, were reading Dante, studying classical Rome, following the news of the latest excavations, and visiting these sites. Miss Jones had targeted such activities on her travel plans—at first. Her change in plans, brought about by her conversion, illuminates the striking contrast between the traveler to Italy who knows nothing of the nation's contemporary politics and only of its past, as captured in visual arts and literature, and one who engages with it politics and people. Prior to Miss Jones's conversion, "it was nothing to her that she walked among a people who were struggling towards life and liberty. . . . She did not understand Italian politics." To Miss Jones, "a modern dweller in Rome . . . was unpoetical, uninteresting, he had no real existence for her," for "she was in the clouds, in the golden-tinted past."[51]

Such interest in Italy's past by tourists interested in seeing and buying art and archaeological artifacts was, in fact, contributing to frequent illness among its poor. Hawthorne had written in his journal and in *The Marble Faun* of the filth in the small streets of the city's lower-lying areas, but the *mal aria* or bad air in these zones was exacerbated by several factors. Archaeological excavations had intensified throughout the nineteenth century, and devastation brought about by the Tiber's flooding in 1870 contributed to the atmosphere. In the year following, as Rome became the new nation's capital, the influx of residents and new plans for the city brought about significant changes through construction of new streets and buildings.[52] In Aunt Friendly's story, the narrator points out, "excavations" concerned with ancient Rome, in particular, were what "fill[ed] the air with death." They contributed to Vittorio's illness, even as they drew visitors such as Miss Jones. Yet the traveling consumers with the "tourist gaze" might, according to the tale, open their eyes to other sites and act to intervene in a life-affirming manner.[53]

The contrasts between death and life, the past and the present, the impoverished and the privileged travelers, become even more illuminating with attention to details of the short story's author, goals, style, publication venue, and larger context—all pointing to its intended impact on readers. The heroine's name, Jones, not only clearly Anglo but also among the most popular, could belong to almost anyone. Thus, Miss Jones, like James's Daisy Miller, represents for Anglo readers a kind of "every woman" abroad. The narrator explains, underscoring the freedom and anonymity abroad that many Americans felt, "no one cared whether she were Smith or Jones, Douglas or Howard."[54] She could easily become lost and forgotten, rather than triumph as a unique individual among the Anglos thronging the streets of new Rome. This common name also speaks to the tale's intended readers, who might put themselves in the place of "Miss Jones," easily substituting their own names for hers.

Certainly not all travelers to Italy, whether male or female, were converted to social activism like Miss Jones. But neither did they all fall victims to poor choices like Daisy Miller. Rather, the two fictionalized heroines stand as antinomies of the extremes, between which stood numerous women facing choices about behaviors. Even Gould, Marsh, and Brewster, who chose action while abroad, were not able to maintain optimism or forgo self-indulgences and fears completely. Indeed, they experienced personal challenges, including concerns with "losing" themselves. Rather than simplistic characters such as the fictional, naïve Daisy or the Miss Jones who returns to the US, these women's lives exhibited complex choices—rational and irrational responses to everyday confrontations. In fact, Aunt Friendly's fictional sketch provides pictures of what might be called "the daily ordinary"—language study, lodgings, interactions with locals and with expatriate Anglos.[55] All assert the importance of both routines and social networks. These means might ensure a healthy life that would sustain an American woman as she engaged with Italy.

Chapter 5

"The Daily Ordinary"

Language, Lodgings, and Hostessing

> The child who translates gradually perceives everything . . . a kind of knowledge without which he would be confined all his life to the circle of his own nation—a circle that is narrow, like everything exclusive.
>
> —Germaine de Staël, 1816[1]

"Miss Jones" provides practical details of travel essential to American women's engagement abroad, such as giving up "furbelows" for simpler clothing, and negotiating languages, lodging, and meals. For Miss Jones, the meals taken in her ample rooms limited rather routine and dull interactions thrice daily with the same English speakers. Aunt Friendly's story explains that the young American woman's linguistic skills added to her sense of independence—she could negotiate the streets, shops, and places to eat. Similarly, Brewster's, Marsh's, and Gould's decisions about languages, lodging, and relationships impacted their vocations abroad. They knew language knowledge was key, just as they knew that socializing with those of their mother tongue and culture could help prevent a sense of isolation or melancholy that might lead one to the "Malinconia." These three women's manifestations of speaking languages other than English typify the diversity of American and British travelers to the peninsula in this regard. Brewster, for example, knew French before she traveled abroad and began Italian studies in full after her arrival in Rome. She studied on her own, as well as with Luigi Lunardi, a member of the private literary and cultural association, the Accademia dell'Arcadia, to which he would later sponsor her elected membership. Even when visiting Florence in 1886, after almost twenty years in Italy, she had an appointment for a language lesson with Angelo Conti, a renowned philosopher and aesthete.[2] Such lessons, then, fostered her connections with well-educated locals immersed in the culture as much as her language skills. For example, Brewster also arranged with her neighbor, Rodolfo Lanciani, to help him with his English. Despite their plans that he would correspond with her in English, most of the letters he wrote to her were in French, including two just after they struck their agreement.[3] Their relationship—essential to both their careers—built upon a mutually shared second language, which trumped any new language teaching and learning between them. Nonetheless, Brewster exercised her learning of languages, copying long passages of George Sand's French and reading in Italian volumes.[4]

Gould studied German but gave it up for French, which she had already learned and found easier. During her summer in Bavarian Germany, for example, as she prepared to move toward Switzerland, she wrote from Heidelberg to her friend Ambassador George Marsh, "Can you tell me of any thing to read on Franconian Switzerland, and where to perhaps procure the same? . . . It must be in French, or Italian, if not in English to benefit me however, for the more I am in Germany, the less German I learn."[5] Nonetheless, ten days later she wrote that she and a traveling companion would "give [themselves] up to German," even moving to another town for the purpose.[6] Six weeks later, she explained her process: "I am studying German, on an excellent plan; taking stories written for ladies and gentlemen of three and four years of age and studying them."[7] The same month, however, Gould expressed frustration at "the difficulty of getting at newspapers in any language excepting the one spoken in this country." She described it as the language "invented by Apollyon"—the Greek deity who in Christian apocalyptic literature represents the dark abyss of destruction. This Apollyon created German "for the express purpose of maddening foreigners," she concluded. "The more one studies, the less one learns thereof."[8]

Gould's slur against German emerged not simply from her desires to order food or talk with the locals. Rather, it arose from her new vocation. She needed to read the local news in order to respond to the flood of requests from US newspapers for reports on political affairs in Italy. She had been asked for more than she was able to write—in part because she was unable to read the German papers, in part because she did not have access to the Roman and Florentine news in French while traveling. As she clarified in the letter to George Marsh, "I intended to subscribe to the Italie [a newspaper in French] as soon as I should arrive in Florence. But will you kindly subscribe to it at once for me, and order it sent to [me] . . . for the next month." Although Gould's "vacation" of the steamy Italian cities for the Alpine fresh air allowed time to pursue this new vocation, her lack of German language skills hampered her plans.

Less like Gould and more like Brewster, Caroline Marsh had demonstrated proficiency with language from an early age. She already had translated *The Hallig* and *The Wolfe of the Knoll*, two volumes from German, Swedish, and French, published before departing for Italy. Marsh's translating contributed not only to her development as a writer but also to her openness to intellectual and ideological transformations, experiences she believed all people should have. These ideas about language appear in Staël's *On Germany*, or *De l'Allemagne* (which was in the Marsh Library), and resonate throughout George Marsh's writings: first, language's integral connection to culture, and second, language study leading to transformation. Staël asserted, for example, "By studying the spirit and character of a language, one comes to know the historical cause of national opinions, customs, and usages." Additionally, she wrote of the value of language study for children, for how it broadens knowledge beyond their "own nation—a circle that is narrow" and "exclusive." She explained, "At first [a child] understands only the words, then . . . advances to the apprehension of the sentence, and soon afterward to the charm of the expression, its power," and so on, until "the child who translates gradually perceives everything" about human communications.[9] Caroline acted on this belief, continuously translating and assisting nieces under her supervision. After Marsh's arrival in the Piedmont region, she wrote of studying Italian with her nieces, first in Turin and then later in Florence and Rome. She continued to study and read in French, she read Horace's poetry in Latin, and her husband George read to her from a "German testament."[10] For her, as for the other two women, language skills went beyond ordering food or a cabman. They enabled engagement with those living around them. Marsh's two decades in Italy illustrated that the most important parts of language study were openness to new ideas and transformations through connection with another culture.

The three women's language skills helped them read the local news, connect with others, and build new relationships. Even so, as their letters, scrapbooks, journals, and libraries demonstrate, they continued to write in English, communicating in other languages as needed. Writing regularly in their native tongues kept them grounded and connected with their audiences in the US. They were not, as Hawthorne wrote of sculptor Hiram

Powers in Florence, "twenty-year exiles" without a sense of "native country."[11] Rather, they maintained double visions, engaged with the culture abroad while writing for US readers. Like the travelers Fuller had described, their engagement abroad helped them appreciate their Americanness more, though they knew not when they would embody their new ideals back in the US.

~

> My bedroom opens on a loggia . . . full of flowers, [with] a bird, [and] carpeted . . . [it is] the prettiest little place!
>
> —Anne Hampton Brewster, 1876[12]

Language skills also affected the women's lodging and household management, as Aunt Friendly's account of Miss Jones depicts. Abroad for longer stays, these women sought lodgings similar to Miss Jones's "sunny suite of rooms, looking out upon a cheerful piazza." Their lodgings were critical to their vocations—as writers with social connections. Brewster, who noted her move from her "wretched rooms" to "Mrs. Gould's" in the summer of 1870, always wrote of new lodgings in her journal. In February of 1873, for example, she wrote of having been terribly ill in January prior to taking her new rooms in the Palazzo Albani in the Via delle Quattro Fontane on the Quirinale hill: "The house I lived in on the Sistina was very unhealthy owing to the bad drains on either side of it. As soon as possible I moved from it into this apartment which is high, healthy and airy."[13]

In addition to reveling in her rooms' spaciousness, elegant décor, light, and views, Brewster noted when they were out of order or needed reorganizing. She wrote in the late fall of 1876, for example, about her beautiful loggia, "glazed in" by windows rather than open to the winter rains, adding that only a month earlier, her "house was in a horrible confusion; it seemed it never could be up to rights. But now thank heaven, it is in order and I have not been so comfortable for years. It is the prettiest sunniest coziest place possible." The loggia, where she usually ate, allowed her to "look out on lovely views"—which she described as "so Italian" and "picture like."[14] Such rooms provided freedom and a beautiful escape from the *pensioni* (Italian lodging houses) and their public meals—disrupting and unsettling situations for introverted and busy writers.

Woolson, for example, who mocked the *pensioni* in her story "A Transplanted Boy," also wrote openly about them in her letters. Because she loathed lodgings where she had to share a table and dinner conversations, she took an apartment where she set up "housekeeping." She wrote from Rome in 1881 of her "little 'apartment' very high up under the sky," essential in Rome for "good air," where she had "a bright little parlor, bed-room, and dinner-room, and balcony with pots of flowers." Even further above the balcony, she explained, was a "loggia . . . a little square room with windows towards all points of the compass, and an arbor outside, made of lemon-trees, plants in pots, and climbing vines. The walls are hung with pretty hangings, and it is prettily furnished. Here among the roofs and campaniles, and under the deep blue sky of Rome, I can sit and write in perfect solitude when tired of my little parlor below."[15]

Woolson also went into detail about the housekeeping. She explained that her proprietress was "an English lady, a governess, whose scholars are of the best Roman families . . . a widow [who] keeps an Italian servant." Of food, Woolson wrote that she prepared her "own breakfast, coffee and boiled eggs, with a little coffee pot and spirit lamp. Bread, butter, eggs and milk are sent in every day. At noon, the Italian servant serves a hot chop. At seven in the evening a very good, but simple, little dinner." Additionally, she made her "own 'five o'clock tea.' " All of this "housekeeping" freed her from the " 'table d'hote' system" with its "long array of courses, half of which" Woolson didn't "touch." Setting up "housekeeping" in an apartment provided her not only "a room with a view," to borrow E. M. Forster's 1908 title made popular by the 1985 film, but also "a room of one's own"—a space insisted upon by Virginia Woolf in the 1920s for all women—for reading, thinking, and writing. Nonetheless, Woolson did socialize occasionally. She wrote, for example, of her plans to go the next week to the Marshes' for "their reception."[16]

Single women like Woolson and Brewster, though of a mature age, did not always have such rooms at their command. They depended on friends and family to help them find lodging, and they often lived with others for short periods. Hosmer wrote to George Perkins Marsh asking for assistance in lodging her friend Lady Ashburton.[17] When Brewster first arrived in Rome, the Read family provided her a social safety net. Then in the summer, to escape the city's feverish heat, she went with the family to the nearby hills of Frascati, where she had lovely quarters meriting attention in her journal. Yet the sumptuous space did not compensate for the difficulties of living with a family's inner secrets. Brewster wrote cryptically in her journal of the challenges Read presented to his own health—most likely excessive alcohol. As she explained, "There are some other causes of anxiety which I cannot mention, not my own, but appertaining to my host & hostess . . . Ah, what skeletons there are everywhere in life!"[18] By October Brewster had found lodgings at 71 Via della Croce, not far from the Reads. Just afterward, she described her rooms in detail, noting the joy her own space brought. These lodgings, however, were never fully her own but shared rooms with the sculptor Harnisch. And, like Miss Jones and Woolson, she had her "servants." Her three *padrone*, or proprietresses, she noted, cared for cooking as well as her laundry.[19]

Several other moves followed for Brewster, always motivated by dreams of better spaces that would serve her vocation. Even when she traveled from Rome, as she did her first summer, Brewster dedicated lines in her journal to her lodgings. In 1873, for example, when she journeyed to the Tuscan mountain resort region of Bagni di Lucca, she described her rooms in the "old ducal palace" as "una vera benedizione"—a true blessing, crucial to her ability to work. She explained, "I have enjoyed the space & elegance of the rooms but most of all the superb view from the windows. I shall have had the place nearly a month when I leave and shall have enjoyed this month most of all the time I have spent at the Bagni. Next summer I may rent this wing—if so I shall come in June and stay until October." When she returned to Rome to new lodgings after a summer away, Brewster devoted energy to having the space appropriately decorated. Another year while away, she imagined changes she would enact upon her return, creating "a coin du feu . . . a cosy corner, with the Barnabo desk, an easy chair and a terra cotta stove for winter evenings." Here she would read in her "salon," stimulating herself for the next day's writing work in her bed room, which she considered her "work room" or "cabinet de travail."[20] As planned, Brewster created this work space, which provided physical comfort as well as beauty.

Likewise, Marsh faced frequent changes in lodging. She moved households several times, writing especially of the moves in the Turin area, from urban to the rural Piobese, and then adjusting to moves to Florence and then to Rome when it became the Italian capital. Even with the transfer to Rome, the Marshes maintained their beloved Villa Forini, just outside the Porta alla Croce in Florence, while they also changed residences several times within Rome for reasons of George's position. During the decade of his career in Rome, they lodged first in the Casa Lovatti in Via di San Basilio near the Piazza Barberini. In 1878 the couple moved to the Palazzo Pandolfi, a forty-room structure by Santa Maria Maggiore, in order to host Ulysses S. Grant's official visit in a more appropriate setting than the smaller Casa Lovatti. The following year they moved to again to a famous site on the Quirinale—the Palazzo Rospigliosi, known especially for Guido Reni's ceiling fresco, the Aurora, in the casino on the property. In this seventeenth-century palazzo, more than one hundred steps led up to the Marshes' expansive rooms with a view of the Colosseum. As the large-framed and aging George struggled with sciatica, he sometimes had to be carried up, just as Caroline had been carried on their hikes through the alps in the 1860s.[21] Perhaps these stairs were one among the many reasons she continued to think of the Villa Forini in Florence as home. Above all, she knew that appropriate lodgings were essential not only to writing but also in her role as a hostess, integral to her daily activities.

~

> We have a big house now, and I know I can make you more comfortable than you could be at a hotel.
>
> —Emily Bliss Gould to George Perkins Marsh, 1870[22]

> She does not only talk well herself but draws other people out which is more than half the art of a good talker. She makes me think of Corinne when talking of Italy.
>
> —Cornelia Underwood, on Caroline Crane Marsh, 1873[23]

Even as lodgings provided Marsh, Gould, and Brewster privacy and a safe haven for their rest and writing, they fostered social relations. For example, when Gould wrote to George Marsh in the fall of 1870, insisting that he visit her in Rome to witness the entrance of Victor Emmanuel to the newly unified Kingdom of Italy, she used her expansive home as a selling point: "We have a big house now, and I know I can make you more comfortable than you could be at a hotel." Not only would the visit be good for his and niece Ellen's health, but, she added, "We have rooms also for your servants at the top of our same house; having taken them for store rooms, servants rooms, or whatever, and they are as yet empty."[24] As such letters and journal entries indicate, the women understood the power and necessity of social networks that interwove with their daily routines.

The networks in which Gould, Marsh, and Brewster circulated included not just letters about private visits but numerous receptions they frequented as both hosts and guests. Each regularly received calls, publicizing the afternoons or evenings on which they accepted guests. They and their contemporaries writing to and about these events referred to them as "receptions"—rather than referring to themselves as a part of salon culture.[25] Carson, Brewster's neighbor, wrote of "the salons" hosted by two prominent American families in Rome, the Storys and the Terrys, but by contrast in the same passage, she wrote of "Miss Brewster's receptions."[26] This word choice likely was a careful one. Salons were considered by some, such as fiction writer Hawthorne, sites for gossip and social maneuvering.[27] Gould, Marsh, and Brewster wanted social encounters of a different sort—engagements that would fuel further social progress and their new vocations. Additionally, women at the center of salons, while considered intelligent and engaged with classical literature and ideas, were known to push the margins of gendered behavior. Staël, for example, lived and wrote in ways that garnered infamy among many Americans. Her autobiographical *Corinne; ou, l'Italie* (1807) was known to have influenced many single women, such as Fuller, who led "conversations" in New England before traveling to Europe. Upon her arrival in France, Fuller met another salon hostess, Amantine Lucile Aurore Dudevant, known best by the pseudonym George Sand. Many thought de Staël's, Sand's, and Fuller's behaviors less than exemplary—especially because of their relationships with men, which broke the boundaries of expected female behavior.

Prior to leaving for Europe, Fuller had participated in the circle of New Yorker Anne Lynch Botta, at the center of US salon culture, which fostered the literary work and intellectual and political ideas of such figures as Edgar Allan Poe, Orestes Brownson, Ralph Waldo Emerson, Helen Hunt, Grace Greenwood, Matthew Arnold, and Bronson Alcott. (Some of these, such as Hunt, would later attend Brewster's receptions in Italy.) In fact, Botta and her husband, Italian political exile Vincenzo Botta, hosted a "reception" for the Marshes in 1861 to celebrate George's appointment to the position in Italy. Such gatherings, referred to as "*conversazioni*" in Botta's memoirs, also were known as "Botta Evenings," underscoring the variety of terms used to describe the events and what happened during them.[28] Regardless of what they were called, the evenings had similar activities and outcomes. The outcomes—furthering social relations, fostering marriages, building professional esteem—outweighed the difficulties and challenges of the obligations, which women such as Brewster, Gould, and Marsh articulated in their private writings. The three continued to participate and benefit from them, although they did not always desire to do so.

What happened during these receptions? Carson wrote of her own hostessing: "I have given two or three tea parties, and I have a reception every Sat[urday] P.M. from 3 to 6. There is a table set out with tea and little cakes, and people drop in, chat and go away quite contented. At ev[enin]g parties it is the same thing, tea little cakes, a glass of wine, talk, music." For Brewster, as Carson noted, the process of hosting receptions involved food, drink, and flowers. While she had a "maid" and other household help to manage these preparations, the expense at times concerned her, especially when, at the height of her popularity, her receptions were twice (rather than once) weekly.[29]

Beyond the offering of refreshments, then, the receptions included conversations. They gave Anglo visitors in Rome, in the days before electronic social media, the opportunity to gather and see each other in the evening, after the day's sightseeing or other labors—such as writing, painting, or sculpting—were complete. Cornelia Underwood, a friend of the Marshes from Vermont, for example, who was in Rome from November 1873 through February 1874 with her four daughters, wrote of "sight seeing" in Rome with the Marshes' niece Mary Edmunds, as her "profession." But she depended on Caroline's "conversation" later in the day, which she found "learned" and "instructive," to keep her from being "judgmental" about what she saw on the streets about her.[30] Such conversations allowed hostesses and guests to exchange ideas.

Participants—both hostesses and guests—also garnered attention through public performance, although they may not have intended to "show off" or put themselves at the center of attention. The ideal hostess was "a facilitator of other people's interactions, rather than as a principal actor on her social stage," Susan K. Harris has explained.[31] The hostess's ideal interpersonal skills were those of "an excellent . . . engaged, listener both to men and to other women," with knowledge "enough about an array of contemporary issues and classical arts to carry on an informed discussion." Finally, "the successful hostess did not 'question' forensically; it was not her job to intimidate. Rather, she encouraged others to contribute to an intellectual community." That is, "she 'drew out' her companion"—"she asked questions in such a way as to make her partner feel that his or her ideas were of the utmost interest and significance, not only to her personally but of the society at large."[32] The hostess also had to operate well behind the scenes, dealing with details such as seating arrangements, topics for conversation, menus, and décor. The ideal hostess was "someone who could demand, coax, and coerce tradesmen, servants, and family members into efficient cooperation and who had the ability to coordinate a myriad of issues simultaneously—and personally self-abnegating, that is someone willing to foreground the interests, and especially the egos, of others rather than her own."[33]

Marsh's behavior at receptions, described by her Vermont friend Underwood, illustrates the characteristics of an ideal hostess but also connects her to Staël's Corinne.[34] Underwood gushed with admiration: "she is the most brilliant talker I have ever heard. She does not only talk well herself but draws other people out which is more than half the art of a good talker. She makes me think of Corinne when talking of Italy . . . eloquent in her admiration of the Italian character and the attainments of the cultivated Italian people."[35] Underwood continued, attributing to Marsh an educational value:

> I find myself judging Italy by what and whom I see on the streets of Rome. Mrs. Marsh says this is not the safest of judgments; she says that the cultural and natural powers of these people are beyond that of any other nation. . . . Certainly no person's conversation could be more instructive as they have lived so long in Italy and have made a study of the country, its real condition and powers. . . . Mrs. Marsh is a great favorite of mine, she is truly elegant and so learned and able to transmit what she knows.[36]

Underwood also connected Marsh in a complimentary light to another literary figure, Elizabeth Barrett Browning: "I think Mrs. Marsh has the same kind of practical enthusiasm for Italy that Mrs. Browning had, and she seems like a poetess."[37] Indeed, at this point Marsh had published her own poetry and translations of others', and she left behind manuscript verses as well. Yet Underwood's choice of the phrase "seems like a poetess" suggests that the *ambasciatrice* had not made herself known yet as a writer of verses; certainly, no record exists of her having read any of her poetry, or calling attention to herself in that light, when hosting receptions.

By contrast, Brewster, at her receptions, may have been more interested in performance and theatrics than in educating or drawing people out. These regular occasions allowed Brewster to reign as "Queen Anne," as New England author Louise Chandler Moulton referred to her in a dedicatory homage poem. Her receptions rose to such prominence in the 1870s that Charles Warren Stoddard wrote of them for the *San Francisco Chronicle* as "a very agreeable weekly diversion" for what he described as "a motley assemblage of natives and foreigners." Another newspaper correspondent writing of them a few years later noted that "one is always sure there of three good things—, a friendly welcome, a refreshing cup of tea, and good society."[38]

In his descriptive account Stoddard invited readers to walk through Brewster's reception with him, noting that the hostess was "a very tidy lady in black velvet and diamonds." (Marsh also wore black, but because she was in mourning for her niece Carrie. By contrast, Brewster, always interested in appearances, noted in a private journal entry that she selected it and her diamonds because they were elegant.) Employing the second person "you" to engage his readers with a "you are there" effect, Stoddard continued: The hostess "greets you with flattering cordiality, even though you be an entire stranger to her and only a friend of her friend." He explained, "she has her hands full, for not one of the multitude that gathers at her receptions but receives some attention from her." Among the guests would be artists and authors, such as T. Adolphus Trollope or Mary Agnes Tincker, or an unnamed Protestant missionary and a Californian philosopher, whom Stoddard described by their beliefs and behaviors. He introduced these celebrities to readers as though they were walking through the reception with him.[39]

Guests would roam through "long, beautiful apartments, crowded with bric-a-brac" and "a thousand lovely objects to look at and admire"—"paintings . . . rare and costly volumes, statuettes . . . odd and valuable bits of furniture . . . a bust of Lizst" from "the musical genius himself," and the like, Stoddard explained. Brewster's reception provided "a well-laden board, to which you are welcomed at your earliest convenience." Amid the din of voices, "music in one of the rooms" would draw those who chose to listen rather than to converse. If Brewster "knows you well," he continued, "you are led into a cozy corner of two or three of your kind, who at once affiliate, and the hour passes swiftly." The flash and show of Brewster's rooms—now in the Palazzo Albani with views from the Quirinale hill—the refreshments, and the arranged music contributed to the festive atmosphere.

Not everyone, of course, was as positive as Chandler Moulton and Stoddard about such gatherings. Hawthorne wrote negatively in *The Marble Faun* of such "weekly receptions" as "common among the foreign residents of Rome" and consisting of "pleasant people—or disagreeable ones, as the case may be—[who] encounter one another with little ceremony." The differences and disagreements arose from rivalries for patronage, which was much more intense among the visual artists than the literary ones. And, Hawthorne added, winning patronage was often an affair of intrigue rather than artistic merit or delicacy of perception among these judges.[40] Brewster's neighbor Carson reinforced Hawthorne's view of the importance of such "affair[s] of intrigue" and recorded surprises as well. For example, she noted that Californian author Joaquin Miller, whom she referred to as "Walkin," was "slap sided, lanky, with a twang" and "hangdog ease." Annoyed especially that "Americans . . . bow to him because he's been with the Princess of Wales" when they knew nothing "about poetry or his poetry, to say the least!"—she described him as highly uncouth when he showed up at "Miss Brewster's" with a letter from Mrs. Gladstone, herself a well-known hostess.[41]

Despite realizing the necessities of these networking occasions for professional outcomes, Brewster's, Gould's, and Marsh's feelings about them were not always positive. Gould both loved and hated the social circles, depending on her day's demands. For example, she wrote to George Marsh in the winter of 1868 of her "duties to [her] husband," explaining "I . . . should be a woman of leisure, were my husband not a doctor." Her responsibility, she noted, was to "keep [him] up," or bolster his professional work as a physician:

> I am entirely out of society this winter. . . . My choice had to be between duties to husband and his patients and the series (unbroken as yet) of diversions of all kinds into which Americans have plunged, and whence Lent has not released them. Eight parties Tuesday night; five Thursday, a steady stream of breakfasts, dinners and suppers meanders through our society. I go up stairs to see the sick and sorrowing, leave cards, and keep up my husband. He never begun to be so busy at home as abroad, and as yet, there is no let-up to it. He had accepted one dinner invitation in six weeks, and had to break it on the day of the dinner.[42]

Gould at this point saw her vocation as assisting her husband by calling on his patients. She visited them and the "sorrowing," likely families mourning the deaths of Dr. Gould's former patients.[43] Sometimes these expatriates "had no friends but ourselves in town," Gould explained. When a Philadelphia couple living in Nice, France, had lost a child, for example, Gould wrote, "The little creature was so full of vitality that it was hard to give it up . . . so that we were the more needed to try and prepare the poor mother for what we saw coming, and soften the blow as much as poor sympathy and tenderness can soften such sorrows." Gould's response and responsibility to these physical and emotional needs of others often trumped the social events in garnering her interest. The beginning of Gould's evangelical activism with the orphanage and industrial school necessitated the social sacrifice. Attempts to keep up daily tasks as well as evening social responsibilities took their toll on mature women and necessitated decision-making for what we now call self-care. Gould explained her approach to the challenges: "By giving up evening company out of the house, and driving out every day, I am doing very well." She was fundraising through a fair advertised in the *Osservatore Romano* and commenting on the Roman government's interference with such activities.[44]

Like Gould, Brewster also noted occasional difficulties in participating in receptions. In addition to the expense of providing "a well-laden board," the socializing and surface conversations concerned her. In the winter of 1883, for example, she wrote in her journal, "Five more Mondays after today and my receptions end. I shall be very glad for they tire me." And then, when that date arrived, "To day is my last reception and I am very glad of it."[45] Contributing to her physical fatigue was the exacerbating financial strain. "My winter is passing without any fruit of work or money," she wrote. "My *Boston Advertiser* letters are all I do. I cannot work as I used to." In addition to needing more rest, she noted that she must be more exacting with bills "due to Harnisch." Several references to the young sculptor housemate in this period complained about his lifestyle. An initial financial and emotional blessing had gone awry, just as the receptions took their toll.

Brewster's neighbor Carson also wrote of the fatigue and emptiness of such socializing: "I can't stand this life much longer. I pine for my children, and vainly do I try to fill my heart with the husks of society, tho' it's very gratifying that people seek me. But daily I feel more and more lonely and weary of it all."[46] In spite of the challenges and emptiness of such socializing at times, Carson also noted the ways in which these events furthered relationships. They extended circles that might lead to formal engagements of marriage. She wrote of casino culture at Bagni di Lucca and of the circles in Rome in this light, mentioning, for example, the Countess Gianotti, formerly "a mature and handsome Washington belle," who "fell in with a handsome Italian younger than herself."[47]

Expatriates like Carson, Gould, Marsh, and Brewster extended their circles by participating in an exchange of visits, even when they did not feel up to it. Just showing up might lead to future results. Brewster's autograph album provides another picture of how people and texts supported each other in these exchange networks. The album not only served the hostess as a record but would allow curious and browsing visitors to see who else attended an evening's circulation. Serving much as a social media page list of "friends" and "likes" does today, others' signatures stood as a material representation of a hostess's networks. Supplementing her letters, journal entries, poems, and newspaper accounts, Brewster's autograph album speaks to her wreath of relations—visitors such as her former neighbor, the civic leader Lanciani, and the Gigliucci family, of concern to Marsh when she left her niece behind in 1869.[48] Any visitor might quickly scan the page upon arrival to see what likeminded friends or new faces were attending.

These receptions also fostered formal political and reform work—sometimes less and sometimes more overtly. Brewster, for example, circulated a petition surrounding a controversial clergyman, the Monsignor Capel.[49] According to Brewster, Capel was a friend of Cardinal Newman, who should have been a "shield" for him but was not, due to a falling out with Cardinal Manning. The petition concerned sermons Capel wished to deliver during the Lenten season and the Duchess Salviato's opposition to them. Brewster had requested that a banker, Mr. Handley, draw up a petition allowing Capel to deliver the sermons, and then send it to a Mrs. Moore and a Mrs. Reggio for their signatures. Brewster planned that after these two prominent women signed, she would have the petition at her reception for more signatures. Although she and Capel both knew the petition's request would not be approved, they went ahead with it, and she procured "over forty names." It was "a protest and declaration of faith in him," she explained. As Brewster compared him to a former "very handsome" suitor, Charles Elmer, she revealed her attraction to him, and a letter Capel wrote to her demonstrates their mutual admiration and trust.[50]

Finally, regarding the petition, Brewster asserted also that she had "no social damnation to fear"—quite in keeping with what Stoddard wrote of her as he concluded his article on her receptions. This "busy" woman, Stoddard explained, was "always in search of new discoveries, gathering facts for future use, interviewing the authorities" but not at "other people's receptions," for "she has no need to visit them." Her behaviors kept her in the limelight when she wished, creating what Chandler Moulton's poem to "Queen Anne" described as the courtly atmosphere over which Brewster ruled as she acted upon her calling. In short, she had set aside some of the formalities of gift exchange invitations.[51]

Brewster's work with the petition at her reception and Gould's choices about social invitations illustrate how exemplary hostesses extended their actions from the private into the public realm to follow their vocations. As philanthropists and activists Annie Adams Fields and Mary Gladstone Drew had "moved from the domestic into the professional arena," transferring skills from one to the other, so, too, did Gould, Brewster, and Marsh. Although "the work they did, in charity and church affairs, had a long history of participation by women," Harris has explained, these women pushed the envelope of change. "The form in which they contributed their labors—what we could call professionally administrative—took them into new gender territory, as they assumed positions of authority in organizations [that had been] dominated by men."[52]

These women's receptions sustained their daily lives, their emotional and physical survival, and their vocations, but they also stretched them. At times they brought delight but at others they delivered despair. Like Arachne's web, viewing the web of relations as positive or negative depended upon position and perspective. For a spinner such as Gould, who wove fantasies of hosting her ambassador friend George Marsh, the imagined power relations invigorated her. For an entangled victim, they could be debilitating. Regardless of the perspective, these relations depended upon economies of gift exchange. Rather than circulating at will as independent and autonomous agents, people moved about as objects of exchange, circulating as currency within social networks. Additionally, the boundaries between people and texts often blur, as the written word often stands in place of absent authors. These circulating texts of informal and formal associational life, considered in the next chapter, reflect the complex webs of relations of Americans in Italy.

Chapter 6

Circulating People, Circulating Texts

Associational Life

Do send me Ellen!

—Emily Bliss Gould to George Perkins Marsh, August 10, 1869

Please whip Ellen. Nothing else will satisfy my wrath.

—Emily Bliss Gould to George Perkins Marsh, August 20, 1869

During the summer of 1869, Emily Bliss Gould wrote several times to George Perkins Marsh from Bad Kipingen, Bavaria, asking and then imploring that he "send" his niece Ellen. The queries had begun on August 7, when Gould asked: "How and where is Ellen? She might write a line if she were lonely." In a mode typical of the time, the letter concluded with a nod to the Ambassador's family: "Much love to her and, always to Mrs. Marsh *when you write*."[1] Tacked on to the letter's end, these remarks about Ellen and Caroline seem almost insignificant in correspondence otherwise filled with Gould's fundraising efforts for the orphanage project and her own summer travel plans. Gould only briefly mentioned her own husband—he was in Paris. The spousal references gain significance, then, as signs of absence—both Caroline and James were away. George could greet his wife on Gould's behalf only when he wrote to her. The separation of both couples—not surprising given their social positions—created an important context for Gould's letters that summer and her requests for Ellen.

Growing in intensity, Gould's requests became more demanding and assertive. She wrote three days later, for example, "Can not I have Ellen? Why not let me?? I will come for her to Wildbad if you choose, or where you choose." Later in the same letter she added, "Do lend me Ellen. I am not bound to anybody, and should be delighted and she shall study and get fat both. Pray think of it." Then, in a postscript amidst a brief reference to her husband, who had recently arrived in New York, she inserted another query, "Can not Ellen write me?" Finally, she scribbled a tag line, "Do send me Ellen." In another letter Gould explained to her ambassador friend, "I write . . . thinking that I may have more hopes of being allowed Ellen. I will come anywhere you say to get her, and keep her until we go down to Florence if you allow it, & bring her to you at any point you wish."[2]

The purposes of Gould's multiple queries and requests for the young Ellen reinforce the myths and challenges of American women traveling in Europe—either alone or with family and friends. On their surface, Gould's requests reflect one mature woman's concern for the well-being of another, in this case a young American living abroad, usually with her aunt and uncle, friends of the correspondent. Ellen's ill health, according to Gould, would benefit from the climate of Rome—more moderate than Florence and significantly warmer than Bavaria. But Gould's insistent and repeated requests merit additional consideration. The letters' temporal context—related to the absent spouses—reveal other interests. Caroline, usually the surrogate mother, had returned to the US, not only to visit family as far west as St. Louis but also to supervise the packing up of the library in the couple's home in Burlington, Vermont. Gould's invitation and plea to send Ellen would lighten George's domestic concerns and responsibilities during his wife's absence. Addressing these responsibilities, Caroline's letters from the period speak to her concerns about Ellen's relationships. She expressed to George that she did not want their niece Ellen "going to the Gigliucci" family; instead, she hoped he "could manage to leave her in some nice family in France or Switzerland" until she returned.[3] Adding to Gould's health concerns about Ellen, then, the niece's situation presents the realities and social challenges for young women traveling abroad in Italy.

Ellen's situation shifted as the summer season transitioned into fall. In a September 23 letter to George, Gould added to the caring language of concern in her closing, "Love to Ellen," with a pointed query about consequences: "Has she had her desserts?"[4] What had happened during the elapsed six weeks to elicit Gould's biting query? An earlier letter provides insights. In August Gould had lashed out with her pen, as she often did in her impassioned letters to the Ambassador. Writing about a dinner George had hosted, Gould fumed: "I am too furious that I might have had Ellen. I wish Miss Blagsden had been anywhere but at your dinner . . . the day I met her there. I could not of course speak to you." The slightly younger Gould saw Isa Blagsden, a mature woman in the circle of Anglo writers in Florence, as a competitor for the Ambassador's attention. Proper social performances prevented Gould from speaking directly to Marsh, assumed to be the protective father figure, about her concern for Ellen's well-being. She explained further, "when Ellen followed me to the carriage, I did speak to her. But she spoke so decidedly of her going to the _______ somebody's that I thought she and you and Mrs. Marsh and everybody but I preferred it. So, I did not speak of it to you the next day." The scene with Ellen typifies a young adult asserting independence and will about social events, selecting where to spend her time while her Aunt Caroline, the surrogate mother, was away. Gould, without the opportunity to speak to both George and his niece without "Miss Blagsden's" presence, had lost the sense of power she wished to assume in Caroline's absence. Through the letter Gould tried to regain some semblance of it. Here and in other letters, her stated desires for Ellen's well-being and her attempts to control Ellen intertwined, as she expressed frustration about the dinner party. She continued with rage, "I am too sorry. Please whip Ellen. Nothing else will satisfy my wrath." Then she concluded the letter, not with the usual "love to Ellen," or "ask Ellen to write," but instead, "With love to Mrs. Marsh and vengeance to Ellen."[5]

Gould's expressed "vengeance" about Ellen's choice, and the desire that the older man, Marsh, "whip" her, scream to contemporary readers for attention, yet other facets of these epistolary transactions deserve consideration. While Ellen's presence would have added to Gould's duties and responsibility as a new surrogate mother and detracted from her labors in writing and on behalf of the school, it would also have given the older, childless woman company while her husband was away. Yet Gould traveled in this period with a "Miss Jordan," who kept her from being alone. Above all, then, hosting Ellen would strengthen Gould's relationship with the Ambassador and, as a result, her sense of empowerment and control while abroad. Ellen, who had not yet reached the "age of majority," and had physical needs about which adult family and friends should have been concerned, circulated among adults as a commodity. Neither slave nor victim of a human trafficking crime by today's standards, Ellen nonetheless stood figuratively in a position like Gould's letters, passed back and forth between adults as a negotiating token in their relationship and its future. Emily's exchange of letters with George reveals how the negotiations of relationships among those abroad, as Leon Jackson describes the "gift exchange" of writing in antebellum America, contributed to the success of their enterprises.[6] Gould saw her connection with the Ambassador, embodied in her expressed written desires for Ellen, as essential to the success of her reform work.

These written desires also reflect the expectation of response typical to letter writing—an "epistolary negotiation" or "epistolary pact." In short, this unstated contract of exchange and expected response extends the relationship's open-ended life.[7] The larger context of Gould's letters to George illuminates this network of exchange and its accompanying expectations. During these months, Emily wrote at least seven letters to George, approximately a third of all their extant correspondence. The letters vary in length from one to several pages, focusing primarily on Gould's work with the orphanage and school project in Rome and on George's health. She encouraged him to travel to alpine locales she had visited, to see a physician she knew, and to take treatments as advised. After his health, the next most frequent topic of concern was Ellen. As for the absent spouses, Gould wrote that she hoped James and Caroline would meet in New York or Rhode Island and that they might travel back to Europe together. Perhaps by linking the absent spouses in her imagination, Gould relieved any guilt she may have felt about her correspondence with George, as she visualized the two couples as a happy foursome, although with partners switched while they were apart from one another.

The correspondence between a married woman and a married man broke the acceptable boundaries as they had been expressed by Philadelphia author Eliza Leslie. Leslie advised in a popular *Ladies' Guide to True Politeness* (1855), "Above all, let no lady correspond with a married man, unless she is obliged to consult him on business; and from that plain, straight path let her not diverge." As Leslie explained the rationale, "Even if the wife sees and reads every letter, she will, in all probability, feel a touch of jealousy, (or more than a touch,) if she finds that they excite interest in her husband, or give him pleasure."[8] While Gould could be said to have written to Marsh "on business" regarding the industrial school, numerous playful comments stray "from that plain, straight path." However, she almost always restrained herself, adding in closing lines her greetings to "Mrs. Marsh" and from "Dr. Gould"—written reminders that each had marital bonds. The context of absent spouses, however, suggests the intensified emotional needs that both writer and recipient might have had—needs that could be met in part by the letters.

Gould was not the only woman writing to the Ambassador in this period. An early September letter written by Rosa Arbesser, a governess and attendant of the Princess Margherita, also gushed with strong hopes of seeing George in Florence:

> I am too much touched at your kindness for writing to me so often to be able to scold you, . . . when I think of your poor eyes, and how much you tire them by writing. . . . Do not hasten back on my account, dear Mr. Marsh, or hurry poor Helen [Ellen], back, from her pleasant stay. I can just as well stay some time with you alone dear Mr. Marsh without being afraid of our compromising ourselves. I go to Florence merely to see you I have not the slightest interest else but I possibly will not have you change your plan's in the least. Stay at Wildbad not one day less dear Mr Marsh than you intended, it would give me so much pain to disturb you any how."[9]

With a bit of "the lady doth protest too much" tone, Arbesser's letter was frank about her desires. Gould's was slightly subtler. Caroline Marsh had been surprised by what she deemed Arbesser's "imprudence" during the early years in Turin when she had become a "confidante" of the German woman. Apparently, George "kept his distance" from her.[10] Nonetheless, Gould's letters to George (and those we imagine he wrote to Gould) stood in the absence of the writers to one another, connecting them safely at a distance, especially through references to their absent spouses and the niece Ellen. With these references Gould avoided appearing dangerously alone. They remind readers of the safety and surveillance of networks in which she and her texts circulated as objects of exchange.

Public Texts and Personal Relations: "For Queen Anne"

> There are some rooms in Rome I shall remember—
> High up a winding stair, like Hilda's tower,
> Where gallant men and gracious women linger,
> And good Queen Anne holds sway with gentle power.
>
> —Louise Chandler Moulton, "For Queen Anne," 1876

As a counterpoint to the private letters that circulated daily in social contexts without Internet and telephones, public texts laid bare the personal relationships negotiated through exchange. One example is Louise Chandler Moulton's homage poem written "For Queen Anne" (Appendix B), honoring Brewster as hostess ruling gently over "gallant men and gracious women" at her receptions.[11] Moulton composed the poem during her 1876 trip to Europe, a literary tour, within two years of Stoddard's article on Brewster's receptions.[12] Among Brewster's papers today, "For Queen Anne" exists in manuscript only, carefully inscribed in elegant handwriting on embossed paper.[13] Yet the poem does more than acknowledge Brewster's "reign" among Anglos in the Eternal City and her relationship with Moulton. As the poem connects Brewster to Hawthorne's *The Marble Faun*, where his fictional

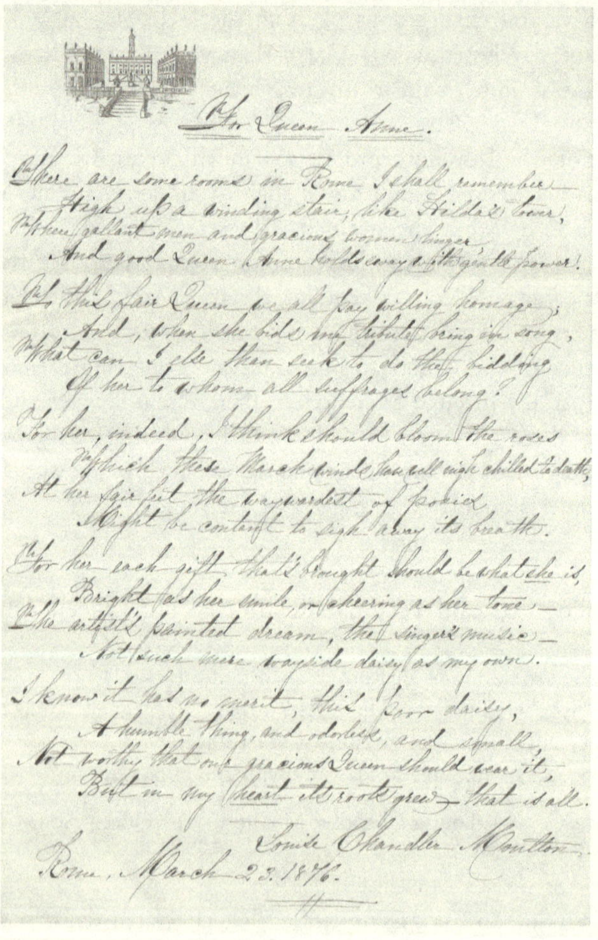

For Queen Anne.

There are some rooms in Rome I shall remember
High up a winding stair, like Hilda's tower,
Where gallant men and gracious women linger
And good Queen Anne holds sway with gentle power.

To this fair Queen we all pay willing homage,
And, when she bids, my tributes bring in song,
What can I else than seek to do the bidding
Of her to whom all suffrages belong?

For her, indeed, I think should bloom the roses
Which these March winds have all nigh chilled to death,
At her fair feet the waywardest of posies
Might be content to sigh away its breath.

For her each gift that's brought should be what she is,
Bright as her smile, or cheering as her tone—
The artist's painted dream, the singer's music—
Not such mere wayside daisy as my own.

I know it has no merit, this poor daisy,
A humble thing, and odorless, and small,
Not worthy that our gracious Queen should wear it,
But in my heart its roots grew—that is all.

Louise Chandler Moulton

Rome, March 23. 1876.

Figure 6.1. Louise Chandler Moulton manuscript poem, "For Queen Anne," Rome, 1876. Credit: The Library Company of Philadelphia.

heroine Hilda lodged in a Roman tower, it places the hostess within American literary culture and the realm of unmarried, virtuous women. Beyond that, the material record also demonstrates the poem's status as a gift and the compositor's pride in crafting it—elevating her position in this circuit of textual exchange. Although the poem's exact use and circulation before it found a place in Brewster's saved papers is unknown, Moulton likely read it aloud at one of Brewster's regular receptions. As Stoddard explained, such entertainment was commonplace.

Within this context the poem illustrates "encounters between . . . people and their poems," which, as Michael C. Cohen has explained, go "beyond the bounds of 'reading'" and "literariness."[14] The writing, reading, and publication of verses now often deemed of little literary worth accrues value within specific venues, as Paula Bennett also has argued. These "moments of substantive creativity" come to light within the context of the authors and their audiences.[15] More specifically, Cohen's consideration of "scene[s] of recitation and exchange" asserts how poems "bring together a mixed company in a private space" that "transform" a poem "from a literary text into a social relation." The poem becomes "a cipher to facilitate what looks like a moment of pure exchange,"[16] but, in fact, it clearly illustrates the complex web of relations—people who gathered at Brewster's home, authors who wrote for a variety of reasons, and imagined characters (such as Hilda) within literature and history. Brewster's decision to keep the poem and the picture it now provides of social relations both contribute to the meaning of unpublished, seemingly simple, manuscript verses.

These five rhyming quatrains are tribute verses, or an homage poem, whose flattering content is both its most remarkable and its most problematic aspect. The speaker's voice as well as the material objects associated with the poem—embossed paper and elegant handwriting—elevate Moulton herself as much as Brewster. The poet's role, in this reading, becomes as significant as the honoree. Following Moulton's title, "For Queen Anne," which designates Brewster's royal stature, the poem continues to flatter in the first stanza with a tower setting that evokes both a medieval court and an illusion to the Rapunzel-like abode of the young, unmarried American artist Hilda. The connection of the much younger Hilda to Brewster, more than fifty years old, is a flattering comparison—imaginative but unrealistic. In addition, the poem praises "Queen Anne" with ennobling adjectives such as "good," "fair," and "gracious." Brewster reigns "with gentle power," a "Bright . . . smile" and "cheering . . . tone." Adding to the ennobling flattery, within the second stanza the poem suggests the humility *topos*, typical of odes, as it refers to the poet-speaker Moulton "seek[ing] to do the bidding" of this royal woman. The commonplace continues as the speaker refers to her own "gift" of poetry as not a "rose" or even "the waywardest of posies" but a "mere wayside daisy," which "has no merit" as an offering. This "humble thing," both "odorless, and small" gains value, however, as it connects the two women. As the poem concludes: "in my heart its roots grew." The poem's sincere, emotional origins in the speaker's heart reflect the bond Moulton feels to Queen Anne and give the poem value.

These common poetic techniques—both the humility *topos* and the personal value statement—ironically call attention to the speaker herself. Within the context of nineteenth-century tribute poems, or what Desirée Henderson labels "friendship elegies," the poem not only honors Brewster as queen but also celebrates the poet and at the same time illustrates "the diverse forms that women's relationships with other women might take."[17] Henderson lists "sororal, tutelary, erotic, [and] textual" relationships as possibilities with "friendship elegies," but only one of these labels fits the Brewster–Moulton pairing. No records of the women's symbolic "sisterhood" exists, nor does evidence of mentoring or erotic relationships between the two in their voluminous letters and diaries. The poem manifests instead the "textual" connection between them, as Moulton "privileges the female community of authors that she clearly saw herself and" Brewster "inhabiting."[18] Perhaps she hoped that Brewster would publish the verses in one of her regular letters that year—to the *Boston Daily Advertiser*, the *Philadelphia Evening Bulletin*, the *Daily Graphic* or the *World* in New York—which would have called further attention to Moulton's work and stature as an American author. The moment of gift exchange in which this poem first circulated—likely a reading at one of Brewster's receptions—would have increased its value as a text with a social life of its own, circulating within the web of relations of these American women abroad.

Gould's, Brewster's, and Marsh's receptions and their moves into the public sphere, where they "assumed positions of authority" and "contributed their labors," further come to light through three other published texts: the collection in which Aunt Friendly's story of "Miss Jones" appeared in 1875, and two adjacent articles in an 1874 issue of an Italian newspaper, *Il popolo romano*. These accounts illuminate how both informal receptions and formal associations enhanced the women's engagement with the world and their literary lives. These networks fed the flow of information within Europe and across the Atlantic. This flow kept afloat their respective interests and goals with their later vocations.

A Wreath of Stray Leaves: Published Textual Networks

The collection in which the tale of "Miss Jones" appeared, published by the Italo-American School in Rome, depicts Gould's network of textual relations in Italy. Entitled *In Memoriam: A Wreath of Stray Leaves to the Memory of Emily Bliss Gould*, it typifies the popular nineteenth-century genre known as "obituary literature," or, more specifically, "posthumous tribute volumes."[19] The volume's composition and publication by friends and family memorialized and idealized the deceased—in this case, Gould, who had established the industrial school and orphanage five years earlier.[20] Rendered eternal through print, the deceased activist Gould lived on through the text's bound pages. This collection, printed on the new press and by the capable students of the school she established, idolized her not only through the words on the page but also through the acts of editorial compilation and publication.[21] However, the tribute volume's composition did more than memorialize Gould. It eclipsed Gould's voice, personality, and career with the voices of Trollope, Howitt, and others deemed of "social or literary significance," who were "solicited" contributors. Gould's words appear only in a few lines included in a biographical sketch. As Henderson has explained, "the work of textual mourning had the effect of shifting focus from the . . . reputation and career of the deceased to those of her symbolic successors."[22] Often a tribute volume editor would contribute more to the collection than anyone else, and thus become "the guiding authorial figure" who would overshadow the deceased.[23] Notably, no written works by Gould appear in the volume dedicated to her; instead, Trollope and Howitt garnered recognition through their work with the collection and in their introductory comments valorizing Gould. Although the title *In Memoriam* recognizes Gould, the editors were the "wreath" makers who gathered the "stray leaves" acknowledged in the subtitle and presented them to the public.

This amalgamation of poems, fiction, historical and pictorial sketches, typical of the genre, differs from them, however, in the volume's planning. Gould herself envisioned it, long before her illness and death. This shift of the posthumous tribute volume's usual origin and purpose prompts consideration of *In Memoriam*'s larger goals and results. According to Trollope, the goal early on, "in the winter of 1874," was attracting financial support for the school by "employing the printing press, and shewing what the pupils could do in that line." Plans included releasing the volume the following spring. After typical publication delays, such as waiting for late contributors, the surprising and "fatalest cause of delay of all" arrived—Gould's final illness and death. Trollope explained that the volume never was intended to provide an overview of Gould's "good work . . . or of the truly rare spirit of entire self-devotion with which it was carried out." In fact, even after her demise, the collection appeared as she and the contributors initially intended—excepting a change in title.[24]

Howitt addresses the volume's fundraising goals in its preface. She explains that despite Gould's death, the volume lives on, embodying both the activist and the children who produced it. Even more, the volume becomes Gould's mouthpiece: "She speaks through it," eternally pronouncing her message, as "she beseeches the friends who love her memory—all the friends of little children athirst for knowledge . . . to stand in her place, pillars as it were of that Home of industry and true instruction of which she laid the foundation."[25] As Howitt concludes, she overtly assumes Gould's voice, preaching for her and appealing through the text: "I speak for her—from the grave. Let the motherless and homeless children, whom she gathered into a home of labour and love, become your children, now that she is gone, so that they—if not others also, may become a living, noble lasting monument, enduring through them to countless generations, to the memory of her who did all that she could—and perished in the doing of it."[26] Such direct appeals for the Italo-American Schools in the volume's introductory materials clearly mark its purpose, which the story of Miss Jones's conversion and the tale's concluding exhortations reinforce.

Notably, and somewhat ironically, Howitt's appropriation of Gould's voice and work parallels the use Gould made of the Italian children and the way in which "Miss Jones's" conversion depended upon the contiguousness of her well-lit lodging in the palazzo with Vittorio's dark, damp home, below and behind it. As Howitt explains, "This volume, every letter of its type set by the agile fingers of little children, whom she loved—whom she rescued from want and ignorance—from crime and degradation, it may be—upon whose heads she had laid her hands in blessing, whom she had led to the Saviour and raised in the scale of humanity—this volume—their work as well as hers, comes forth as an appeal for *them*."[27] These multiple voices of and for social improvement—Howitt's, Gould's, and Trollope's, followed by those of the contributors—illustrate the ongoing power relations associated with social reform, like layers of Russian dolls nesting within each other. The collection demonstrates the magnetic and cumulative nature of these efforts, instigated by only one woman who felt she "must do something." Gould's work gathered force and momentum as others were drawn to the utopian ideas from which they, too, garnered a sense of pleasure and power. Howitt's participation as a spokesperson, and the voices of others joined to the cause, exemplify the expansive networks of Americans and English abroad who were concerned supporters of Italian social reform but also depended upon their beneficiaries to buoy themselves.

The book's contributors were Anglo, except for Pasquale Villari, a political and educational leader who also advocated for social reform of all types and had married an English woman.[28] Other contributors included George Perkins Marsh, a star in the orbits of many Americans on the peninsula, and Matthew Arnold, along with Howitt's husband William, their daughter Anna, Trollope and his wife Theodosia, and sculptor William Wetmore Story, known not only for his artistic work but also for his circles, captured in James's biography, *William Wetmore Story and His Friends* (the same volume that describes the "marmorean flock" of female artists in Rome). Another contributor was Charles Isidore Hemans (son of popular poet Felicia Hemans). Hemans lived most of his adult life in Rome, established the English Archaeological Society, published several books on Roman history and monuments, and published the first English newspaper there, the *Roman Advertiser*.[29] Literary scholars Mary Cowden Clarke and her husband, Charles Cowden Clarke, who lived in the Genoa area, an important port and stop for Anglo travelers on the Grand Tour and hotbed for political changes in the era, also contributed.[30] These contributing figures corresponded with each other, shared books, and met face-to-face—illustrating the textual networks of the time, not unlike social media tendrils today.[31]

The collection's contributions by the Howitts and Villari, written from positions of those highly invested in educational reform, address Gould's role as an engaged activist abroad. In addition to being popular poets, the Howitts were leaders in the industrial school movement in England.[32] Gould's efforts followed this model and attracted donors who already knew of the Howitts' works. William's essay, entitled "Progressive Steps of Popular Education," provides a sweeping transnational history to create a context for Gould's Rome project. His overview revises the typically accepted foundation of Sunday schools in England, attributing instead the beginnings to the American Sunday school of Ludwig Hacker, leader of the Ephrata cloister in Lancaster County, Pennsylvania.[33] The revision allowed him to introduce Gould's work by national affiliation: "The noble-spirited lady, who is now introducing the principle of working-schools into Rome, and from whose school-press the present volume issues, is an American, and it is a notable fact that the originator of popular education was also an American, at least, by residence." Referring to Gould in the present tense, the essay indicates that Howitt drafted it before her demise.

Howitt's overall emphasis—educational reform—transcends national and religious boundaries. He notes, for example, Johann Heinrich Pestalozzi and Philipp Emanuel von Fellenberg in Switzerland and Andrew Bell in India, whose efforts went beyond education, to "the improvement of the popular condition." And he credited utopian visionaries Charles Fourier, Henri de St. Simon, Robert Owen, and George Birkbeck for advocating "social amelioration" of problems. This historical overview of reform poised Howitt to turn to the recent past: "Technical Institutions" supported by the British House of Commons in 1867, and Gould's place within the situation in Italy.[34] The revelation was "that out of twenty-six millions of people, seventeen millions could neither read nor write." The situation in the former Papal States was bad—with "eighty to ninety percent of the population . . . in . . . utter ignorance. In the Neapolitan States the case was still worse." But thanks to "the new Italian government," he reported, 11,137 schools had been established for boys and girls in five years.[35] Because schooling was not compulsory, however, "individual efforts" such as those by Gould were essential "to bring within reach of reformatory discipline the neglected children of the ignorant and indifferent." Gould and Julie Salis-Schwabe in Naples were "the most conspicuous and efficient labourers in this cause," he explained.[36]

Rather than leave these lesser-known women's names standing alone as reformers, Howitt drew a culminating comparison to another woman well known and favorable in the eyes of readers: Lady Byron. She supported "pioneer" working schools when she lived at Ealing in England, where "the boys were taught agriculture, horticulture and other arts, as those of carpentry and smithwork, the girls knitting, sewing, washing, and cooking."[37] Harriet Beecher Stowe had celebrated this school and reform work in *Lady Byron Vindicated* (1870), published only five years before *In Memoriam* appeared. Finally, while Howitt waxed nostalgic about his visits to such schools, he also conveyed a blessing to Gould's work: "May Whitechapel School be the harbinger of equally happy results in the school and school press, from whence this volume issues in Rome! May the boys print themselves into self-supporting and prosperous citizens, and at some very far distant day, may they erect a tablet of equally grateful recognition of the beneficent services of Doctor, and Mrs. Gould!"[38] Monuments recognizing "Mrs. Gould's" services did, in fact, appear after her death.[39]

In contrast to Howitt's tribute, Villari's contribution to the volume did not mention Gould's work. He focused on education, but with an emphasis on Vittorino Rambaldoni da Feltre, whom Villari labeled "il primo educatore moderno," the "first modern educator" in Italy. Typical of political reformers, Villari celebrated past achievements on the peninsula, but with a reminder to readers that much gleaned from the Italian past should be applied in the present. This sixteenth-century leader, Villari explained, opened a school in Venice, attended by famous rulers such as the Duke of Urbino. But in this otherwise Edenic atmosphere of learning, division reigned. Not only were the social classes divided but secular students were separated from clerical students, as were boys from girls after elementary school. Those in disciplines such as architecture were separated from those in medicine, law, and engineering, and in their requirements with languages. Above all, though, Villari noted that the school's educational leader provided a message for the present on education's value.[40]

Villari's contribution and its publication in Italian underscores not only a transnational readership but also the linguistic facility and efforts extended by many Anglo-Americans and Italians to break national boundaries in the interest of social improvement. Villari had been involved in the Risorgimento in 1848 and had left his home in Naples, becoming active as an author and professor of Italian history in Pisa and Florence. His publications on controversial historical figures such as Savanarola contributed to his appointment to the council of education in 1862 and then in 1869 as under-secretary of state for education.[41] According to historian Lucy Riall, he blamed the failure of the peninsula's earlier unification attempts not on any radical leaders, such as Mazzini, but on the uneducated masses and ignorant politicians and bureaucrats who fell prey to rhetoric.[42] His marriage to an English woman as well as his correspondence with Americans such as Brewster and George Perkins Marsh demonstrate his and their beliefs in the power of this transnational network.[43]

In Memoriam, one example of a network of friends and supporters in Italy, connected by texts, also imagines a supportive audience elsewhere. The material object, published by the Italo-American School Press, stood as a manifestation in the US and England of the skills of its students and the results of Gould's visionary dreams and labors. Although ascertaining the volume's impact on readers is impossible (WorldCat only locates about thirty copies), *In Memoriam* remains as a record of transnational and collective efforts to achieve utopia: improving the situation on the peninsula through improved education. Announcements of the volume's publication preempted its appearance, and advertisements afterward reminded readers of Gould's cause. For example, *The Rutland Daily Globe* announced in December 1875 "an interesting statement of the proposed 'wreath in memory of Emily Bliss Gould,' a niece of the late Hon. George T. Hodges, and a former resident of Rutland." And less than two weeks later, the *Burlington Weekly Free Press* explained,

> Last winter, a somewhat ambitious venture was made by Mrs. Gould's students in the printing of a handsome volume, composed of contributions of friends of the school then in Rome. . . . Mr. Trollope now writes to the New York *Tribune* to say that it is desired to bring out an edition . . . in the United States, to aid in some measure a fund for the permanent establishment of the school and the home. To any who are interested in the growth of Italy to a higher national life, the opportunity for charity thus offered will be readily welcomed.[44]

The volume revises a popular vision of American women in Italy when limited to fictional accounts such as those by Hawthorne and, later, James. Gould's social reform work, as much as Gould herself as valorized subject, lived on after her death, memorialized through this circle of contributors and their writings, which reinforce the multifaceted nature of Anglo networks on the peninsula.

Il popolo romano: Varieties of Formal Associations

American women's varied associational life, also prevalent in the new Rome, appears in two adjacent stories of the "Roman News" section of *Il popolo romano* in January 1874. One story features an event at Gould's school, headlined "La scuola americana." The other, entitled "La festa degli arcadi," describes a celebration of the Accademia dell'Arcadia, of which Brewster was a member.[45] Additionally, *Il popolo romano*'s presentation of the two events underscores differences of opinion about such organizations and their purposes. While Gould's school supported social reform through educating impoverished Romans and giving them training in "industrial" skills such as printing and sewing, the Accademia dell'Arcadia supported education and literary activities among an already well-educated group of elite adults. The

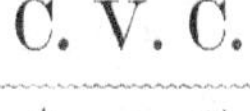

AGESANDRO TESPORIDE

CUSTODE GENERALE DELL'ARCADIA

Alla Illustre Signora
Anna Hampton Maria Brewster
di Filadelfia

L'Arcadia nell'intendimento di onorare le valorose, che per la eccellenza dell'ingegno, unita al merito di eletti costumi e alla coltura degli ottimi studî, van segnalate per l'ornamento delle Lettere e della Erudizione, a proposta dei gentilissimi e valorosissimi nostri Compastori *Eristeno Nassio* e *Arcandro Termideo* ha voluto dichiararvi Pastorella Arcade, ed annoverandovi nel Catalogo dei componenti questa antica letteraria Repubblica, vi ha dato, secondo il nostro uso accademico, il nome di *Clicera Samia*

L'Arcadia nel dichiararvi aggiunta al suo Comune, confida che non solo manterrete la osservanza delle sue leggi, ma darete opera eziandio perchè sempre più fiorisca con la dignità delle lettere l'onore dell'arcadico istituto.

Dato dal Bosco Parrasio addì 31 gennajo dell'anno 187

Dalla Restaurazione dell'Arcadia anno 183, della Olimpiade anno

Il Custode Generale

Registrato al vol. VIII, num. 201.

Figure 6.2. Accademia dell'Arcadia membership certificate. Credit: The Library Company of Philadelphia.

longstanding Roman association, whose origins go back at least to the late seventeenth century, had welcomed not only Brewster but also, for example, John McCloskey, Archbishop of New York, who became a member in 1873, the same year Brewster did. And honorees of the Accademia, such as Longfellow, reinforce its highly literary nature.[46]

The thriving press, which consisted of more than 350 periodicals in Rome alone between 1870 and 1875, captures such activities.[47] The adjacent stories highlighting these organizations confirm the political stance of *Il popolo romano* as "moderate" and "of the center left." The paper's proprietors, Guglielmo Canori and Leone Fortis, who had previously published *La nuova Roma*, provided a voice against the leaders of the conservative right through details and commentary on the many problems associated with transformations of the city as a new capital. Through agreements with communal authorities, *Il popolo romano* regularly published the official acts of the city with its new leadership and its "Camera di Commercio," or Chamber of Commerce.[48] As in many Italian papers, the writers voiced opinions strongly and with vitriolic humor, as the story of the Accademia dell'Arcadia event illustrates. As the story unfolds, the reporter's biting sarcasm emerges, culminating with powerful punning in its final lines. There he connects the "cells" of the priestly cloisters with those of the city jail, where he believes priests should be housed. His stance clearly affiliates him with the new secular government and monarchy.

Setting the stage for this conclusion, the unnamed reporter first mentions that he has sacrificed an invitation to attend the annual and important inauguration dinner of the Christmas tree at the Quirinale, formerly the Pope's palace and residence, but now the residence of the new king and queen, in order to write of the Accademia's event. He was asked to write on behalf of the organization's "Custodian General," Stefano Ciccolini, to whom he refers first as "Signor" but quickly corrects to "Monsignor." This revision of the equivalent of the English "Mr." to the clerical title also firmly establishes the reporter's anti-clerical stance. He continues the jabs at this traditional learned society by adding an overview of participating clerics. He counts and names nine priests (monsignors, canons, and abbots) and two "brothers," but only four non-clerics, including a doctor, a lawyer, and two women.

The women, Adele Bergamini and Maria Rosa Pieromaldi Biroccini, esteemed popular writers at the time, remind us that Brewster's membership in the Accademia as a female was not unique. In fact, the esteemed Pistoian poet Maria Maddalena Morelli, crowned on the Campidoglio in Rome for her extemporaneous verses, was named within the Arcadia as Corilla Olimpica beginning in 1775 and credited with reviving the society.[49] And during the years Brewster was a member, she sponsored at least four additional American women to join: Harriet Waters Preston, Olivia Rigby Seward, Sara Carr Upton, and Lucy White Jennison (Brewster would later encourage Jennison, a popular author who wrote under the pseudonym Owen Innsley, to write a sonnet honoring Longfellow after his death, an invitation she deemed herself incapable of accepting).[50] Brewster also sponsored several American men's memberships: Richard S. Greenough, Eugene Schuyler, Thomas Davidson, and Edward Wheelwright, all reflecting her stature as respected within the Accademia.[51] These and other members, such as Longfellow and McCloskey, speak to the association's highbrow and traditional desires in an era of change. These elements, however, are exactly what the reporter ridicules.

The reporter's critical stance highlights what they see as unnecessary and impractical theatrics at the gathering. For example, each "pastore" and "pastorella," as male and female Accademia members are known, has an associational name, contributing to a silly and "otherworldly" performative environment. Ciccolini is "Agesandro Tesporide." (Brewster, not mentioned in the story, becomes Clicera Samia within the Accademia.)[52] The story acknowledges dual identities and clerical positions as it proceeds with criticism of theatrics. Following his opening "elocution," Ciccolini delivered a piece written by a member who was unable to attend because he took cold at the previous meeting, held in the Bosco Parrasio, named for a wooded spot in Greece. The reporter here mocks the Arcadia's tradition of celebrating the pastoral age of Rome by meeting outside, even in the winter months, in its exclusive garden temple on the Janiculum hill, just above Trastevere and St. Peter's. The evening program continued with entertaining poetry declamations in Latin and Spanish, followed by "an injurious allusion to the monarchy" delivered with frank liberalness. The declamation asserted the "infalliblity of the Vatican" and noted that the new monarchy's power "must be dispersed like leaves in the wind"—both statements met with resounding applause. The declamations continued with members who "went to battle with verses." The imagery of poetic fighting underscores the members' desires for approbation and self-elevation—a stark contrast to the goals of military battles and bloodshed that had helped establish the new Kingdom of Italy just a few years earlier.

The reporter's stance comes most openly to a point in the story's conclusion. After noting how "remarkable" the discourse of the "priests and brothers" and the presence of the "aristocracy and Borghese clericals" has been in contributing to the event's "discrete success," he explains that this success has been "in the arcadian sense"—which is incomparable in its "ridiculous show of human vanity and these reminiscences of a fossilized literary school." "Discrete success" here signifies small and insignificant, then, rather than modest or careful. Counter to the political changes of the day, the literary association celebrating the classical past reflects the flowery and sometimes privileged habits of the sacristy and convents. The reporter concludes with a humorous warning: that the Accademia's leaders might move from one type of cell to another—from the cells of the comfortable church cloister, where "unmentionable pleasures" might have occurred, to the secular and uncomfortable cells of the Questura, or city jail.

Adjacent and in striking contrast to this account, the brief and non-satirical report of "La scuola americana" points to civic and social action. It describes a party "of the Christmas tree" held the previous night at the school "founded and directed by the philanthropist Mrs. Gould, an American." About 150 young students, the story explains, receive a free education there, and among these, ten of the "orphaned and abandoned" children are "fed and clothed" by Gould. During the celebration the students received gifts of toys and clothes from under the tree, but only after a reading and "remarks" by leaders, among whom were Italians and "foreigners." Englishman "Signor" Shrubb, Director of the *Italian News*, for example, attended, but the Mayor, former political exile Count Luigi Pianciani, who was invited, was unable to attend due to his many obligations.[53]

As these two accounts reinforce *Il popolo romano*'s views of events in the new Rome, they speak to differences among citizens and readers of the city and among Americans abroad, such as Gould and Brewster. While Gould hoped to build from the energy of anti-papal leaders through her newly established school and reform efforts, Brewster wished to insert herself into a centuries-old tradition, based on literature and the arts. Their desires, both affiliated with formal associational life, were worlds apart. Nonetheless, as historian Stephen Soper has explained, all types of formal associational life in Italy had a "civilizing role," regardless of the stance. In the 1840s popular collective social actions, such as gatherings in casinos, piazzas and cafes, reading rooms and libraries, as well as participating in Carnevale, the celebratory season before Lent, or resisting it, raised concern and suspicion among those in power. Control of these activities, whether by religious or secular authorities, had begun in 1847 in Turin with press and assembly laws. Additional regulation through formal associations appealed to many, to ward off the damage uncontrolled mobs could deliver. Without formal associations and their organized reform, collective chaos might ensue.[54]

Formal associations offered a positive alternate view of social forces. Many appeared in the 1860s, drawing leaders from elite families who saw their abilities to reform the impoverished. That said, the stated purposes of these newer associations were never merely social or recreational, as casinos and alpine clubs had been a generation earlier and continued to be.

(George Marsh was a member of an alpine club and enjoyed hiking, but he refused to join a whist club, for example, during the first part of the 1860s in Piedmont.) Socializing did not disappear but "so-called productive association" emerged overtly in an "ideological turn against recreation after 1866 by Italy's leading liberals."[55] The types of new formal associations varied greatly: some religious, some mutual aid societies, some focused on books and literature, some artisan groups—and members did not always mix well.[56] Many of these societies, along with economic exhibitions and fairs visited by the masses (not just merchants and industrial leaders), contributed to the goal of "transformation . . . of the ragged poor."[57] One example, the Italian equivalent of the YMCA, was a cause with which Gould affiliated. While this association might be considered a religious one concerned with saving young men's souls, its goals included keeping men off the streets and providing them places to go to improve more than their spiritual lives. With gifts and funds channeled through the New York YMCA, the association established a "Christian Training School for Young Men."[58] It included a library with popular texts (rather than rare books for show) and hosted lectures. This type of association, which Gould celebrated and supported—part of "Christian Work in Rome" described in a published report of 1873—differed immensely from Brewster's membership in the Accademia dell'Arcadia.

Brewster's neighbor Carson provides another example. In 1876 she became a member of an artisan group—the Società degli Acquarellisti—"the only woman and only foreigner elected to its membership" that year when it was formed.[59] She and Brewster both participated occasionally in the Circolo Dante, led by Michelangelo Caetani, the Duke of Sermoneta. Longfellow, another among the many Anglos who adored Caetani for his knowledge, genteel spirit, manners, and excellent English, also participated in the "Dante Circle" when he was in Rome.[60] But Gould also associated with Caetani, writing to him for assistance with her industrial school, and he attended some of its festivities. Later, he would marry the sister of one of Gould's teachers, Enrichetta Ellis. This correspondence complicates any neat divisions among the Americans and their associations—affiliations illustrating these tangled networks.

Caetani's leadership and his relations with the Anglo community in Rome also illuminate the concept of "exemplary ownership" popular in this period of transformation. Exemplary ownership illuminated the power of private book and visual art collections of elite families, opened to the public. Description of these collections "flourished" in guidebooks for tourists, demonstrating Italy's rebirth and elevation to those who had the ability to travel. Such elite collectors took action with political reform rather than remain aloof as a disengaged, dissatisfied wealthy group.[61] American authors such as Sedgwick and Brewster described these collections for their readers back home, just as Longfellow also embraced Caetani's position when he visited Rome.[62] Brewster, who became a collector herself, showed off her holdings in her private apartments, as she made them public during her weekly receptions. But for Brewster, who gained rights to read and borrow at the prestigious Accademia dei Lincei and its Corsini Library as well as the Arcadia, these collections were about her own improvement and advancement in elite culture and privilege.[63]

Notable in this associational work, of course, was the objectification of the lower classes by the upper classes and reification of class stratification through the process. A growing "gospel of benevolence" in fact reinforced "class hierarchies" and reinscribed "differences of race and ethnicity" associated with national views, as Harris has explained. Wealthier Americans and English believed "the poor only descended into misery when they . . . refused to practice a set of economic and physiological behaviors that met the demands of a capitalist economy." Without "the prime virtues" of "thrift, temperance, regularity, and self-control," those in Italy would remain in misery—especially because of impositions of the Papacy, such as stifling education.[64] Marsh, Gould, and even the Roman Catholic Brewster often inscribed this perspective of American exceptionalism and privilege, although Marsh came to realize and question it while abroad.

These perspectives on improvement through associations provide a framework for the "social action" of these women. Brewster's place among the Dante Circle, the Accademia dell'Arcadia and the Lincei—the "elite" and cultured—as well as Gould's evangelical work and Marsh's more modest efforts demonstrate the differences among associations' specific goals. At the same time, the movements of local leaders such as Caetani and American visitors and residents underscore the fluidity of relationships beyond the boundaries of formal associational life. Rather than marking relationships as merely "formal" or "informal," the terms "programmatic" and "proximity" associations, which Soper employs, also help. In the former, such as the YMCA, the orphanage, and the industrial school movements, members were drawn together by common ideals. Without ever seeing each other, they sent funds or circulated reports and letters of appeal for financial support. In the latter, members knew each other through face-to-face gatherings and participation.[65] Proximity shaped the ongoing powerful but informal relations of receptions and salon culture. Both the proximity associations of Brewster, Gould, and Marsh as hostesses and guests and their participation in formal associational life supported their work as women engaged abroad.[66] Their behaviors during gatherings, their writings about these events, their pushing of the envelopes of leadership from positions of privilege—all provide examples of the women's utopian visions and actions. But did these utopian visions come to fruition? As Moulton's traveling partner to Europe, Sherwood Bonner, suggested in her poem, "The Radical Club," the visions of many formal associations never did. However, the next part of this book provides stories of how some of the women's visions *did* bear fruit, as well as reasons for why some did not.

PART III

VARIETIES OF UTOPIAN EXPERIENCES

Chapter 7

Utopian Visions, Reform, and Religious Beliefs

> In their wild Eutopian dreaming and impracticable scheming
> For a sinful world's redeeming, common sense flies out the door,
> And the long-drawn dissertations come to—words and nothing more,
> Only words and nothing more.
>
> —Sherwood Bonner, "The Radical Club," 1875

An inscribed gift copy of "The Radical Club," a literary and satirical view of high-minded idealism in verse, remains among Brewster's papers. It raises questions for inquiring readers of the value of "social dreaming" in the era's religious sectarianism, especially for Brewster, Marsh, and Gould as they traveled across the Atlantic and settled on the Italian peninsula. The poem by Sherwood Bonner, published in pamphlet form in 1876, depicts club members humorously and in thinly veiled language, such that they were recognizable to readers of the time.[1] Club members' names scrawled in the margins of Brewster's copy include Amos Bronson Alcott, co-founder of the Transcendentalist and experimental Fruitlands community; abolitionist and women's rights advocate Julia Ward Howe; and education reformer Elizabeth Palmer Peabody. When the poem appeared, Marsh was six years beyond meeting Howe in Newport, where she witnessed the forthright activist delivering one of her regular Sunday discourses at the Unitarian Church. When Howe and Peabody visited Rome in 1871, they interacted with Brewster and Gould. For example, Howe attended at least one of Brewster's receptions, wrote to her, and passed along a copy of her "Appeal to Womanhood Throughout the World" (1870), and Brewster later noted a dinner they shared together at her neighbor Carson's.[2] In 1872 Peabody visited Gould to learn more of her educational work with Roman children.[3]

Bonner's poem ridiculed reformers such as Peabody and Howe, especially in the final stanza. The club members' "wild Eutopian dreaming and impracticable scheming / For a sinful world's redeeming" all "come to—words and nothing more." Simply put, associations such as the Radical Club manifested the vanity of verbal actions alone and led to no concrete results. By contrast, other reform activities such as literacy campaigns among Sunday school workers and temperance unions in cities seemed to be bearing fruit. Active reform associations—for abolition, prison improvements, and women's rights, for example—likely enjoyed the verses for their satirical rendering of the more philosophical ones, such as the Transcendentalists, of which the Radical Club was a remnant.[4]

Bonner's satire may have been influenced by the failures of many utopian communal attempts in New England, such as Transcendentalist George Ripley's Brook Farm, Adin Ballou's Hopedale, or Bronson Alcott's and Charles Lane's Fruitlands, well known not only among reformers but also among those skeptically watching them. But the critiques also included some dreamers judging the world as "sinful" and in need of "redeeming." Whatever the cause, Bonner's satirically critical stance sounds loudly within the context of American travelers to Italy, for she was among them. The pamphlet version of the poem explains in a concluding note, "THE AUTHOR of this Poem is now travelling in Europe, in company with Louise Chandler Moulton, and is writing a series of entertaining letters to the Boston Sunday Times."[5] (Moulton wrote "For Queen Anne" in March of 1876, the same year the pamphlet appeared.) The *Times* editor's note signals entertainment rather than political and utopian action as Bonner's goal, pointing to a contrast between her work and that of Marsh, Gould, and Brewster.

Brewster's gift copy of the poem teases out this topic of contrasting utopian associations and writing for entertainment. First, the copy's inscribed message, "From Thomas Davidson to Miss Brewster Rome, May 3rd 1878," speaks to texts as exchange objects that possess life and meaning beyond the verses.[6] Davidson's inscription confirms the poem's provenance as a gift but, at the same time, raises questions of the relationship between the two and their visions of social reform, for a gift text often is more than a mere token of exchange; it usually embodies beliefs the benefactor believes will be appreciated by the recipient. In this case, Davidson likely assumed Brewster would appreciate the poem's humor and view of the impracticality of club members' "wild Eutopian dreaming . . . For a sinful world's redeeming." This view also suggests that Davidson and Brewster saw themselves as different from the Radical Club. They were, perhaps, anti-utopian, more pragmatic and down-to-earth. However, Davidson's life and views, alongside the Roman Catholic convert Brewster, complicate any easy reading of the poem's status as anti-utopian.

In fact, Davidson's prior affiliation with the club suggests instead his self-aggrandizement by circulating a publication about a group with which he had associated during two periods in which he lived in Boston. Although not referenced in Bonner's poem, Davidson participated in the Radical Club while Alcott and Ralph Waldo Emerson were members, as Howe noted in her *Reminiscences*.[7] The club, established in 1867 and continuing until 1880, continued the Transcendentalists' tradition of conversations, essays, and publications promoted by Emerson and Fuller. The membership, consisting of ministers of various denominations as well as lay persons such as Alcott, Peabody, and Howe, swelled from an initial thirty to almost two hundred who attended meetings. Topics of discussion moved from religion in the early years to science and education in the 1870s—all with attention to social concerns and their implications. As Mary Elizabeth Sargent described in her *Sketches and Reminiscences*, the group sought "larger liberty of faith" and "the freest investigation of all forms of religious thought and inquiry."[8] These topics were also central to many Americans engaged with the "Roman Question," so it is not surprising that the club flourished in the period of heightened American interest in Italian unification, the secession of the Papal States to the secular monarchy, and the chaos surrounding it.

The satirical poem, then, raises the question of whether Brewster and Davidson thought "Eutopian dreaming" merely "long-drawn dissertations" expressed in "words and nothing more." Or were utopian visions expressed in writing of value? Davidson and Brewster did not consider words vapid. In fact, both Davidson's and Brewster's utopian visions, fleshed out in their voluminous writings, stimulated their respective transatlantic movements. Later, writing influenced their theological and intellectual movements. In sum, Brewster's and Davidson's relationship and lives reveal an ironic twist to the concept of "Eutopian dreaming" as rendered in the poem. They parallel in some regards the relationship between Transcendentalists Emerson and Fuller and their later divergent views. While Emerson advocated an active life, in which each individual would be an ethical reformer, his activism primarily was of the pen. He despised reform societies.[9] Fuller, like Emerson, used her pen as a tool, but she honed her focus more keenly on social concerns as she interacted in the public realm with those in need. Similarly, for Davidson and Brewster, words and pens played important roles in both their "Eutopian dreaming" and the social actions which followed. According to Brewster, Davidson's ideas exposed her to the varieties of beliefs within Roman Catholicism. Although differences in their beliefs later threatened to push them apart, their engagement with words and ideas kept them connected.

Davidson, himself a visionary and activist, was also a spiritual seeker with a love of learning and affinity for words, which connected him to Brewster in Italy. He, like Brewster, had been motivated to transatlantic travels by his own utopian visions, drawn perhaps from his impoverished youth with an unknown father in rural Scotland, a love of learning and intellectual quickness recognized by his village schoolmaster, and a lighting of "a divine fire" within him at age twelve, followed by scholarship-supported studies at the University of Aberdeen. Cycles of spiritual searching and unbelief moved him through Protestantism, Greek Orthodoxy, Roman Catholicism, and Transcendentalism, with teaching appointments in Scotland, England, Toronto, Boston, and St. Louis before heading back to Massachusetts and then Europe in 1877.[10] At the most intense time of his relationship with Brewster (ca. 1876–82), he was writing of religious figures St. Thomas Aquinas and Antonio Rosmini Serbati, and of Greek archaeology—all subjects of interest to Brewster as well.[11] He went on to write of several well-known intellectual figures who pushed against political boundaries: Aristotle, Jean-Jacques Rousseau, and the Italian heroes Dante Alighieri and Giordano Bruno. In these works Davidson emphasized free thought and educational practices and ideals.[12] In short, Davidson, like Brewster, continued to use "words" and create "long-drawn dissertations" throughout his career as a writer on the Italian peninsula—with the belief that they would impact social reform.

Brewster's early letters to Davidson in the spring of 1878, after they had been neighbors in the same palazzo for almost a year and he had departed for England, speak most to this relationship, as they resonate with the tone of love letters. Just shy of sixty, the single woman begged the much younger intellectual to return to Rome, to take the apartment above her once again, where he could write his book. She referred to his letters as "charmingly fresh & spontaneous," like Davidson himself; they "delight[ed]" her.[13] She noted his writings and their mutual interests, as well as their differences. She wrote after reading his article on Rosmini that such philosophical writing was lovely for the stimulus it provided on occasion, like her "cold bath in the mornings or [her] constitutional walk." It gave her "a fine exultation of spirit afterwards, a lightness of heart, a lofting up above mortal cares as if . . . walking with the gods."[14] Brewster liked the *idea* of the ideas, although she expressed not having the mental fortitude to pursue them, because they lifted her "above mortal cares" of the material world of life abroad.

Yet she labeled Davidson an "ultra rationalist" and was disappointed in his public treatment of Roman Catholicism in an article published in the *Fortnightly Review*. The problem, Brewster explained in response to a letter from American consulate member Eugene Schuyler, was that Davidson treated "Rosmini's religious convictions in a bitter malignant manner," which she found "most ungrateful." As she noted, "the Rosmini Fathers are highly indignant as they may well be—."[15] They had hosted him in their inner circle, the monastery at Domodossola, likely with no expectations that he would write harshly of their beliefs and practices. The article was an "unmasking" of what Davidson considered the unethical and dishonest elements of the religious community's practices, similar to the many apostate narratives written in the nineteenth century by former Shakers and Mormons, although neither the Rosmini fathers nor Brewster noted the popular genre.[16] Davidson's writing went beyond apostasy to abuse, Brewster believed. He took advantage of their "kindness" and generous hospitality "for his own selfish purposes [and] for his own vanity: to gain notoriety and find a subject for articles." He even possessed the gall, she noted, to return to Domodossola, the hosts he had snubbed through his writing.

Nonetheless, a few months later Brewster wrote of the loneliness that Davidson's departure instigated.[17] Clearly not wanting to let go of the relationship, she wrote to Davidson soon after that she and "a friend" had "talked of" him. The friend, likely Father William Lockhart, a Rosminian, visited and corresponded with Brewster during this period. The friend thought "with grief" that Davidson was "an atheist"; she, however, "assured him to the contrary in vain." The foundation for the controversy was Davidson's refusal to profess belief in the supernatural. Finally, despite this spiritual flaw, Brewster justified the behavior by telling the visiting friend that Davidson had made her a better Catholic.[18] He pushed her to acknowledge that her faith was not based on reason.

The ways in which these religious differences with Davidson refined Brewster's faith become more apparent in their ongoing correspondence during the next several years. By October of 1880 Brewster referred vividly to the differences, writing to Davidson, "You are like a little terrier with a bit of leather: you hang on to trifles." Diving into an argument about saints, including a defamatory comment about the Paris Bishop Saint Denis, who according to tradition "carried his head under his arm a great distance" after his decapitation, she concluded, "I fancy no one knows . . . Neither Butler nor your authority can decide the matter. The only authority to a Catholic is the Church."[19] Perhaps she had pulled from her bookshelf a copy of Alban Butler's *The Lives of the Fathers, Martyrs, and Other Principal Saints*, which had been a gift from her brother Benjamin in 1849 and a key reference throughout the years. Yet it contained nothing on St. Denis.[20] She explained to Davidson that she would remain fixed in her stance and "of the same opinion still," noting that "Such futile questions are not worth arguing about."[21]

Eighteen months later Brewster read what she referred to as Davidson's "deplorable article on Rosmini" and described its impact with shock and sadness. First, she explained, "I had no idea he felt so malignant and bitter against my beloved church." She mourned his "blindness and darkness on the subject" as "lamentable." To her it seemed "evil" that Davidson had "so much intelligence"—a gift from God—but that he "willfully" ignored "the truth." She noted a sense of betrayal and loss: "I felt as sad as if I were meeting death." Yet despite the pain that this reading rendered, Brewster extolled one positive outcome of "such attacks" on the church: "they send careless Catholics . . . humble and penitent to the foot of the cross and cause faith to be more likely in our hearts." This emotionally based faith would trump all reason, as Brewster embraced her religion of choice. Finally, writing to Davidson, she prayed, "May God help you in your outer darkness." Brewster signed this and the letters after 1880 with more formality and less familiarity than the earlier ones, closing "Very truly, Anne Hampton Brewster," rather than "your madrina," or godmother, a signature she had used more often.[22]

Nonetheless, the two continued to correspond, to communicate face-to-face when Davidson was in Rome, and to consider political and religious changes going on in the world around them. Davidson sent Brewster his works on Rosmini and on the Parthenon; she read them, even later referring to his "heretical introduction to Rosimini" as "fine." She invited him to visit and talk over old times with her and to help her entertain guests.[23] Granted, she now was too tired to host guests alone, as she had done when Stoddard wrote his article on her receptions. She knew Davidson possessed the conversational and intellectual skills to stimulate a party. The next year they communicated about the possibility of Brewster taking his apartment on Capri for a few months; she thought it would be perfect for her health and writing and planned to ask her physician, Dr. Taussig, his opinion. The possibility of Capri did not come to fruition, however. Instead, she traveled north, spending time in France and England. Brewster's numerous journal entries about these travels and sightseeing neither mention Davidson nor explain what might have happened with the plans. By November, having returned to Rome, she expressed disappointment in Davidson's religious beliefs.[24] Relevant to their relationship's trajectory, however, Brewster and Davidson continued to correspond and to share writings, despite these theological differences. Each believed in the value of verbal expression for their readers.[25] The transformations in their relationship during almost a decade demonstrate how for Brewster the words and ideas, rather than being "nothing," were everything. They were integral to Brewster's actions as a news correspondent in Rome, which were utopian in her attempts to share knowledge with readers in the US, if not to enact larger and more radical social reforms.

Similarly, words were essential to the works of Marsh and Gould, who attempted to record and share their utopian visions. While not a part of "The Radical Club" that Bonner and others thought ineffective, these women held dreams of making the world a better place and used their words and networks to do so. Significantly, their "social dreaming"—or "utopianism"—did not purport to "redeem" a "sinful world." They never wrote of "sin" and "redemption," although they were not without judgmental comments—ringing of American exceptionalism—which arose from their diverse religious stances. The women's varieties of religious experiences, to borrow a phrase that psychologist William James would coin later, and their shifting utopian visions influenced the ways in which each was motivated to act in Italy. In this chapter I elaborate on these visions and actions through anecdotes about the spiritual world and its relationship to material realities.

Brewster, for example, an adult convert to Roman Catholicism, initially saw Italy as an idyllic escape, where she imagined participating in a culture in which women had more freedom than they had in the US. Her utopian vision, not merely one of personal indulgence, was also of a world where she could live financially independent of her brother and supported by her writing. This vision was not overtly connected to her Roman Catholic faith. While her first novella, *Spirit Sculpture*, focused on conversion and faith practices, the autobiographical novel of her time in Naples in 1858 referred to the "*nobile ozio*" (noble idleness) in Italy, more frequently known as the *dolce far niente* (sweetness of doing nothing), with brief references to religious practices. In Rome she regularly acknowledged the necessity of laboring intensively as a writer to reach her goals.[26] She would not be living in a Golden Age dream world, where rivers flowed with milk and honey and grapes landed in her lap without labors. She had to write to survive. And Brewster's writing for American newspapers focused on the temporal world in Italy, rather than on a spiritual afterlife or a "perfect place" that did not yet exist.

Varieties of Religious Experiences: Miracles, Mariology, and Missions

> In these days we are so liberal. . . . There are no more Auto da Fés, no more burning of Quakers by Puritans. A man can announce himself Turk, Mormon, Jew, or Christian, and if he does it for a sensation he finds himself sadly mistaken, for no one notices him. . . .
>
> —Anne Hampton Brewster, *Philadelphia Evening Bulletin*, 1869

Despite her disappointment in Davidson's supposed loss of faith, Brewster's liberalism seeped out of her *Philadelphia Evening Bulletin* letters. In 1869, for example, she commented that "no one notices" or cares when a "man" professes he is "Turk, Mormon, Jew, or Christian," revealing a view she assumed of her readers.[27] Imagining an educated elite readership with nonchalance toward religious affiliation, she poked fun at Charles Hemans, a Roman Catholic convert who had reverted to his early Protestant faith. Her humorous letter, not far removed from Bonner's view in "The Radical Club," expressed that religious beliefs and utopian visions no longer mattered. Pointedly and poignantly, though, this published liberal view starkly contrasts with Brewster's private writings. The *Evening Bulletin* passage, when placed alongside comments in Brewster's journals and letters to Davidson, presents a created public persona, much as Fuller maintained a persona of optimism and utopian possibility when writing of the Roman citizens for readers of her *Tribune* dispatches. Fuller wrote privately, however, of despair about the common people's capacity within the political situation.[28]

Brewster's writings for American newspapers show that she was sifting popular perspectives—especially among Roman Catholics. She regularly visited and corresponded with leaders, such as the Rosminian Lockhart and Monsignor Cataldi, a close friend and adviser of Pope Leo XIII. These men influenced to some degree their counterparts in the US, who took strong political positions and held sway in the elections there.[29] As she discussed ideas with these men, Brewster, a longtime southern sympathizer, also followed the ongoing political upheaval in the US, rejoicing over Rutherford B. Hayes succeeding Ulysses Grant as US president and later hoping that James Garfield would be defeated in his candidacy for the office. Brewster's views as a Roman Catholic stimulated her engagement with the religious politics of Rome. She appreciated the city's ancient history and aesthetic traditions. But her faith and utopian visions did not motivate her to social reform through religious practices—she was too liberal for that.

In contrast to her public statement of no one caring any more about a person's faith, Brewster wrote privately of caring very deeply about both faith and religious practices. Her mixed expressions confirm what William Vance has written of American visitors to Rome in the later nineteenth century. They "were not . . . fanatical Puritans" but held a variety of religious views: "they were Deists, Unitarians, and covert agnostics, with a few Episcopalians and a Catholic convert or two." Although most had lost a "fervor of belief" that might be associated with American Protestantism, however, they maintained some of "its habits of refusal." These engrained perspectives, Vance aptly asserted, emerge in the writings of Henry James, Charles Eliot Norton, and even Catholic convert and novelist Francis Marion Crawford. Non-Catholics, he wrote, saw nothing in the art, architecture, and religious symbols "to suggest that Catholicism [was] a vital contemporary force." Nonetheless, in spite of some diversity of views toward religious art, many Americans held "a belief in the progressive modernity and ethical superiority" of the US national culture and still considered Roman Catholics "a threat to American assumptions about history and about the future."[30] Vance's nuanced study of numerous Americans abroad is well substantiated, especially for the later nineteenth century. Yet contrasting views, especially earlier in the century, emerge in these women's writings.

Some views of the lack of vitality in Roman Catholicism, as well as growing fears of arriving Roman Catholic European immigrants in the US and the split over slavery, sat alongside each other. Paola Gemme and William McGreevy, writing more recently than Vance, have contributed to a deeper understanding of both the diversity of views and the complexities of American engagement with the Italian situation of unification, even pointing to Roman Catholicism as a global force. They highlight the roles of liberal Catholics and intellectuals, such as Orestes Brownson and John Courtney Murray, alongside the Ultramontanist.[31] Examining periodical records of the 1850s, Gemme notes the "thorny" visit of Gaetano Bedini, former governor of the provinces of the Papal States, to New York and elsewhere in the US, where he was met with rioting. The American and Foreign Christian Union (AFCU), for example, saw Bedini as a "true representative of a despotic Catholic Church attempting to extend its influence over the free United States."[32] This organization later would support and publish news about Gould's work in Rome and Marsh's in Florence, and it would track and report on local non-Catholic religious leaders throughout the peninsula.[33] McGreevy provides a rich picture of political debates and publications of the antebellum years and just afterward, describing Jesuit revivalism, anti-Papist sentiment, and reactions against Jesuit exiles in such places as Ellsworth, Maine, and Westphalia, Missouri. Gould's, Marsh's, and Brewster's utopian visions for Italy emerge within these religious and political controversies and, in sum, their writings reflect a variety of intertwining but sometimes polarized attitudes.

The polarizing messages of Protestant leaders Theodore Parker and John Cheever illuminate the political divisions. Parker, a well-known "liberal Protestant" Unitarian, was disliked by "American evangelists" due to his disavowal of miracles and literal readings of the Bible, and his celebration of "reverence . . . faith . . . [and] gentleness" among Roman Catholics in the 1840s, although he was concerned about their influence in the US. Parker's friend Fuller influenced him to see the beginning of Pius IX's rule as optimistic. By contrast, Cheever, a Congregationalist in Maine, opposed Unitarianism and built allies among English Scottish and Swiss evangelicals against Roman Catholics. He became a leader in interdenominational associations, including the AFCU, which promoted "Religious Liberty, and a pure and Evangelical Christianity, both at home and abroad" in the 1840s.[34] AFCU leader Leonard [Woolsey] Bacon, a Congregationalist colleague of Cheever's, later would write Gould's biography, *A Life Worth Living*, a fact illustrating these webs of connection and influence. (The biography was an imprint of the religious publisher Anson D. F. Randolph, who worked initially with the American Sunday School Union.[35]) Illustrating his anti-Catholic stance, Bacon gave a speech at the 1853 AFCU annual meeting in which he "defined 'absolute religious liberty as a doctrine for the world,'" drawing from US history as a foundation.[36]

Thematically, then, a topic central to these US discussions of Roman Catholicism—central to discussions of utopian communities for decades—was freedom, or individual liberty, in relationship to anarchy and order. Anti-Jesuit arguments of the age centered on "the freely acting self" or that "the individual was presumed sovereign" and that a Jesuit "'loses his individuality' through vows of obedience to his order and to the pope." Within discussions of Roman Catholicism, the topic intersected with other political issues, such as education and slavery. The opposite extreme of individual liberty—anarchy and the loss of "civil order"—was among the greatest fears that infiltrated all religious groups, not just Roman Catholicism. The US Constitution's First Amendment offered a foothold, many Catholics and Protestants alike argued, but the proper balance between freedom of religion and respectful, participatory citizenship remained difficult to articulate. Additionally, views of the miraculous or the supernatural also factored into these debates and intertwined with anti-Jesuit beliefs that the pope and the Vatican were against education and controlled people's minds.[37]

Holdings in Brewster's and Marsh's libraries also illuminate these controversies. The women—linked by their progressivist, nationalist views of freedom—were not identical in their religious views and practices. Brewster had an elaborately illustrated folio edition of Gustave Doré's *La legende du Juif errant* (1862), a version of Eugène Sue's *Le Juif errant* (*The Wandering Jew*, 1844), a highly popular anti-Jesuit novel. According to its American publisher James Harper, it "sold eighty thousand copies immediately upon publication." First published serially and a best seller in France as well as elsewhere, the story contributed to "the second wave of Jesuit expulsions" from Europe.[38] As McGreevy has explained, the book's "plot revolved less around Jews than crafty Jesuits uniting from all corners of the globe to maneuver a vast fortune away from an honorable but needy French Protestant family." Brewster's possession of the folio edition, a gift received long after her conversion to Roman Catholicism and almost two decades after the book's initial serial publication, indicates both its ongoing popularity and the gift giver's assumption of her stance toward Jesuits—not unlike that of some Protestants.[39] Brewster's stance likely was similar to that of some other Catholics who "criticized the Jesuits" on two accounts: "for thwarting the union of Catholicism and modern nationalism" as well as for "bolstering antimodern factions within the episcopacy and in Rome." One Italian Catholic contributor to this view was Vincenzo Gioberti, whose *Il gesuito moderno* was "an influential attack on the Jesuits."[40] Brewster did not have a copy of Gioberti's work, but the Marshes possessed another by him: *Il Piemonte 1850–52*. The volume suggests their knowledge of Gioberti and his political stance toward Roman Catholicism, although *Il Piemonte* provided them historical and geographical information on the region where they first settled. The region had been the first to support religious freedom with laws established in 1848.[41]

Another thread connecting Marsh and Brewster to these diverse sentiments about Roman Catholicism was the Jesuits' mission work in the US, which infiltrated rural areas, not only near the Atlantic but also throughout the South and what is now the Midwest. In Ellsworth, Maine, for example, a town of approximately four thousand residents, a young Protestant woman named Mary Agnes Tincker was among the converts of Jesuit missionary Johanne Bapst, founder of a Catholic school in which she "became the first teacher." When she later became a novelist, she wrote autobiographically about the events in Ellsworth as well as her time in Rome.[42] Perhaps Tincker became a friend of Brewster's because both were single women who converted to Roman Catholicism in adulthood. This background on Tincker and Ellsworth deepens an understanding of Brewster's network and brings to life the tangible results of Jesuit missions and the complex web of reactions to them.

Another example emerges in the history of Missouri, a region Marsh visited because of family ties. Although the rural town of Westphalia, a seat of strong Jesuit mission work, lies a hundred miles from St. Louis, where Marsh's closest sibling, Lucy Wislizenus, settled, its location resonates with the group's powerful presence west of the Mississippi. There Archbishop Peter Kenrick took a staunch political stance after the Civil War, directing priests under his jurisdiction not to swear loyalty to the US.[43] Extensive correspondence between Marsh and her sister reinforce how the ambassador's wife in Italy remained connected to the political situation in the US—beyond the Eastern seaboard cities of New York and Boston and rural New England to her family located in Indiana and Missouri.

Within the context of these religious controversies, Gould's, Brewster's, and Marsh's utopian visions come to light. They were immersed in these ideas, which seeped into their writings, their libraries, and their personal lives. Of course, literary works by well-known American Protestant authors such as Hawthorne and Stowe exude these controversies of Christian missions, Mariology, and miracles. While these authors' works do not support the supposed Papal and Jesuit control of religious teachings and spiritual development, they do celebrate the power of women, drawing from the role of the Madonna and female saints in Roman Catholic traditions.[44] By 1850 in *The Scarlet Letter*, for example, Hawthorne gave his readers Hester as a type of Madonna figure, celebrating her strength of spirit and relationship with her daughter Pearl. Stowe's *The Minister's Wooing* (1859) oozes with comments about Roman Catholicism and motherhood, especially in conversations about the French character Virginia. In 1860, the popular author and travel writer Anna Jameson released *Legends of the Madonna, as Represented in the Fine Arts*. The ideas reach further fruition in Stowe's *Agnes of Sorrento* (1862), written after her travels to Italy. Such works by Protestant authors point to Mary as the admirable Madonna without affirming miracles, such as the virgin birth of Jesus. Instead, they acknowledge a sacredness that arises from the role of motherhood in general—the role accessible to all women, whether with biological or adoptive children.

These ideas about Roman Catholicism provide a backdrop for considering Gould's, Marsh's, and Brewster's comments on motherhood and the miraculous, the supernatural and the spirit world. Their verbalized visions illuminate a common concern of utopian literature—the degree to which those visions related to the present moment—what might be called the here and now or immediate future—and how much they project an imagined immaterial otherworld or afterlife. And these movements in time or space, between the present and an imagined future of social change, depend upon memories of the past provoking them. Gould's, Marsh's, and Brewster's experiences demonstrate these movements.

Brewster: Miracles, Mysticism, and the Vatican

Brewster's journal entries, correspondence, and newspaper writings reveal that, as for the other women, her personal faith was constantly changing, with twists and turns contributing to a complicated but not unusual account. Influenced by the ideas she came in contact with, Brewster was looking to "other worlds" for possibilities, as most utopian visionaries do. Roman Catholicism provided the young Brewster such possibilities—independence from family, mystical traditions, and the powerful female figure Mary. Brewster's mother's name was Mary, and upon her conversion, she adopted the name Anne Maria. But the place of miracles and the mystical in Brewster's faith, as her communication with Davidson and other writings reveal, is less clear. Her novel *St. Martin's Summer* (1866), based on her time in Naples in 1858, contributes to the complications with a chapter on séances and the spirit world—a popular mid-nineteenth-century topic—and depictions of the miracle of St. Januarius's blood, all of which the autobiographical female character in the fiction seems to believe.

Likely Brewster included these controversial items because of her own experiences with dreams, séances, and the celebration of the miraculous liquefaction of St. Januarius's blood during the short period she lived in

Naples. Within two years of Brewster's time there (and before her novel was published), the annual celebration of the city's patron saint had received attention in the US press. The popular political cartoonist Thomas Nast caricatured it in "The Saint and the Hero," wherein the military hero Garibaldi drove a despairing Januarius out of Naples. Published at least in the *Illustrated London News* and then *Harper's Weekly* in October 1860,[45] Nast's cartoon would have been understood by readers, many of whom had visited Naples or had read of scientific explanations for the liquefaction. Similar to debates over creationism or climate change today, the topic evoked serious conversations as well as humor. An undated note to Brewster from the Jesuit father Torquatus Armellini, discussed in more detail below, underscores the contemporary interest in the controversial miracle.[46] Armellini, among the Jesuit exiles who had arrived in the US in 1848, due to the new and temporary secular Roman Republic, had become a Professor of Logic and Metaphysics at Georgetown. His father was a successful and well-respected attorney, Carlo Armellini, an "upright" and "moderate" figure "known for his sober judgment." The two reflect the well-educated and liberal leaning among Jesuits and other Roman Catholic leaders and illustrate the diversity of Catholics in Italy and the US at mid-century and afterward, as they wrestled with views of relations between church and state and of beliefs in the supernatural.[47] After the younger Armellini's return to Rome, he was for many years a part of what was known as the Gregorian University or Collegio Romano in central Rome, an important Jesuit institution.

In 1870 Torquatus Armellini wrote to Brewster, advising her on corrections to theological and church history errors and Italian place names in her novel *St. Martin's Summer*, of which she had sent a copy to him. Additionally, he asked Brewster to welcome to Rome Edmonia Lewis, "the coloured American Artist" and "recent convert," from whom he hoped she would "induce some wealthy Americans" to order work.[48] This exchange of novel and response indicates a collegial comfort level between the Jesuit leader and Brewster the convert. Likely in the same period, and perhaps in the same letter, he enclosed the undated message mentioned above. It discussed the annual miracle of the liquefaction St. Januarius's blood, an event described in Brewster's novel. He recommended that she read what Friedrich Hurter had written about it in the second volume of his *Geburt und Wiedergeburt.* Armellini even provided Brewster the citation for a shortened version, published in the *Univers*, the conservative or "ultramontane" periodical published by Louis Veuillot, which circulated Jesuit ideas throughout the Catholic world.[49] Also in Brewster's papers, scrawled on a scrap, is an 1839 "apologetical dissertation on the miracle of St. Januarius," which includes a chart showing "the temperature at a little distance from the vial and the space of time, which was taken by the blood to melt." The "observations" taken in September 1794 and May 1795 indicate that the ambient temperature appeared to have had no impact on the time needed for melting—whether two minutes when "under 76 F" or more than a half hour when "under 80 F."[50] Whatever the source of the scrap—it may be Brewster's transcription from the article, or, it may be a copy Armellini inserted for her—one point remains clear: the educated possessed a desire to understand the miraculous through science, and believers in the mystery wanted to supply evidence that the miraculous could not be explained away.

In keeping with Brewster's interest in St. Januarius and her writings about it, séances, and dream interpretation in *St. Martin's Summer*, she noted in her journal occasional mystical moments in Rome. In January of 1871, she wrote of being awakened "from a sound and dreamless sleep as if someone had touched me." Mistaking that a robber had entered her room to seize her watch and diamonds, she realized the time was "nineteen years to the day and hour" since her mother "passed off into Eternity." Awakened by "her memory, [which] had been acting," Brewster described it as a "curious experience." She concluded, "It is so strange to feel these hidden powers."[51] But two days later as the experience continued to niggle at her, she confessed, "I wish I knew some wise cool headed man who felt interested in psychology so that I could talk it over with him. It interests me greatly. Spiritists would say my mother had come to me and that the nervous trembling & irritability I have felt since then was occasioned by a certain amount of nervous fluid passing out of me because of her touch." Attempting to shake off the ideas of "spiritists," Brewster rationalized in another paragraph: "But I believe in no such thing." Instead she believed that "memory and imagination are uncontrolled" while asleep. During waking hours, she would not allow herself to consider the past, attempting to avoid such painful memories but, Brewster explained, "in my dreamless sleep my memory was as sure as the hand on a dial plate of a clock" as it recalled that moment losing her mother and the start of "longing and regret & tears."[52]

As Brewster wrestled with her beliefs about the spirit world, she relied not completely upon herself but rather wanted "some wise cool headed man," such as Davidson or Armellini, to discuss the possibilities with her. The man need not know psychology but only to be "interested in" it. As she attempted to rationalize her experiences and the Roman Catholicism's many mystical stories, she imagined that a dialogue with a learned man would help her understand them. During her first years in Rome, Brewster explored these teachings as a convert to Roman Catholicism, especially amidst the discussions of papal infallibility. She trusted the Jesuits' learning and rationality as well as the traditions of the church. She realized that experiences deemed mystical might have a rational or scientific explanation and wanted to grasp such understandings. This questioning stance appeared in her 1869 and 1870 journal pages, in particular, shuttling between descriptions and analysis of Roman Catholic leaders, critiques of their sermons, and stated desires for a stronger practice of piety and faith.

In a September 18, 1870, journal entry, for example, just before the Italian army's entrance to Rome, Brewster outlined three diverse opinions on the relationship of church to Unification: Silas Chatard, vice-rector of the North American College at Rome; Anatolia Scifoni, whom she described as a friend, an artist whose father was patriotic revolutionary in 1831 and a leader in the 1849 Roman Republic, imprisoned and later exiled; and James Clinton Hooker, from Vermont, secretary of the American Legation in the 1850s, who had established a bank in the Piazza di Spagna that most Americans used.[53] Brewster explained, "Scifoni argues from the Liberal anti-Catholic point of view, the Dr. [Chatard] from the Ultramontane one. . . . [Hooker] is the midway and has just as positive ideas as the others." They are "each very wide apart from the other," she explained. "The Dr. has *a sort of mystic belief* that the Italians will never enter Rome and if they do a curse will rest on them. . . . Scifoni hopes to see the Catholic religion entirely effaced, believes its end is approaching and hails the destruction of priests & convents."[54] The journal entry attempts an even-handedness, as Brewster's newspaper letters also do, but her negative stance toward the ultramontane Chatard shows through.

As Brewster wrote about these debates for the public in her newspaper correspondence, maintaining the even keel needed for ongoing financial support, she wrestled privately with her faith and religious practices, the loss of her mother, her relations with her brother—whose life would constantly provide a thorn in her side and challenge her spirituality—and her place as a writer needing to circulate abroad. Despite describing herself as "not . . . devout," while she was depressed and faced aging in December of 1869, Brewster wrestled with the afterlife, and with "unchristian feelings." The autumn of 1869 had not only brought challenging Americans such as Mrs. Hicks, "a filthy rich widow," to Rome; it also delivered news of her brother Benjamin's troubling professional situation in the US.[55] Hicks sought advice and counsel about converting to Catholicism, and Brewster found it amusing that Hicks, whom she considered a loud, obnoxious New Yorker with plenty of fashionable devotees, preferred "a quiet, studious, unfashionable woman"—as she considered herself.

Brewster's brother had been appointed Attorney General of Pennsylvania in 1866 but was forced to resign in October of 1869 with the election of Governor John W. Geary. The resignation built from differences preceding Geary's election, during his campaign months, and public attention in the press.[56] Brewster, disturbed by what appeared as slander in the press, believed the governor had grossly insulted her brother. Bound by sibling sympathy, she wrote in her journal, "At such a moment there are no differences between us—we are brother and sister." This reparation of differences leaps from the pages, since Brewster so often wrote with detestation and loathing about his behaviors, including his treatment of her. She concluded, "What wounds him wounds me." As she described the impact, "the mortification of the insult touches me also, and although I am to control myself, live up and over it, as I have over other bitter trials, still I succumb."

To treat the "very natural depression" that ensued, Brewster turned to her faith, writing, "But our dear Lord is merciful he never gives us more trouble that we can carry and this trial comes when I am surrounded with agreeable occupations and living in the very center of everything that is gratifying to my intellect & tastes." Confident that her depression would pass and determined that her "religious duties"—such as "more constant confession & communion" and life "closer with God"—would provide "firmness & independence," she continued: "To live in society and yet be detached from all that is wrong & injurious; to be in a whirl of work and engagements and yet be capable of placing the soul in retreat." She confessed, "Far far above all pettinesses and mortal troubles, mortal injuries and slights and insults is the real child of God." The passage ran on for several paragraphs, as Brewster reflected on past wrongs and the wisdom she had gained with age. Yet within a few months her brother sent a letter she described as "full of haughtiness and desires for revenge." It suggested he had no need of her sympathy and rekindled her dislike of him. Later in the year she wrote of his engagement to a young, divorced woman with four children, and soon afterward, she became ill—perhaps impacted by her brother's marriage.[57] Brewster attempted to treat her ongoing pain by acknowledging "rage, resentment & hatred & all unchristian feelings" as natural, human experiences, yet she also curbed her emotions, writing that she should give grace and forgiveness.[58]

In sum, Benjamin's problems contributed to Brewster's plummeting spirits. She wrote of herself as being "quite gray and depressed . . . suffering from a revulsion of feeling."[59] The next month she had bounced back, writing of her confirmation and her new "friend" Mrs. Hicks's baptism and confirmation, followed by Holy Communion. They visited with Monsignor Paolo Angelo Ballerini at the Casa di Convertende and then the American College, where they "paid . . . respect" to the Bishops.[60] And she recorded in her first entry of 1870 that she had "thrown off the old Adam." Noting that she had been too consumed by her agreements with the newspapers and accomplishing her writing goals, she determined to "take Sunday as a rest day, go to Mass and . . . rest." Planning to punctuate her writing with Wednesday and Saturday visits to galleries and studios, she added "but above all rest all my desires—all my work on God! Do nothing of myself—just as He pleases!"[61]

That month Brewster attended mass weekly, often commenting in her journal on the sermons. On January 7, for example, likely full of New Year's fervor, she listened to two sermons. Perhaps she had little else to do, or perhaps she sought fuel for her fires as a correspondent, despite the goal written earlier of making Sunday "a rest day." Her notes reflect Brewster's interest in the power of speech, the church's authority and its position about indulgences and miracles, and the stance of the speaker toward these controversial topics. She wrote of the Bishop of Rochester, Archbishop McCloskey, for example, as "the cleverest & ablest among our American Bishops," and of Bishop Kenrick of St. Louis as "one of the best Theologians." Her most telling comment was about Bishop McQuaid, who was "pretty outspoken" and "not in favour of the Infallibility." And she noted his dislike of "my dear Jesuits." Although Brewster employed the possessive "my dear Jesuits," suggesting her affinity for them, she followed up with "But maybe I might not [like them] politically"—she would not side with the more conservative group in this historical moment. Instead, she noted with delight that McQuaid "was pleased with" her letter written for publication and that he "had sent it to Rochester." The next week she commented on the content of Monsignor Capel's message, without any judgment of it, noting that he "proved the necessity of Infallibility in the Church."[62] And the following, she noted contentment with the message from the English Cardinal Dr. Henry Edward Manning, Archbishop of Westminster: "The way in which Dr. M. disposed of Calvinism was refreshing and the delightfully self-convinced manner with which he informed us that there were no new heresies in the world was equally cool. The Church has been attacked all along the line."

He concluded that "the Reformation which forced the Council of Trent" was seeing "its natural conclusion"—all due to "rationalism" and "infidelity."[63] That someone in power would articulate this persuasive argument soothed Brewster's soul as she wrestled with the place of the mystical. The next two Sundays she wrote of the church's stance on indulgences and miracles, noting, for example, that a group of Franciscans had asked the archaeological expert Giovanni Battista de Rossi, mentor of her friend Lanciani, about the corporeal assumption of Mary. After that lecture, she heard Capel preach again, this time on indulgences—a topic she thought most converts found difficult and about which she wanted to hear more.[64]

Despite Brewster's expressed desires to know more about these church practices and to be a better Catholic, the duties of her life as a newspaper correspondent seem to have taken over. Her journal entries ground to a halt. When they picked up again in March, she wrote only about interactions with Anglos in Rome and reactions to the Vatican Council. These spring journal entries make the January spiritual fervor appear fleeting, if not less than sincere. Yet Brewster carefully presented herself as a Roman Catholic, even if she only occasionally wrote in her journal about not attending mass regularly. Not a supporter of Jesuit extremism and Jesuit missions, either nearby in Rome or throughout the world, she believed that faith and practices were important on an individual level. Brewster's utopian visions were not evangelical "social dreaming" or "for a sinful world's redeeming"—although she stood firm in her commitment to the church long after discussions of papal infallibility waned. Brewster's utopian stance in her public writings sought to educate elite readers on the excavations in Rome and the rich traditions of a civilization she deemed worthy of study. This intellectualism could liberate individuals in the present age, regardless of their precise beliefs about the miraculous and the afterlife.

Marsh: Mariology without Mysticism

Marsh, like Brewster, wrote of mystical events—but without curiosity. She outright denied them. Nonetheless, she saw their place within religious traditions, just as she recognized the value of art and sensual expressions within religious practices. Throughout her years abroad, she walked a tightrope of faith. While holding consistently to rationalism on the one hand, she held art and openness to new ideas on the other. She maintained her balance by staying focused on the here and now rather than gazing toward an unseen spirit world. These views come to light through her first interactions and correspondence with Elizabeth Barrett Browning in 1853. While both women believed strongly in serving the needs of children and people around them, Barrett Browning's letters to Marsh reveal differences in their religious beliefs—especially regarding Spiritism and séances, an interest moving through both the US and Europe during the decade.

Barrett Browning commented of spirits and "turning tables" during séances—they had "come to very different conclusions." The women responded also to writings by men of science Alexander von Humboldt and Michael Faraday, who had attempted to reconcile science and faith.[65] Works by Faraday in the Marsh library, although they were published later, suggest the interest that the *ambasciatrice* had in science as it rationalized miracles.[66] Yet Barrett Browning's letter explained that she believed Faraday and von Humboldt lacked the "divine humility" of their esteemed predecessors, such as Francis Bacon and Isaac Newton. She wrote, "We know so little in this world! For my part, nothing overwhelms me with the sense of our absolute ignorance, as when the wise and learned among us say arrogantly: 'This is not; this cannot be.' "[67] While Barrett Browning left herself open to the inexplicable, Marsh, like Brewster, wanted the mysterious explained. However, as she wrote later in her journal, Marsh remained open to new truths.

Overall, in contrast to Barrett Browning's desire to connect with people in the spirit world, Marsh wanted to attend to what the famous poet had labeled "The Cry of the Children" at hand, in her 1843 poem with that title. In addition to this poem advocating on behalf of victimized child laborers, Barrett Browning had written poetry against slavery. And, just before meeting Marsh, her *Casa Guidi Windows* focused on the Italian people she witnessed thronging the piazza of Florence's Pitti Palace in protest. Marsh, like Barrett Browning, was concerned with these humans surrounding her in the here and now. This concern, along with her poetry, linked Marsh to the widely published poet as an undeclared mentor and exemplifies the utopian practice emerging from her liberal faith.

Although the exchange between the two women about communication between the spirit world and the observable, material world of the living occurred several years before Marsh settled in Italy and was surrounded by Roman Catholics, two elements of their relationship speak to Marsh's later period living in and engaging with the culture. First, Marsh continued to present herself as a rationalist, not believing in miracles and an active spirit world. This approach connected her to her husband George. Yet distinct from George's rationalism, she, like Barrett Browning, maintained a reverence for the "divine," for mystery and the unknown. For Marsh, the unknown prompted and inspired further exploration of truths. This second element of Marsh's link to Barrett Browning—a utopian visioning of better worlds—would continually appear as she wrote within Italian and Roman Catholic culture. As Marsh would express of both Catholics and non-Catholics in the Turin area in the 1860s, she was frustrated that they did not let education help them let go of their past beliefs in order to move forward with actions in the present that could change the future. She wrote of Vincenzo Botta and Massimo d'Azeglio, for example, that they changed their minds about politics and philosophy but about religion they never did; they hung on to their "superstitions."[68]

Marsh's political and religious views were not identical to her husband's, yet his views on faith provide a backdrop for understanding the connection of the *ambasciatrice*'s faith and practices to her utopian visions. George's New England heritage caused him to label himself and his ancestors as "desperate heretics" as early as 1844, although he was a "Congregational Calvinist" who "never formally professed . . . but did not repudiate" the teachings. Fiercely independent, he "mistrusted all organized religion." He "spurned Catholicism, both Roman and Episcopal," was "nominally Trinitarian" and inspired by James Martineau's and Edmund Sears's Unitarian writings. Yet George's liberal stance also meant that he did not deem individual Catholics to be corrupt. He wrote of some "Catholics [as] superior to Protestants in 'the minor morals' "; with regard to their "mannerisms in social intercourse [they were] 'superior' to 'the bluff, oppressive address of the Englishman, the offensive self-sufficiency of the German, and the rude self-assertion of the American.' "[69] Nonetheless, he wrote about the "threat" of Roman Catholicism to US ideals with a response to the 1864 Syllabus of Errors and the proclamation of papal infallibility, "The Catholic Church and Modern Civilization."[70] After appearing in an 1867 issue of the *Nation*, it received "a torrent of abuse from the [American] Catholic press." Then, after the Marshes had been in Italy more than a decade, he wrote of what he saw as the problem of miracles, published anonymously by *Harper's* in 1876 as *Saints and Miracles*. The book, according to biographer Lowenthal, was "written in wrath" and consisted of "a potpourri of diatribes" against "Mariolatry, the confessional . . . the evils of Pius IX" and the like.[71] These views of specific aspects of Roman Catholicism were not atypical of liberal Protestants in the US, although not all expressed themselves with George's vitriol and through a public platform.

These views were not the *ambasciatrice*'s, of course. Specifically, the "Italian Tale" she wrote demonstrates that she did not seem as opposed to Mariology. This children's story set in several mountain villages of Tuscany also celebrates religious art—both music and statuary.[72] The tale's hero artist not only played the church organ for thirty years but also carved crucifixes and several Madonna and Magdalen figures. The story shows that unlike many nineteenth-century American Protestants, the "Progressivist" author Marsh recognized the place of religious art in reaching peasants in rural regions. Her view appears more like that of American authors Stowe and Hawthorne, who acknowledged the power of the female imagery. Another significant point of contrast between wife and husband was his concern with US Protestant culture back home, while she focused more on doing what she could to change the Roman Catholic culture surrounding her. Marsh's vision of a utopian future focused not on the afterlife or the individual's eternal salvation bur rather on improvement of the material circumstances of the impoverished, illiterate, and uneducated through her work with the school in Florence.

Marsh believed, like her husband, that studying the past helped in contemplating the world's present problems and envisioning possible futures. She did so especially by reading in other languages and about other cultures. While her husband, an avid hiker and explorer of physical geography and topography, became known as an advocate for environmental actions that would impact the future, Marsh's utopian visions emphasized, rather than physical geography, changing personal habits and social structures to improve spiritual, religious, and moral life. These visions emerged, as typical with utopianism, from the present moment's material needs—but not without an understanding of the past and a willingness to look forward, dreaming about a better world. She later would uphold Matthew Arnold for this characteristic openness when she met him in 1873, although she did not go as far as accepting all the ideas in his *Literature and Dogma*, which she had read a few weeks earlier.[73] Like Brewster with Davidson's beliefs, Marsh did not believe all of Arnold's proclamations about religion. Yet the exchanges exemplify her desires to keep looking. She would write of the importance of "everyday acts" as the proper steps for moving toward that unknown future, even with the humble stance that not all truths had been reached. Marsh's reading and writing about other cultures would help her move toward this future.

Gould: Avoiding Miracles, Engaging in Missions

Gould's shifts in her utopian visions moved from an early emphasis on the afterlife and salvation as goals to a concern with journey and process. These paralleled her growing personal agency. Both were evidenced through her writing, beginning with her earliest work, the short story "Little Caroline," published anonymously in a slim volume entitled *Little Pilgrims* comprising four tales designed for young readers. The volume was published by the American Tract Society in 1866, several years into Gould's time in Rome. "Little Caroline" and all Gould's publications do not give the author's name, indicating that her goal was never to gain fame or attention. She followed the practice of women writers within the bounds of female behavior, writing pseudonymously or anonymously, although some authors, such as Stowe—and even Brewster—eventually set the convention aside.[74] Gould's early stated utopian visions did not include individual agency; instead, eternal salvation was central to the vision she emphasized in "Little Caroline." It does not merely focus on the one impoverished girl of the tale's title but also brings in the eternal salvation of many, as it conveys the evangelical work of its narrator, who teaches Sunday school among the urban poor in Brooklyn.

The tale reads autobiographically, as the young woman has begged her father to let her stop participating as a student in an adult Sunday school hour so she can teach a class for "little girls," all of whom "were too small to read." The young teacher explains how she nurtured students with a motherly posture, "tak[ing] one on my lap, and put[ting] my arm around another," as she taught them with Bible verses, hymns, and "the never-ending story of the Good Shepherd," who cured ills, comforted woes, forgave sins and "died for all."[75] In sum, the didactic tale focuses on the evangelistic gift of a heavenly afterlife to the little "sheep" with less-than-ideal "pastures" at home—they will be tended by the Good Shepherd above. This atonement theology, though not expressed as such, continues through the narrative and emerged also in Gould's proclaimed non-sectarian work with the Italo-American schools. The tale testifies to Gould's eagerness to evangelize through literacy on two levels: first, by teaching young children to read while employing stories of Jesus as a "good shepherd" who would care for them in Heaven; and second, by having young students leave Sunday school to become teachers—or good shepherds themselves—as the tale's narrator had.

The "good shepherd" imagery emerges not only through the tale's title figure, Caroline, but also through several children among the urban poor who become ill and die, all within a few pages. They waste away in conditions fostering contagion and disease—overcrowding, poor air, light, and water, and late intervention of medical care. For these children the afterlife is "the Kingdom of Heaven" where the "good shepherd" abides. Using a brief statement about "little Louisa" and the afterlife as a foundation, the narrator then describes Caroline with a "white robe," "crown of gold," and "harp"—before flashing back to her illness and death. At a physician's advice, the chronically sick "little Carrie" travels to the country, which brings some recovery, yet on her return to her urban home, she contracts whooping cough. Next the tale makes a mystical turn as it describes a physician's supernatural visions. The physician "loved little Carrie dearly" but was unable "to make her well." Yet, the narrator explains to readers, "he has seen her since we have, in her happy, heavenly home."[76] The story continues with language of a material afterlife of perfection and beauty, ending with an image of Carrie's brother Frankie, who spoke to his sister in the night, and not long after went to be with her in the spirit world, where they live "side by side in their happy, heavenly home."[77] The story's message contrasting earthly and heavenly conditions should succor small children who read or hear the story, knowing that they or their siblings might also suffer such illness and loss. Published after Gould had arrived in Italy, the tale may have been prompted by children she witnessed there, triggering memories of young people she had seen in New York. Such dialogic movement from present, to past, to imagined future of a better world typifies utopian visions.

Upon Gould's arrival in the Piedmont in 1860, having traveled overland from Le Havre, through Paris, up the Rhine and over the Alps at Chamonix before arriving at Turin, she was moved to action by the Waldensians' work in the region. In addition to touring Roman Catholic sites and learning local legends and stories of saints' lives, she met well-educated and multilingual Waldensians, one of whom spoke of the New Yorker Mrs. Lenox having donated $10,000 for support of their work.[78] This substantial gift from another New Yorker, equivalent to more than a quarter million dollars today, may have provoked Gould. Not long after, as she traveled south to the port city of Genoa, Gould noted with sadness the underground lifestyle of the lower-class Genovese, whose homes were built into the hillsides, but with optimism she wrote of the patriotism and loyalty of the young Garibaldini boys she witnessed at breakfast. These ideas of Italy, which she had seen only in books and newspapers prior to travel, began to reveal themselves in front of her.

When Gould arrived in Florence in early December, she met people from the US, England, and Scotland—active in Protestant churches throughout the week. The congregations' leaders, dependent on the wealth of their attendants, competed to attract members. Likewise, local Italian politicians sought to ingratiate themselves with expatriates of influence living in the growing and changing city. Journal entries from that winter—Gould's first on the peninsula—demonstrate this new tension in her life: engagement with non-Catholic religious communities and participation in expatriate social events of the Anglo expatriate circles. In preparation for a New Year's fête, for example, a young female traveling companion helped her dress. Cornelia Mitchell (later married to Marsh's nephew Alick) devoted several journal pages of details to Gould's gown and headdress. The invitation from an important figure in the expatriate community was one Gould would not decline. Yet by Christmas 1867, Gould wrote to the AFCU leaders to secure funds for the schools she sought to support. Her goals for education soon would overshadow her socializing.

As Gould's writings attest, her utopian visions differed from Marsh's and Brewster's. Yet like theirs, hers shifted as she witnessed cultures new to her but considered ancient, cultures whose ruins surrounded modern Rome. She retained a residue of her own early visions of educational and spiritual improvement as she began to work with local children. While Gould wrote in her reports that her mission work was not on behalf of any Christian denomination, her writings seeped anti-Catholic sentiment, most of which underscored the church's lack of emphasis on literacy and, specifically, on biblical literacy. A key player in improvements of Italian children, Gould emerged from behind the scenes as an anonymous author and unnamed narrator of "Little Caroline"—emphasizing the afterlife—to become an active agent, asserting her "wants and needs" in the here and now for readers in the US.

Chapter 8

Emily Bliss Gould

"Works and wants"

We beg you to come over and help us. . . .

—Emily Bliss Gould to Dr. Thompson, President, American Foreign and Christian Union, 1867[1]

I did not lose the main object . . . which was to . . . give the cheer of my sympathy to Mrs. Gould's noble work in Rome.

—Elizabeth Palmer Peabody, 1871[2]

Emily Bliss Gould's letter to Dr. Thompson in 1867, written from the Marshes' dining room in Florence, stands as a historical marker in her life—her first plea from Italy written to an American male leader on behalf of a cause she had taken up. But before and after Gould wrote this letter to the President of the American and Foreign Christian Union, her transformations in voice and growing rhetorical confidence emerged through other writings. Following "Little Caroline," the articles in *Hours at Home* and the *Overland Monthly* first demonstrated her early stance as a Protestant woman abroad, developing a public voice. Then, in official documents of the Italo-American Schools, established after Rome became the capital of a unified Italy, Gould's voice reveals her decreasingly veiled position in religious imprints as a public spokesperson. And, finally, private letters, illuminated by letters men sent to her, reflect her voice in "epistolary negotiations."[3] Gould's correspondence with George Perkins Marsh and Waldensian leader

Matteo Prochet illustrate the ways in which women's writing, even privately in journals and letters, fostered their reflective and imaginative processes, often feeding their activism in the public and international realms. Gould's writings fueled her fires for reform, rekindling sparks that at times may have been smoldering due to doubt and seemingly insurmountable obstacles. Gould's negotiations and transformations revealed in these documents enhance recent studies of American women abroad, in the fields of journalism, travel writing, and global missions by demonstrating in detail how a trip for health at midlife transformed her into an activist, intensified by the needs she saw at hand, the support community surrounding her, and the one she imagined at home in the US.

Details of Gould's labors abroad, which reveal these tensions and transformations, also appeared in two full-length volumes published soon after her death, as well as in numerous short sketches others wrote for periodicals during the years preceding and following it. Unpublished works, such as Brewster's diaries and education reformer Elizabeth Palmer Peabody's correspondence, also reference her. Peabody wrote of her travel to Rome, "I did not lose the main object of it which was to . . . give the cheer of my sympathy to Mrs. Gould's noble work." The published memorials link Gould with Mary Lyon, founder of Mount Holyoke Female Seminary, and with Italian education reformer Ermenia Fuà Fusinato. These records focus on her involvement with impoverished children in Florence beginning in 1866 and then, motivated by the Florentine work, her establishment in 1870 of the Italo-American Schools for orphans and poor children in Rome.[4] The value of records of Gould's life and work lies in the revised understanding they provide of nineteenth-century American women in Italy during the years of Unification. Gould's writings—from her earliest journal entries and published accounts, through reports of the Roman school during her last years—reveal a steady and then an exponential increase in her literary production, sense of audience, and strength of voice—quite "noble" for a woman who went abroad without these intentions. These records illustrate how the political climate engaged and fostered the transformation of understudied Anglo women abroad whose lives contribute to the diversity of experiences among transatlantic travelers.

Gould's writings of her later years especially reinforce and extend concepts described by Sarah Robbins and Karen Sánchez-Eppler in their analyses of American Christian mission work, and of women's labors in particular. The latter explains that Sunday school tracts asking children to give "merge the sentimental, feminine, religious basis of domesticity with the aggressive, masculine, economic, and military project of imperialism."

While "devotion" is stressed, "collecting money" is "the primary activity." She concludes, "the goal of missionary work is quite literally the multiplication of the [capitalist], American Christian family unit . . . especially the organization of gender and idealization of motherhood."[5] The process and cycle Sánchez-Eppler describes is recreated on Italian soil within Gould's writings. Robbins, focusing on the missionary mother image, describes the figure's transformation from a woman who teaches a boy (who becomes preacher), to a woman accompanying a preacher-husband abroad, to an "individual woman" in the field who taught women. Robbins illuminates "celebratory accounts of single women who trained native . . . women, built schools, taught native children, guided newcomer missionaries, and (eventually) administered large-scale community enterprises (including corporate-like fund-raising campaigns)."[6] Robbins's depiction, with an emphasis on literacy, independence, and fundraising, provides an apt frame for Gould's work with the Roman schools. Gould first visualized more schools for teaching children to read, then nurtured students to become teachers, and, finally, raised funds and provided financial reports.

Nonetheless, Gould's situation differs from what Robbins describes in that Gould went abroad for her health, with her husband in support of her needs, rather than as a missionary wife or independent "missionary mother" from the beginning. Additionally, Gould's labors pre-date the period Robbins describes in the 1880s. These differences underscore how Gould's experiences, rather than being the exception that proves the rule about nineteenth-century female missions, demonstrate ways in which some women did not fit exactly the idealized "missionary mother" image. While public images, such as Gould's portrait with the Venetian Bartoli children, undoubtedly were posed carefully for purposes of persuasion through the mothering role, and accounts memorializing Gould uphold images of accepted gender roles and American imperialism, the textual residue remaining of Gould's life reveals her to have been a woman who went outside the bounds to a certain degree. Gould at times took risks with her behavior and forthrightness, based on her utopian visions of reform. These assertive behaviors emerge especially in her private letters.

Travel Writing, 1866–67: *Hours at Home* and *The Overland Monthly*

Although Gould's writing career began with the evangelistic sketch "Little Caroline," her travel sketches, which appeared soon after, manifest a completely different tone—often humorous. Nonetheless, they are peppered with poignantly Protestant comments, appropriate for one venue in which they appeared—the *Hours at Home* monthly magazine, a Scribner's imprint edited by James M. Sherwood, author of numerous religious works affiliated with the Presbyterian Church, especially in Brooklyn and New Jersey. As the periodical's subtitle noted, it was "Devoted to Religious and Useful Literature." Gould's five sketches, published with the title "Rambles Among the Italian Hills," appeared between March of 1866 and May of 1867. Gould's confidence in her experiences as exemplary and educational must have motivated her to write, as she imagined an audience of eager readers "at home" who learned while enjoying armchair travel. These readers kept Gould connected to life and culture in the US. Without a regular pattern of appearance, the "Rambles" sketches suggest that Sherwood likely made decisions about publications dependent upon what he had available for an issue. For example, the first sketch, published in March 1866, refers to an excursion to Subiaco the previous May, just after Easter. The sketch was written as a reflection from memory or travel journal entries, perhaps delayed in receipt by the international mail, or perhaps held by Sherwood until he was ready to publish it. Whatever the reason for the delay, the timing of the sketches' publications did not matter as much as the content, if they were to be "Religious and Useful" to readers. Overtly, the descriptive and anecdotal sketches—similar to those by Washington Irving, Margaret Fuller, and other nineteenth-century travel writers—lack clear narrative patterns of dramatic tension and resolution. Yet they reveal writers' prejudices and concerns, as Bailey has explained.[7] Gould's emerge sometimes with humor, sometimes with literary flourishing, sometimes with bald pronouncements. Gould's opinions strike through her anecdotes, shifting slightly through the years, as she transformed from the woman who wrote "Little Caroline." Not giving up her desire to take charge and change a situation she believed worthy of redemption, she began to open her eyes, heart, and mind to a world whose ways were much larger than her initial vision.

"A Ways and Means Committee"

In Gould's first sketch, for example, of a trip beyond Tivoli in the hills east of Rome to visit the Benedictine sites at Subiaco, she described the mountain people, or Saracens, as a potentially untapped or wasted resource and presented herself as someone ready to establish and direct "a ways and means committee" to improve the situation.[8] The land surrounding Subiaco was a "garden of Eden," but unfortunately these beautiful people around it lived in poverty and filth, she wrote.[9] Reinforcing the people's proximity to nature, Gould noted their close relationships with their pigs, which they treated almost like pet dogs. She saw the village as "an infinite succession of piggeries," reminiscent of Constance Fenimore Woolson's "The Front Yard," wherein a New England heroine views her hillside home in rural Italy with dismay. Although Woolson's heroine is duped by the local people's dishonesty, Gould is struck by their honesty. One boy finds a ring and returns it, first to his father, then to their priest, who returns it to the group in Rome. Gould notes the village priest was "seemingly as guileless as the flock he leads." But she is struck even more by "their powers of discernment."[10] The people treated her admirably, wanting her to ride a donkey instead of walk, although she refused to do so without saddle or bridle. When they entered the church for service that evening, "the services closed by a prayer written in Italian in a simple style, suited to the understanding of the worshippers." Gould glossed with her positive, optimistic vision, "I never attended a Catholic service where there seemed so much simplicity and sincerity."[11]

As Gould's sketch progresses, the prejudiced language increases, as did Gould's actions on site. Within the priest's house where they lodged with his family (his mother and brother), as was the "customary" practice in these rural areas, she makes herself a "ways and means" committee in order to help get supper. Instead of allowing her host family to serve her, she prepares the tea and "rescues a pigeon" from boiling water. Instead, a spit over an open fire leads to a healthier repast—as American domestic and scientific cookery texts attest. Boiling would diminish the bird's nutritive qualities.[12] At the travelers' prior lodging, at Vicovaro, where they had visited the Winking Madonna, they had refused to eat anything prepared where the dirty hillsides served as the inn's walls. Gould prepared a meal from wine and eggs she had requested—so twice she stepped in to cook in her American way rather than to eat as the villagers.

In addition to this cultural difference with food and cleanliness, Gould notes "the want of sympathy between the high places of this religion and their supporters."[13] She recognizes that female saints offered idealized love and concern that the villagers needed—in contrast with the male-dominated church hierarchy and clerics. Gould pardons Saint Benedict's "error" of messages that "gentle Agnes or lovely Cecelia ministered" to the villagers, and she concludes her sketch with a message reinforcing this sympathetic view. A co-pilgrim's poetic composition refers to a beautiful plant that has survived on this cliffside, "not . . . by Heaven alone" but due to "earnest life":

> "Oh wondrous power of earnest life!"
> . . .
> Could blossom thus with beauty rife
> Yet were no canker at the root,
> Not flower alone had been, but wholesome fruit.[14]

Gould includes no judgmental discussion of these people as lost in their faith; rather, she sees them as oppressed in their poverty and ignorance. While judgmental about their uncleanliness and their lack of appropriate food, Gould makes overt that the cause is the oppressive and controlling rule of the Roman Catholic church. It caused the "canker at the root" of rural life that would otherwise bear "wholesome fruit" instead of merely beautiful blossoms. She concludes, "God help the good sheep wandering over these hills, for surely the shepherds act the wolf's part."[15] Here, in contrast to "Little Caroline," "the Good Shepherd" does not protect the sheep-like people, who remain duped by Roman Catholic priests.

Gothic Riffs on Earthly Realities

> "How we laughed at the sensation we might create at home—a party of Protestant ladies from America hidden away in the convent of Valambrosa [*sic*], and locked up in an obscure corner thereof!"
>
> —Emily Bliss Gould, "Rambles among the Italian Hills," August 1866[16]

Other accounts in the "Rambles" highlight local people and their potential as resources, under the shadow of Roman Catholicism and history of classical sites. Writing of a trip to the area of Albano, the Capricene convent, and the Franciscan monastery of Palazzola, east of Rome, at first she describes the foliage and vines swaying in the breeze like feathers.[17] Gould recognizes the natural surroundings as "a glorious temple of verdure" providing a contrasting backdrop to civilization's corruptions. The Temple of Hercules in the mountains contains "great blood-red serpents . . . hissing and coiling and uncoiling in the dark vaults," while "swarthy figures seized them and drew them into hidden recesses" and "huge fires gleamed and glowed in the distance." Gould resolves this eerie, gothic description of the group's visit to the ancient Temple with an explanation that the structure was "a large blacksmith's shop." Reminiscent of Rebecca Harding Davis's *Life in the Iron Mills*, published in the *Atlantic Monthly* (1861), with contrasting scenes of the hellacious mills and a Quaker home and cemetery in the countryside, Gould also opposes the blacksmith's shop with the countryside, the mountains, the Claudian aqueduct ruins, and the villagers. These rural folks are clean—although their villages are dirty and look better as they perch on hillsides in the distance than up close and from within. The women's hair, clothing, and jewelry are nicely tended, and the women are kind to the travelers passing by on donkeys. But the most revealing portion of this sketch focuses on education, forecasting interests Gould would embrace fully in Rome in 1870.[18]

As the group arrives at the village Monticelli, led by a geology professor, on donkeys laden with hammers and picks, they meet the local abbot, also a geologist and teacher. Gould contrasts the two learned men, the almost immobile abbot and the Anglo expert, who "was able to gratify his refined tastes and further increase his stores of knowledge by foreign travel." The abbot's confined "sphere" consists of a "poor, miserable suite of rooms over a stable, filled with peasant children, to whom he is imparting the mere rudiments of education." The abbot "most kindly" invites them into his home and "a small room"—his study, full of specimens of rocks and fossils—"in which it was evident most of his leisure hours were spent." Gould's description underscores misadministration by the Roman Catholic hierarchy: this learned Italian abbot, known even in the US, is not paid well enough to wear decent clothes, and his task teaching impoverished boys is inappropriate to his intellectual level:

> [B]ent with toil, as he commenced prematurely the descent of life, [he] was dressed in a rusty cassock, whose pockets were torn and frayed, a hat which had scarcely a particle of color and but little form left, and those of the coarsest worsted. His very bands showed that the greatest economy was used even in his weekly wash-bills. And this man of eminent science, known as such through Europe and American, is forced to earn his living, and spend the time of which the world has need, in teaching peasant children to read and write, for a pittance which does not clothe him decently.[19]

Gould's view of misadministration of education emerges even more in her later fundraising reports for the industrial school.

Gould's second published sketch, also describing an excursion, differs from that to Subiaco, Albano, and Monticelli in that it adds gothic humor to minimize Roman Catholic power. It does, however, often attend to food preparation and consumption. To escape the heat of Florence's Via Maggio, where the Hawthornes and the Brownings had lived near the Pitti Palace, where the stone streets and piazzas broil in the summer near the low-lying Arno, the travelers headed to the cool air of Vallombrosa in the Tuscan hills. There they witnessed—as observers rather than participants—the celebratory feast of the Assumption of the Virgin. Arriving late one afternoon in this "valley of shade," they learned that as *forestiere*, or outsiders, and as women, they would not be able to visit the monastery, a site of men on this sacred feast day. (Gould also notes such gendered exclusion at Subiaco.) Not satisfied with disappointment, she successfully begs a visit and even lodgings at the monastery. To succeed Gould played the "sick-dodge," she boasts to US readers, telling the clergy that she came to Italy in order to improve her ill health. The air of a village at a lower elevation had made her even sicker. She desperately needed the air of Vallombrosa. Her pleading led the cleric in charge, whom she labelled Padre Decano, to have beds arranged. Because other visitors—local peasants who had arrived early so as to not miss any festivities—already occupied the barn, the brothers set the beds in a curtained-off corner of the large room in which another cleric oversaw the cooking, already under way.

Gould gloats, employing adventurous language of danger—referring to "parricide" and "pirates"—to describe the way they are "locked up" and fed in their corner of the room. She glosses her triumph for US readers with a humorous riff on popular gothic tales of Roman Catholic imprisonment, such as *Maria Monk's Awful Disclosures of . . . the Hotel Dieu Nunnery at Montreal*.[20] "How we laughed at the sensation we might create at home—a party of Protestant ladies from America hidden away in the convent of Valambrosa [*sic*], and locked up in an obscure corner thereof!"[21] But she eradicates any fear and increases the humor by noting that they were able to unbolt the door from the inside.[22] At the same time, Gould's words reinforce stereotypes of clerics' sexual liberties, extended as she describes the following day's feast. The "Protestant ladies" observe an almost bacchanalian scene with locals of all ages indulging in sweets filled with liquor, ices, and cold drinks. Young women, she notes, wear long strings of pearls—signs of wasted luxury rather than purity. Yet the American females safely observe all from their window, where they remain "silent, mysterious, and almost ghostly."[23]

Yet Gould does not silence herself as she rattles on in print about the mesmerizing feast of the Assumption, witnessed as a distant observer rather than a participant. Safely poised at the window, Gould distances herself as well as through humor, expressing her delight and good wishes for the Virgin with a wry remark: "We have rather enjoyed the Assumption of the Virgin (whatever that is) and only hope that she does." Gould's statement merits feminist elaboration on the Virgin's victimization: "The pictures of that event [the assumption] generally represent her [the Virgin] as pushed about in a way which might be disagreeable."[24] Rather than viewing Mary as venerated, surrounded as she often was in paintings by human crowds and divine beings who thrust her up from the earth into the heavens, Gould sees her as victimized. Perhaps the reformer considered Mary's earthly work as more important than a divine position in the heavens. Or perhaps she believed that Mary should not have been "pushed about"—a feeling Gould would express about herself later in her life, as she negotiated with men in efforts to support her Italo-American Schools in Rome.

Rather than continuing the reflection on Mary's virginal and heavenly state, though, Gould returns to earthly situations at Vallombrosa. Judging by the large quantities of food and wine given and consumed, which she enumerates, she summarizes that all those who participated in the feast enjoyed it. She confesses that the Protestant women "were all six feet deep in love" with their chief host, Padre Decano—except for those with husbands, who were "only half a degree less than those who had not." Gould's concluding statement oozes with earthly rather than heavenly desires: "Oh! To be a lay brother, or a Madonna, or a Padre Decano, or a sacred relic, or a pine-tree, or an any thing or any body that could remain at Valambrosa [*sic*] indefinitely!"[25]

Heavenly and Eternal Visions

Another travel account, lacking Gould's gothic humor, touches on the heavenly realm and eternal life as it moves back in time to the years prior to the Roman church's influence. In this sketch of a visit to Veii, an ancient Etruscan site north of Rome, Gould describes the ruins of a painted tomb that had been excavated only a few decades earlier. The sketch opens with Gould inviting readers to time travel as they move from the Pincio hill, looking west on "modern Rome," with St. Peter's and the sites on the Janiculum hill—"the triple fountain of St. Paul" and the imposing "entrance to the Villa Doria"—to classical Rome. Then, readers journey with her north and further back in time, stopping a dozen miles away at Veii. En route they see the beautiful countryside, where farmers work hard, but often lay down beside their fields in the evening never to awaken, due to the noxious gases emanating from the soil and vegetation. The travelers begin their ascent to Veii at Isola Farnese, "a poor little village," where the women are "homely and haggard; wrinkled in their youth, their eyes sunken and bright, their cheeks hollow and burning with fever." As in the other villages Gould visited, she notes positively their religious practices, free from corrupt Baroque influences. She describes "the church, which was bare of decoration, but strewn thick with sweet-smelling boughs, its doors and windows were hung with garlands; and in this simple manner the villagers had dressed it for one of their church ceremonies, or festas, as they call them here."[26] Rather than criticize, she admires the simplicity, reminiscent of an era before St. Peter's and the pope's power in "modern Rome."

From this simply decorated early Roman church, Gould transitions to praise the Etruscans' technology, passed on to the Romans. Drawing heavily from George Dennis, whose *The Cities and Cemeteries of Etruria* had been published in 1848, she describes Veii as the greatest among twelve Etruscan cities, retelling accounts of its many wars with Rome.[27] Gould veers from Dennis, however, as she provides a glimpse of her own time travel and reconsideration of her faith. As she describes the elaborate tomb of a prince and his wife, imagining their deaths and burials, Gould interprets a painting on the tomb's wall with references to Christian traditions of eternity. The painting depicts a boy traveling on horseback, "unarmed and unclothed," who represents "the soul of the warrior . . . setting forth upon its long journey." His judgment awaits, as "The attendants [riding with the warrior] are the good and evil spirits, to one of whom he is to be delivered. The animal who rides behind him is the memory of his past deeds." But the young boy knows no fear. His "countenance" as well as "his firm posture, his steadfast, onward gaze," and his unashamed nakedness show that although "alone and unarmed, he trusts and is safe." As Gould interprets, "Surely, gleams of a better faith; surely, hopes of a higher life are portrayed here. And around all . . . are portrayed garlands of lotus-flowers, the emblems of immortality." She concludes with a question: "May it not be said of these who sleep here, and of those who laid them to their rest, that they obeyed the command, 'That they should seek the Lord, if haply they might feel after him and find him?' "[28]

Gould quotes from the biblical account of the missionary Paul's message to leaders of Athens, in which Paul acknowledges that people across time and space have access to the deity, regardless of the language used, because language and material icons cannot capture the divine.[29] She draws from Dennis when writing about the tools the travelers carry, the lotus-flowers, and the boy on horseback. Dennis interprets these items as part of "the passage of the soul into another state of existence," connecting the funerary emblems to Greek, Egyptian, and "Mexican" civilizations.[30] Yet Gould extends Dennis's reflections, indicating a departure from traditional Christian views of an afterlife to a larger vision, connected to cultures beyond classical Rome. This sketch from 1867—only a year after "Little Caroline" and its heavenly sheep, shepherd, harp, white robe, and gold crown—suggests either a shift due to her imagined audience or a shift in her faith. Although Gould had not relinquished her views of impoverished rural Italians in need of education and freedom from the pope's powers, and she continued to believe Paul's message—that those who sought "the Lord" would "find him"—she acknowledges in this sketch that paths to an immortal end might be diverse.

Political Visions in "Gossip Abroad"

> Would-be monarchs are as plenty as blackberries.
>
> —Emily Bliss Gould, "Gossip Abroad," |*Overland Monthly*, January 1869

> Bleeding Poland, prostrate Hungary, and mangled Greece . . . big nations eat up little ones [as] the minnows swim about merrily in the hearts of their devourers.
>
> —Emily Bliss Gould, "Gossip Abroad," *Overland Monthly*, March 1869

Two years later, in the winter and early spring of 1869, Gould's "Gossip" letters—briefer than the "Rambles"—began appearing in Bret Harte's *Overland Monthly*. The four published accounts—primarily politics, with some attention to the natural forces of weather and social circumstances—all focused more on political affairs than on the social lives of American expatriates in Rome. Likely not published in the order in which Gould wrote them, these accounts resemble Fuller's and Brewster's letters in that they present political insight while exhibiting an engaging literary style and including self-referential first-person pronouns. Gould's first account, for example, published in January 1869, but written from Rome on November 1 the previous year, opens with events in Spain, as Queen Isabella II had begged the Emperor of France to "save her throne," a "plea" she had made "in vain." Similar to Fuller describing Romans in the street at the time of the 1848 revolutions, Gould described "the frantic joy" during which "the people found themselves free!" from being caught between the powers of "libertinism and superstition." And she noted "a curious sign of the times"—"that universal suffrage being demanded, the ladies of Andalusia have applied for the privilege of the ballot." Although no other commentary appears, it suggests Gould's attention to arguments about freedom and democracy, even for women. A string of short sentences summarizes the situation with the staccato of revolutionary gunfire, demonstrating Gould's flourishing rhetorical force, demanding political change: "There is much else to be done. The Jesuits must be driven out. The system of police spies abolished. Taxes are to be reformed. The censorship of the press is to cease. Religious liberty must be established. In short, the system of government must so be reformed that the people shall be free."[31]

Continuing with reflections on Spain's next leaders, Gould listed the possibilities among the "could and would-be monarchs . . . plenty as blackberries"—from England, Savoy, Austria, and Portugal—before concluding, "she cannot but be better off than she has been." She applauded "the revolutionists" for removing "a crafty and resolute monarch from her throne" and "a tyrannical government." Even more, the revolutionaries paved the way for "an ignorant and priest-ridden people" to live with "the blessings of free government."[32] In the column's second half Gould turned to Italy, with attention to flooding in the north rather than to politics. Here the lack of a reportorial "I" suggests Gould's political sources were either other newspapers or eyewitnesses who corresponded with her.

Her second account, however, opened with an overt recognition of audience and authorial position, although she noted "less of interest to communicate to our readers, this month, than was furnished in our last review of political and general news in Europe." After summing up the fallout from Spain's political shifts, and discussing Europe in general, Gould turned to details of the Prince and Princess of Piedmont arriving in Naples, to which she refers as "here," suggesting her eyewitness position. The royalty were welcomed with a large reception and fireworks but "without enthusiastic applause," for "Naples has not learned to love her princes." She added, "when Republicanism takes possession of this country—as it doubtless will ere long—its fountain-head will be found on the shores of this bay." Gould turned next to personify the volcano Vesuvius, as she vividly summarized the eruptions and lava flow of November, 1868, which she had observed first from the city and then with a group who had "ascended the mountain" to witness an "impossible to describe" scene.[33] Gould's "Gossip" then returned to politics in Rome. Attention to "the vice rector of the Scotch College," Campbell, provided a touchpoint for religious reform, Protestant sacrifices, and martyrdom. Campbell had been "seized by brigands at Grotta Ferrata," where the grounds would close. Additional political commentary followed before she concluded with the weather—"uncommonly rainy" but with "consolation . . . that after all it is worse elsewhere" since "upon the whole, we have a very fair proportion of sunshine."[34]

Gould's March column, written in January, included more social "gossip" than any other, including holiday events at St. Peter's, social affairs surrounding Longfellow's stay in Rome, preparations for the Vatican Council, and brief references to activities of the royal families in Genoa and in Florence, including a birth of King Victor Emmanuel's second son and the king's fall in favor since the battle of Aspramonte. It also opened with the most dramatic and sensational metaphors, describing the European political situation: "Bleeding Poland, prostrate Hungary, and mangled Greece" and "big nations [who] eat up little ones" as "the minnows swim about merrily in the hearts of their devourers." As Gould continued with literary humor, she demonstrated her growth as an opinionated and persuasive rhetorician. She wrote humorously of "Old Mother England . . . in an especial state of mind, running from side to side of her tight little island to survey matters, wringing her hands, and exclaiming: 'Have done there, you foolish, greasy, little baby. Stop kicking your big brother. He will be knocking you down the first thing you know, and who is to be everlastingly setting you on your feet!' " This "Old Mother England"—unable to act and only able to fret—"mourns over Jonathan, the prodigal son who never returned"; "weeps over Johnnie Crapaud, whom she hates with all her heart, and would surely bully, only she is afraid of him"; and "bites her nails as she contemplates the great game of soldiers . . . her Teutonic neighbors are forever playing."[35]

Gould's readers may have seen political news elsewhere, she acknowledged, thanks to the telegraph. But she elaborated nonetheless, giving accounts of the death sentence of "liberals" Ajani and Luzzi, following the previous execution of revolutionaries Giuseppe Monti and Gaetano Tognetti, which had "the whole Peninsula" stirred up. The Roman military government after Garibaldi's defeat had searched the factory owner Ajani's house for arms. The public wondered whether the pope would extend a pardon from the death sentence.[36] She referred to Parliamentary debates over the mill tax, or

"Macinato," and resistance to it with mill closures and demonstrations. She wrote of rioters who "attacked the millers who had opened their mills, sacked the palaces, burned the archives, poured out the wine from the wineshops, and resisted the troops sent to disperse them." Gould continued, "the opposition party in Parliament knows that the people are on its side." She concluded the column with references to the troubles in Greece and Turkey, Spain, and France, noting that otherwise, "things generally in the little European world are rather quiet." Gould's diminutive phrasing—"little European world"—reeks of American exceptionalism. In fact, as she wrote of Spain, she referred proudly to the monarchy being "for the moment only; a temporary bridge between absolutism and republicanism. And then the man! A kingdom for the man!"[37] This echo of Shakespeare's King Richard III crying for a horse in order to save himself even with the sacrifice of his kingdom, attacked the monarchical governments that reigned in Europe, as it reinforced Gould's support of the US model of a more representative government as ideal.

The abrupt conclusion of this final "Gossip Abroad" column, along with its prolonged gap between the January writing and the May publication, raises questions about what caused Gould to desert these "Rambles" and the "Gossip" after only eight publications. The records reveal little, but the titles themselves suggest an answer. Gould became more direct in responding to her later vocation. No longer a mere "rambler" or writer of "gossip," Gould had become a woman on a mission. Her daily engagement on the ground with her schools—urgent daily tasks such as recruiting teachers, securing food and clothing for students, and locating rooms for the classes won her energy and attention. When she turned to pen and paper after 1869 and her summer in the Alps, her words focused on immediate needs of the "dear children" and their schools rather than on self-indulgent travels to tourist sites or the political news from the European papers, which plenty of others, such as Brewster, were providing. Gould's primary calling had become writing on behalf of industrial education in Rome.

Published Documents of the Italo-American Schools

> [A] "cry of the children," pleading . . . that they may be enabled to grow up men and women instead of machines, Christians instead of infidels or bigots, must find its ways to every benevolent heart. . . .
>
> —Emily Bliss Gould, report of the *Italo-American Schools*, ca. 1871[38]

As in the travel sketches, Gould's name did not appear on the title pages of the Italo-American Schools publications between 1870 and 1874. Instead, the institute itself and its male board of directors shone in print as the prominent authority figures. However, the power of Gould's calling, visions, and voice erupted in the first report's pages and became more apparent in each. The transformation leaps out dramatically, from the first report—an unsigned and undated document around 1870—to a published letter in 1874 with Gould's signature above her authoritative title, "Directress of the Italo-American Home and Schools."[39] Her portrait with two Venetian children makes her public position even more prominent for readers (see figure 2.8). Between the late 1874 publication (less than a year before her death) and the first document, where male leaders framed and deeply embedded Gould's voice, lie several rationally conceived but emotionally forceful narratives, which also include lists of contributors and expense reports. Gould's steady increase in textual production, sense of audience, and strength of voice appear not only in these formal reports of the Italo-American Schools but also in private letters she composed during the period as she worked to secure her wants. These transformations in voice and growing rhetorical confidence demonstrate "the definitions of self, other, and situation" that Toby Ditz labels "acts of power" revealed in "commercial" as opposed to private and personal letters.[40]

The first publication, a three-page pamphlet entitled *Italo-American Schools in Rome: Mrs. Gould's Work and Wants*, introduces Gould by defining her in relationship to powerful men—first as "daughter of" a well-known physician and leader of the American Tract Society and then as "wife of . . . American Physician in Rome, formerly of the United States Navy." After providing these defining relationships, the report continues referring to Gould in the third person "she" as it lists her significant skills—speaking Italian and demonstrating sympathy for the impoverished. The report again refers to Gould's husband, explaining that he is in the US "seeking aid," before quoting "a letter just received from Mrs. Gould"—likely passed on by the doctor. Notably, the doctor was merely messenger rather than author and activist. In fact, Emily's voice speaks through quotations throughout the pamphlet, providing the school's history and her desires to teach the children to love labor and despise idleness. The last paragraphs, however, return to the report's institutional narrative voice, which lists basic items Gould "wants" for her "work," such as maps, furniture, a printing press, and a model of a steam engine to aid in teaching young boys and men the advantages and systems of mechanized power. The pamphlet concludes with a list of the (all-male) undersigning committee members, including the poet William Cullen Bryant, the Reverend Howard Crosby, and Professor Vincenzo Botta. Bryant, a renowned poet in New York literary circles, and Botta, a political exile from Italy's Piedmont region who became a language professor at Columbia, mark the wide range of supporters and beneficiaries—beyond the expected religious figures. Crosby, foremost among the latter group, was the powerful pulpit voice of the wealthy Fourth Avenue Presbyterian Church, where he eulogized Gould after her death.

The next year's report, *Italo-American Schools in Rome* (1871), swelled to sixteen pages from the prior year's three. In addition to an increased size, the report opens with another notable change—an introductory message signed "E. B. G." In this message "E. B. G." acknowledges the preference and propriety of private letters and apologizes for writing in this impersonal manner and in a public medium deemed improper for a woman: "The impossibility of writing so many letters to friends, and the necessity of laying the needs of Rome before the . . . public, have compelled me to print this communication." She steps beyond the bounds even further by asking for a larger public media presence: "I beg my friends, and the friends of Italy, to circulate" the report. The apologetic stance, a rhetorical pose, underscores the blurred boundaries between private and public realms for women of the era. Gould, like Fuller and Stowe, recognized the traditional views of propriety for women as well as the potential power of their writings. Many, including female missionaries, often kept journals and letters knowing that they might be preserved for posterity and possibly published. They also knew that the letters would be circulated among friends and family.[41]

Gould assumed another rhetorical pose within this report as she described her involvement with male leaders of the Waldensian church. Humbling herself, she recognizes the valuable relationship and her "great obligations to Reverend Messrs. Ribetti and Pons," who had "generously allowed . . . use of their rooms, and given personal aid in the . . . instruction of the children."[42] These "obligations to" Waldensian leaders later would become points of contestation and negotiation, Gould's private letters reveal, in which she did not bow to the male leaders' wishes. While they wanted her energy and enthusiasm, they desired "her work" to be controlled—channeled to their "wants" rather than hers, as this chapter's final section brings to light.

The reports increased lengthwise each year, reaching forty pages in 1873. The growth partially was due to an extensive and growing "treasurer's report" and list of contributors, which Gould's name notably headed in 1873—demonstrating not only her financial prowess but also her growing authority. The reports also increased in rhetorical sophistication, moving beyond basic history of the school's founding and increasing enrollment, to instructions about how additional copies of the annual report might be acquired for a growing circulation of readers, to explanations of how and when reports would be released. These aspects of Gould's report writing also underscore her increasing responsibility. She added to her reasoned and detailed financial accounting numerous emotional and humanizing stories of the school's successes and troubles, meant to garner sympathy in readers, who were potential supporters. For example, the *First Annual Report* describes the curriculum and educational process—adherence to the Froebel method (also advocated by Peabody), employment of Italian-speaking teachers, and curriculum that included some English. For the English classes, teachers used Gould's "The Children's Manual for Speaking and Writing the English Language"—published in Florence by the Claudian Press and dedicated to Erminia Fuà Fusinato, a leader of Italian educational reform.[43] These several details about instructional methods complement stories of specific teachers, students, and their needs.

Rhetoric within the reports typifies sentimental, religious literature of the period as it points to the extreme physical and emotional needs of the children. Gould drew from nineteenth-century Scottish epistemology and educational philosophy, which had been influenced by John Locke's *tabula rasa* theory. She wrote in her first report, for example, of the children whose "minds are perfectly blank" and followed in later reports with the possibilities for them. After describing their lips, hands, and hair in detail and noting the challenge "to avoid all shrinking from poor, diseased, deformed little bits of humanity, such as many of them were," she exclaims in summary, "Poor little things! They were so ready to be loved." Like farm animals, they were "very docile" but had experienced "nothing but blows" when it came to discipline. By contrast, the school's methods "produced a pleasant effect upon the child's temper, seeming often to awaken intelligence and affection in a surprising degree." Rather than punishment by blows, a reward system of earning positive marks and tickets offered positive attention rather than fear. Rewarded students "put a penny into a box"—not for their family's bread—but for a sister institution, "the Orphan Asylum at Florence."[44] The children responded well to this domestication, Gould explained, which also included gender roles. All children learned to read, sing, and pray; additionally, boys learned to work at press, and girls learned to knit and sew.

The curriculum also included patriotic support of unified Italy, with songs and salutes to the flag and to military leaders such as Garibaldi. The school's end-of-year celebration intentionally coincided with Italy's new birthday. Civic leaders showed their support by participating as guests at school festivities: Garibaldi himself, Fuà Fusinato, and Michelangelo Caetani, the Duke of Sermoneta and leader of the Dante Circle in which Brewster and Longfellow participated. Fuà Fusinato wrote glowingly of the school in *L'Italie*, and Sermoneta "called upon the directress, and left a subscription for the funds of the schools." He insisted that "in any difficulty," they should contact him "without hesitation." Gould took him up on the offer, writing letters requesting aid. Also reflecting the patriotic and politicized reform rhetoric, Gould concluded one report with an allusion to Barrett Browning's "Cry of the Children": "I appeal to all who sympathize with the new day of liberty which has dawned upon Rome for aid to continue and multiply our labors. It seems to me that such a 'cry of the children,' pleading for the ordinary blessings of childhood, that they may be enabled to grow up men and women instead of machines, Christians instead of infidels or bigots, must find its ways to every benevolent heart."[45]

Gould's increasingly sentimental rhetoric included humanizing touches, such as naming specific children and describing unexpected problems with the European-born instructors. Professor Gotelli, for example, an Italian, had a German wife, who also taught. He had been called to Sardinia by church leaders and, Gould explained, Madame Gotelli was having voice problems. As a result, Gould made a managerial and financial plea for support of their replacements. In addition to teachers from Europe, the school welcomed Americans, such as Mary Ellis from Mount Holyoke Female Seminary, who joined the work in 1873.[46] Gould described exemplary students, such as four girls who were brought by their father, "a poor hard-working man [who] was abandoned by his wicked wife," and a "deformed" girl (also mentioned in the prior report), who was now flourishing through "nourishing food, good air, and kind treatment." She had become "a most loving little thing, an excellent student," and "a girl of high principles." Another had demonstrated such promise that she had been sent to Torre Pellice in the Turin region for education at the Vaudois seminary. This girl and others like her would return to Rome as teachers in the school.[47]

Among the most emotional of Gould's reports were virulent anti-papal messages. In an early report she wrote, "The parish priests oppose us, it is true, but they are almost powerless, and where one child is removed [by its parents] for fear of excommunication, ten stand ready to take its place." A later report embedded intense descriptions of opposition from the ultramontane party. Harassment by the school's neighbors included yelling epithets and "an infernal dance" on the roof above, resulting in not only "really frightful" noise but also falling mortar. They feared, Gould wrote, that "the ceiling would come down bodily upon our heads." The account culminated with a kidnapping story that demonized the Society for the Promotion of Catholic Interests—with more gothic detail than Hawthorne's fictional account of Hilda in *The Marble Faun*. An ill, impoverished girl whose infirmity was blamed on being in Gould's Protestant school was removed by her mother and then, soon after, snatched and put "under the charge of the nuns of St. Agatha. Here . . . in company with far from repentant Magdalenes, this poor girl went through experiences . . . quite too shocking to repeat." The "shocking" events must have been true, Gould attested, for they "could never have been invented by a young girl not yet thirteen years of age."[48] The gothic tale reverberates with rhetoric of the period's other anti-Catholic fictions, as well as that of news accounts of the forced baptism and kidnapping of the Jewish Edgardo Mortara, which may have been a source for Hawthorne.[49] For more than a decade following Mortara's baptism, his education and the pope's attitude toward it became the center of conversations not only about some Roman Catholics' attitudes toward Jews but also about the lack of religious and educational freedom under papal control.

The actions of ultramontanes culminated with the school's forced move from the neighborhood. As Gould reported, "two Catholic women, interested in the school, exerted themselves" to find a larger space and successfully found rooms to rent. The Catholic women's actions on behalf of the school underscore Gould's proclaimed interdenominational albeit evangelical goal: "*Our aim is to christianize and civilize, not to propagandize*."[50] Even the lower-case "c" emphasizes what Gould hoped would be a unifying work for the good of all, rather than a sectarian and divisive enterprise. Yet when the proprietor of the new rooms learned of the women's educational intentions, she refused. Apparently, the proprietor had assumed "immoral purposes," such as establishing a brothel, Gould explained: "the Roman ultramontanes may let their houses for dens of infamy . . . but not for schools."[51]

Gould's strong, emotional requests climaxed publicly in a thirteen-page handwritten letter, printed and distributed with a request for further circulation on behalf of the schools: "Please to have this letter read in your Sabbath School, and ask for help to carry on the work." A striking portrait captioned "Mrs. E. B. Gould and Marietta and Pepino Bartoli" (see figure 2.8) complements this instructional prefatory comment. While Gould embraces the Bartoli children and looks directly at readers on one page, her letter opens to them on the following. Dated the third week of December, the letter sets the stage for the holiday, year's end, and a winter appeal to help those in need. Gould asks each child to "consider this letter as written to him or herself," and she includes a call to action: "as you listen to it make up your minds to answer it in some way." Gould opens with a question, followed by an accessible story. "Did you ever hear of Briareus? He had a

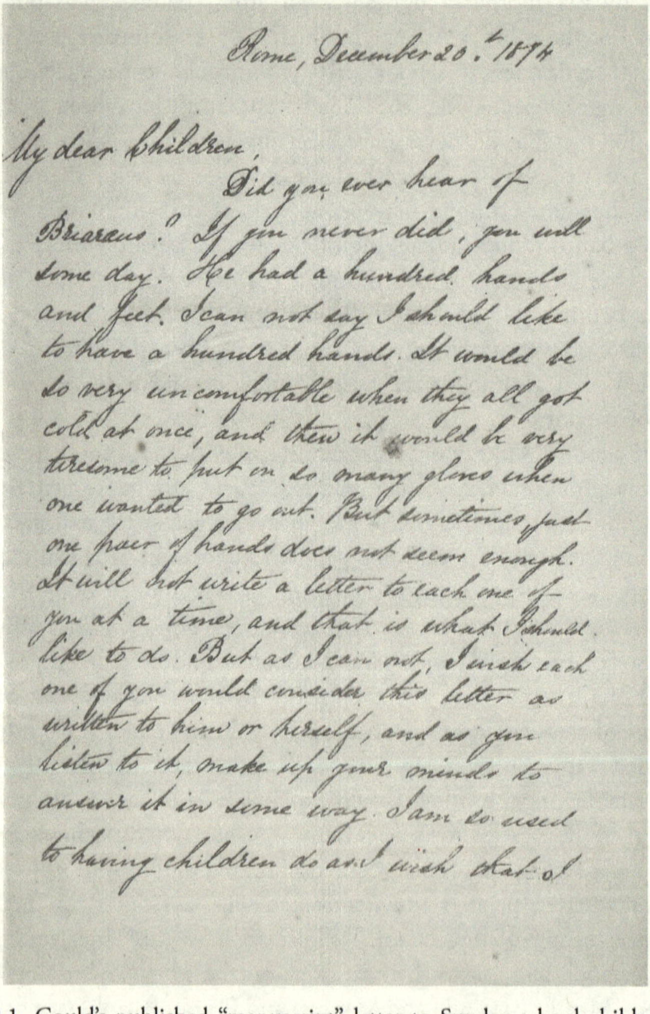

Rome, December 20th 1874

My dear Children,

Did you ever hear of Briareus? If you never did, you will some day. He had a hundred hands and feet. I can not say I should like to have a hundred hands. It would be so very uncomfortable when they all got cold at once, and then it would be very tiresome to put on so many gloves when one wanted to go out. But sometimes just one pair of hands does not seem enough. It will not write a letter to each one of you at a time, and that is what I should like to do. But as I can not, I wish each one of you would consider this letter as written to him or herself, and as you listen to it, make up your minds to answer it in some way. I am so used to having children do as I wish that I

Figure 8.1. Gould's published "manuscript" letter to Sunday school children, from *Italo-American Schools at Rome* [1874], New-York Historical Society. Credit: Photography © New-York Historical Society.

hundred hands and feet." The figure from Greek mythology, she explains, must have been miserable in the winter with so many cold hands. How "tiresome" it would be "to put on so many gloves" before going out, she notes. Then she expresses the need for many hands to do the work in Rome. She begs American children to help.[52]

Supporting this plea, the pages unfold with descriptions of several hungry and dirty children who come to life through the school's efforts. The Bartoli children of Venice, Marietta and Pepino, shine among them. They "never ate anything but polenta . . . made of coarse corn-flour"; though it was "not good at all . . . they could not get enough even of that." But the Waldensians took them in, gave them a "warm bath" and "clean night clothes," and put them "in a nice bed," prior to bringing them to the schools in Rome. Having recounted the Bartolis' sad past and their current progress, Gould appeals in conclusion, "I ask you to hear the blessed command, 'Come ye blessed of my Father, inherit the kingdom prepared for you from the foundation of the world.' Remember, your Savior will one day say 'inasmuch as ye did it unto one of the least of these, ye did it unto me.' " Here the promise of a future reward—so much a part of Gould's earlier "Little Caroline" tale—appears again. Added to the heavenly afterlife (that "one day" when the "Savior" speaks), however, Gould's message employs the language of financial investment with a payoff of inheritance.[53]

Noteworthy in this final publication, Gould signs the letter with a dual identity: "Your friend" and "Directress of the Italo-American Home and Schools." The signature presents her as both in relation and authoritative—a sympathetic, friendly mother-figure of the domestic realm as well as an effective, assertive, and militaristic manager of funds within the public realm. She combined the two images that Sánchez-Eppler and Robbins have described as integral to American missions abroad, as noted in this chapter's opening. Similarly, the portrait of Gould embracing the children in a motherly pose complemented the economic goal of the letter's rhetoric. While she asked readers to imagine cold hands, empty bellies and warm beds, she asked them to respond financially, just as the school children in Rome were rewarded for good behavior with "tickets" that allowed them to give to the needy children in Florence.[54]

Gould's behavior builds from American exceptionalism, what Amanda Porterfield recognized years ago as the tension between ethnocentrism and beneficence. Porterfield, writing of Lyon's direction of female missionaries from Mount Holyoke, explains that ethnocentrism at times blocked attempted good works "and lay at the root of the reputation for hypocrisy that missionaries . . . acquired." Lyon, of course, "did not anticipate any of the ways in which the ethnocentrism of her religious vision would undermine its credibility" and contribute to a "problem" that "beset every foreign mission in which her students worked."[55] Porterfield's study, focused on "nonwestern peoples" with whom American missionaries interacted, remains valuable as it reminds readers that a knowledge of the situation in a specific locale, such as the Italian peninsula, complicates a colonizer–colonized binary. Each locale may shed a slightly different light on American missions and women's work in a global context. Studies of Italian reform associations, for example, explain that both the resident middle classes and the elite of the peninsula not only were ripe for reforms supported by associational life following Unification but also invited it. In fact, they contributed to fervor for and the growth of such associations.[56] These reform traditions went back to the revolutions of 1848 and the works of women such as Fuller and Cristina Belgioioso, and they continued later with the efforts of Jessie White Mario and others. Often these movements sought to decrease poverty and improve education and health. Nonetheless, as Harris has written of beneficent civic reform efforts, they also often reinscribed and reinforced class differences and hierarchies. Records of specific reformers, however, reveal the diversity of attitudes about whether and how changes should be implemented. Gould's writings illuminate such controversies about reform.

Seeing Gould's work merely as unwanted imposition of Western capitalism, imperialism, and American exceptionalism upon impoverished Romans overlooks the fervent advocacy of "native" groups thick in the Piedmont and Lombardy regions who also moved south to Rome. The Waldensians and Masons, for example, welcomed the assistance of Anglo non-Catholics such as Gould in their educational reform work. Yet in the case of the "industrial education" Gould advocated, records reveal that Piedmont-based Waldensians and "free church" leaders such as Ferretti differed with her in some of their approaches. More so than in the published records of the Italo-American Schools in Rome, Gould's private correspondence makes overt what Gaul has written of the posthumous reconstruction of Harriet Gold Boudinot and her Cherokee husband, vis-à-vis her private letters: an "idealized feminine nature stands in tension with the political meanings her life signified."[57] Gould's final published letter and its intended circulation—which reinforces the "missionary mother" imagery and the "American Christian family unit" with its gendered organization—stands in contrast with her private letters. In these letters her "aggressive," opinionated, and "masculine" style emerges and, in so doing, it provides a new understanding of the diversity of American women in Italy at the time of Unification and their interests in engaging local political culture.

Private Letters and Their Political Meanings

> Tell the altar man that the Pope sends him malediction and says he is an ass.
>
> —George Perkins Marsh to Emily Bliss Gould, August 3, 1868

> Try & infuse a little of your fire into Ribetti's, Bosio's & Garnier's veins.
>
> —Matteo Prochet to Emily Bliss Gould, November 24, 1874

The "political meanings" of Gould's life emerge partially in letters she wrote to George Perkins Marsh between January 1867 and the summer of 1874 and in letters Waldensian leader Matteo Prochet wrote to Gould and to other Waldensians about the Rome school between 1871 and 1874. Even in the absence of letters Gould wrote to Prochet, his rhetoric suggests the fervor and directness of the voice that would have provoked his responses.[58] Both Prochet and Marsh held their positions of power for lengthy stints. Marsh, US minister plenipotentiary to Italy from 1861 through his death in 1882, held the position longer than any other American appointee, retaining the decision-making role despite changes in US presidents and the political parties they represented. Prochet, president of the Waldensians' Evangelism Committee, served from 1871 until the twentieth century—well beyond the period of his correspondence with Gould. Prochet's title alone does not convey the persuasive power he possessed. In this leadership position, Prochet spoke and traveled internationally for the Waldensians, with appearances in Scotland, England, France, Switzerland, Denmark, Germany, the US, Uruguay, and Argentina. In addition, he was a Mason—a politically important association in Italy at the time. This association connected Prochet to politically influential US Masons, and in 1893 he received the title Commendatore of the Order of the Crown of Italy. Twenty years earlier, when he was not yet forty, Prochet was well enough known in the bustling seaport city of Genoa that he wrote to Gould, "My name and Genoa are quite sufficient for any letter or parcel sent to me."[59] Correspondence between Gould and these powerful and prominent men speaks to her strength of vision, character, and behaviors that led others to respond to her work. Both Marsh and Prochet believed Gould had the ability to accomplish much. They entrusted her to influence ministers—or an "altar man," as Marsh wrote of one who was particularly troublesome, "an ass" with whom she worked. And Prochet noted her infectious "fire" as beyond that of Waldensian ministers Giovanni Ribetti, Enrico Bosio, and Giovanni Garnier, who lacked her enthusiasm and energy. At the same time, however, both men employed imperative verbs, direction commanding Gould to "tell" and to "try & infuse" these men. These letters and Gould's rhetorical negotiations reveal that, as a woman, she was as much a pawn of their games as an independent agent. Nonetheless, she did what she could in this difficult position.

Most of Gould's approximately thirty letters to Marsh were written in 1869 and '70, a period in which she was asking for his help, as she worked with men who frustrated her because they were not very savvy about the culture in which they lived. Gould's letters to Marsh began with an intensive focus on the political situation of the "persecuted" and fearful community of American Protestants in Rome, but the relationship transformed through the years, as they bonded through their leadership skills—George as political minister and Emily as fundraiser for the orphanage and school efforts, first in Florence and then in Rome. Thematically, the letters focus on Gould's attempts to raise money, frustrations with the postal system when sending money, infighting among Protestant groups in Rome, and her anger with male church leaders wanting to take over. While the topics are not surprising, given the cultural context, Gould's language is. She sometimes playfully and often bitterly names enemies and asks Marsh for help—a tone seldom seen in her published works. And even when these emotions emerge in the publications, Gould directs her anger only at papal authority.

In a private letter to Marsh, for example, Gould railed against the heroic Ferretti, writing that he "is evidently a child about money and yet anxious to spend it like a prince." She was better than he at ethically managing finances. She explained that he "should [be] put . . . down first [in a class to] . . . teach the A. B. C. of truth telling." However, "he would never get beyond his Ab Abc." She continued, expressing her view that Feretti needed to be reined in, even if it meant coming under the Wesleyans, a branch of Protestants with whom she was in discord:

> One thing is certain, he would have been made to behave himself, had he come under their rule. There is nothing for it now but to let him feel that he has a master. *I always knew it*, but now he has kindly proved it. . . . *I will with all my might* protect against one cent being given them unless and until we do have proper control. . . . *If I were living in Florence*, so that

> *I could do a big bit of the work, we could get up a Committee* through whom the money should pass, and who should keep matters straight.[60]

Just as she had written of getting up "a ways and means committee" when disappointed in the kitchen and food preparation in the priest's home en route to Subiaco, here Gould's confident repetition of "I" exuded her desire for control. She knew she could accomplish much—if only she did not have to deal with incompetent male leaders.

Similar complaints and anger had appeared earlier in the year as she wrote to Marsh about an unnamed man coded only as "B. E.," who attempted to take over her work by "put[ting] the Orphan House under the charge of the Am[erican] S[unday] S[chool] Union." When B. E. assumed the institution's direction and tried to place it under this organization run by men in the US, he had created a following. Gould's jealousy erupted on the page as she explained that "B. E. had had a meeting of . . . little B. E.'s at his house" with the purpose of "endeavoring to get each child to contribute one penny to its support." Gould, who had a more ecumenical vision for education, including Catholic teachers in the Rome school, responded vehemently, "B. E. has not grown suddenly wise." She had stepped in "to go forward as if B. E. had never been born." The result, she explained to Marsh, was that "everybody was satisfied as soon as I said I should write to you, and agreed to my decision." Gould's frustration and anger grew, as she explained forcefully, "I can not help considering B. E. '*Raca*.' I can not forget his behavior in America this summer. I can not forget that he has '*Our* church' on the brain. I can not forget that he thought the 100 £ sent by good Mr. Lockwood in answer to an appeal for our charities was for '*our* church' " (emphasis mine). She employed the equivalent of a curse word, "raca," calling him a stupid fool, as she ironically and repeatedly used the plural possessive "our" to emphasize B. E.'s attempts to wrest control of the project and perhaps channel funds into the church rather than school. Finally, she concluded, "you know what B. E. does in the simplicity, goodness, and *utter stupidity* of his heart."[61] Such raging language about his "utter stupidity" crossed the bounds of appropriate female behavior, of course, and did not appear in her public reports.

Gould's correspondence with Marsh also at times demonstrates the playful repartee among the two friends, rather than a one-sided rant from female supplicant to male official. In response to a complaint Gould lodged, Marsh wrote of "the altar man" as "an ass,"[62] leaving unclear his identity and imitating Gould's approach to B. E. As Lowenthal has described "Marsh's private communications" and "personal notes"—they "were vigorous and sparkling"—in contrast to his impersonal publications,[63] Gould's likewise scintillating prose undoubtedly fed Marsh's style, and vice versa. The letters point not only to their growing relationship but also to Gould's strength and accomplishments as a woman abroad—often going outside the bounds some might consider proper, such as writing letters to a man not her husband, with lines that strayed "from that plain, straight path" that Leslie advised in her handbook on female behavior.[64]

Gould's willingness to assert herself and her dreams through negotiations with another powerful man who was not her husband become even more pronounced through her correspondence with Prochet. Prochet had risen to his long tenure as president of the Evangelism Committee from a childhood of *contadini* parents. His education in the Waldensian schools near Turin, two years in the Sardinian military campaign of 1860, and studies in Florence and in the Presbyterian seminary in Belfast preceded his 1862 ordination. Soon after, complementing his international and multilingual studies, Prochet's marriage forged an important link in his career. Prochet's wife was Milca Caffarel, daughter of Turin industrial chocolate magnate Pier Paolo Caffarel and Olympe Gay, with whom he had nine children. He served as Waldensian minister in Lucca, Pisa, and Genoa (among congregations including many Swiss), where he lived when appointed president of Evangelism. Prochet continued in Genoa through 1883 and served after that in Rome until 1906.

Prochet and Gould met in October of 1870, when Prochet was in Rome for the first services of the Waldensian church there. Gould requested the leaders' assistance with her school, and the Waldensians agreed to provide room for it in their mission locale of 51 Via dei Pontefici, not far from where she and Brewster lived, without charge for the next thirteen months.[65] By the summer of 1871 Prochet was writing to Waldensian ministers Ribetti, Garnieri, and Giovanni Pietro Pons, all named in Gould's published reports, about the school and the importance of Gould's project—*her* work, not theirs. In the *First Annual Report*, for example, Gould named Garnier as in charge of the school in the original locale, when she noted a second venue had been established for the girls. In the following year's *Second Annual Report*, she labeled Garnier "director."[66] Prochet's six letters to Pons in 1871, nine to Garnier up through the winter of 1874, and twenty-seven to Ribetti between June 1871 and August 1874 (almost all in French) make up only part of the correspondence during these years that concerns the schools in

Rome.[67] All of these point to the investment of the Waldensians in what was described early on as Gould's work but now was simply "the school," with Garnier and Carolina Dalgas as "Director" and "Directress." Where, then, was Gould during these years, and what had become of her authority?

The chaos in 1870s Rome contributes to the difficulty of answering such questions. Letters in the Waldensian archives contain gaps relative to Gould's work. From 1871 forward, with Prochet's move into the position of president of the Evangelism Committee, correspondence is clearly recorded. Prior to that date the Waldensians in Rome, with whom Gould worked, did so independently of direction from the leadership seated at Torre Pellice.[68] For example, early on Gould's organization hired and paid Garnier with funds she raised. From 1871 on, the Waldensian leadership oversaw the work in Rome by sending and removing teachers, providing pay and housing, and the like. By late summer of 1871, Prochet encouraged a unified effort which, from his perspective, Gould resisted. From her perspective, he behaved a bit like B. E.

Another factor challenging contemporary understanding of Gould's position in these years is the sheer number of missions in the name of Christianity, which mushroomed following the breach of the walls at Porta Pia. According to the 1873 report *Christian Work in Rome*, at least five distinct organizations with diverse goals arose, but the players involved crossed boundaries. The report refers to the American Union Church, the English and American Christian Association, the Italian Young Men's Christian Association, the Church Among the Soldiers, and the Christian Training School for Young Men. It also explains that "through the efforts of its pastor and the younger members of its congregation," the "Christian Association" was formed by "English speaking people resident and visiting in Rome." This organization designed specifically for young people provided a library and reading room, lectures, and readings. Serving as a model, it motivated Italian young men to create the Italian Young Men's Christian Association, or "Associazione Cristiana della Giovenì [*sic*] di Roma." Although aided by the pastor of the American Union Church, the president was Waldensian Giovanni Garnier and the secretary was Ernesto Filippini—also a Waldensian minister.[69]

The report continues with attention to forty "representatives of all the denominations in Rome" and "all of the Italian pastors resident in Rome," who were "a powerful aid in giving intellectual life to our Association" through "a Christian Training School for Young' Men." They provided a "social evening" for members' families every two months. The report provides similar descriptions of the soldier's church and the training school. Despite overlaps in leadership and teachers, the report also underscores the independence of each organization. For example, the Christian Association was "existing upon a basis of perfect independency" from the Union Chapel, which "has given constant aid and sympathy."[70] Because these "independent" organizations shared leadership and teachers, keeping boundaries distinct and demarcating clear lines of responsibility and agreement were difficult. In fact, in this early period a kind of "communitas"—to use Victor Turner's terminology—existed. Well-intentioned and visionary people who did not want to duplicate efforts built from strengths and "shared the wealth" of available talents. But it did not take long for the community spirit to rankle as differences, and perhaps power hunger, flourished.

Nonetheless, within published reports of these works, Gould appears as an important leader, fundraiser, and negotiator for the "Italo-American Schools." While she presented herself through photo and signature in the last published letter as "Directress of the Italo-American Home and Schools," at this point, the Waldensian Evangelism Committee, under Prochet's direction, managed much of the on-the-ground details for the institution. Prochet's correspondence with Gould and other Waldensians in Rome bears out the situation. Among the nine letters Prochet wrote to Garnier between July 1871 and September 1874, one letter mentions the potential interests of American children and reveals his understanding of the importance of maintaining Gould's position as a figurehead and conduit to these financial and emotional supporters.[71] And a chronological overview of the references to Gould's work and the schools within the nine letters also reveals that what began as a mutual agreement—that educating the poor young children was most important—mutated from a unifying work to one fraught with controversies. The controversies included what was to be taught (i.e., the degree of evangelism to any specific Christian denomination or doctrine); who was in charge and had the final word (Gould and an American board of directors, or the Waldensians); and who was responsible financially. While Waldensian leaders understood they wanted at least financial assistance from wealthy Americans and others from outside the peninsula, they did not agree with all the theological views some of these benefactors held. At the same time, Gould and other non-natives of Rome and Florence recognized that assistance from Europeans who understood the cultures and spoke French and Italian better than they did was essential to the success of "their" projects. Nonetheless, they wanted to assume and maintain ownership of them.

Despite both sides realizing their needs to negotiate and come to mutually beneficial agreements, the negotiations often fell short for Gould.

The first point of negotiation emerged in June 1871, when Prochet wrote to Ribetti of the importance of work in Rome, for the city and for the church. The most important questions, he asserted, were about the school. Letters in July and August continued the topic, including the significant comment that Gould did not want to unite "her work" with that of the Waldensians. Then early in 1873 a conflict with the teacher Buffa erupted. It continued for more than a year. Prochet wrote to Buffa, for example, "I tell you only that it appears that you will do you better to continue in the school of Signora Gould until the relation . . . returns to good. In a couple of months I will find myself . . . in Rome to explain my thoughts better and face-to-face, and I am convinced that you will see that I am right." Ten months later he wrote again to Buffa, explaining that he was sent to Rome on behalf of Mrs. Gould's request. But by February of 1874, the Evangelism Committee had accepted Buffa's request that he might leave Rome. By March 10, Buffa had moved to Guidizzolo, near Mantua.[72]

During the same period, Prochet's twenty-seven letters to Ribetti gave much attention to the recently formed "superior school" for females and its teachers and director, along with commentary about the related Waldensian congregations. The letters reveal above all Prochet's involvement from a distance, his impact on decisions about day-to-day directorship in Rome, his interest in and dependency on American financial support, his impatience with specific pastors, and the rhetorical directness of his private letters. The topics include needing to find space for the school, determining which women will work in what positions (Martha Sommerville Desanctis, Carolina Dalgas, and Josephine Arnoulet were key figures), inquiring about possible part-time teachers and what they might be paid, and commenting on congregations specific pastors serve.[73] By mid-August 1874, in spite of decisions having been made about Dalgas as directress and Arnoulet as teacher, he wrote to announce that the opening of the women's school had been delayed, due to "the news . . . of the financial state in America."

Prochet employed carefully crafted prose—typical of someone in international diplomacy and an educated leader with fine linguistic skills. His letter about the state of Pastor Meille's sore throat is one example. Meille's illness prompted a brusque comment and query, noting that Prochet was still waiting for the letter in English about the Rome school. "I have asked him to loan it [the letter] to me and I don't see anything. Is his throat so bad that it keeps him from writing?" His rhetorical flourish (and perhaps restraint) emerges in all four letters to Gould. The first, dated two and a half years after their initial meeting in Rome, he addressed directly to Gould rather than through Waldensian Pastor Ribetti as a mediator—the process he had chosen when addressing Meille. By content as well as address the letter indicated that their relationship had been well established. Prochet thanked Gould for a letter of introduction she had sent to pave the way for his upcoming journey to the US.[74] This gesture had "provided already a little brightness to the somewhat dark prospect of a visit to a land where I scarcely know a person." Prochet then turned to Gould's request for teachers. She wanted someone part time and indefinitely—a position which seemed untenable to Prochet, from a practical standpoint. He apologized: "I am sorry not to be able to point out one who would be fit for such a work." He also apologized that the Waldensians had "somewhat neglected the training" of their teachers. The plans were "to have a school for them in Florence similar to the normal school at Torre Pellice" before long. Prochet finally excused himself with a "not-in-my-job-description" phrase—his position over Evangelism excluded him from the group overseeing theology and education. However, he "trust[ed] no real difficulty" from the men in that "department." In conclusion, he returned to his generally supportive position, "So far as I am concerned I shall not make any difficulty at your having one of our teachers."

Four days later Prochet wrote again, apologizing for a lack of communication, and blaming poor mail service and lost letters. He reinforced the value of Gould's correspondence and "counsel," begging excuse due to his "haste" and imminent departure for the US.[75] The letter indicates that Gould had followed up with persistent inquiry and "counsel," which, along with Prochet's concluding lines in "haste," underscore the forthright but careful negotiations and exchange between two birds of a feather. Both Prochet and Gould, driven by distinct visions they labored to achieve, kept busy schedules with travel and correspondence. Their mutually beneficial and somewhat competitive relationship appears more overtly eighteen months later, in the last and longest letter Prochet wrote to Gould.

Prochet's attempted manipulation and patronizing phrasing culiminate this 1874 letter, which also reveals the evolving relationship. He opens with what could be read either as a friendly regret about her absence from Rome when he was there, or a passive-aggressive barb about her travels: "Had you been in Rome on the beginning of this month you would have saved the trouble of writing and given to me the great pleasure of a good long chat with you."[76] Stories in American newspapers, such as the *Congregational*, the *Observer*, and the *Evangelist*, he explained, touched his "nerves" and increased his desire "to bring twice the attention of American people" to their efforts in Rome. After uniting the two in their labors with these opening phrases, Prochet turned to teachers and justifying the Waldensians' actions, including Buffa's relocation: "Now, about Buffa: Remember my dear Mrs. Gould that I took him when he was out of your employment & you well know that I did not bribe him away. When he told me you wanted him, it was when it was impossible to spare him, being as he was the only agent in one of our missionary stations. I don't know whether it will be possible or not to let him go next year, but I will try and get some one for you." The passage opens with a direct but almost informal tone, a casual one that would be used among friends or equals ("Now, about Buffa"). Prochet quickly shifts to a gently apologetic reminder ("Remember my dear Mrs. Gould"), then to the rational explanation ("I took him when he was out of your employment"), and finally to a pointed remark that may have been written in response to an accusation ("you well know that I did not bribe him away"). Prochet concluded with a remark suggesting that Buffa was indispensable to the church's larger works—Prochet's priority as president of Evangelism. And he concluded the passage by assuring her of his ongoing efforts on her behalf: he "will try" to locate another.

Then Prochet changed the subject with a clever transition which suggests that "dear Mrs. Gould" had written a letter admonishing him. Prochet continued with a simile claiming humility: "As to my not going to Rome, you are not the only one who has loaded me with reproach. I bow my head as the tiny flowers when the sirocco is blowing & take it with patience." He then shifted to a comical and irreverent reference to the Roman Catholic Saint Anthony: "Reasons for not going! . . . I wish S. Antonio were still living & would kindly sell me his skill." Prochet mocks Anthony's mystical abilities of "being two places at one time" and his subsequent sacral position, continuing with humorous images and wishful thinking: "Sometimes I think it would be of a great worth to have more than one head & two or three right hands—I suppose I should not look very handsome, but in keeping inside of my study, nobody would know it & my work would get on better." Prochet's vivid and somewhat grotesque comic imagery of himself with multiple heads and hands seems to have resonated with Gould. Only two weeks later, she wrote her letter for Sunday school children, opening with the tale of the many-handed Briareus (figure 8.1). Rather than employ humor, she replaced the Roman Catholic St. Anthony with a figure from Greek mythology—perhaps less offensive and more appropriate to her didactic storytelling for Protestant children. But, like Prochet, Gould implored children to understand how diligently she labored, hoping they would feel the need to assist with her works and wants in Rome.

Prochet's striking imagery moved through a skillful series of rhetorical steps, just as Gould's did, in concluding the letter. He asked Gould's assistance, flattering her by appealing to her strengths before suggesting how she should proceed. Then he agreed with her about what should be done, prior to concluding with an attempt at unifying by reference to Divine love:

> Do you know what you can do for our congregation in Rome? Try & infuse a little of your fire into Ribetti's, Bosio's & Garnier's veins. Add to them Bari who is now also one of us. You may not succeed at once, but . . . if you undertake one thing at a time, forming committees, for example, or mother's meetings, you will see that one after the other all the necessary reforms will come. I quite agree with you—some kind of work ought always to be given to church members. There is no better way for keeping out idle gossip disputes & other evils and meanwhile foster a greater love & zeal for whom [*sic*] loved us.

This persuasive tactic of request, flattery, suggestion, and agreement scalds with patronizing phrases about the work she might do as a woman: "forming committees . . . or mother's meetings." Through these behaviors, she would "infuse a little . . . fire into" the ministers' "veins," building up the Waldensian congregations, "keeping out ideal gossip disputes and other evils."

Prochet's culminating appeal in the letter tapped into the ideal of American liberty: "Excuse me for writing freely," he apologized, explaining that he has been influenced by his "five months & twenty days in America, quite enough to . . . drink in a good lump of freedom!" After reiterating his belief in her "work" in the "direction" he advised, for which she would "be blessed," he appealed again for assistance with the American periodical the *Evangelist*. He asked that she use her connections to secure a complimentary copy and publishing venue for him. As Prochet explained, "three other papers, I receive from America, [are] kindly sent by their editors & in return I write one or two letters per year." His desire was to be "*au courant* of what it pleases those gentlemen to say about us." The plural pronoun "us" may be an exclusive reference to the Waldensians, but it also may be an inclusive collective noun, connecting Gould with the missions under Prochet's leadership.

A week later Prochet again brought up the American newspaper subscriptions and his desire to place articles within them. In this final letter to Gould he stated that he did not want to duplicate either her efforts or those of his colleague Pons.[77] Prochet's final letters demonstrate the Waldensian dedication to promote the cause of the Italo-American Schools in the US through a unified work. But, in fact, the Prochet–Gould correspondence as a whole and other Waldensian records reveal that the two were negotiating leadership of the Roman institutions. Gould's negotiations depict a self-confidence and motivation that resulted in the letter she wrote to Sunday school children in December of 1874 and the volume she planned in 1875, the year of her final illness, published posthumously as the *Wreath of Stray Leaves*. Gould's position in that volume, and the dramatic increase in power, responsibility, and voice it manifests, remain within the confines of ideal womanhood, as do other publications. The private letters with the powerful married men Prochet and Marsh, however, reveal her position as one who pushed the boundaries. Transformed by her negotiations and experiences in Rome, Gould was codified ideally after her death by those who memorialized her, first in the *Wreath of Stray Leaves* and then in Bacon's *A Life Worth Living*. But her private writings help her speak from the grave, revealing the strength of a woman determined to fight for her utopian visions.

Chapter 9

Anne Hampton Brewster

A Catholic Correspondent Negotiates New Rome

> I am somewhat like the Empress Catharine of Russia when she was in her youth, working for her empire. I in my mid age am working for an empire of peace and good will.
>
> —Anne Hampton Brewster, Journal, January 1872

> Keep thyself free as an Arab of thy Beloved.
>
> —Anne Hampton Brewster, Journal, quoting Ralph Waldo Emerson[1]

Not long after Emily Bliss Gould's death late in 1875, Anne Hampton Brewster proudly noted in her journal that she was writing for "two of the best" American newspapers. Like Gould, she had been developing her public voice as a reporter and correspondent about affairs in Rome for several years. And, like Gould, she carefully balanced public and private life, keeping light what went on the published page but pouring out sometimes dark and heavy emotions in her letters and journal entries. In this journal entry of 1876, Brewster let her pride roll, boasting, "I have now 11 letters a month and am the correspondent of two of the best journals in America." These were not only "the best" newspapers but "also . . . two well-known ones," she continued, naming the four: the *Boston Daily Advertiser* and the *New York World* were among "the best," and the *New York Daily Graphic* and *Philadelphia Evening Bulletin* were the "well-known."[2] Since this entry was for Brewster's eyes only, the record may have served as an indulgent self-pinching, as Brewster assured herself that she was not dreaming about her professional position. It may have also served as private self-stroking, in which she savored pleasures that, if shared publicly, might be deemed gloating—inappropriate for a genteel woman.

Whatever the purposes and results, the passage indicates Brewster was at the peak of her career as a correspondent in Rome, busy with laboring to meet numerous writing commitments that had begun in 1869. When she arrived in Rome in November of 1868, she had possessed only one agreement—to send regular letters to Gibson Peacock's *Philadelphia Evening Bulletin*. By the end of the next decade, Brewster and her letters were so well known among readers in the US and those who traveled to Europe that she was satirized in Tincker's *By the Tiber*. What happened during that decade? She made choices about relationships that impacted both her professional and personal health. Some of Brewster's actions, judged in light of the bounds of appropriate behavior then, illuminate the challenges nineteenth-century American women faced abroad as they responded to their callings. More importantly, they explain why Brewster's name does not appear among histories of women in journalism, and why it is little known among those recovering nineteenth-century American women writers.[3] This chapter extends and revises studies such as Alice Fahs's, which comments on American newspaper women writing internationally about political events. Although Fahs justifiably challenges the claim that "relatively few American journalists, male or female . . . reported from overseas in the nineteenth century" and successfully argues that they "eagerly embraced such work," she does not mention Brewster, a figure with a twenty-year career in Italy.[4]

Yet as we will see, Brewster's highly gendered behavior, as well as her Roman Catholicism, both contributed to and limited her success. Brewster at times adhered to nineteenth-century mores for women, outwardly and deferentially bowing to men with whom she associated, including career-driven personalities such as Ernesto Nardi, who hoped to become pope, and the Roman civic leader Rodolfo Lanciani. This behavior opened doors for her, but only so far. The story of the initially mutually beneficial relationship with Lanciani, and Brewster's decision to sever it, told elsewhere in more detail but summarized here, sets the stage for her behaviors.[5]

Lanciani, in charge of excavations in Rome and increasingly gaining civic power, was one of the "friends" to whom Brewster regularly referred in her published letters. He wrote her more than sixty letters after their initial meeting in 1869. Mostly undated and written in French, the letters confirm Lanciani's role as a "useful" informant, if not a dear friend. They refer to news of the Vatican Council, who received gifts from the pope at public ceremonies, the ongoing excavations, and Lanciani's granting Brewster access to sites. By the date of her last published reference to him in 1887, Lanciani was well beyond his 1880 receipt of the 10,000-franc prize from Rome's prestigious Royal Academy of the Lincei for his *Topografia di Roma antica*, one among more than 250 works published with his name.[6] Throughout his long career Lanciani was also known as an engineer, professor, and internationally recognized expert on excavations of classical Rome.[7] But he had not always been at that high point. He was self-created, professionally speaking. A "precocious" professional climber and "certain" in his "self-promotional skill," he was little more than "twenty-something" when his opportunities opened up in the years 1867–71 in the "new," secular Rome.[8] Brewster was a significant rung on the ladder of his professional climb. More important here than her impact on *his* career, however, is what the relationship reveals of Brewster's behaviors and their impact on *her* career.

Lanciani was among Brewster's first neighbors in Via del Babuino. A letter Brewster wrote to author Helen Hunt Jackson in 1869, thanking her for "the lost key" and "for his acquaintance," suggests a serendipitous start to the relationship.[9] Two American women, unable to enter their lodgings as they looked for a lost key, likely with fatigue from the day's outing, and perhaps late, were assisted by the young local, a Roman gentleman, who allowed them access. As Brewster continued her thanks to Jackson, "I have made several interesting items in my letters from his delightful bits of information." In that first year of their "acquaintance," she referred to Lanciani as a "charming agreeable eminently *useful* young man" and "a most *useful* friend."[10]

Although not emotional love letters, many of Lanciani's letters to Brewster in French illustrate the mutually "useful" and "personal" relationship between the two as it progressed. Additionally, they reveal a significant turning point in the relationship, quite strained after the failed publication of a book translation Brewster undertook. During the summer of 1873, Brewster's professional labors included translating into English Lanciani's popular *Guida del Palatino*. His guide to the Palatine Hill, serving the numerous tourists traveling to Rome, had launched Lanciani higher into what was quickly becoming a successful social and professional flight. Although references to Brewster's translation and its publication appeared in print, the guide was never published. The manuscript remains almost untouched in her extensive papers.[11] The story surrounding the unpublished-but-translated manuscript speaks to the non-amourous relationship between an American woman and a Roman man in the first decade of the newly unified Republic of Italy. More importantly, Brewster chose to have her name removed from the title page when the publisher offered to pay her merely "a paltry gift and 20 copies" of the inexpensive volume. She believed her "friend" Lanciani, who brought the publisher's offer to her, would reap immense financial benefits from the publication and hid his part in the negotiations, which left her little. He placed the burden of the agreement of the "gift" of "paltry" pay on the publisher, with whom he served only as messenger rather than a broker, Brewster suggested. In the same period, Lanciani became a competitor to Brewster by sending articles on excavations to the *New York Herald*. Brewster took revenge on her "false" friend, deciding to "punish him" by removing her name from the title page of the translation. The plan backfired, however. His continuing professional rise overshadowed her professional demise. His name appeared frequently in John Murray's popular travel guides to Rome between 1875 and 1894, and as author on the title page this last year. He also appeared once in K. Baedeker's popular volume. The books directed Anglo visitors to find him at an office on the Palatine, where they could seek his assistance—in English—with entrance and understanding the site. Brewster's name appeared on no guidebooks after the reference to the forthcoming English translation.[12]

The relationship's relevance today lies in its illumination of studies of nineteenth-century authorship and of women in journalism. The Lanciani–Brewster relationship demonstrates how authorial success often depends on events of "social bonding," which might not seem to be an economic activity, but are a form of "gift exchange," as Leon Jackson has explained. Breaches in the economic circuit of the "gift exchanges" with Lanciani limited Brewster's career.[13] While Lanciani's name is well known among those who study classical Rome through its nineteenth-century excavations, Brewster's name, as mentioned earlier, does not appear among histories of women in journalism.

Brewster's absence from these histories is in part a result of her previously noted gendered behavior, articulated in a letter she wrote to Thomas Davidson after Lanciani received the prestigious Lincei award, for example. Her recounting of the event for Davidson opened, "Lanciani and I have buried the hatchet and are good friends." Brewster also explained that after Lanciani presented her the signed first copy of his prize book, they "said nothing of the past, shook hands, and each felt better for the forgiveness of the little troubles." "Little troubles" are hardly of the magnitude to demand Brewster's warrior-like battle imagery of a buried hatchet. In fact, Brewster's ambivalent imagery included courtly coquetry as well, when she wrote to

Davidson of how Lanciani "behaved so prettily" to her "when his great success came." She explained, "I gave in, woman like" and forgave him.[14] The story of this disagreement and Brewster's highly gendered surrender speaks clearly to her chameleon-like negotiations and the dystopian end to what had been a utopian beginning to her career in Rome.

Other negotiations Brewster brokered in Rome also illuminate her professional path, while they illustrate her habits and writing style as a female correspondent abroad in light of women such as Margaret Fuller and Louisa May Alcott. These two, well known for having crossed gender boundaries as correspondents, succeeded nonetheless. Brewster's negotiations reveal her keen understanding of the place of newswriting and publishing to create and feed an audience. And they underscore choices Brewster made about socializing and career, revealing that in her attempts to be in control of relationships in ways she thought would be beneficial to her calling and utopian visions, Brewster made some decisions that damaged rather than advanced her career. She eschewed intimacy with men as well as with women, following the words of Emerson she wrote in her journal in the winter of 1872—she remained "free" from relationships that might control her, living the last few years of her life almost alone in Siena. In short, Brewster's most intimate relationship was with her pen. Sadly, her position as a newspaper figure *and* a woman choosing a single life pushed her into relative obscurity today. Her life differed significantly from that of better-known news correspondents such as Fuller, Alcott, Sara Jane Lippincott (Grace Greenwood), Jessie White Mario, and Elizabeth Cochraine Seaman (Nellie Bly). The path she chose—as she turned aside both women and men—included several notable points, among them decisions that launched her across the Atlantic to begin her rise in Rome's circles.

Anxieties of Arrival—Creature Comforts Compromised

> I am very weary and wish to reach Rome or some place where I can sleep at night without anxiety, where I can undress like a Christian and take my bath like a civilized being.
>
> —Anne Hampton Brewster, Journal, 1868[15]

Brewster's position had not always been such that it garnered both fame and infamy. She had arrived among the dust and noise of Rome in November of 1868 feeling herself "a mere atom," dependent on the welcome of fellow

Philadelphian and family friend Thomas Buchanan Read. Although she had been on the Italian peninsula a decade earlier, the sights and sounds at the Termini station overwhelmed her. They were new to her in many ways. She had never been in Rome. Her first European trip in 1857–58 had been prior to Italian unification, and, when she had first traveled abroad a decade earlier, her creature comforts had not been as strained as they were in 1868. A short voyage on the steamer *Arago*, with maid Lina and dog Beauty, a letter of introduction from US consul Robert Dale Owen in hand, contributed to her security as she journeyed overland through Le Havre, Paris, and Lyon to the posh resort of Vevey, Switzerland, which became the opening setting of her 1866 autobiographical novel, *St. Martin's Summer*, more than a decade before James set the opening of *Daisy Miller* there. The lake and surrounding Swiss Alps dealt her stimulating summer weather and vistas, experiences she wrote about into the fall. After several months in Vevey, Brewster had journeyed south to Naples, hosted by the American consul Owen and his wife and daughter for a leisurely winter.[16] The physically and emotionally challenging autumn and early winter months surrounded by the mountain air were followed by a glorious spring and summer in Naples, full of *dolce far niente*—"the sweetness of doing nothing," as she read, wrote in her journal, socialized with the Owens, and took in the sights of the Bay of Naples and its historic environs. She had composed extensive diaries and letters, as well as parts of two novels, which appeared in the decade after her return to the States in 1858.[17]

Now, in 1868, she was ten years older—almost fifty. And she was traveling differently. With ongoing publishing agreement in hand, Brewster saw herself as leaving the US indefinitely, an expatriate—exiled not so much from country as from family. In early September as she awaited departure, she reflected on the preparation of recent weeks—the goodbyes said, the taking of Holy Communion, and visiting her mother's grave. She lost patience with the ship's captain, whose family was not ready for departure. She expressed with dismay, "I found to my consternation that the Captain's wife and three children are to sail with us. The wife is a blessing, but the babies I am afraid will be a nuisance. They are all babies, too; the eldest only 5, and the youngest 4 months, the middle one only 22 months!" As she waited in a "filthy hotel" for the captain's family's preparation, she reminded herself, "Patienza!" Having chosen the hotel, captain, and ship to save money, she turned her time, energy, and emotions to her profession. She planned to write "an article for Lippincotts on the 'Pains & pleasures of preparing for a sea voyage,' " in which she described the "dreary desolate dirty loneliness" endured while waiting, after the excitement of preparation.[18]

Brewster had selected a freighter with sails rather than a more luxurious passenger ship that relied more on steam. In this vessel the Atlantic and Mediterranean crossing was at a significantly slower pace—forty-nine days, rather than ten. She chose it not only for the lower fare (half the cost) but also so that she could take as much luggage as she wished. She did not plan to return. The time at sea allowed her to read twenty-six of Shakespeare's plays between the Straits of Gibraltar and Sardinia. Despite careful financial planning, Brewster nonetheless expressed desire to speed up the crossing: "Seven weeks to morrow since we have been out at sea! Forty nine days! Heigho! Blow Eolus a fair wind!" Brewster's call upon the Roman keeper of the winds reveals that her patience wore thin as she anticipated the beginnings of her new future. Later, just before reaching the port of Messina on the Sicilian coast, she made her concerns even more apparent. Eager to be rid of the close quarters, with the captain and his gaggle of small children rather than a steamer-full of elite passengers, she noted, "I am very weary and wish to reach Rome or some place where I can sleep at night without anxiety, where I can undress like a Christian and take my bath like a civilized being."[19] Although she remained confident with her contacts, such as the Reads, and with her contract with a US newspaper, she was ready to be settled abroad. The fatigue of travel dissolved into anxiety about her new home and this new phase of her professional life.

After a stop in Messina, the freighter sailed to Naples. From there Brewster departed in the early morning on November 8 for overland travel by train. Not far north of Naples, the train stopped at Caserta, where she sat alone in her "carriage" most of the day, and finally rolled into Rome after 8 p.m. It was "quite dark," she noted, in early November. Even worse, "every person had someone to greet them or someplace to go. In a few minutes all the compartments on the carriages were empty. I stood there alone. It was a desolate outlook." As the peninsula had begun moving toward unification, and the Papal States' future was uncertain, the city was in chaos. Stazione Termini was not what it is today. As she described, it was "an unfinished Barrick—heaps and piles of stones everywhere. Great ruins also—the baths of Diocletian." Not only were the sights desolate, the sounds were a "Babel" to her—"Porters, tourists, cabmen, each and all talking at once. . . . Every language under the sun was screamed out in various tones each equally impatient." These made her "loneliness greater." In the midst of the loneliness, a porter took her "bundle of wraps and traveling bags"—fulfilling his duties rather than merely assisting her—and ordered her out of the carriage and into the chaos.

"Wondering what to do, and where to go," Brewster thankfully "heard a familiar voice cry out." Her friend Read brought a "flow of words, each one pleasant to my ears," she wrote. His "warm welcomes" and "sympathetic inquiries" related to her journey and fatigue provided a sense that she "was being cared for after the tiresome solitude of a long and dangerous voyage." As Read swept Brewster into his home in the Via del Babuino, just off the Piazza di Spagna, she was transformed from freight to full-blooded human. The flower-filled room, honoring her arrival, moved Brewster to write of herself, "Who had been of so little consequence for some time past! A mere atom! A simple, unimportant human parcel to be sent from one place to another!"

Next a mesmerizing moonlight tour of the city brought to life the scenes Brewster previously had known only from reading—St. Peter's, the Colosseum, the Arch of Titus, the Palatine and Capitoline hills, St. John Lateran. Brewster wrote during her first weeks of touring Roman sites associated with not only church history but also artistic, literary, and political traditions. Although much of her first month was devoted to seeing sights, her journal reveals that her professional situation was also on her mind. She wrote with confidence of her plan, trusting that a way would be paved for her: "I am allowing my sight seeing and every thing else to shape the way for itself."[20] Other entries speak also to this constant tension between rest and labor, personal edification and thoughts of sharing insights with others.

Through her relationship with the well-established Reads, Brewster almost immediately entered the fray of social and political circles of new Rome that became the fuel for her fire as a journalist. Her lodging with them offered keen views. From their home on the palazzo's third floor (by US counting), she observed in the coming months the departure of French soldiers and the entry of the Italians, as well as several public processions. More importantly, the Reads introduced her to many people who gave her career abroad a kick start. She met right away the sculptor Thomas Crawford's daughter; his wife's sister, Louisa Ward Terry; a Mrs. Macpherson (whom she described as "Mrs. Jameson's niece"); a Mrs. Church (described as "the artist's wife"); and Mr. Cushman (Charlotte's brother). Her interactions with Nardi and Lanciani, however, provide the most keen insights to Brewster's professional negotiations.

Despite the numerous introductions, Brewster wavered between appreciation for what Read and his wife offered socially and physically and the challenges posed by being their guest. Delighted not to be alone in Rome, she was disturbed nonetheless that they insisted on covering her expenses, which, for a woman attempting to be independent, was troubling. Additionally, she wanted to talk "business" with "Mr." Read, but "Mrs." Read was always around. Finally, distressing issues about her "host & hostess"—"skeletons" in the closet that created "anxiety"—went beyond what she would expose in her journal.[21] These might have been Read's excessive use of alcohol, or his financial troubles, both which manifested themselves more fully later in Brewster's journal. Just as the sea voyage was marked by the antinomies of careful planning and uncomfortable events outside Brewster's control, a tension between personal desires and professional obligations marked her life with the Reads. Such tensions continued throughout her time in Rome—as she negotiated relationships with men, encounters with women, and the realities of living abroad as an unmarried, older female seeking independence as a writer. She was caught in a crevice between two types of lives—one more traditional and the other more radical—neither of which attracted her enough to ground her fully on either side.

Nero Nardi and the Vatican Council

> My conversation . . . proved that he will be of no use to me in the matter of council information, only for ceremonies, special views of functions and the like.
>
> —Anne Hampton Brewster, Journal, 1869[22]

Often one to boast about her social circles, Brewster claimed friendship with Cardinal Giacomo Antonelli, chief adviser to Pope Pius IX.[23] But her relationship with Ernesto Nardi, known as the "Grand Inquisitor," reveals more of Brewster's pursuit of her utopian visions. Given various titles throughout his life and career, the "nero" Nardi, who was editor of *La voce della verità* and the *Rota* (two Roman Catholic publications), was "a fervent champion of the pope's temporal power."[24] The records of Brewster's and Nardi's interactions reveal that he had high hopes of achievement, just as the female correspondent dreamed of her professional climb in Rome. The relationship—female and male equally striving to reach their goals—parallels that of Gould with Waldensian leader Prochet.[25] Instead of politely ignoring Nardi's secretive political stances, Brewster attempted to pry them open for the American public.

Her understanding of Nardi emerged in her journal, where she also described his "tall, thin, august" build, "awkward . . . movements," "intelligent face," and "amusing and interesting . . . conversation," which all attracted attention. As she explained, "He is a welcome visitor at the Vatican," because his humor "amuses his Holiness." She elaborated on his rhetorical flair and engaging personality: Nardi "knows every thing that is going on at home and abroad [and] speaks all languages." She compared him to Shakespeare's Sir Andrew Aguecheek of *Twelfth Night*, adding that outside the Vatican, Nardi's "sharp mots about people and things fly like stinging quills all over Rome, wounding and irritating long after the Mgr has forgotten them." He would forget them because he was "neither spiteful nor bad hearted." His talking, instead, like some contemporary political figures on social media, was "to amuse himself and others." Although "sharp tongued" and "intolerant," primarily his "delights" were "in giving the last bit of news, sketching aloud in words an absurd story or saying an epigrammatic bit no matter at whose expense."[26]

When Brewster met Nardi in 1869, at the dinner the Childs hosted for Longfellow upon his arrival in Rome, the monsignor had come to the attention of American politicos because of his involvement with the unstable situation in Mexico, where Napoleon III had attempted to further his empire during the American Civil War. Five years earlier, when the US was distracted by its own divided union, France under Napoleon III had brought about the fall of Mexican President Benito Juárez and claimed it was under the rule of Maximilian Hapsburg. The US sided with Mexican liberals who were fighting French rule. As Napoleon III sought European support, Nardi, part of the Roman Catholic leadership, collaborated with the European leaders. At least one of the Italian leaders thought that uniting with France in the cause could be a good idea, although the approach ignored the 1823 Monroe Doctrine, which the US had established. The doctrine stated that the US would not ignore European intervention in the West.[27] When George Perkins Marsh learned of possible Italian involvement in Mexico, he shared the information with officials in Washington, which brought attention to Nardi's position in the scandal. It likely contributed to the view of him as a shrewd politician. In the worst light, Nardi might be compared to Aaron Burr, who had hoped to gain political power from Napoleon I's desired foothold in New France.

Brewster elaborated on Nardi's tenuous but eager political position in her journal: "A short time ago Monsignor Nardi seemed to have a fine future before him. His office is in the line that leads to the purple, and he was apparently going rapidly towards it. . . . In every Roman prelate's pocket is a Cardinal's berretta [*sic*]. . . . But it is pure luck. If the tide runs suddenly to an open empty sea and leaves the poor priest stranded high and dry, he rarely finds another chance. . . . So it has been with Mgr. Nardi." His interactions in Mexico had led to trouble, Brewster mused. For "the prelate who managed the Roman affairs of poor Maximillian," his luck ran dry. "If the Mexican [Empire] planned by the Emperor of France had succeeded, Mgr Nardi would now be an Eminenza. But luck was against the whole affair. Maximilian lost his life, Carlotta her wits and poor Mgr Nardi his berretta."[28]

Brewster's comments on Nardi's position appear among the records of their interactions, all written during the first five months of 1869—within Brewster's first six months in Rome—indicating the importance of the negotiations to the beginning of her career abroad. These records consist of Brewster's two journal entries and, from Nardi to her, a handful of letters and two calling cards. Within the journal entries a recommendation to view activities from Sant' Andrea's balcony in St. Peter's stands as a sad symbol of what their relationship came to be for Brewster—not an open book of a political insider's insights but merely a pass for a surface view of ceremonies within the basilica.[29] In sum, this residue remains of Nardi's and Brewster's mutual understanding of the values of exchanging knowledge of language and culture as well as the power of wisely negotiating professional relationships. Brewster in these early days believed she did well, especially upon their first encounter at the Childses' dinner. Childs, publisher of the Philadelphia *Public Ledger*, influenced Brewster's connections with other newspapers, but Nardi's presence that evening also contributed to her published letters during those months.[30] While the evening may have been merely a "fortunate event," Brewster played the event to her favor, so that it prepared a pathway for future encounters of more depth. This behavior became a pattern with others, such as Lanciani, who gifted her with china dolls and busts as well as numerous important articles and information on Roman politics.

What happened that evening, during which Brewster thought she performed very well? The evening's conversation stimulated Brewster so that her journal entry a week later swelled to a nine-page retelling, including embedded dialogue, prompted by preparations for attending another dinner party on the evening of the journal entry. She would be going to sculptor Harriet Hosmer's, a gathering to which the Childses' circle had been invited. The past week's event had been "a splendid dinner" and "superb," she recalled. She remembered that after Nardi escorted her into the dining room, where they were seated together, she asked him several pointed questions. "We talked first about the unfortunate Emperor of Mexico and the unhappy

Empress [Carlotta]; of Nardi's visit to them at Miramar and their visit to Rome." She acknowledged that "his account was simply a surface one, but interesting all the same. He revealed no diplomatic secret, never alluded to the French Emperor, avoided all mention of the murder of Maximilian and the sad insanity of Carlotta." Although disappointed with this meager, surface description from one who "was behind the scenes," she understood his politeness and political restraint: "How much he could have told! . . . It was a nice study . . . to observe how cleverly this experienced Roman prelate treated the subject and kept out of everything tragic and historical."[31]

In her reflections, Brewster turned from Nardi's restraint to her own clever behavior: "I let him handle it without interference, made no remarks, but listened with deep interest," but "what would I have given to have been at liberty to question him!" Brewster took liberty, however: her desire to "have a little amusement" overpowered her own restraint. As she explained, "When Mgr. Nardi was through, I thought I might repay myself for my self denial. . . . I selected the subject of the coming Council." She imagined that "Nardi prepared himself to talk well-bred platitudes," but she "sent his banalities up into the air by coolly asking" where she might "get a copy of the Syllabus" then under discussion by the Vatican Council.

Brewster at this point in her journal notably changed her narrative style to direct dialogue, capturing more dramatically Nardi's voice and their performative tête-à-tête. When he asked her why she wanted the Syllabus ("not available in any bookstore"), she explained that Childs, their host, had assisted her with "several engagements for journal correspondence in the United States," that the Council's operations were "the most novel and interesting subject of the moment," and that "naturally" she wanted "to be well informed as to its meaning and intention." She saw the document as "the best source of information." Almost immediately Nardi's visage became "as good a study as his account of Maximilian & Carlotta. He forgot his Italian savoir faire and burst—with a loud laugh."

Apparently, the male author and editor thought the female "was jesting" or perhaps ignorant. Capturing this dramatic performance, Brewster scripted, he "turned and looked me squarely in the face." In response, she "met his look without flinching and with a cool surprise." He attributed her brashness to her citizenship: "Ah you Americans are incomprehensible." Brewster continued her posing by asking "innocently," "Have I been indiscreet?" Longfellow, seated nearby and intrigued by the laughter, inquired of the conversation, to which Nardi responded: "She has asked me for an ecclesiastical document meant only for the private use of bishops as frankly as if it were the program of a concert." When Brewster explained to both men her desire for the Syllabus, as well as the Encyclical that accompanied it, "Longfellow was amused but . . . a little uneasy." Nonetheless, she believed her "apparent innocence and Nardi's bon homie . . . were reassuring."

However, as Nardi acquiesced to her good intentions, he merely threw her a bone. Instead of offering the important "papers" she requested, he granted her access to "all the functions and celebrations at St Peter's from St Andrea's balcony." From this location, "high up on the left hand pier of the dome," she and her friend Mrs. Read would have free entrance "not only all this season but also next year during the Council." Nardi asserted to the female correspondent, "descriptions of those . . . ceremonies will interest the general reader more than summaries of dry theological documents." The monsignor and editor concluded his polite gesture by turning the conversation to "less risky subjects," but not before he reminded her, "I am a journalist, you know, and can give you good counsel."

Nardi's patronizing advice emphasized an important gender distinction and a social reality. The position for a journalist as an eyewitness to events in St. Peter's would be important to sending engaging stories back home to interested readers, as Nardi noted. According to Grace Greenwood's accounts of Anglo visitors to the Vatican, the competition for views could get quite fierce, with some women sticking each other with hat pins to gain positions.[32] At the same time, however, his comment points to the surfaces of ceremonies—the flash rather than the foundation for potential political and religious changes. As Maurine H. Beasley has noted of nineteenth-century female reporters in Washington, DC, who wanted to write more than for the social pages but were relegated to the public galleries, Nardi effectively relegated Brewster to the balcony rather than giving her an insider's account of the action behind the scenes. Yet women such as Jane Gray Swisshelm, Mary Clemmer Ames, and Mary Abigail Dodge determined diversely how they would access political information to share with the public—whether through personal relationships and apart from the press rooms, or by pushing for access to political spaces. Brewster, like these contemporaries back in the US, continued to push to get the information she wanted.[33]

Brewster's conclusion to the entry magnified her strategic negotiations with Nardi, who, as he reminded her, was a journalist. She labeled him a careful, "clerical politician." This summation implicitly linked the male Italian Nardi and the female American Brewster as professionals and writers as much as Catholics, concerned about the fūtures of their careers. Brewster believed she outdid Nardi with her sly questions, for after he departed the Childses' festivities, she confessed to Longfellow—"to his great amusement"—that the Syllabus and Encyclical both were already in her possession, thanks to "a Dominican friend." She had queried Nardi "in order to sound him." Noting that Nardi "has no intention of showing his hand to anyone," she continued, "My conversation . . . proved that he will be of no use to me in the matter of council information, only for ceremonies, special views of functions and the like."[34]

Despite her recognition that he would be "of no use" toward gaining the political information she sought, Brewster did enjoy "studying one of the most astute prelates of the Roman curia," and she sought further interactions. A letter from Nardi soon after the Childses' celebration of Longfellow indicates that Brewster quickly composed a follow-up note to the monsignor as well. It and three others written between January 30 and June 4 mark their engaged and playful relationship—not unlike Gould's with George Perkins Marsh. Nardi moved between English and Italian—a sign of the "epistolary pact" and comfortable exchange between the two.[35] There were playful comments about Brewster's perhaps indiscreet questioning over dinner. Nardi noted that he "never felt the slightest hesitation about the discretion," and referred to Brewster as "my dear and excellent friend." They exchanged ideas about language and about Greek literature. He asked her assistance in helping a "poor American friar," and he wrote of religious rituals such as fasting and used them as an excuse for not visiting her. And Nardi wrote of a potential later visit "to see this dear hospital at 107 Babuino." The "dear hospital" was Gould's work, which began in the palazzo where Brewster lived with the Reads.[36] This wide range of topics—from politics, to religious holidays, to cultural differences in religious fasting, to literature, to greeting friends, and to ongoing invitations—indicates the ways in which both Nardi and Brewster viewed themselves and their relationship. It consisted of much more than narrow political and religious journalism. Yet their desires as professional climbers certainly undergirded the communication. Despite the polite and friendly exchanges in these spring letters, however, their relationship went awry. Nardi would later banish Brewster from "the Papal precincts" for three years, due to her "enthustiastic report" of the Italians' entry to Rome on September 20, 1870, published in the *Newark Courier*.[37] That is, she supported the overthrow of papal secular power and the establishment of the Italian monarch's rule. Although Brewster temporarily lost access to the Vatican, however, she had not set aside completely her Catholic faith.

The APOSTATE!: Negotiating Roman Catholicism

> This is not the place to discuss whether this state of public feeling is right or wrong and whether it should be called indifference or Christian charity. I simply state a fact.
>
> —Anne Hampton Brewster, *Philadelphia Evening Bulletin*, December 9, 1869[38]

Despite claims she would "simply state a fact" rather than take a judgmental stance in her published correspondence, by the late fall of 1869, Brewster's writing for the *Philadelphia Evening Bulletin* demonstrated otherwise. She acknowledged—with her own biases—that many news writers were biased as she commented on various contemporary European newspapers and their highly opinionated stances in support of or against the doctrine of papal infallibility.[39] Especially evident in the months leading up to the decision on papal infallibility in the summer of 1870, her published letters in the *Boston Daily Advertiser*, the *Cincinnati Commercial*, the *Philadelphia Evening Bulletin*, and occasionally a paper under the Bishop of Rochester's jurisdiction reveal her political stance as a liberal American Catholic. Not surprisingly, all these publishing locales had large Roman Catholic populations. But throughout her two-decade career abroad, Brewster's more than 750 letters appeared in many more than these four papers. Roughly sixty newspapers throughout the US published her writing. While a dozen of these venues were ones with which Brewster had agreements, others were not. The latter papers would follow a common professional practice—lifting what they wished from her letters to fill pages and please readers. Content of both the authorized and unauthorized publications, discussed elsewhere, speaks to the image of Italy in the press by a Catholic female journalist and the publishers who were manipulating material for their readers.[40] Brewster's three contractual agreements in 1869 and 1870 provide an ample window to her career development and, at the same time, the skills successful women writers employed to meet challenges they regularly encountered.

Brewster's writings on the pope and the Vatican assert the expected stances of many American Catholics, as Paola Gemme has described them. American Catholics explained events in Rome in quite differently from the non-Catholic "liberals" who associated the pope with despotism and slavery and expressed "nativist" and "xenophobic" fears. Catholics wrote of what they saw as the anti-Republican elements emerging in the liberal and secular arena. Brewster contributed not to the progressive, liberal *Tribune* or the *Nation*, to which Fuller, Charles Eliot Norton, and George Perkins Marsh contributed, but sent stories to the *New York World.* She tried to maintain a moderate stance as a Catholic—yet her more liberal stance often slipped through, as her "disembodied," objective journalistic voice give way to the voice of the "eyewitness." Similarly, two decades earlier Fuller, and then Elizabeth Stoddard in the 1850s, had developed their followings with overt attention to themselves as eyewitnesses. Fuller developed a clear "persona" (differing from what appeared in her private letters) as she wrote about herself in Italy, and Stoddard "insert[ed] herself, in a thoroughly performative way," calling attention to "the widening canvas of individuals" who were Americans as she published in the *Daily Alta California*.[41] Though not the full-fledged stunt reporting of the 1880s, cultivated by writers such as Seaman (better known as Nellie Bly), eyewitness accounts had flourished during the US Civil War, with authors such as Alcott participating. As Edelstein has explained, Alcott exhibited multiple personae in her writing—a moralistic and didactic voice in her children's fiction, a sensational voice in fiction written pseudonymously as A. M. Barnard, and a reportorial voice for her Civil War *Hospital Sketches*.[42] Brewster also adapted to her situation, as Alcott, Stoddard, and Fuller had, always with a view to the financial end she needed. This chameleon or "chromatic" behavior did not signify a lack of belief or that she was void of opinions; she rendered her beliefs and feelings quite clearly, despite her claim to just state facts. Brewster's style, like that of other women reporters, had enough consistency and personality to be recognized and followed by regular readers. Overall, the breadth and variety of topics in Brewster's letters, along with her recognizable reportorial but personal voice, enabled news publishers to print her works as needed—whether on the front page, on the second page of international news, or in the women's section—all of which were locales in which her letters appeared.

Brewster's first letter, written in March, appeared on the front page of the *Philadelphia Evening Bulletin* on April 6, 1869—as did almost all. That month alone, she saw eight stories published, and in May and June combined eleven letters appeared. In August, September, and October that year, in the heat of the Vatican Council and the Italian soldiers' march on Rome, ten of her letters were published—an average of almost one per week. Only three among them appeared on the second page during this year. By the summer of 1870, paper editors bumped her accounts to the second page—but notably not to the "women's page."[43]

A December 9, 1869, letter, in which Brewster claimed to "simply state a fact" rather than take a stance about "Christian charity," captures the tone of others she wrote during the period as it provides examples of her self-revelation within the published correspondence and her sense of an interested American audience. At the same time it demonstrates her ongoing social negotiations to further her professional status—all as it focused on her interactions with Charles Isidore Hemans, whom Brewster had wanted to meet. Hemans, son of the well-known English poet Felicia Hemans, was "author of very valuable works on Rome and Mediaeval Art." Her account also reflects the humor with which Brewster wrote of Anglos traveling to Rome—perhaps influenced by Greenwood, whose humorous *Haps and Mishaps of a Tour in Europe* had appeared in 1854, and Mark Twain, whose *Innocents Abroad* had appeared as a book in 1869 (but had appeared first in serial form in the *Alta California*, and New York's *Herald* and *Tribune*). In another story of this period, Brewster overtly referred to Nathaniel Hawthorne, Fuller, and an American "Jonathan" character—a caricature Fuller had used to describe Americans abroad. The term had been popular since the years of the early Republic. Brewster, like Fuller, employed it to comment upon Americans' notably rough edges—especially when compared to other Anglos and Europeans.[44]

In the letter about Hemans, Brewster wrote of having attended a reception where she noted a striking figure—a "gentleman" who, in spite of his otherwise noble physical features, looked like "a Melmoth or Wandering Jew." That is, Brewster visualized him as a character type, likely drawn from Charles Maturin's gothic novel *Melmoth the Wanderer* (1820) and traditions of the European legend of a man cursed to be forever homeless. She learned from a Catholic English woman, "more Papaline than the Pope," that the man was "THE APOSTATE!" Brewster employed the Catholic English woman and Hemans to discuss humorously the contemporary status of religious diversity. Most people, she explained, were no longer bothered by "such spiritual . . . tumblings" of conversions and apostasy. Furthermore, as a news correspondent, she was "not . . . to discuss whether this state of public feeling is right or wrong" but rather to "simply state a fact."

Notably, Brewster described this encounter on public pages—not in her private journal as she had when revisiting the dinner with Nardi. Here she overtly explained her strategies to readers. By conversing with the English woman, she negotiated an introduction to Hemans, whom she immediately flattered. "I told him of his mother's poems always occupying one apron-pocket when I was a young girl, and of the instruction I had received from his books. With such an appreciated beginning, what man would not succumb! So we sailed off on what Jean Paul [Richter] called 'a high cool sea of conversation.' I think I was inclined to be a little more expansive than I should have been under other circumstances." Her "expansive" gushing with "the apostate," Brewster suggested, was an intentional performance meant to impact her "more zealous English sister," who politely said her goodbyes "with an expression of pitying sorrow on her face." Brewster confessed that the departure "amuse[d]" her "greatly," relishing for her readers her position as untroubled by Hemans's deconversion.

In fact, Brewster continued with his visit to her home "within a few days," in which she outstaged Hemans in two ways. First, when he arrived, she just "happened . . . to be reading his new book, 'Mediaeval Christianity and Sacred Art in Italy.'" She had carried it with her to greet him, pointing out "how far the leaves were cut."[45] As they visited, Hemans "amused" her with "his constant and sharp little grumbles" about the church's censorships, including the confiscation of "a box containing several copies of one of his works." Brewster laughed as she explained her view: "If we are willing to go through the proper private channels all difficulties disappear." She easily found "forbidden book fruit" whenever she wanted. Hemans, by contrast, "would scorn to use means that were not open to all the world." He summarized with regret, "'Ah, indeed! Yes! Here in Rome law bows to interest and influence.'" Brewster's response revealed her ethics: "All over the world, my dear Sir! . . . Laws are only meant as outlines on a very broad margin. Discreet persons can always walk freely on the margin, if they please."

Brewster's anecdote about her encounters with Hemans reveals much about her strategies as a news correspondent. Her outward persona in this published letter was one of professional drive and success. She saw herself as "discreet," able to "walk freely on the margin," and as one to whom "Rome law bows." She differed from the norm and deserved preferential treatment. Yet unlike the newspaper "stunt women" and "sob sisters" who later in the century influenced writers such as James to create characters such as Stackpole, she emphasized not her body but her brain. In sum, Brewster illuminates Fahs's depiction of female journalists who supported themselves through foreign correspondence and engaging in American "*expansionism*." The writers "not only observed the customs of other countries in ethnographic-style pieces, but also, in a number of intriguing cases, wrote extensively about politics—including both U.S. foreign policy and the internal politics of other nations."[46]

However, Brewster's writing also reveals her understanding of *creating* the news. As she reported regularly in the spring and summer of 1870 with updates on the Vatican Council and the Italian soldiers' entry into Rome, she referred more than once to the cable news her American readers would have received already. To maintain their interest and her appeal, Brewster's letters had to elaborate in feature style on what readers already knew something about. Similar to today's *Washington Week* or *Sixty Minutes*, Brewster provided a weekend in-depth discussion for those with time and interest. The story of her interactions with the zealous English Roman Catholic and "THE APOSTATE!" Hemans is merely one example of her entertaining accounts.

Another glimpse of Brewster's understanding that newspapers and journalists created the news appears in accounts of the Vatican Council and the Italian soldiers' march on Rome. She quoted from *L'Opinione*, the *Official Gazette*, and *L'Italie*, noting differences of details in each, wondering which contained the truth, as they contradicted each other.[47] Some US papers had more interest in this reporting than others. Stories she sent to the *Cincinnati Commercial*, for example, are more detailed about the council than the ones for the Philadelphia and Boston papers, which focus more on arts and which socialites are visiting—perhaps because Brewster knew her audiences. Additionally, as the council and news of the new government waned, she wrote increasingly about excavations—sensing that she could continue to cultivate her readers with history and the arts—and drawing extensively from her relationship with Lanciani.

Brewster's professional stance comes to light as well in her journals. As she readied letters for publication, Brewster for the most part used copybooks to prepare her letters with careful crafting, although occasionally (such as the dinner with Nardi celebrating the Longfellows) she repeated items almost verbatim from her journals. The journals were more personal accounts, and they often differed drastically from the published revelations. For example, as the published story on Hemans disclosed Brewster's liberal reflections on faith and "spiritual tumblings," her journal entries during the same period demonstrated, as discussed previously, her anxieties and concerns for spiritual success. This divided attitude emerged also in writings about her relationships with women, whom she considered as necessary but as problematic as men to her sense of success.

Women Loving Women: A Necessary Circle of Admirers

> Decidedly this journal must be a locked one if I mean to put in it all the curious experiences I have.
>
> My life a moi is no one's. . . .
>
> —Anne Hampton Brewster, Journal, January 1872[48]

Brewster pursued relationships with men such as Lanciani and Nardi because of her professional visions. The same was true for men whom she encountered only briefly on social engagements, such as Hemans, or with appointments to visit their artist studios or to study Italian. But there were others—both men and women—with whom the relationships reveal values beyond the professional. Her relationship with Davidson is one example. Brewster's letters to Davidson included not only gossipy and biting comments about Lanciani and Tincker but also on theology and philosophy, reflecting her need for intellectual stimulation. But significantly, they developed at a period in which her relationship with Lanciani was on the rocks. She was in need of an admirer—one who would bolster her esteem, motivate her professional work, and prevent her from feeling isolated. With Davidson, as with Lanciani, Brewster exhibited an intense desire to be in control. Her use of parental terms of endearment in the relationship reflects this urge, as she regularly wrote to the man twenty years younger as "mio figlio" (my son) and signed herself "your madrina" (your godmother).[49] In fact, Brewster continually surrounded herself with younger men, and she took advantage of this difference. In one letter to Hunt Jackson, Brewster referred to Lanciani as "the dear boy" who "rub[s] his hands with delight and say[s] in baby like English, 'Oh so nice, so nice!' "[50] Another example is the American sculptor Albert Harnisch, who also was twenty years younger than Brewster, and with whom she shared lodgings for almost fifteen years.[51] Quite different from the deeper intellectual engagement with Davidson or the professional gift exchange with Lanciani, the relationship with Harnisch provided financial support; similarly, it provided emotional esteem and a sense of control. He often traveled with Brewster, as in 1873 when she lived in Bagni di Lucca and translated Lanciani's book. This company also provided her a sense of safety and assistance. As she expressed, "travelling without 'maid or man' is no pleasant business for me."[52] These companions contributed to Brewster's "pleasant business" by offering her a sense of authority, surrounded by others she believed she controlled. Sometimes—as with Lanciani and Harnisch—Brewster's sense proved erroneous.

Brewster's relationship with these men illuminates the circles of women with whom she interacted, revealing value beyond social and professional negotiations. Brewster wrote of her dependence upon such "friends," for example, in a long journal entry that noted not only the young Anna Vernon but also Brewster's "new friend" Grace Bristed, who was "delicious: soft voiced refined, clever, witty and a lady in every sense of the word."[53] Brewster explained with dismay, "I shall never see as much of her as I should like, because she is a young rich widow . . . younger than I by some twenty yrs." The sensuous language reverberates with Brewster's relationship earlier in her life with the older Charlotte Cushman. Most important, however, the conclusion of the entry on the younger Vernon and Bristed suggests the endpoint to which all these relationships delivered Brewster. It provides a key that unlocks the numerous journal entries about women—the "curious experiences"—which Brewster chose to not write about publicly. The revelatory key is that Brewster was a woman devoted to her vocation more than to intimacy with another. This end is the one to which her initial utopian visions led her.

Brewster capped the entry on the two younger women with her inability to go out because of her age, as a woman in her mid-fifties:

> any one who sees much of me must come to me as I am less and less active every day I live. Next year I must find a house or apartment more convenient: on a lower floor in a more easy position. It was all well enough when H[arnisch] was willing to wait on me; but he is prosperous, busy, and indifferent. . . . I have not accepted the fact that he has been growing out of all need of me.[54]

Brewster needed a circle of admirers—whether male or female—who "needed" her more than she needed intimacy. This need and her marriage to her work appear most forcefully in Brewster's writings about women.

Among the signs of Brewster's needs are numerous jealous jabs at female literary figures. Brewster interacted with many of these women socially—for professional ends—although she did not necessarily admire them. She wrote bitingly in her journal of "those Yankee literary women," such as Louise Chandler Moulton, who had written the 1876 poem in her honor, and of "Miss Peabody." As she explained, "They live in little compartments of intellectuality, are always en evidence always regarding themselves in the little mirror of their tiny reputations and strutting accordingly." She wrote of "Miss Preston the authoress . . . from Salem Mass: She has lately gone into the Catholic Church. . . . she belongs to a little set where she is an oracle." And Brewster wrote of a gift volume of poems by Annie Adams Fields, wife of the Boston publisher: "they are very pretentious and shallow, no originality in them and an immense deal of classical gush. Mrs. Fields was always a tremendous poseuse."[55] Brewster did not like the performances and posing she saw around her, which she saw even Preston attempting, as the recent convert discussed Davidson's falling out of favor with Roman Catholic leaders. Of course, Brewster regularly posed to accomplish her professional goals—as her published account of Hemans and her journal entry about Nardi acknowledged.

Among the Anglo women such as Carson and Tincker, who lived in Rome for longer periods and with whom Brewster had the opportunity to develop more intimate relationships, a pattern appears: initial bonding, followed by a relationship gone bad, like fish and guests after the third day. With Tincker, the relationship became challenging because of Brewster's concerns with the fellow Catholic convert's illness and her fictionalizing of Brewster. Carson wrote kindly of her neighbor in the palazzo soon after the South Carolinian's arrival in Rome in 1872. But after June 1882 their relationship degenerated, in part because of Harnisch's commission for the John C. Calhoun memorial statue, which both Carson and Brewster claimed credit for engaging. The conflict became even more challenging, as Anglo-Italian circles were small. Seeing male visitors calling on the neighbor, such as Roman Michelangelo Caetani, the Duca di Sermoneta, and the Anglo social set such as the Terrys and the Storys, the two vented about each other in their letters and journals. As Brewster wrote in February of 1885, "My neighbor Miss Carson is a cross to me also. I shall be so happy to be where I need not run the chance of meeting her on the stairs."[56]

Most telling, however, are the entries surrounding the women Brewster met through Cushman's circle, such as sculptor Harriet Hosmer and the novelist Amelia Edwards. Hosmer almost immediately embraced Brewster upon her arrival in Rome in 1868. They attended vespers at St. Peter's, enjoyed long, leisurely afternoon rides about the city, and took tea together in each other's lodgings, laughing over Hosmer's humorous anecdotes. Brewster even wrote of crimping Hosmer's hair on one of these occasions, upon learning that Hosmer had never seen crimping pins before casting eyes upon them at Brewster's home—most likely in the room where she groomed herself, a rather private and intimate space. They traveled together outside of Rome, taking a week-long "frisk" to Orvieto in the spring of 1874. And they attended the races together, where Brewster watched Hosmer's horse Blazer win the steeplechase. By the winter of 1875, however, Brewster wrote of fatigue with Hosmer's and William Wetmore Story's "theatricals." Hosmer had written a futuristic play, entitled *1975*, which Brewster deemed "dreary, tedious & stupid"—in script as well as in performance.[57] Hosmer inscribed a gift copy of the published script for Brewster, to "My Diana," with the request, "Pray accept a copy of my play with much love from the author."[58] After the performance Brewster summed up her fatigue with the Anglo-Italian social circles, an attitude that frequently appeared in her later writings: "I am very tired of it this year and pose for an invalid so as to avoid invitations and to be able to stay at home. I do so enjoy my solitude, my studies, my leisure and myself!"[59]

Nonetheless, Brewster continued to write periodically of meaningful interactions with Hosmer. In June of 1876, for example, the two took an invigorating drive to Albano, in the hills southeast of Rome. The morning sun on the poppies and the beautiful sunset later stimulated Brewster, but even more so she fed on the conversation. Brewster's reflections the following morning ranged over more than sixteen pages in her journal:

> Hattie and I talked, and talked, and talked as we always do. She is very fresh and vigorous, like a clever little man. There is no pettiness in her; a deal of worldly wisdom, an immense amount of reticence, an entire freedom from trifling confidences, no feminine gushes and outbursts, no loose feminine thinking aloud. She is just a cunning charming little man in her mode of talk and thought and intercourse with others.[60]

Brewster described the day's activities as though she might have been envisioning a future article. The length of the drive, the arrival time at mid-morning, the ruins along the way, the gardens, luncheon at 1 o'clock, resting in their rooms afterward, and other moments are weighted with descriptive details. The account oozes sensuality as well. For Brewster, the time passed quickly when she was with Hosmer and, she noted of their conversation, they "seize[d] the thoughts out of each other's mouths."

Among the topics were "politics of the day," "public news," "art matters," and George Eliot's new book, *Daniel Deronda*. The characters of Grandcourt and Gwendolen's family, with their "free manners," surprised Brewster, as did the author's seeming "acceptance" of them—a contrast to Brontë's Jane Eyre and her "refusal of Rochester's money during her engagement." Brewster asked Hosmer whether the world "had grown less nice" in the twenty-five years that had passed between the two novels' publications, but Hosmer would not answer—in a manner that "showed her cunning." Brewster continued, "Hattie is no stream. She is solid, sagacious and deliciously wise." In fact, "to avoid agreeing or differing with" Brewster, Hosmer cleverly changed the subject, sharing an anecdote about Eliot's "mode of composing." For Eliot, writing was "laborious" rather than "easy work"—it was "a torture."

She crafted "every sentence in her mind before putting it down on paper," an idea that Brewster avowed as a misunderstanding, employing her "own mode of writing" as her evidence. For Brewster, her perspective stood as the center of truth.

Brewster's and Hosmer's conversation that day also touched on the woman who brought them together—Cushman—and her relationships with women. Reflecting on her own time with Cushman twenty-five years earlier, Brewster noted the older woman's desire to "reign" in any relationship. More recently, the victims had been Matilda Hayes and Emma Stebbins. Cushman and Hayes "fought like cat and dog"; they would "throw brushes & combs at each other." Hosmer "had heard of the private fisticuffs between the two women" and had "counted them as gossip," until she witnessed an altercation prompted by jealousy over Stebbins's arrival in Rome. Brewster recounted the event in her journal, employing labels such as "victorious amazon" to describe Hayes, who spouted hateful words toward Hosmer, as Hosmer tried to remove Hayes from the fray. Hayes attempted reconciliation in London years later but Hosmer refused. However, Hosmer "did not seem to feel any [lingering] disgust against C. C."

Brewster, by contrast, wrote with judgmental comments and outrage about both women. Not only were they "women over 40 yrs of age!" but also were "people of nice intellectual culture and good social associations." Brewster wrote more positively of Stebbins, who moved in with Cushman after Hayes left. She was "a soft . . . quiet ladylike woman, a good woman" who "yielded to C. C. blindly." The relationship lasted through Cushman's death, and was good for both women, although the ever-reigning Cushman "let out the tiger in other ways." As Brewster summarized, "she was bitter and abusive and full of hate towards many persons." But expressing sympathy for Cushman's final illness (breast cancer), Brewster concluded, "Poor poor woman! How she suffered those last years. She had everything her fondest, wildest ambitions had craved. Position, reputation, great wealth but was ravaged devoured by a cruel malady—Poor poor Charlotte Cushman!"

Brewster's reflections on Cushman and the trip to Albano—on changing attitudes toward marriage, authorship, and relationships among women—likely were fed by her recent experiences. Cushman's death that year had touched her, of course; but only two years earlier, in 1874, she had mourned the death of her musical friend Mary Howell, with whom she had corresponded passionately during her first trip abroad and for years afterward. Brewster expressed longings for Howell in her journal, both before and after the musician's death. Brewster's early financial successes in Rome brought her hope that she could write to Howell, "here is a home whenever you are tired of hard work & dependence on others." After learning of Howell's death, she wrote, "Oh my darling my darling how am I to live without you. . . . She was more to me than anyone living. Her letters were the joy of my existence. She was my audience."[61] Also prompting reflections in the winter of 1871–72, Brewster had opened her eyes to female–female relationships as she briefly and intensely intertwined her life with novelist Amelia Edwards. Brewster met the English author of "Barbara's History" and other "agreeable clever" romances late in 1871. The sculptor Percival Ball, who was creating a bust of Edwards, put the two women "en rapport." Fifteen letters and a copy of Edwards' *Ballads*, which she gifted to Brewster in 1872, provide a window on this relationship, which waned after the winter months that year but continued through November of 1873.[62]

Edwards wrote first in response to "beautiful flowers" Brewster had sent to the novelist's lodgings at 26 Piazza di Spagna. Notably, Brewster instigated the relationship. Whether Edwards served as a source for future published news or as an inspiration, Brewster would learn about another woman writer's life and profession through this connection. Edwards gushed of her flowers, "I have had nothing so lovely to keep me company since I left my Gloucestershire roses to their long solitude." She planned to call on "Miss Brewster" the next day. The letters that followed this note of thanks lost their formality, as greetings and closings became more passionate. One began "My dearest" and apologized for not having been able to visit. Edwards had hurt her back "jumping over a fence the day before yesterday" and had "not felt well since." But she underscored that she would visit Brewster "somehow" before leaving for Naples. Another apologized for having returned home at midnight to find she "had taken up & carried off" a couple of Brewster's letters, which she would return the next morning. Was it the intimacy of sharing private letters or Edwards's questionable behaviors that caused her removal of them without Brewster's knowledge? She did not explain but only concluded, "miss your lovely little hands half a million times." Edwards also tried to arouse jealousy, writing in another letter to Brewster about a young woman named Lucy, whom she referred to as "Miranda," in relationship with a "Caliban" in the Anglo social scene: "I am in a bad way with regard to that young woman just at present. Her hands, as small as yours—& her hair won't be any comparison—but it is a delicious hand for all that—soft, Warm, yielding, like herself. Oh my!" She continued sharing her admiration of this other woman, "I have a vast mind to take Miranda serious, right away, for good & all—for better or for worse, to cleave to her in a serious legitimate way, & settle down abroad. What do you say? Oh my! When I come back from the Della Valle, & have dropped her at her hotel, I will . . . tell you all about it; her, the theater, etc., etc., etc."

Complementing these letters, Brewster's journal serves as another source of information about the quickly developing relationship, providing thick details of multiple encounters. Like those with Hosmer, these encounters prompted long, reflective journal entries with a tone of shock, scandal, and surprise. Brewster frequently compared Edwards physically to Stebbins, but her demeanor was nothing like the latter's "soft" and "quiet ladylike" behavior. Based on Edwards's novels, Brewster had expected "a tall muscular imposing woman." But to the contrary, Edwards was "middle size younger & prettier than . . . expected." She "impressed" Brewster "as being rather pretty & not more than 30." She had a face "something like Mary Howell's & something as Emma Stebbins." Even her conversation differed from Brewster's expectations: "positive" and "enunciations of opinions, assertions quite after the manner of Emma Stebbins." Edwards demonstrated "a shrewd smile on her really pretty mouth" and gave off what Brewster saw as self-confidence which said, "I am contented." Although she praised this "general appearance" that was "unassuming but self collected," admirable because "as if entirely apart & with herself," the woman who preferred her black velvet, diamonds, and pearls scorned Edwards's dress—"as a guy of course," in the style of Englishwomen, plain and "not well fitting." Brewster also sensed something negative in Edwards's "shrewd smile" and the "cautious look in her eyes"—something "antipatica"—not nice—perhaps too calculating and "not spontaneous."[63]

These tensions between Brewster's expectations and surprise, between what she deemed pretty and admirable and what seemed too harsh and direct, run through her journal entries that winter. After this first encounter, the development of the relationship during the coming weeks and months pushed Brewster to write of what she labeled "women and women." She reacted emotionally to Edwards having "fallen desperately in love" with her and expressing it through "the oddest things" she "says and does." Edwards's behavior caused Brewster to write in January of 1872, two weeks after the two met, "Decidedly this journal must be a locked one if I mean to put in it all the curious experiences I have."[64]

The passages on Edwards waver between delight and dismay, as Brewster wrestled with her emotional reactions to the attention. She described Edwards's behavior as "passionate in her caresses," as she playfully called Brewster "old woman" because she was "over 53." Of this attention Brewster exclaimed, "beautiful! Oh dear how droll it is—women always fall in love with me—always have; more than men." She quickly added, "yet I have had my full share of masculine adoration." She continued boastfully, "Miss Ed. is the second woman this winter who has paid me this compliment." But then, as though recalling a poisonous snake in the weeds, she drew back, noting, "Mme Gaggiotti Richards frightened me out of my wits one Sunday—since then I have lied and avoided her in fifty ways." Although Gaggiotti was "beautiful," she had not the characteristics of Edwards, who "au contraire is gentle delicate and refined." Brewster gushed about Edwards: "I like her extremely—indeed, I love her after my fashion, which is a sort of maternal older sister way."[65]

As Brewster elaborated on her view of "women and women," she described her own position as regal and Empire-interested, rather than devoted to a single lover:

> How unnatural it is for women to adore women passionately. Now I love my own sex dearly, but as I said before, it is in a maternal sisterly way. I never make them jealous—I never interfere with their aims or ends except to further them if possible. I am somewhat like the Empress Catharine of Russia when she was in her youth, working for her empire. I in my mid age am working for an empire of peace and good will. I have a serene happy air with everyone. I extend politeness and attentions to all.

Brewster continued, boasting of her ability to be indifferent and of others envying this detachment. She believed she exuded "a sort of sympathetic atmosphere which surrounds every one caressingly," and that "almost every one feels its influence." She bragged about the way she had been able to establish herself in Rome, "without fortune or connections—and not by brains alone either, but mostly by kindness, generosity, putting myself aside thinking of others and knowing how in the center of the world to live alone."[66]

The irony of Brewster's comments sparkles, for she *did* have "connections"—her Philadelphia contacts such as the Reads and the Peacocks gave her a kick start. And although she may not have considered herself to have a "fortune," the property her family owned and of which she inherited a portion provided her partial support and financial freedom as she set out to follow her later vocation in Rome. Her "brains" contributed to her successes, as she noted her strategies. However, what she considered "kindness, generosity [and] putting herself aside," some such as Tincker saw as the opposite. Brewster kept herself at the center of this decision "to live alone." Other writings about the news correspondent reinforced Brewster's comments. For an article in *Lippincott's Monthly Magazine* years later, for example, J. R. Corson described Brewster not only as a journalist of "spirited and well digested articles which we so heartily welcome" but also as "one of those full-souled woman whose very presence made sunshine in a circle," who gave "at once the impression of a very amiable person." Corson went further to explain that "her forte lies in a discriminative charity and a genuine and sympathetic kindness toward all men."[67]

But confirming a view of herself as separate and apart in her journal, Brewster twice cited Emerson, author of the essay "Self-Reliance," as she reflected on relationships. First, she quoted erroneously from his poem "Fate." Emerson's lines emphasize the maternal and domestic nature of one who chooses *not* to go to war: "Who bides at home, nor looks abroad, / Carries the eagles, and masters the sword." The person focused on domestic life forgoes weapons of violence and battle and instead *nurtures* eagles, who will later potentially soar. Brewster wrote, "Who bides at home nor goes abroad / Masters the Eagle & carries the Sword."[68] Brewster's point was that she remained separate; however, her twist of the poem's closing line presents her as dominating by brandishing a weapon within a domestic space. Her pen was her sword. Notably, the masculine weapon imagery Brewster chose in 1872 would shift when she wrote of Lanciani in 1881 that she "gave in, woman like" and had "buried the hatchet."

Brewster's second channeling of Emerson, "Keep thyself free as an Arab of thy Beloved," cites his poem "Give all to Love." The poem shifts from directing readers to "Leave all for love" to the final lines' imperative, "Keep thee to-day, / To-morrow, forever, / Free as an Arab / Of thy beloved." This directive applies, the poem's speaker explains, when an ever-beloved and adored "maid" rejects the speaker by suggesting that her heart lies elsewhere—with "a joy apart from thee." Then the lover should let her go, for she is merely one of many "half-gods." Her departure alone will allow room for the full "gods" to "arrive."[69] Brewster applied what she labeled Emerson's "wise môts" to her own status: "My Beloved now is a little choice refined society, the admiration of a certain set of cultured people—I get it but I keep myself free as an Arab—My life apart, my life a moi is no ones and so enough of myself and good night dangerous little book—good night."[70]

Instead of closing the entry and her "dangerous little book," however, Brewster continued with thoughts she believed she "must mention," revealing ambivalences that kept her from sleeping. She wrote of Edwards,

"She is perfectly fearless, she glories in danger, carries a pistol about with her. It seems so droll in a little delicate creature, as she is refined and quiet to have such mannish ways." This surprising and "mannish" energy caused Brewster to confess, "I must say, while she interests me greatly—indeed I feel a strong drawing to her." While the "exaggerated developments of hers do not please me," Brewster continued, "they amuse me greatly—But it is not nice to feel amused where we wish to respect & love."[71]

Even the next day Brewster was unable to set aside the previous evening's musings. As she prepared for a ride, she "fell into a reverie over women and women." Witnessing poet Mary Howitt's daughter visiting her parents, Brewster observed the younger Howitt's "prim little figure undulating and floating along." She contrasted the daughter—"dear, healthy minded intelligent . . . little woman as she is"—with her parents, whom Brewster found "so intelligent and so dull. So good and so stupid." Yet Brewster praised their life for its "sweet sweet odour" and its having "been honest and quiet and pure." Although their simple life was "a little unripe and raw," it was "healthy and strong." The Howitts were momentarily admirable in contrast to Brewster's own temptations with Edwards. As she noted her own struggles:

> Ah what perils and quicksands I have been graciously led over! Sometimes falling while deep in the mud but forever holding up the borders of my mantle from soil. Very beautiful is this power which holds and guides us. It is a certain proof of immortality, of the existence of a Supreme Being—this sense we feel that some strong good influence takes hold of us and brings us all right when we have been all wrong. We go on in evil doing & evil feeling & suddenly awaken and find ourselves lifted over into the right path as by an unseen hand. We go into our memories & hearts from the remembrances of anger and wrong and find the whole washed out and nothing but love and peace & goodwill. It is very wonderful. It is God!

Brewster's reflections continued, describing a declined invitation to ride with Mary Healy and her mother. She "shivered with repugnance" at the invitation, because Mary was "intelligent" and "bright" but also "so hard and sharp and spiteful." She was "the rose branch full of thorns and no flowers." The mother was no better—"ordinary, good as gold but fat & vulgar." Undermining her commentary on being Empire-interested, Brewster elaborated with snobbery and self-protection, carefully choosing her social invitations.[72]

Within this series of journal reflections, Brewster's repeated phrase, "Oh women and women!" . . . "Oh women and women!" indicates her unresolved obsession. In fact, she turned again to Edwards, who had written "the drollest letter" earlier that day. Brewster's typical ambivalence reigned. She wrote first, "I really loved this clever woman," and then, "I shall try to place our relations on a more sensible footing." She explained the rationale—"otherwise they will end as violently as she is beginning them. May God help me with her, for I really wish to keep her as a friend." That evening, the two visited. Rather than being "overpowering," as Brewster had feared, Edwards "was fascinating and charming," and her presence lifted Brewster's fatigue. The next morning Brewster summed up in her journal, "She refreshed me greatly—amuses me by her foolish adoration of me, which is very senseless, but I can easily draw her into her natural good sense, and then she is ravishing." Brewster reflected dreamily on the prior evening. Edwards had described the painter Giovanni Costa's landscapes with poetic vividness, gazing with half-closed eyes in the firelight. She had demonstrated her understanding of multiple instruments, discussing musical composition. And she had talked of her 5000-volume library. Although engaging and admirable topics, the ever-judgmental Brewster added, "She has had curious experiences, I fancy with women. After all, human nature is as rampant in my beloved sex as it is in our master Man, and yet I like to forget it. I like to think of women as half angels, as we should be."[73]

By early February, Brewster had had enough of Edwards, writing "When she is with me, she bores me to death." In her as-yet-unlocked journal, she confessed:

> Miss Edwards' star is setting in my heaven. I never have been so woefully disappointed in a person. She is painfully exaggerated & absurd, drinks too much wine, keeps herself in a state of unnatural excitement all the while; makes indecent love to women; in short, is disgusting. So there's an end of her—I am trying to slip her off easily without a noise. Luckily for me she has fallen in love with another woman—has married her regularly with a ring—that is, as regularly as such a thing can be done; had a wedding dinner and they both made great asses of themselves, I've no doubt.

Indeed, Brewster even expressed delight with this marriage: "I am enchanted, for it relieves me from her overpowering love." Then she turned the entry into a dramatic dialogue, capturing Edwards's typical behavior: "She flounders down on me with her hungry eyes and asks me if I love her every little while." Edwards would then respond, "I'm awfully fond of you. But you don't care a tu'pence for me—No you don't—You are cold, changeable without devotion. I know it. Still all the same I'm awfully fond of you." Brewster would laugh and attempt "to turn off the disagreeable absurd questionings." She summed up: "How absurd between a woman of forty odd and a woman of fifty odd! This love making between women at any time is frightfully unnatural—it is positively indecent and disgusting."[74]

A final reference to Edwards appeared in late February, with a record of dinner at William Wetmore Story's home, which Hosmer also attended. Noting Edwards was "egotistical and insufferable," Brewster revealed her ongoing obsession with "women and women" by continuing for two paragraphs about Edwards's "silly twaddle & stuff." Brewster wrote that she wished she "might never see her again," concluding "she bores me so frightfully."[75]

Lines scrawled in the poetry volume, *Ballads*, which Edwards gave to Brewster, sum up their relationship. The author inscribed on the title page, "from her faithful & attached friend." But a telling inscription in Brewster's hand lies deeper within the pages. A lyric entitled "For Ever" recalls Emerson's poetic imperative to "be free," which Brewster had cited in her journal. The speaker in Edwards's poem, for years "a silent suitor," promises eternal love to his beloved, "A cold and careless mistress." In Emerson's poem, the lover is commanded to let go of the "beloved." By contrast, Edwards's speaker vows his love is eternal, whether returned or not. Brewster wrote her thoughts at the poem's end: "Pretty much a fool that man."[76] Reinforcing her view of independence and non-intimate relationships, Brewster unwittingly foreshadowed the arc of her career.

She surrounded herself with women but also eschewed female social circles focused on marriage and getting married. Even when considering the popularity of "Boston marriages" in the period, it is impossible to overlook how Brewster's journal accounts in Rome, marking her joys at spending time with women such as Hosmer, also include entries recording her fears of intimate relationships with others, such as Edwards. Her most intimate relationship was with her writing. Yet Brewster preserved the gift books and letters—rather than destroying them—suggesting that she needed these icons of adoration as much as a circle of physical admirers. They stood for her as memorials of this period of success early in her utopian venture abroad.

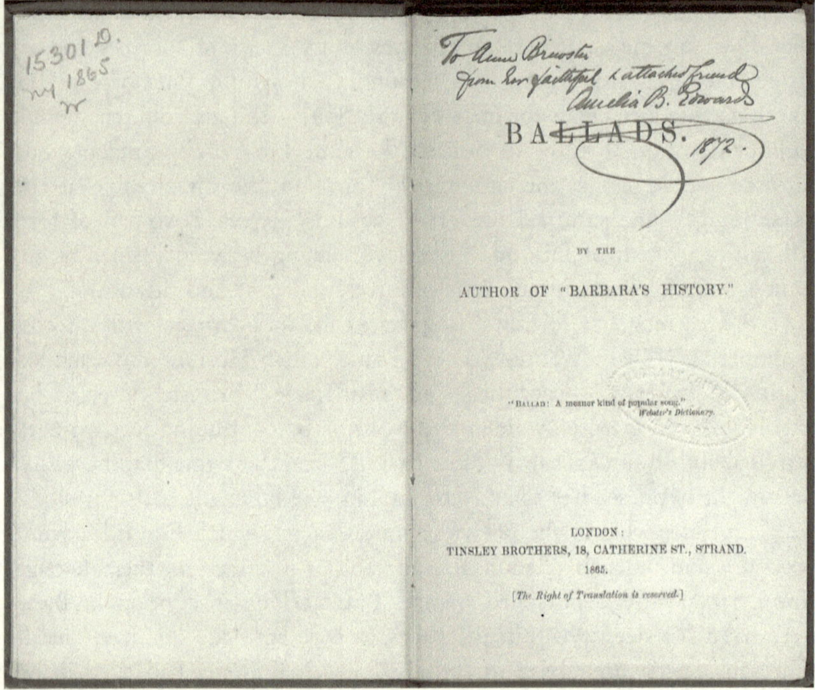

BALLADS.

BY THE

AUTHOR OF "BARBARA'S HISTORY."

"BALLAD: A meaner kind of popular song."
Webster's Dictionary.

LONDON:
TINSLEY BROTHERS, 18, CATHERINE ST., STRAND.
1865.

[*The Right of Translation is reserved.*]

Figure 9.1. Brewster's gift copy of *Ballads*, from author Amelia B. Edwards, "her faithful & attached friend." Credit: The Library Company of Philadelphia.

Brewster's Life Alone: Utopian and Dystopian Visions

In spite of her diligence and competence as a writer, Brewster's self-positioning as a genteel and self-righteous woman caused her to be left behind. Both betwixt and between, she did not want to leave behind the mores instilled since childhood, or to be as brazen as she considered other female professionals abroad. Despite her numerous journal entries about Cushman, letters to Howell and from Edwards, and her numerous conversations with Hosmer, Brewster shied away from female–female intimacy. She was not interested in women's rights, although she accepted from Julia Ward Howe a copy of her "Appeal to Womanhood Throughout the World." As Brewster wrote to her friend Davidson, she did not follow the path of her "Boston sisters." Rather, she believed "men were made to be our masters"—even when in communication with one she thought had "no logic" and was "a stupid man." This deference to men and a maintenance of the carefully guarded, genteel female figure stayed with Brewster to the grave. And it took her to the grave, professionally speaking, when other newspaper women were making new careers for themselves.[77]

During the decade in which American journalism was increasingly commercialized and depoliticized, Brewster was fully engaged with the politics of Rome. Her numerous imprints from the bustling city—both authorized and unauthorized—reflect a woman abroad fully engaged with national issues, near at hand in Rome and in the distant US. While women writing for newspapers have been described as absent from the international scene until the 1880s, Brewster clearly was present. As a female Catholic, Brewster wrestled with roles not only of papacy, monarchy, and new parliament, but also of sexuality and gender. Quite poignantly, Brewster's private writings throughout her career underscore the difficulties of a single professional American woman abroad. For Brewster, Italy fostered a career full of challenges, rather than providing an easy Arcadian escape from family and social conventions which she may have imagined initially. Her quick thinking, flexibility, dedicated labor, and negotiations necessary to a literary life emerge when her published writings are laid bare by more personal ones. Likewise, they shine a small light on the newspaper work of post–Civil War, Reconstruction, and Gilded Age America, illuminating how one woman attempted to fulfill her utopian visions with her calling abroad. Despite her efforts, and in large part due to her choices about societal gender expectations, Brewster realized utopia was ever beyond her reach.

Chapter 10

Caroline Crane Marsh

"The Power of Doing a Great Service"

> Knowing that you are in the way of seeing so many persons & have the power of doing . . . a great service . . .
>
> —Mrs. J. Haight to Caroline Crane Marsh, 1868[1]

Mrs. J. Haight wrote to Caroline Crane Marsh in 1868, putting on paper the view the Anglo-American community in Italy held of the ambassador's wife. Haight knew that because Marsh came in contact with "so many persons," she had "the power of doing . . . a great service" for those in need. Her position prompted many to write as Haight did, asking for assistance. Haight's letter did ask not that Marsh relieve the needs of the impoverished by providing food, clothing, or shelter. Nor was it about organizing "a ways and means committee" as Gould had, or about raising funds for Salvatore Ferretti's orphanage or school—all works with which Marsh had been involved during that year and would continue in the coming decade. Instead, Haight asked that Marsh hire a piano instructor, Dina Vannuccini, whose family needed help. She offered Marsh the double opportunity for doing service to both society and her family, as Haight knew that Marsh was parenting her niece and that piano instruction was deemed important to female education. She explained that the capable Vannuccini would provide much to the Marshes. As niece of Luigi Vannuccini, conductor of the orchestra at La Pergola, Florence's opera house, the young Vannuccini had fine musical abilities.[2] Additionally, she was also a capable dressmaker, providing fashionable clothing for their friend Madame Corsani in Via Castellani. Marsh's role, Haight's letter suggested, would be not just providing some financial assistance by employing Vannuccini but, as important, managing a young, unmarried woman whose family was unable to provide the guidance and supervision they deemed necessary. Marsh would serve as a surrogate mother for not only her niece but also for the Italian woman in her employ.

These recommendations to hire the young woman capture the numerous requests Marsh received for rendering her "great service"—especially among families connected to the Anglo community abroad. In 1874 a Mrs. Hamilton would write asking for practical advice on funding a music school in Milan, prompted by Marsh's involvement with the Ferretti School. The same year, Marsh's niece Mary Crane would write asking for advice on clothing for her upcoming trip abroad. Then, in 1875 Marsh would become involved in a complicated case involving a large sum of funds "borrowed" by a family in need. The funds were never returned. The sad situation, not clearly articulated in the archival materials, touched several in the Anglo community in Italy.[3] The letter from Haight, then, captures the varied textures of the *ambasciatrice*'s life abroad. Written almost a decade into Marsh's time in Italy, when the Villa Forini in Florence was her home, the letter renders both the reputation she had gained as well as the vexed position of a woman whose interests went beyond the domestic and social to the literary and political. These myriad interests and abilities would continue well beyond her husband's death in 1882, which prompted Caroline's return to the US and the writing of her third and longest work, George's biography, only one volume of which was published.

In addition to responding to numerous requests for help from friends and family, Marsh regularly assisted her husband. In fact, her position as dutiful wife both enabled her activism abroad and required that she assert herself within the confines established by his career. She balanced these numerous requests for service, her duties to George, her roles as surrogate mother, and her literary inclinations and aspirations. One poignant example of Marsh's balancing acts occurred the year after her receipt of the Haight letter, when she was back in the US dealing with the Marshes' home and library in Burlington. Then as throughout her time abroad, she wrestled from afar with her responsibilities as a surrogate mother.

Surrogate Motherhood: The Power and Service of Letting Go

I have advised her . . . and I trust her good judgment for the rest.

—Caroline Crane Marsh to nephew Alick,
on his sister Helen, 1876[4]

Within the convincing letters Marsh wrote to her husband in 1869 about the library, when Marsh referred to "our young people here and elsewhere" she employed a possessive phrase that speaks to the vision she held of herself as responsible and accountable teacher and surrogate mother. Numerous nieces and nephews, as well as other young people, would be enriched by the loaned volumes. Such parenting and teaching played a significant role in Marsh's self-understanding as an *ambasciatrice* and activist abroad. Even without biological children, Marsh understood herself as a mother, as she became a mother first to George Ozias, George's young son by his first wife, and to numerous nieces and nephews, who traveled, visited, and lived with the Marshes during much of their time abroad. At the time of writing the library letters, niece "Carrie," Caroline Marsh Crane, traveled with her aunt.[5] Carrie had been with the Marshes in Piedmont from 1861–65 before returning to the US. Another niece, Elinor, known as Ellen, daughter of Caroline's youngest brother, Abiathar of Indiana, went to live in Italy for five years when she was thirteen.[6] Great niece Mary Edmunds visited in 1873 and was "very happy in Rome . . . with her aunt."[7] In addition to these family members, Marsh "adopted" children or "wards" associated with the orphanage and school in Florence.[8] One of the mother figure's greatest challenges in this role was relinquishing the power and positive influence she wanted to have in their lives, especially as they became adults and she extended service to them as a wise and caring older woman. And it was difficult from a distance, when the Atlantic separated her from family members in need.

Such letting go was not without pain. And it did not mean that Marsh relinquished her interests. She wrote to nephew Alick in 1876, for example, of previous advice for Helen, Alick's sister and Marsh's niece, who later married the European Guglielmo d'Arcais:

> I have advised her if she would conveniently manage it, to spend a couple of weeks with Mr. and Mrs. Edmunds, in case

> they repeat their invitation. Of course, I could not press it too much, as I am too far away to know all the circumstances, but I have advised her from the only point of view I can have, and I trust her good judgment for the rest. We must after all live our own individual lives, and I never feel it right to over advise one who has come to Helen's age and who has always shown good judgment thus far.[9]

Voicing her view that it was "never . . . right to over advise," Marsh extended and continued the advising, however, by recounting to Alick her desires that Helen visit the Edmunds, George's US congressman nephew and his wife, in Washington. Marsh's writing on the subject suggests that she likely hoped that the brother Alick, knowing his aunt's concern and efforts, might exert some sibling pressure as she wrestled with such letting go.

That is, all these "children," despite blessings they added to the Marsh household, also added concerns. The stepson George Ozias, whom Marsh had gained upon marriage to George, died tragically in 1864 in his early 30s, estranged from his father.[10] Earlier, in the 1850s, while George Ozias and Marsh lived in Burlington and George was in Washington, DC, the parents corresponded about their son's troubles. Niece Carrie, who had planned to join her aunt and uncle in Italy for a second stint abroad in 1875, died when the *Schiller*, the boat on which she was crossing the Atlantic, went down. Niece Ellen succumbed to her fragile health soon after leaving her aunt and uncle, with whom she had lived for several years in Italy, upon her return to the US. And Marsh wrote of a nephew, Milton Crane, "after a most exemplary early youth, which gave a very brilliant promise, he fell into bad habits while in the army, which ended in ruin and death."[11] Marsh's writing about all of these exude poignant, heartfelt emotions.

As young women the nieces also brought with them to Europe interests typically accompanying young people approaching adulthood. Helen had written home to Alick in the fall of 1871, for example, asking him to share information with his wife: "Tell Laura to be in the fashion, she must make her hair look as if it hadn't been brushed for six weeks—the more snarls the better—more of fashions next time—."[12] But less humorous and more serious is a letter of two years earlier that Ellen received—a love letter from Mario Gigliucci, written in the spring of 1869, partially in Italian and partially in English. Knowing that she would be en route to Paris, he asked her to stop in Bologna so that he might see her at the station.[13] For some reason ripped into pieces, the letter remains in the archives, preserved for present

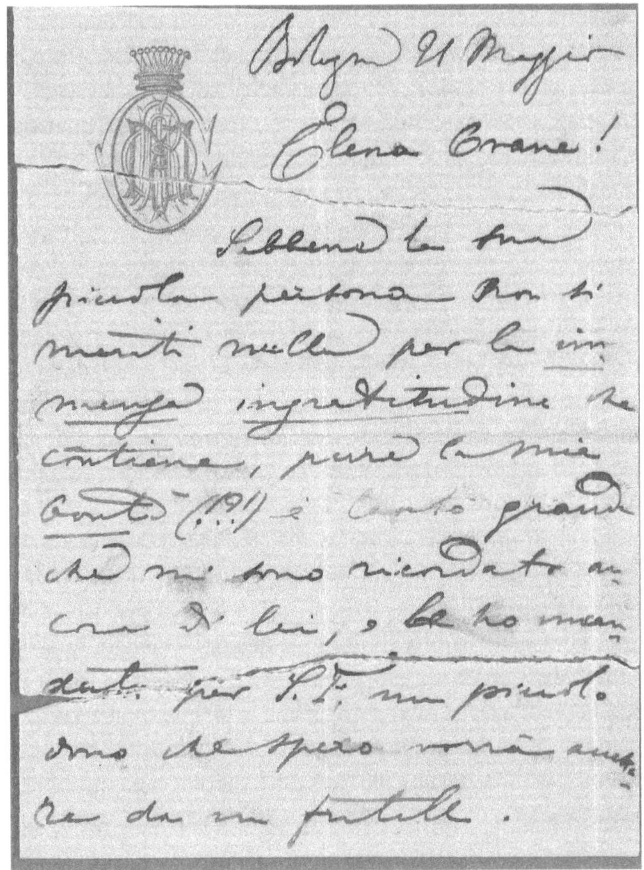

Bologna 21 Maggio
Elena Crane!
Sebbene la tua
piccola persona non si
meriti nulla per la im-
mensa ingratitudine che
contiene, pure la mia
bontà (!!!) è tanto grande
che mi sono ricordato an-
cora di lei, e le ho man-
dato per P.T. un piccolo
dono che spero verrà accetta-
ta da un fratello.

Figure 10.1. Torn letter from Mario Gigliucci to Caroline Crane Marsh's niece Ellen (addressed as "Elena"). Credit: Manuscripts and Archives Division, the New York Public Library.

readers as a remnant of a romance. The scraps raise some questions: Why two languages? Why torn? Why saved? The letter meant something to the young woman who chose to save it.

Information on Gigliucci fleshes out the letter's context and illuminates its content. His father, the Count Giovan Baptista Gigliucci, Governor of Fermo, had married English opera soprano Clara Novello in 1843. Clara's sister was the well-known English author Mary Cowden Clarke; they both were entrenched among the Anglo communities in Rome and Florence. Clara's new international family soon consisted of not only sons Giovanni

(1844–1906) and Mario (1847–1937) but also daughters Porzia (1845–1938) and Valeria (1849–1945). (The latter two attended Brewster's receptions and signed her autograph book.) Although Clara had left the stage when she married and began to have children, she returned to it for financial reasons after the Count lost property in the 1848 revolutionary upheavals.[14] Having birthed four children in six years of marriage, and in spite of her prominent position among Anglo circles, Clara was not considered appropriate in all her behaviors, likely not providing as much motherly guidance as some women such as Marsh deemed beneficial. The second son, Mario, was about twenty-two years old when he wrote playfully to Ellen in the spring of 1869.

The letter's date, May 21, fell just before Marsh set off for the US and left Ellen in George's charge. Marsh's second letter to George, written from Burlington while she worked with the library and household possessions, shows an equal preoccupation with this "daughter." Marsh worried that George would place Ellen in a bad situation. First, she asked that he "tell dear Ellen her letters are an immense comfort to me, though I cannot answer them." Her comments indicate that Marsh responded to her husband rather than to her niece but also that Ellen had written to her aunt about a possible visit to the Gigliucci family. Perhaps without a satisfactory rationale to send directly to the young woman, Marsh explained to her husband, "I must . . . say a word about her not going to the Gigliucci. It seems to me better that she should remain with you—and if you could manage to leave her in some nice family in France or Switzerland till I return I should make no objection, but of course you would only leave her where you felt most sure that everything was right."[15] Marsh's suggestion that Ellen might be left with "some nice family" and not with the Gigliuccis resonates with parental concern.

Mario's language in his letter tells more. Opening it in formal Italian, he attempted to guilt Ellen by referring to her as his "evil little sister" and by noting that she had not sent even one line acknowledging a photo he had sent her. Then he added, "I can't go on giving da Lei to you"—the formal mode of speaking and writing—and so "must try and finish in English." Attempting to bridge a gap in their relationship, he wanted to write in her mother tongue. Sarcastically he added, "I suppose your diplomatic duties didn't allow you to darmi ricevuto [acknowledge receipt] of my photo." But Mario, like a good salesman, provided a means of resolving that excuse by enclosing some paper—the equivalent of a self-addressed stamped envelope. "Now that I have sent you some paper," he wrote, "I hope you will find time just to tell me you pardon my ardor in send [*sic*] you such a gift." Finally, he expressed his desire to see her and to maintain their thoughts of each other: "I hear you are going to Paris. Will [you] be such a ~~goose~~ (I beg your pardon, duck, I mean) as to let me know when you pass by Bologna that I may see you at the station. Goodbye, Helenska; I hope you remember some times your brother Mario."[16]

Gigliucci did not disappear from the Marshes' lives after writing this letter. He reappeared in the *ambasciatrice*'s journal entry of November 6, 1873, when she wrote that the young man was "with them much," adding that it made her "sad to a degree he can't imagine." At this point he was connected with another niece, Alick's younger sister Helen, who had been in Italy since October of 1871. Nine months after the journal entry, in the late summer of 1874, Mario's mother, Clara, wrote to Marsh, acknowledging three letters received, Helen's sudden departure back to the Marshes, and Gigliucci's departure for London due to "his youthful impetuosity." Writing of the falling out, Clara was "provoked" at Helen's sudden departure but, ever the doting mother, she blessed the son who, in her opinion, had done nothing wrong. Decades later Gigliucci entitled his memoir *Reminiscenze d'un uomo inutile ovvero "Reminiscenze inutili d'un uomo più inutile"* (Memories of a Useless Man or, more truthfully, "Useless Memories of an Even More Useless Man.")[17] The volume does not mention the young Crane, but the title suggests one reason that Marsh did not want her niece "going to the Gigliucci." Perhaps directionless and without parental guidance, the young Gigliucci likely did not exhibit the New England drive that the surrogate mother wished for any of her nieces' potential future partners.

This string of correspondence among the two families provides a glimpse of not only Marsh's concern for her nieces' well-being but also her concern for her husband—and perhaps for herself as an often-distant spouse. These concerns typically emerged as negotiations in her correspondence. She wrote from Burlington that stressful summer of 1869, "As to your plans I am too far away to advise you and will not trouble you by asking why you do this or do not do the other thing—all I have to say is be careful of yourself, *for my sake*; that you will be careful of our dear Ellen I am very sure." Was the care to which Marsh referred about her husband's health? Or about his reputation and relationships? This period was the one in which Gould's husband also was away in the States, and she wrote frequently to George. The letters from the period stand as extensions of the writers' lives, revealing how Marsh had to let go of ideals for both her niece and her husband, while she continued to present herself as a dutiful wife and mother figure.[18]

Marsh's surrogate children magnified the sheer burdens of managing the household's physical needs. Even with the household help the privileged *ambasciatrice* enjoyed, ongoing and frequent guests later in life added to her responsibilities. While George "was delighted," and "far from resenting" what might be considered an "incursion" when nephew Alick's six children arrived in 1881 with their governess (also a relative), the expanded responsibilities were part of Caroline's expected duties in nineteenth-century culture. While he chatted with the children at teatime, she ensured teatime occurred. And she also saw that the children either studied or got out the door to keep from distracting her husband while he worked in his library.[19] These management labors only intensified as Marsh aged.

Another example from these later years emerges in accounts of the Swedish boy Carlo, whom the Marshes adopted in 1877, when Caroline was in her sixties and George was nearing eighty; Carlo was then two. They called him "Young King Karl," and George "spoiled him inordinately." This "constant source of amusement" to the ambassador in his later years, however, was not necessarily one for the *ambasciatrice*. She wrote in her journal one rainy August day in 1880, for example,

> Held a serious family council as to the best way to correct some of our little Carlo's worst faults. With all his sweetness of temper, which is unparalleled in our experience, & all his strong love for us, he seems to have no power to resist temptation. . . . [He] breaks promises about what he will do and not do . . . accepts punishment, very sorrowful about it, then wakes up and does the same thing the next day—so as to never appear to learn in a way that will change his behavior. . . . [I am] also having trouble teaching him to read. In everything else his intelligence is unusual.

Marsh sought advice from the head of the kindergarten in Florence, who responded that she had "never known so clever a child who was so unteachable."[20] Letting go of feelings of responsibility associated with this service of mothering was an ongoing process for her.

Serving Schools: Fundraising at Home and Abroad

> If I could spare a couple of weeks here I could get a good deal. As it is I hope to do something.
>
> —Caroline Crane Marsh to George Perkins Marsh, 1869[21]

> [W]hat a great business man or woman rather you would make. What profession would you have followed?
>
> —Mrs. C. Allen to Caroline Crane Marsh, September, 1869[22]

> Yesterday went to a meeting of our Orphanage Com. Debts over 7000 frcs!
>
> —Caroline Crane Marsh, Journal, 1873[23]

Marsh not only wrestled with her service as a mother figure, overseeing the adopted Carlo as well as another "ward" a few years earlier, she also struggled to balance her domestic responsibilities with those as a social activist. When she was in the US in 1869, overseeing the library move and also writing to George with concern for niece Ellen, Marsh was also fundraising for Italian causes. Letters of the period illustrate the vocation begun intensively in Florence the previous year. Marsh had been prompted in part by Gould's infectious behavior—which continued throughout the decade—and was noted by those who wrote to Marsh with their financial contributions. While her time in Turin and Piedmont had introduced her to European life and salon culture, by the late 1860s after she and her husband had moved to Florence, Marsh had found a calling with Ferretti's school and orphanage. Marsh's goals focused on females in particular, as the Florentine project "aimed to 'teach Italian females to respect themselves by compelling men to respect them.' " During the period, Marsh wrote in her journal less as she engaged more with needs around her, as "an active reformer" devoted to "secular schooling, and succoring scores of wretched wives, woebegone daughters, and abandoned infants."[24] At the same time, Marsh's journals and letters—especially beginning in 1873—voice the questions and despair with which she faced these tasks. By 1875, when Gould died, Marsh was in the thick of family losses, such as Carrie's tragic death, and ongoing struggles with the local school. From that point, Marsh seems to have directed her energies more toward literary work over which she had more control and toward her family.

The first letters about the Florence school appear in 1868, from Anglo women prominent in Europe, such as New York philanthropist Augusta Astor (wife of John Jacob Astor III), the Tuscan "Queen Bee" Janet Ross, and Martha P. Wurts, of Delaware, who spent much time in France. The latter wrote to Marsh, for example, of having received "the interesting report of 'the Orphan Asylum in Florence.' " She had sent a copy "to Le Comte de St. George, who interests himself in all good works," she explained, and it would "give . . . pleasure to distribute" additional copies. A Miss Forbes likewise promised to share the information, writing to Marsh, "My sister and I are very willing to take an interest in the schools & we shall mention the project to any one we know." She also ordered one ticket, with a promise to pay for it as soon as they saw each other face to face—she didn't trust the post with the money.[25]

The fundraising intensity grew with Marsh's trip back to the US in 1869. Letters to and from prominent US and British families refer to financial contributions to the work and to Marsh's role on committees. For example, Cyrus West Field, founder of the Atlantic Telegraph Company, responsible for the first transatlantic cable connected in 1858, sent funds through Marsh's nephew Alick.[26] Marsh wrote to her husband from Newport, almost boasting of being hosted on opposite ends of "the island" by Mrs. Bull and Mrs. Paine. The latter, with whom she discussed her "plans to do something for the orphan school," had "promised . . . her best help though she thought there were few people here likely to give for such an object." The result was a luncheon for "about forty people . . . invited on purpose to meet" the ambassador's wife. Marsh wrote, "I am satisfied that if I could spare a couple of weeks here I could get a good deal. As it is I hope to do something." Marsh listed names of important guests and fundraising prospects: Boston business magnate and philanthropist Gardner Brewer and his family, who owned a villa in Newport; a Mr. & Mrs. Wales; activist Julia Ward Howe with her niece Annie Crawford, who had been raised in Italy; and critic, essayist, and travel writer Henry Theodore Tuckerman, who knew Italy well. One guest, a Dr. Thayer, offered very specific non-monetary help. He "was most kind in promising to put any statement I would make into the hands of the wealthy residents & visitors in Newport." While Thayer promised to spread the word, others offered to host events where they would collect funds. For example, the wife and daughter of prominent New York attorney Dudley Field, both named Jeannie, wrote to Caroline about the cause, apologizing that everyone was scattered from the city in August. Instead, daughter Jeannie offered as she wrote from Germantown that she would like to host Caroline in New York before her departure for Italy in October. She would then "transmit" afterward all funds collected for Marsh's "good cause."[27]

A few days later, after leaving Newport and arriving in Burlington, niece Carrie wrote to George as a scribe for her aunt, with "regard to the villa for the orphan school." She noted, "Mr. Edmunds asks if there is no way in which the property can be secured to American residents by trust.

That is as near what he said as I can remember. I dare say I have said it wrong—do you know what he means?" Carrie's humble inquiry indicates how much this project was on her aunt's mind. Marsh sought to troubleshoot such issues as securing a property for the school, and she engaged the minds of men such as George's nephew, the congressman Edmunds, to do so. Carrie closed the letter with an important message to her uncle. "You must not be anxious about Aunty," she explained, noting how "surprised" everyone was "at the wonderful way in which she bears all these many demands upon her strength." Marsh appeared "lovelier every day" that she was in the US. This new vocation seems to have strengthened the *ambasciatrice* as she asked for aid, although she may have gained strength from being back among supportive family and friends in the US.

News of Marsh's work continued to spread. In September that year Miss L. T. Wheeler sent "a mite for the Florentine House," and Mrs. C. Allen wrote, "What a great business man or woman rather you would make. What profession would you have followed"? In fact, Marsh's activism inspired others. Allen continued, for example, "I do long to see more of you. You always incite me to good, and I think I should be a better woman for the companionship." Family member Mrs. Lyndon Marsh wrote from Woodstock, Vermont, in December of 1870 that she had read an account of "the schools in which you expressed such an interest" that appeared "in a New York *Observer*." She added, "I trust you are prospered in your good work."[28]

Throughout the 1870s letter writers in Europe, such as Luisa Gadda and Augusta Limone, as well as those in the US, sent words of good wishes, emotional support, networking tips, and financial contributions. Josephine Graham, for example, offered in 1874, "make any use of my name you choose in regards to the Orphanage and the Fair." Gadda, likely the wife of Senator Giuseppe Gadda, wrote of her support, "I promise you to do for your generous cause all that is in my power," and encouraged Marsh to proceed: "we desire the continuance of your precious benevolence." Limone wrote twice from Rome in 1874, referring to sixty lottery tickets Marsh had promised "to dispose of" and to a drawing on Easter, following two days of "Exhibition of the prizes" that were tentatively planned to be in "the hall of the Scuola Superiore Femminile" in Via Palombella. Limone's letters speak to the ongoing link Marsh had to Gould's work in Rome, as the *ambasciatrice* was expected to distribute so many lottery tickets, either by purchasing them herself or selling them.[29]

In contrast to such records of fundraising successes and strength in the letters, however, Marsh's less-frequent journal entries and a few letters provide another picture. Entries from the fall of 1873, in particular, erupted with trials—of arranging teachers, of debts, and of troublesome committee members. In July her sister-in-law, Mrs. E. Crane, had written from East Greenwich, "I wish the Bostonians would build their church for 200,000 & give the other 200,000 to you for your orphanage—they will spend I fear more than they now say 400,000." Crane's vented expressions about local expenses for a mere building may have been prompted by knowing the orphanage's financial need.[30]

Marsh picked up a similar thread about obtuse indulgences in the face of social needs when she wrote in her journal in November, while George was in Rome and unable to hear her concerns. She began with dismay over debt: "Yesterday went to a meeting of our Orphanage Com. Debts over 7000 frcs!" Three days later, she picked up the thread again, writing of the same meeting, and one out-of-touch, self-indulgent committee member, labeled politely as "Mme Blank."

> At our Committee the other day when the alarming balance sheet was produced there was much discussion as to what should be done to raise money to pay off the debts. A Fair for Christmas had already been decided upon—but one lady proposed a concert besides—another something else etc. At last one proposed to ask some ladies who were arranging for giving private theatricals, to hand over to the orphanage the proceeds of one of their evenings—the person who made the suggestion added, 'Mme Blank told me these theatricals would be very fine—not a dress was to cost less than 1500 frc.' Not a very brilliant change for the Orphanage I fancy—

Based on calculations of 1500 francs as about 300 dollars for a dress in 1873, or more than 6000 today, the price of each dress needed for the performance would be exorbitant.[31]

Simultaneous to such challenging meetings, Marsh was reading works on approaches to religion and social reform. Just after referencing the theatrical fundraiser's expensive costumes, Marsh remarked on her reading with comments that reveal her reconsideration of approaches to social activism. She wrote of Fénelon's assertion that "everyday acts" should have "a religious character"; of the "very suggestive" material in [James Anthony] Froude's "Philosophy of Catholicism"; and about "a curious book" by Charles de Ribbe, *Les familles et la société en France avant la révolution*, that "ought to be read by all of us Progressivists."[32] The string suggests more than Caroline's ability to read French and to keep up with the latest literature. This self-directed advice points to how French authors' ideas intertwined with Marsh's activism, combining to manifest uncertainties and frustrations. Would she give up her reform goals or revise them? Would she hang on to old methods, infusing them with new ideas, or employ new methods but attempt to teach old "truths"? Or should she give up entirely? Overall, Marsh's comments in the fall of 1873 indicate her openness to ideas that crossed national and cultural boundaries. They reflect theories of translation that George had inscribed more than a decade earlier and which she had experienced as she published her two translated volumes from German. She would live and act in ways that manifested her desires to understand and learn from the culture in which she lived.

Transformations of a Reformer and Litterateur

> Translation forces us into new trains of thought, demanding new forms of phrase; lifts us out of the rut.
>
> —George Perkins Marsh, 1860[33]

> Instead of talking oracularly like so many litterateurs, he is evidently trying to collect new truths.
>
> —Caroline Crane Marsh on Matthew Arnold, 1873[34]

Marsh expressed her desires to continue learning as she reflected in her journal on Matthew Arnold and his *Literature and Dogma*. A few weeks before the fundraising committee meeting, she wrote that although she did not find Arnold's ideas compelling, she read them "with infinitely more pleasure for knowing him personally." It was not the relationship with the author alone that moved her. Marsh explained that the touchstone was witnessing Arnold himself: "how completely he possesses the spirit of a learner. . . . Instead of talking oracularly like so many litterateurs, he is evidently trying to collect new truths." Notably, Arnold appealed to her because of his being "a modest listener where he might well assume to teach."[35] His openness to "new truths" reverberated with ideas George had published in his essay on "Translation," drawn from lectures he had delivered at Columbia during the couple's stateside stay after leaving Turkey and just before they left for Italy.

George wrote that translation "forces us into new trains of thought, demanding new forms of phrase; [it] lifts us out of the rut." Additionally, related to the concept of newness, George referred to "extemporaneous translation"—not preparing poetry for publication but rather "reading off into English a book or a newspaper in a foreign language." This type of translation engaged his wife constantly while she lived abroad, since daily demands with letters to local political figures, responses to invitations, and reading newspapers occupied much of her time. This "extemporaneous translation," George explained, "confers the power of readily calling up familiar or less habitual words and combinations," in the process "securing us against contracting a restricted personal dialect . . . which reacts injuriously on our own originality and variety of thought."[36]

George's ideas about translation providing "newness" and opening up a "variety of thought" echoed Germaine de Staël, who emphasized the role of translating for broadening a child's knowledge beyond "his own nation—a circle that is narrow" and "exclusive." Language study, the European linguist, historian, and philosopher explained, "combines precision of reason with independence of thought." She connected geographical region to language, and language to national character. This integral connection of language with "a particular culture" and "national character" lay at the heart of translation work, in her eyes.[37] Staël saw the translator's work as "negotiating universality through particularity." The "universal" would be the tool that would "do good for the human race."[38] Yet the translator must also maintain a sense of the particular. As Colleen Glenney Boggs has described the views of Staël and her American follower, Margaret Fuller, these women continually acknowledged difference, or the particularities within the universals, as they translated, even while attempting to recognize human connections across cultures.[39] Marsh, too, in the translating process, would acknowledge the importance of difference and gradually shed some of the judgmental American exceptionalism she originally manifested. Her private writings demonstrate this increasing awareness of her limitations as an American woman living abroad. Marsh's experiences in Italy and her translating, at both extemporaneous and literary levels, recognized and negotiated cultural differences without eliminating them.

In this period in which Marsh wrote of Arnold and an openness to new truths, she also read several works in French on Roman Catholicism and reflected on social activism in Italy—specifically, with the school and orphanage. At the same time, she was engaged with what it meant to be literary—a private author or one more publicly known. She had been a part of Anne Lynch Botta's salon culture in New York in the late 1850s and had written and translated. Now in this period in Florence, Marsh returned to thinking about what it meant to be a "litterateur," as she received letters and visits from those viewing her as an author, including literary figures such as Bayard Taylor. Taylor enclosed proofs of his poem "Lars" for her perusal and asked that she share it with Mary Howitt while he was away in Germany. Whether he was asking her advice or hoping for her support through stroking and distribution, his letter shows his respect for her position in literary circles. Also reflecting Marsh's stature as a literary figure, she had received a letter two weeks earlier from an admirer, who had confused her with author Anne Marsh-Caldwell. Marsh-Caldwell's publications included the novel *Ravenscliffe*, the short story "Emilie Wyndham," and works on the Protestant Reformation. As the admirer explained to Marsh, the mistake was "not unnatural," having "often heard of your talents in this line."[40] These figures indicate a belief in Marsh's "power of doing a great service" in the literary realm as well as in social and reform circles.

Another letter that arrived in 1873, from Marsh's sister-in-law, Mrs. E. Crane, likely prompted nostalgic revery and a rethinking of the *ambasciatrice*'s stature in Florence. Crane mentioned having found a poem Marsh had written in 1858, celebrating the thirtieth anniversary of the Kingsbury School in Providence. The poem, "Life's Lesson," was read at the event and then published in a history of the school that year—apparently Marsh's first publication. The poem celebrates women's roles and power to change the world—inviting alumnae to step up their efforts. The memory of that literary work, prompted by a dear family member, may have pushed Marsh ahead with her endeavors in Florence. But it may have caused her to retrench, as it invited her to rethink the optimistic "Lesson" she had delivered in verse more than fifteen years earlier. The poem applauds the "heroic" woman who will "leave her native shores" to "stand calm" amid "war" and "pestilence" where "heaps of tombless dead are lying." This generic woman abroad "tends the wounded, soothes the dying, / and lo! At her blest presence cease / The groan and curse, and all is peace!"[41] The didactic and optimistic poem invites comparison of Marsh's work to other litterateurs on her mind that year and her other imaginative compositions.

In addition to Arnold that challenging autumn, Marsh referenced the highly popular Fénelon, represented in the Marsh library and well known for the moralistic didacticism of his best-selling novel *Telemachus*. Marsh's journal entry about Fénelon's belief that "everyday acts" should have "a religious character," and knowledge of his method of teaching children through moralistic fables, provide a lens for interpreting her lengthy unpublished tale set in the Tuscan mountain village Pruno. The year's struggles, alongside views of translation as an act that opened her to new truths, suggest reasons that Marsh's tale remained unpublished.[42] The untitled and undated tale, featuring the hero Nastaggio, likely was written early in her time in Italy. Its setting, its characteristics, and her journal suggest that this moralistic and didactic literary endeavor was influenced by a collection she read while living in Piedmont, just after she had moved from the bustling urban capital of Turin to a more remote and rural area, Piobesi, outside the city.

When Caroline arrived in Turin in 1861, she brought with her not only her translating skills and past experiences abroad but also a pre-established view of Italy's oppressive subjugation to other European powers and the Roman Catholic church. She and other American Protestants were celebrating the religious liberty non–Roman Catholics in the Piedmont regions had been enjoying since 1848, ushered in by European revolutions.[43] For her as for many Americans who observed the political changes from afar, "Italy" provided a playground for enacting what they believed was the best America offered as model: democratic leadership, accessible education for the masses, and, through these two venues, alleviation of poverty.[44] This idea of "Italy" and its possible futures shifted for Caroline as she, who labeled herself a "Progressivist," religiously speaking, gained new information about the culture in which she lived.[45] Marital relations and covenants were ignored. She believed the problem was associated with—if not caused by—marriages arranged for the ends of economic and political power.[46] Within journal pages expressing shock, however, many also reveal Caroline being moved by a thread of human sympathy that tugged at her heart. She transformed from "moralist" to "informant as participant sociologist," letting "her rigidly egalitarian rustic New England Puritanism" soften, so that "she became less critical and more compassionate, less censorious and more self-deprecating."[47] While she maintained her American Protestant "Progressivist" stance and her view of companionate marriage, several journal entries reveal Marsh gradually let go of her ideals about missions and social reform. These changes emerged through extemporaneous and private, rather than published, translations.

Soon after their arrival in Piedmont, for example, Marsh met "Mr. Bert," a leader of the non-Catholic Waldensians, and was impressed by his knowledge of many languages. The next day she wrote of parliament at

Turin discussing the kidnapping of Jewish babies and other "evil" works of the Roman Catholic priests, "a story too scandalous to be believed," she explained, except "for the evasions" of those testifying, which gave the stories "substance." But by 1863 any simple anti-Catholic/pro-Catholic binary was confounded in her journal. She expressed frustration about political leaders, such as the Marshes' friends Vincenzo Botta and Massimo d'Azeglio, writing that such men changed their minds about politics and philosophy, but about religion they never did. Even when educated—that is, knowledgeable of other languages and cultures—they hung onto "superstitions" from their childhood. But by April of 1863, when the Marshes were settling in to a rural manor house at Piobesi southwest of Turin, Caroline negatively critiqued one of Waldensian Bert's colleagues, Meille, for a funeral oration he delivered. He did not understand that taking the public opportunity to make negative comments about Roman Catholics to an audience of primarily Roman Catholics was neither persuasive rhetoric nor the best practice for realizing religious reform. Other entries during the period when the Marshes had undergone the somewhat isolating move to the rural area on the plains of the Po demonstrate her changed household management, relationships, and cultural views. The move decreased urban visitors while it increased reading and writing time and opportunites for interactions, or extemporaneous translations with the gardener's family. When the village priest arrived to bless the Marshes' new home, for example, she did not pay him to perform the rite, which, for her, had no efficacy. She did, however, communicate with and pay the priest to bless the gardener's house. A month later she swapped tales with the gardener's wife. When Marsh confessed sadness due to missing family, her new confidant expressed surprise that even the *ambasciatrice*, with her material abundance, felt the pain of personal loss.[48]

Not long after both of these events, Marsh wrote of reading "a little anthology of Italian tales"—likely Temistocle Gradi's *Racconti popolari*, a volume of Tuscan stories—which was in the Marsh library. She explained that the three tales she read underscored challenges of village life. Two elements of Marsh's journaling merit attention. First, she transcribed into her journal rhyming lines of proverbs from the book without translating them. That is, some she paraphrased in English, and others she copied in the original language, suggesting she wanted to remember the latter to use as needed. Also, they reflect her understanding of the area, as she noted details of the proverbs unique to each village, such as the Baron Ricasoli's reputation in and around Siena. The tales point to regional isolation and difference, maintained through fear and warfare, even as Marsh recognized that unification was shifting long-ruling families' power.[49]

Whatever her reasons for reading, Marsh's extemporaneous translation of the published collection and the gardener's advice when he saw her reading them moved her. He recommended that Carrie, who was living with the Marshes, study tales from Piedmont rather than Tuscany, because they would help her fit in to the region, and he offered to find a local teacher for her. And it seems likely that these tales led to Marsh's creation of the lengthy moralistic story with the rustic setting, the mountain village Pruno, and its rags-to-moral-riches hero. Its topics include the value of literacy, the necessities of hard work and shunning frivolous parties, the challenges of arranged marriages, the power of the domestic realm, and the responsibilities of parenting—all topics central to Marsh's journals. But the tale includes also another theme: religious art as a vocation. Early on, the hero played his fiddle at dances. When he fell ill, a friar told him he "deserved it for going out to play at night-frolics." He then "broke" his "fiddle" and channeled his love of music into becoming the church organist. In addition to developing musically, the hero also became a visual artist. Enduring patience, hard work, and criticism, he carved first a crucifix in wood, then with marble. He left a Madonna on a hillside, then created a Saint Michael and a "Conception," based on pictures he had seen of "a young girl with her hands clasped, a crown of twelve stars on her head and the half moon and the serpent under her feet." Next he created a St. Anthony, another Madonna, a Martha, and a Magdalen. The story demonstrates that Marsh now shunned neither Roman Catholic aesthetics nor Mariology. The hero's concluding deathbed message reverberates with Marsh's transformed, more inclusive view, even while it rings out remnants of her New England ethic: "As to me I have always seen that he who works hard, and does all the good he can will get on somehow,—he'll get on, and never come to a bad end. God is for us all."[50]

Through her translations and her interactions with locals, Marsh's views of religious life, reform, and her own art evolved, especially as she recognized her limitations. The lack of a record of the Italian tale's circulation suggests that she may have lost faith in the efficacy of such moralistic stories as a means of reaching children. Instead, Marsh's reading and writing in 1873 reveal that she continued to believe in extemporaneous translation as a means of collecting new truths. Poetry had a place in that process.

"In Vain Have I Labored": Ideas of Italian Reform Revised

> Who saith the grief is light,
> To toil for years, and see no fruits requite!
> To feel thy o'ertasked powers untimely waste,
> To know their highest energies misplaced,
> To have labored in vain! (ll. 31–35)
>
> —Caroline Crane Marsh, "Frustra Laboravi!," 1860[51]

In that difficult year of 1873, where literary work complemented challenges of the Florentine school and orphanage, Marsh read—extemporaneously translated—Horace's first and second odes. She and George owned copies in Latin, Italian, English, and German, as well as a book on Horace's metrical style.[52] The odes range broadly in theme from artistic skill and patriotism to love and loss and war and peace. Marsh's references to Horace do not point to specific content, but her journal entries that November do express common themes of his poetry as well as those from a poem she had written more than a decade earlier. Marsh wrote pointedly of past sorrows while trying also to look ahead. While grateful for the eye physician Dr. Meurer, whose skill and treatment allowed her to be able to read again, she poured out on the prosaic pages: "The sorrows that have gone over our heads have not, I trust, either hardened or embittered our hearts, & while the gray of life's winter has settled down upon us we are still grateful for so much left, & not without the glorious hope of finding again all we have lost."

The poem "Frustra Laboravi!," published at the invitation of Abby Maria Hemenway in her anthology *Poets and Poetry of Vermont* (1860), captures similar emotions and is eerily anticipatory of the despair and hope Marsh balanced in the mid-1870s. The poem also speaks to the place of poetry writing for her. The writing process "functioned as a craft, where making—not being—was the dominant mode," as Paula Bernat Bennett has explained of female poets in the period. These "moments of substantive creativity" come to light within specific venues, the context of which illuminates the writing's value for the authors and for readers.[53] Marsh's poem captures the way in which she employed translation and literary craft to make her way through life's difficult periods and to visualize a different future.

The poem's Latin title, "Frustra Laboravi!," evokes the biblical phrase from Job 9:29 rendered in English as "in vain have I labored." The poem acknowledges past difficulties but refuses to give up hope for the future, anticipating entries that filled Marsh's journal pages in 1873.[54] Although no overt self-references appear in the poem, she seems to have written it in a moment when forceful waves of failed idealistic ventures washed over her. Indeed, the period of composition was that of intense financial need and future uncertainties, when she labored with her translations and wrestled with family responsibilities, such as George's young adult son George Ozias. The son remained financially dependent on his father and implicated in business problems in Vermont, where Marsh translated while George was in New York. The verses would have helped her process such experiences, just as translating Horace's poetry did. Notably, although the title suggests a religious tone, the verses include no appeal to the divine for delivery. Instead of a heavenly, spiritual, or transcendental realm, the poem exudes a connection with humanity writ large, while it grounded problems in allegorical examples.

Of typical verse style, the poem's eight five-line stanzas each end with repetition that lends the poem hymn cadence. Variations of "I have labored in vain" serve as a refrain, emphasized with a shift from the regular iambic pentameter of the previous lines to a break with fewer feet. This repetition, a broken anaphora, creates not a pleasurable, ecstatic experience but rather, as it is repeated throughout the poem, one of dulled numbness linked to grief and despair.[55] The first stanza, in fact, opens with these feelings of pain as common to every "human" whose "voice" will exude a "bitter cry" of weariness:

> "My strength is spent for nought!" This bitter cry
> Oe'r all our earthly moanings riseth high;
> For ah! No human voice shall ever fail
> To swell the mighty chorus of this wail,
> "I have labored in vain!" (ll. 1–5)

Following the first stanza's image of humanity in general, spent by laboring in vain, the sensations of despair continue with slight variation, as images of people who have labored in vain emerge. In the second stanza, for example, "The farmer sows in hope the golden grain" (l. 6), but "The torrid heavens withhold the latter rain," such that "The shriveled ear a sickly color shows, / And the poor husbandman no harvest knows; / He has labored in vain!"

(ll. 6–10). The next four stanzas turn respectively to merchant, parent, artist, and reformer, all of whom have "labored in vain!" for wealth, children, art, or social change.

Although Marsh was neither farmer nor merchant, she passionately noted in her journal the poverty of Italian farmers, who ate primarily grain. While in Turin, Florence, and Rome, she would witness Italian merchants struggle, but the merchant's description, "with pallid cheeks" and "Dark in his brow, [as] despair doth gnaw his heart" (ll. 11–12), also reflects what she wrote of her nephew Alick, as she saw him weaken and age under duress and encouraged him to visit Italy to relieve stress.[56] And she sympathized with any parents holding a "tortured memory" of "children" who met difficult ends, "Disgraced by folly and with crime defiled" (l. 17), as she had felt the pangs caused by her adopted children. Marsh wrote of her own experiences as she described the artist "with a strong passion stirred" who labored over "the thought . . . in . . . [her] soul" that often resulted in "the feeblest shadow of . . . lofty dreams" (ll. 21, 23–24). And, as the despairing reformer the poetic lines depicted, she would later attempt reform "with a noble zeal" (l. 33), while seeing "trusted weapons shattered in [her] hands" (ll. 26–27). The poem returns in its penultimate stanza from specific despairing laborers to the general situation of any "son of man" who "know[s] their highest energies misplaced, / To have labored in vain!"

Finally, though, the poem's last stanza turns to consolation through admonition. Marsh turned the poem from one focused on the vanity of labors to present an essential element of a meaningful life—suffering while laboring for what is deemed a just cause. The speaker explains, "there is a plaint more sad than this, / Breathing of darker, deeper, hopelessness— / 'In vain I have suffered!' " (ll. 36–38). Marsh's speaker directs the "mortal" reader to "take . . . heed / That of these fearful words thou have no need! / Else thou hast lived in vain!" (ll. 38–40). Through the poem's concluding stanza, Marsh justified the pain she had experienced while laboring—as surrogate mother, artist, and reformer.

The poem predicted the challenges Marsh faced in Italy and her adjustments to what she learned about her own limitations. Translating languages of other cultures contributed to that knowledge and her recognition of ongoing cultural differences. Its tone is a far cry from the optimism she exuded in her poem of 1858, "Life's Lesson," although it appeared in print only two years later. Her experiences turned to verse in that brief period stateside, before leaving for Italy, were a chrysalis containing the beginnings of what would develop further as she lived abroad again, engaged with Italy's political upheaval and Americans' desires to be a part of the changing cultural fabric.

The poem's positive final stanza also crystallizes Marsh's actions just before and after George's death in 1882, as she prepared to move on from doubts and despair with hope, into a new segment of her life. Marsh turned from emphasizing the education of Italians broadly to focus more specifically on the education of family members and the help she could give her nephew and nieces. She wrote on May 22 that year to her nephew Alick, for example, explaining the arrangements she was making for him and his wife, Laura Cornelia, to visit and the ongoing plans for their children's education abroad under governess Laura Vernon's care. She wanted Alick to assuage Vernon's anxieties about expenses, explaining how she and her husband had everything organized. They were looking for the perfect villa high in the Tuscan hills, where the price would be less expensive. She responded to her nephew's concern not only for Vernon's well-being but also that the stay of the large family not stress the older couple. Marsh insisted that she and George wanted everyone to join them.[57] Even this late in her time in Italy, she had "the power of doing a great service" for her family. Marsh's husband died in July 1882, while Alick and his family summered with the couple at Vallombrosa. Marsh's physical relationship with her husband ended there in the Tuscan hills—one of George's favorite spots and the site Gould had visited and written about two decades earlier for *Hours at Home*. Marsh, moved by the loss of her husband but not destroyed, within the year would supervise the packing up of the library once again, leaving the Villa Forini that had become her beloved Italian home, and find new ways to focus her utopian visions.

Coda

Residual Ripples

Hidden Lives & Unvisited Tombs

> Her full nature, like that river of which Alexander broke the strength, spent itself in channels which had no great name on the earth. But the effect of her being on those around her was incalculably diffusive: for the growing good of the world is partly dependent on unhistoric acts; and that things are not so ill with you and me as they have been, is half owing to the number who lived faithfully a hidden life, and rest in unvisited tombs.
>
> —George Eliot, *Middlemarch*, 1872[1]

> She hath done what she could.
>
> —Epitaph, Emily Bliss Gould memorial stone, Woodlawn Cemetery

When Marsh crossed the Atlantic a final time, she returned to the US to live near Alick and his family in Scarsdale, New York. Soon after, she began rereading her previous writings, her husband's writings, and many of their letters, in order to craft George's biography.[2] She wrote about political life, published in the *New York Evening Post,* and continued to study poetry, philosophy, and languages such as Greek. And, when her nieces traveled abroad again, they visited many of their aunt's friends in Rome, writing back to her about encounters with them. During these last twenty years, Marsh continued to read, to write, and to learn—sharing insights with those around her—most especially her family members, who looked to her for assistance.[3] She followed her lifelong vocations, demonstrating that to the *ambasciatrice*, transformation through reading and writing was not a singular event; it was an ongoing process. She gave voice to new insights about ethics and social action to her nieces, nephews, and a broader public through her private letters, newspaper articles, and her husband's biography. This voice lives on in archival materials that remain almost untouched, ripe for researchers interested in how an American woman's life was enriched by her writing and how her activities, including writing, had an impact upon many. Like the fictional character of George Eliot's *Middlemarch*, Marsh conducted many "unhistoric acts" that had their "diffuse" impact on the world. Her body was laid into the earth in the cemetery of St. James the Less Episcopal Church in Scarsdale, where a stone marks her grave. Beside her memorial stone stand those of nephew Alick and niece Elizabeth Green Crane. Marsh's husband's monument lies across the Atlantic in Rome's Cimitero Acattolico and in the company of John Keats and Percy Shelley—undoubtedly more visited than hers.

Brewster, who remained in Italy even longer than Marsh and wrote as voluminously, never sailed back across the Atlantic as a living correspondent. Instead, she retrenched from her Roman life to a quieter one in Tuscany around 1890. Resettling in Siena, where she had visited her friends several times throughout the years, Brewster perhaps was called by the familiarity of a place where the pace was slower than that in Rome. Her records suggest, however, that lower expenses, rather than a slower pace, attracted her. Once again she found lodgings, the Casa Bellugi at 25 Via del Casato, that lent her the space she needed for what she imagined would be continued writing—perhaps fiction this time. And she continued to have the privilege of some household help. Although she died in Siena without family, Brewster's final transit across the Atlantic was similar to Marsh's—in that her body traveled with books. Her extensive library, more than three thousand volumes when Philadelphia's Library Company acquired it, remains with her manuscripts as a record of the world that surrounded her in Rome. They speak of the networks she negotiated as much as of the ideas she admired. Together they reveal the relations and the unnoticed "effect" that her work had on the world. Notably absent from Brewster's collection is Eliot's *Middlemarch*, which she read in the winter and spring of 1872. Although she did not find it as good as *Adam Bede*, Brewster remained intrigued by Eliot's writing process and ability, manifest in her journal notes and her possession of John Walter Cross's 1885 biography of Eliot. Perhaps Eliot's powerful conclusion to *Middlemarch* did not sit well with Brewster, who, at the time she read the novel, was on the rise in her career abroad. Perhaps she could not anticipate that her life would be full of what would later be deemed "unhistoric acts"—"a hidden life"—or that her body would rest in Philadelphia's Woodlands Cemetery, next to her mother and her brother, in what would become one among several "unvisited tombs."

Gould, on the other hand, passing away in Perugia in 1875, at the height of her work in Rome, would become relatively sanctified—compared to Brewster and Marsh—through a memorial service, a memorial stone, and the institution that she left behind. Perhaps her surviving husband—something Brewster and Marsh lacked—was responsible. The memorial service honoring Gould after her death, held in one of lower Manhattan's imposing churches, and publicized on finely printed announcements, included speeches by prominent men such as the Reverend Howard Crosby. Within a few years of Gould's death, James determined to leave her work to the Waldensians, who continue to operate the institution bearing her name. Upon their guest house wall in Florence, a small plaque recognizes her generous spirit, and their archives at Torre Pellice include her among those featured in their online biographies. Gould's body was interred in Woodlawn Cemetery, then on New York's northern outskirts. Elsewhere in the cemetery, stones honoring the likes of Elizabeth Cady Stanton, Herman Melville, and Nellie Bly stand decorated with flowers left by visitors. Meanwhile, Gould's memorial, like those of Marsh and Brewster, appears largely unvisited. Neither flowers nor flags adorn it. Yet the stone's noted engraving, on the eastern face, speaks to Gould's life: "She hath done what she could." Sunrise or sunset, the message may resonate with hopefulness or shadow, depending upon how onlookers know and understand her life's work. Gould's actions with her pen—like those of Brewster and Marsh—revise stories of women abroad. Many were more than consumers, artists or mere spectators.

Eliot might well have written of Gould, "the effect of her being on those around her was incalculably diffusive." She, like Brewster and Marsh, contributed "to the growing good of the world" not only during their lives but through the little-noticed residual ripples their actions left behind. Less apropos of Gould than of Brewster and Marsh, but relevant nonetheless, each of the three may be said to have "lived faithfully a hidden life." While Longfellow's poems were recited publicly for decades, his houses in Cambridge, Massachusetts, and Portland, Maine, are open as museums, and his tomb in Mount Auburn Cemetery is visited regularly, these three "rest in unvisited tombs." Perhaps these pages recounting their stories have helped to bring them back to life, however momentarily, so that we today might contemplate how best to live.

Mrs. Emily Bliss Gould.

Memorial Services.

Services in memory of the late Mrs. Emily Bliss Gould, well-known as the founder of the important Christian Schools in Rome, Italy, and whose remains have been recently brought to this country, will be held at the Fourth Avenue Presbyterian Church (4th Avenue and 22d Street), on Sunday afternoon, November 12th, at 3 o'clock. Appropriate addresses will be made by Rev. William Adams, D.D., Rev. Howard Crosby, D.D., and others. The relatives and friends of Mrs. Gould, those interested in her Italian work (now permanently established as the "Gould Memorial Home and Schools"), and the relatives and friends of her husband, Dr. James B. Gould, are respectfully invited to be present.

Figure C.1. Announcement of Gould's memorial service, Fourth Avenue Presbyterian Church, with address by Rev. Howard Crosby. Credit: Manuscripts and Archives Division, the New York Public Library.

Figure C.2. Gould family tombstone, Woodlawn Cemetery, NY, with inscription, "SHE HATH DONE WHAT SHE COULD," from Leonard Woolsey Bacon, *A Life Worth Living*. Credit: General Research Division, the New York Public Library.

Appendix A

"To ____ ____."

From Caroline Crane Marsh, *Wolfe of the Knoll, and other Poems.*

BELOVED! Thou whose tender care hath fed
My flickering lamp of life for many a year,
Thou who hast watched beside my weary bed,
And dried with loving hand the frequent tear,—

Who, when each healing art had proved in vain,
With a strong arm thy helpless burthen bore,
Despite the threatenings of the stormy main,
To milder breezes on a foreign shore,—

Sweet was our rest in Arno's lovely vale,
Amid her olive groves, her orange bowers,
And if health came not on the balmy gale,
Better than health the memory of such hours!

Nor sight of Nature's fairest scenes alone
I owe thy love, O friend most true and wise!
Art's highest wonders, old and new, thou'st shown,
And taught me how to see, and how to prize.

And thy beloved voice hath charmed mine ear
With many a sage's, many a nation's lore,
Lifting my soul above each selfish care,
When on the page sublime these eyes could look no more.

Lo, now the humble offering that I make!—
A poor return for culture—well I know!—
Given with such liberal hand—yet do thou take!—
And may some future day fruits less unworthy show!

Appendix B

"For Queen Anne"

Louise Chandler Moulton, Rome, March 23. 1876

There are some rooms in Rome I shall remember—
High up a winding stair, like Hilda's tower,
Where gallant men and gracious women linger,
And good Queen Anne holds sway with gentle power.

To this fair Queen we all pay willing homage;
And, when she bids me tribute bring in song,
What can I else than seek to do the bidding
Of her to whom all suffrages belong?

For her, indeed, I think should bloom the roses
Which these March winds have well nigh chilled to death,
At her fair feet the waywardest of posies
Might be content to sigh away its breath.

For her each gift that's brought should be what she is,
Bright as her smile, or cheering as her tone—
The artist's painted dream, the singer's music—
Not such mere wayside daisy as my own.

I know it has no merit, this poor daisy,
A humble thing, and odorless, and small,
Not worthy that our gracious Queen should wear it,
But in my heart its roots grew—that is all.

List of Abbreviations

Books, Newspapers, and Periodicals

BDA *Boston Daily Advertiser*

PEB *Philadelphia Evening Bulletin*

Manuscript Collections, Archives, and Libraries

AFCU American and Foreign Christian Union Series II, New York University Fales Library and Special Collections

AHBP Anne Hampton Brewster Papers, Library Company of Philadelphia

ATV Archivi Tavola Valdesi, Torre Pellice, Italy

CFP Crane Family Papers, New York Public Library

NYHS New York Historical Society

UVM George Perkins Marsh Collection, Silver Special Collections Library, University of Vermont

YUL Papers of Thomas Davidson, Yale University Library

Names

ABC Alexander B. Crane

AHB Anne Hampton Brewster

CCM Caroline Crane Marsh

EBG	Emily Bliss Gould
GPM	George Perkins Marsh
TD	Thomas Davidson

Notes

Introduction

1. Madden, "American Anne Hampton Brewster's Social Circles" and "Travels, Translations and Limitations."

2. [EBG], "Gossip Abroad," March 1869, 288; May 1869, 479.

3. [EBG], "Gossip Abroad," May 1869, 479.

4. [EBG], "Gossip Abroad," May 1869, 479.

5. AHB, Journal, January 1869.

6. Lamberts, *The Black International*, 7–9; Kertzer, *Prisoner of the Vatican*, 127–128.

7. Longfellow to Jane Norton, 9 May 1876, in *Letters, Vol. VI*, 137.

8. AHB, Journal, January 1869; Nardi to AHB. On Brewster's career, see Larabee, *Anne Hampton Brewster*; Fisher, *A Gentle Journalist Abroad*; Larabee, "Brewster, Anne Hampton."

9. "An Outrage at Rome"; Bacon, *A Life Worth Living*, 117.

10. Kertzer, *The Kidnapping of Edgardo Mortara*, 154–166; Kolich, "Miriam and the Conversion of the Jews," 430–443; McGreevy, *Catholicism and American Freedom*, 11–14.

11. Hopkins to CCM, 18 February 1867; EBG to Dr. Thompson, 22 December 1867.

12. [Mitchell], "Miss Mitchell's Journal."

13. Gould's earliest preserved communication with Caroline Crane Marsh appears in 1870, but she began writing to George as early as 1867, and almost always greeted "Mrs. Marsh" in the letters. To distinguish wives from husbands and to foreground the women, I generally refer to them by last name, Marsh and Gould, and refer to their husbands by first name or professional title.

14. CCM, Journal, 9 November 1873.

15. "Centri Educativi Gould e Ferretti."

16. AHB, Journal, 7 November 1868.

17. Fuller, "Things and Thoughts."

18. Urry, *The Tourist Gaze*, 1–7; Buzard, *The Beaten Track*, 155–216; Schriber, *Writing Home*, 2, 12–14.

19. Bailey, *American Travel Literature*, 17; Matteson, *The Lives of Margaret Fuller*, 64, 428; Marshall, *Margaret Fuller*, 45, 56, 80–81, 110, 136, 215; Steele, *The Essential Margaret Fuller*, xl; Salenius, *Set in Stone*, 74, 78–80; Bergland, "Emily Dickinson's Italy"; Herbert, *Dearest Beloved*, 215–217.

20. Fisher, *A Gentle Journalist Abroad*, 8.

21. E. Crane, *Caroline Crane Marsh*; Quartermaine, "Views from Beyond the Alps"; Lowenthal, "The Marriage of Choice," and Lowenthal and Quartermaine, *Un'americana alla corte dei Savoia.*

22. Martin, "Two Women," 115; Bacon, *A Life Worth Living*, 8.

23. Alison, *History of Europe.*

24. AHB, Journal, 7 November 1868.

25. Fuller, "Things and Thoughts."

26. Emerson, "Self-Reliance," 198.

27. Emerson, "The American Scholar," 85, 88–89. Bergland, *Maria Mitchell*, 92, employs this aspect of Fuller's writings. Bailey, *American Travel Literature*, 157–158; Bailey cites Steele, *Transfiguring America*, 3–11; see especially 10–13.

28. AHB, "Letter from Rome"; *Catalogue of the Library of George Perkins Marsh* cites "Sara Margaret Ossoli (Fuller)," in Villari, *Saggi di storia*, 508, 703; AHB, Journal, 28 March 1872.

29. Salenius, *Florence*, 89–105, and Vance, *America's Rome*, vol. 2, 93–96, also discuss types of Americans abroad.

30. AHB, Journal, [14 January 1872].

31. Mitchell, "Maria Mitchell's Reminiscences of the Herschels," *Century* (1891): 909, qtd. in Bergland, *Maria Mitchell*, 112.

32. Sargent, *Utopianism*, 5.

33. AHB to TD, 27 January 1881.

34. AHB, Journal, [14 January 1872].

35. GPM to W. Seward, 20 January 1868, no. 200, in Ducci, *George P. Marsh Correspondence*, 139.

36. Schriber, *Writing Home*, 2, 12–14.

37. Marshall, *Margaret Fuller*; Ciampi, *Miss Uragano*; S. Mitchell, *Frances Power Cobbe*; Snailham, " 'The Reality Is Far Removed from the Ideal' "; Dabakis, *A Sisterhood of Sculptors*; Salenius, *An Abolitionist Abroad*; Culkin, *Harriet Hosmer*; Buick, *Child of the Fire*; and Rioux, *Constance Fenimore Woolson.*

38. Smith, *The Gender of History*, 7, 10.

39. Kaplan, "Manifest Domesticity," 581–606. Kaplan connects "domestication" to empire- and nation-building in the 1850s, works that unified white men and women in spaces outside the "home" as they forced their views and beliefs upon "uncivilized" others. White Americans approaching Italy applied a similar view to assisting the fragmented peninsula (savage and uncivilized) to unification.

40. Barolini, *Their Other Side*; Salenius, *An Abolitionist Abroad*, 144. Boyd and Bergland have written about the freedom of the female "genius" embodied in the title heroine, Corinne, of Staël's novel. Bergland labels "woman of science" Maria Mitchell a "professional," as opposed to a "vacationer," to underscore her purpose in traveling. Boyd, *Writing for Immortality*, 149–150, 190–199, 216–220; Bergland, *Maria Mitchell*, 93. Similarly, Dabakis has explained that female artists "who travel[ed] or expatriated to Rome composed the first truly professional class" of their type. *A Sisterhood of Sculptors*, 10.

41. Mitchell, "Maria Mitchell's Reminiscences of the Herschels," qtd. in Bergland, *Maria Mitchell*, 112, emphasis mine.

42. *Oxford English Dictionary*, s.v. "vocation."

43. Pritchard, "The Way out West," 45–72, embodies postmodern feminist thought that considers political exiles and the oppressed to stand firmly against utopian language and thinking. Elsden, *Roman Fever*, 105, refers to those "compelled for philosophical, political, or practical reasons to remain abroad," limited in their mobility. She draws from Joan Myers Weimer's introduction in *Women Artists, Women Exiles: "Miss Grief" and Other Stories* (New Brunswick, NJ: Rutgers University Press, 1988).

44. Fuller, "Autobiographical Romance," 31, 28, 24–43.

45. Salenius, *Florence*, 98–99. In addition to the primary sources, she draws from Ziff, *Return Passages*, 258.

46. Kertzer, *Prisoner of the Vatican*, 8.

47. Kertzer, *Prisoner of the Vatican*, 8.

48. Gemme, *Domesticating Foreign Struggles*; Vance, *America's Rome*, vol. 2, 94; McGreevy, *Catholicism and American Freedom*; McGreevy, *American Jesuits and the World*.

49. Berthold, *American Risorgimento*, 1. See also Reynolds and Belasco Smith, *"These Sad but Glorious Days."* Additional works on American writers in Italy also discuss these topics: Bryant, *Facing Melville, Facing Italy*; Martin and Person, *Roman Holidays*; Livorni, "American Writers in Rome"; and Rockwell, preface to *Spellbound by Rome*.

50. Berthold, *American Risorgimento*, xi.

51. Bailey, "Fuller, Hawthorne, and Imagining Urban Spaces in Rome," 175–190. Bailey underscores how well-known authors Fuller and Hawthorne differed in their views of the possibilities for change.

52. Claeys and Sargent, *The Utopia Reader*, 1–4; Moylan, *Demand the Impossible*, 10, 44–46; Wagner-Lawlor, *Postmodern Utopias and Feminist Fictions*, 7–9, 123–125; Atwood, "Dire Cartographies," 85.

53. Mortara, *Writing for Justice*, 20. Dowling, *Charles Eliot Norton*, and Sutcliffe, *Victorian Radicals*, similarly intertwine intellectual and social history and influenced this project.

54. Cohen, *The Social Lives of Poems*, 7.

55. Sutcliffe, *Victorian Radicals*, 1.

56. Sutcliffe, *Victorian Radicals*, 2.

57. Soper, *Building a Civil Society*, 157, 256 n. 40.

58. Harris, *The Cultural Work of the late Nineteenth-Century Hostess*; Soper, *Building a Civil Society*.

59. Bonner, "The Radical Club." Inscribed "From Thomas Davidson to Miss Brewster Rome, May 3rd 1878," Library Company of Philadelphia. Bonner was a pseudonym for Katherine McDowell.

60. Gemme, "Republican Debates II: The Religion of the Republic," in *Domesticating Foreign Struggles*, 131–155; McGreevy, *Catholicism and American Freedom* and *American Jesuits and the World*.

61. Gaul, introduction, *To Marry an Indian*, 64. Gaul writes that Harriet Gold Boudinot's letters reveal that an "idealized feminine nature stands in tension with the political meanings her life signified," drawing from what Susan K. Harris refers to as "epistolary negotiations," 66; 40–42.

62. Sánchez-Eppler, *Dependent States*; Robbins, *Managing Literacy, Mothering America*.

63. Journalism studies overlooking Brewster are Fahs, *Out on Assignment*; Lutes, *Front-Page Girls*; Beasley, *Women of the Washington Press*; and Edelstein, *Between the Novel and the News*. Madden asserts this argument in "American Anne Hampton Brewster's Social Circles," 117–144.

Chapter 1

1. Larabee, *Anne Hampton Brewster*, 27; Fisher, *A Gentle Journalist Abroad*. See also Larabee, "Brewster, Anne Hampton," 134; Wright, *American Novelists in Italy*, 108–114; Atkinson and Grippe, "Anne Hampton Brewster Papers."

2. Bacon, *A Life Worth Living*; "Gould, Emily Bliss"; Martin, "Two Women," 107–120; "Memorials of Mrs. Gould of Rome," 723–724.

3. Crane, *Caroline Crane Marsh*, 4–8.

4. Caroline Crane Marsh to her brother, January 1850, qtd. in Crane, *Caroline Crane Marsh*, 10–14.

5. Crane, *Caroline Crane Marsh*, 22, 37, 7.

6. Crane, *Caroline Crane Marsh*, 22, 37, 7.

7. Crane, *Caroline Crane Marsh*, 16.

8. Crane, *Caroline Crane Marsh*, 22, 32, 37

9. Both poets' collections were in the Marsh library. See *Catalogue*, 92.

10. Crane, *Caroline Crane Marsh*, 38.

11. Crane, *Caroline Crane Marsh*, 43.

12. CCM, *The Hallig*; *Wolfe of the Knoll*.

13. CCM, *The Hallig*, iii–v.

14. [CCM], "To ____ ____," *Wolfe of the Knoll*, 324–327. Although the poem is unsigned and its title anonymous, its venue and content suggest it is by Caroline and about George.

15. Crane, *Caroline Crane Marsh*, 8; CCM, *Life and Letters of George Perkins Marsh*, vol. 1, 427–428.

16. Lowenthal, "The Marriage of Choice"; Quartermaine, "Views from Beyond the Alps"; Lowenthal and Quartermaine, introduction, *Un'americana alla corte dei Savoia*, 5–6.

17. Bacon, *A Life Worth Living*, 8.

18. Martin, "Two Women," 114.

19. [EBG], "Little Caroline," 5–15. The publication seems to have played off the popular monthly newspaper *The Little Pilgrim*, edited and published in Philadelphia by Grace Greenwood (Sara Jane Lippincott) and Leander K. Lippincott, from 1854 through 1868, with contributors including Mary Howitt and Mrs. S. C. Hall.

20. Bacon, *A Life Worth Living*, 30, 45; [Mitchell], "Miss Mitchell's Journal."

21. Martin, "Two Women," 116.

22. Bailey, *American Travel Literature*, 74–75, 165–169.

23. Bacon, *A Life Worth Living*, 53.

24. Whitman, "Europe."

25. Bacon, *A Life Worth Living*, 55.

26. Bacon, *A Life Worth Living*, 57, 71–113.

27. I have located five sketches, published between March 1866 and May 1867, listed in the bibliography under Gould's name, although none is signed. Bacon, *A Life Worth Living*, 51–59, refers to six sketches and quotes extensively from them.

28. All are listed in the bibliography under Gould's name, although none is signed. WorldCat cites several letters from Harte to Gould about her submissions to him, first requesting the letters and then providing these responses (OCLC 16700642, 16700687, 16700568, 16728808).

29. Boyd, *Writing for Immortality*, 149–150, 190–199, 216–220; Elsden, *Roman Fever*; Kohn et al, *Transatlantic Stowe*; Salenius, ed., *American Authors Reinventing Italy*.

30. Bacon, *A Life Worth Living*, 141–142; *Christian Work in Rome, 1872–73*, 14.

31. Bacon, *A Life Worth Living*, 129, 172–173.

32. Larabee, *Anne Hampton Brewster*, 23, 34–36.

33. AHB, Journal, 19 October, 23 November, 10, 18, 19 December 1857, and January 1858.

34. Larabee, *Anne Hampton Brewster*, 8–10, 15; Markus, *Across an Untried Sea*, 15–16, 20, 41, 60–61; Merrill, *When Romeo Was a Woman*, 46–47, 52–53, 56–62, 73, 163–165, 183–185; Atkinson and Grippe, "Anne Hampton Brewster Papers," 7.

35. Thanks to Katrin Horn for a reference to the entry about Cushman's letter, AHB, Journal, 17 July 1867; AHB, Journal, 19 August, 3 and 27 November, 20 and 28 December 1868.

36. AHB, "Letter from Rome," 13 April, 25 May, 11 November 1869, 25 January, 31 May 1870; AHB, "Miss Cushman"; AHB, "Miss Cushman The Youth and Early Friends of the Great Actress (News), 26 August 1878.

37. Larabee, *Anne Hampton Brewster*, 16, 35–36.

38. AHB, Journal, 14 February 1858.

39. Larabee, *Anne Hampton Brewster*, 8–10; 15–25.

Chapter 2

1. EBG to Dr. Thompson, 22 December 1867.
2. EBG to Dr. Thompson, 22 December 1867.
3. EBG to Dr. Thompson, 22 December 1867, emphasis mine.
4. EBG to Dr. Thompson, 22 December 1867, emphasis mine.
5. CCM to GPM, 15 August 1869.
6. *Catalogue*, vii.
7. CCM to GPM, 15 August 1869; CCM to GPM, 19 August 1869.
8. CCM to GPM, 15 August 1869; CCM to GPM, 19 August 1869.
9. Lowenthal, *George Perkins Marsh: Prophet*, 318, 363–364, 379.
10. CCM to GPM, 19 August 1869.
11. CCM to GPM, 19 August 1869, emphasis mine.
12. CCM to GPM, 19 August 1869.
13. CCM to GPM, 19 August 1869.
14. *Catalogue*, iv.
15. Liming, *What a Library Means to a Woman.*
16. Tincker, *By the Tiber*, 66–67. On Cromo's link to Brewster, see "Life in Boston," 10. Some readers believed Tincker also had fictionalized Brewster in *Signor Monaldini's Niece* (1879)—a charge Brewster denied. Brewster asserted that the novel's Mrs. Brandon was "Miss [Julia] Beers," who had the same initials: "The apartment is exactly like Julia's . . . Julia did half ask Miss T. to live with her, then discovered her peculiar temper, and drew back. Miss T. never forgave her. Julia was soft, gentle, and very popular. She and Miss Tincker knew the same set of people among Catholics and Miss T. was very jealous of Julia. She accused Julia of impugning her literary interest with Father Hecker when on the contrary Julia tried secretly to befriend her. So I read Mrs. Brandon sorrowfully as meaning Miss Beers and am astounded that anyone should take it for me." AHB to TD, 30 March 1879. The fictionalization and accusations contributed to the fracture in the women's relationship, exacerbated later by Tincker's emotional and psychological tailspin.
17. Tincker, *By the Tiber*, 66–67.
18. Tincker, *By the Tiber*, 66–67.
19. Lutes, *Front-Page Girls*, 96.
20. Lutes, *Front-Page Girls*, 95, 100, 7, 106, 95–108. Lutes especially emphasizes Stackpole's transformation from the 1881 edition to the later 1908 version,

explaining that the latter version epitomizes a transition that scholars such as Nina Baym referred to as "the systematic vulgarization of Henrietta Stackpole" (98). She is a "monster" in both versions but becomes more than monstrous in the second (95, 100). The second Stackpole writes travel accounts, like the first, but she also writes spectacular crime accounts, stunt reporting, and "sob sister" stories, prevalent in turn-of-the-century journalism. James also changes Stackpole's physicality, "deflect[ing] attention from her sexual attributes" to become more "machinelike and even as a newspaper itself"—"equating her body with her text . . . both agent and object of the news" (106).

21. AHB, Journal, 12 January 1872.

22. Lutes, *Front-Page Girls*, 2.

23. Edelstein, *Between the Novel and the News*, 94, 108–109.

24. Rush, *Letters of Benjamin Rush*, quoted and explicated in Madden, "To Make a Figure," 262–263.

25. For information on nineteenth-century portraiture in Italy, I am grateful to email correspondence with Professor Claire Kovacs and the resources in Johnson, *Nineteenth-Century Photography*. For comparative images of the era that illuminate these, see Becchetti, *Fotografi e fotografia in Italia, 1839–1880.*

26. Sansay, *Secret History*, 64–67; Sedgwick, *Clarence*, 265.

Chapter 3

1. EBG to CCM, 12 September 1870.

2. Huemer, "To be Remembered and to Please," 11. The Keats-Shelley House today includes a map, included in Huemer's work, plotting where famous authors lived.

3. AHB, Journal, 7 July 1870.

4. Calculations were made on July 29, 2019, using the CPI Inflation Calculator, http://www.in2013dollars.com/1870-GBP-in-2016, and Currency Rate Today, https://gbp.currencyrate.today/usd/944.

5. Goddard to AHB, 9 May 1870.

6. CPI Inflation Calculator, http://www.in2013dollars.com/us/inflation/1870?amount=600, accessed July 29, 2019.

7. Brann, "The American College in Rome."

8. AHB, Journal, 30 January 1870; "Letter from Italy," *PEB*, 1 July 1870.

9. "Housekeeping in Rome"; "The Ecumenical Council"; "Hans Andersen at a Child's Party"; "(Jesuits have nearly all left Rome)," *Home Journal*, 17 November 1870; "About Women"; "Roman Catholic or Infidel." Johanningsmeier, *Fiction and the American Literary Marketplace*, 26, 27, 29, 34–44.

10. Hare, *The Story of My Life*, cited in Frapiselli, "Harriet Hosmer," 313–323; Edelstein, *Between the Novel and the News*, 89–92, 94, 108–109.

11. AHB, Journal, 16, 20, 30 August, 7 September 1870.

12. Bailey, *American Travel Literature,* 74–75, 165–169.

13. AHB, Journal, 16, 20, 30 August, 7 September 1870.

14. Vance, *America's Rome,* vol. 2, 209.

15. AHB, "Letter from Rome," 12 August 1870, refers to readers having received news already via "cable telegram." McGreevy, *American Jesuits and the World,* 5–6.

16. "Salvatore Ferretti"; McGreevy, *American Jesuits and the World,* 43–48.

17. EBG to GPM, 29 September [1870]. The entrance of the king to Rome was in July 1871. It is possible that many were anticipating an entry that did not occur until the next summer.

18. EBG to CCM, 12 September 1870.

19. EBG to CCM, 12 September 1870.

20. EBG to CCM, 12 September 1870.

21. EBG to GPM, 29 September [1870].

22. GPM to H. Fish, 27 March 1870, in Ducci, *George P. Marsh Correspondence,* 164.

23. ABC to CCM, 21 January 1870; Edward A. Crane to CCM, 1 February 1870; Wislizenus to CCM, 8 May 1870; Sabatier to CCM, 25 March 1870; Sabatier to CCM, 9 April 1870. Ministero della Pubblica Istruzione to CCM, 17 February 1870.

24. Crane, *Caroline Crane Marsh,* 70.

25. GPM to H. Fish, 12 August 1870, in Ducci, *George P. Marsh Correspondence,* 173.

26. AHB, "Letter from Rome," 29 September 1870; AHB, "Letter from Rome," 11 October 1870.

27. Aunt Friendly, "Miss Jones," 217; Trollope, *In Memoriam,* xi. Within the tale Dr. G., "the physician who had won the affection of many strangers in Rome," seems to be Gould's husband.

Chapter 4

1. Aunt Friendly, "Miss Jones," 209.

2. AHB, Journal, 5 March 1885.

3. [Mitchell], "Miss Mitchell's Journal"; Carson, *The Roman Years,* 116, 129–130, 31.

4. Boyd, *Writing for Immortality,* 117–118, 191, notes "American Women Abroad" and "Shall the American Girl be Chaperoned?" as contributions to this milieu. They appeared in the *Galaxy* (1876–77) just before *Daisy Miller.*

5. Boyd, *Writing for Immortality,* 191.

6. Boyd, *Writing for Immortality,* 156–157, 177.

7. "Online Books by Sarah S Baker."

8. Aunt Friendly, "Miss Jones," 205–220.

9. Dean, *The Complete Letters of Constance Fenimore Woolson*, 150.

10. Bischof, "A Summer in England," 152–171.

11. AHB, Journal, August 1867–May 1871.

12. [Mitchell], "Miss Mitchell's Journal"; Carson, *The Roman Years*, 116, 129–130, 31.

13. AHB, Journal, 10 February 1873; Madden, "American Anne Hampton Brewster's Social Circles," 126; AHB, Journal, 25 July 1875; AHB, Journal, 5 March 1885.

14. AHB, Journal, 14 March 1875.

15. Schriber, *Writing Home*.

16. AHB to TD, 12 June 1878.

17. Herbert, *Dearest Beloved*, 225, 229–234; Milder and Fuller, *The Business of Reflection*, 253 n. 20.

18. Hawthorne, *The French and Italian Notebooks*, 230, 78, 157. Hawthorne refers to Hosmer in his 3 April entry, 158–159; and to his concerns about Una on 23 May 1858, 211, 192, 204.

19. Dunlavy, *Sophia Peabody Hawthorne*, 112–115, 149–184.

20. Emerson, Clarke, and Channing, *Memoirs of Margaret Fuller Ossoli*. For recent scholarship on Fuller in Italy, see Marshall, *Margaret Fuller*; Matteson, *The Lives of Margaret Fuller*; and Reynolds and Smith, *"These Sad but Glorious Days."*

21. Hawthorne, *French and Italian Notebooks*, 155–156.

22. James, *William Wetmore Story and His Friends*, vol. 1, 260.

23. Norton, *Notes of Study and Travel in Italy*; Dowling, *Charles Eliot Norton*, 106, 109.

24. Dowling, *Charles Eliot Norton*, 116, 119, 125–134.

25. Hawthorne, *French and Italian Notebooks*, 230; Lutes, *Front-Page Girls*, 95–108; Rioux, *Constance Fenimore Woolson*.

26. Damon-Bach, "My Readers Will Thank Me."

27. Elsden, *Roman Fever*, 7–8.

28. Sedgwick, "An Incident in Rome," 104–108; see also Bailey, "Tourism and Visual Subjection."

29. Wordsworth, "The Excursion," 1814.

30. Rioux, *Constance Fenimore Woolson*, 8; and Rioux, "Introduction," xxvi–xxvii.

31. Jenkins, "Mary Agnes Tincker."

32. The Italian word means melancholy. AHB, Journal, A10, 12 September 1874, 14 March 1875, 28 February 1877, and 14 November 1878.

33. AHB to TD, 30 March 1879 and 13 November 1878.

34. AHB, Journal, 28 March 1872.

35. J. Hawthorne, *Nathaniel Hawthorne and His Wife*, Vol. 2, 372–374; Herbert, *Dearest Beloved*, 218, 253.

36. Only one Hawthorne work—*Passages from the English Note-Books* (Leipzig: Bernhard Tauchnitz, 1871)—is catalogued among Brewster's library.

37. AHB, Journal, 30 April 1871.

38. AHB, Journal, 5 May 1874.

39. AHB, Journal, 7 April 1874.

40. His *Life Amongst the Modocs* (1873) had appeared just before he arrived at Brewster's apartments in Rome. The autobiographical adventure tale also took a stance for Native American rights. Miller's poetry collection *Songs of the Sierras* (1871) won him the titles "Poet of the Sierras" and "The Byron of Oregon." English literati noted "his wild Western appearance and manners." Lawson, "Miller, Joaquin [Cincinnatus Hiner]," 771.

41. Mario Gigliucci to Elena [Crane], 21 May 1869; CCM, Journal, 1 October–1 December 1873.

42. Other nineteenth-century publications discuss these concerns. See Boyd, *Writing for Immortality*, 105–125.

43. Aunt Friendly, "Miss Jones," 209, emphasis mine.

44. Aunt Friendly, "Miss Jones," 209.

45. Aunt Friendly, "Miss Jones," 209–210.

46. Aunt Friendly, "Miss Jones," 213.

47. Aunt Friendly, "Miss Jones," 217–219.

48. Aunt Friendly, "Miss Jones," 219.

49. Aunt Friendly, "Miss Jones," 205, 209, 210, 211.

50. Aunt Friendly, "Miss Jones," 220.

51. Aunt Friendly, "Miss Jones," 208.

52. Huemer, "To Be Remembered and to Please," 9–11. For images of the extensive excavations disrupting Rome in this period, see *Rome in Early Photographs*.

53. Aunt Friendly, "Miss Jones," 208.

54. Aunt Friendly, "Miss Jones," 210.

55. Susan Cahill, *Desiring Italy*, xi–xii, employs this phrase to describe the "embodied fact of life" as she distinguishes between living abroad and being a tourist.

Chapter 5

1. Staël, *Politics, Literature, and National Character*, 289, 301.

2. Salenius, *Florence*, 89–93; AHB, Journal, 22 June 1872, 3 February 1873, 28 January 1874, 3 May 1877, 5 March 1885; AHB to Angelo Conti, 22 December 1886; Bacci, "Il Fondo Angelo Conti," 79–91; AHB to Helen Hunt Jackson, 5 July 1869.

3. Rodolfo Lanciani to AHB, 24 August 1869; Rodolfo Lanciani to AHB, 26 August 1869.

4. Madden, "American Anne Hampton Brewster's Social Circles." Brewster inscribed passages from and comments about George Sand's *Histoire de ma vie* in Liszt's biography of F. Chopin (Paris, Escudier, 1852), Library Company of Philadelphia.

5. EBG to GPM, 11 July 1869.

6. EBG to GPM, 21 July 1869.

7. EBG to GPM, 8 September 1869.

8. EBG to GPM, 23 September 1869.

9. Staël, *Politics, Literature, and National Character*, 289, 301.

10. CCM, qtd. in Lowenthal and Quartermaine, *Un'americana alla corte dei Savoia*, 176 (Notebook IX, 23 April 1863); CCM, Journal, 4, 9, 13, 15, 19, 25 October, 9, 22 November, 1 December 1873.

11. Hawthorne, *The French and Italian Notebooks*, 4 June 1858.

12. AHB, Journal, 20 November 1876.

13. AHB, Journal, 10 February 1873.

14. AHB, Journal, 20 November 1876.

15. Woolson to Henry Mills Alden, 8 April 1881, in *Complete Letters*, 162.

16. Woolson to Kate Livingston Mather (WRHS/Mather), Rome, Easter Even 1881, in *Complete Letters*, 164; Woolson to William Dean Howells (Houghton), Rome, 4 May 1881, in *Complete Letters*, 165–167.

17. Hosmer to GPM, 1872.

18. AHB, Journal, 7, 23 November 1868, 27 April, 4, 17 August 1869.

19. AHB, Journal, 6 October 1869.

20. AHB, Journal, 18 October 1873, 21 September, 22 October 1881.

21. Lowenthal, *George Perkins Marsh: Prophet*, 335, 359. On the history of the Villa Forini and the Marsh's access to it, see Pacini, "Firenze capitale d'Italia," 75. For descriptions and pictures of famous structures in Rome where Marsh and Brewster lived, see Rendina, *I palazzi storici di Roma*: Villa Pallavicini Rospigliosi, 200–202, 393–396; Palazzina Pandolfi, 592; Palazzo Albani, 8–9, 87–88; Villa Arrigoni in Frascati (where Brewster lived with the Read family), 265–266; Palazzina di Villa del Bosco Parrasio, 506–509.

22. EBG to GPM, 29 September 1870.

23. Qtd. in Daniels, "In Italy with Mr. and Mrs. George Perkins Marsh," 192.

24. EBG to GPM, 29 September 1870.

25. Daniels, "In Italy with Mr. and Mrs. George Perkins Marsh,"191. Daniels uses the term "salon" rather than reception but his sources, letters written by Cornelia Underwood of Woodstock, Vermont, do not.

26. Carson, *The Roman Years*, 46.

27. Hawthorne, *The Marble Faun*, 131.

28. Botta, *Memoirs of Anne C. L. Botta*, 16 n. 1, 30; "Literary Folk Once Found Pleasure in a 'Botta Evening,'" cited in Oliva, "The Circles of Anne C. Lynch Botta," 6.

29. Carson, *The Roman Years*, 51; AHB, Journal, 19 March 1883.

30. Cornelia Underwood to Levi Underwood, 5 December 1873, qtd. in Daniels, "In Italy with Mr. and Mrs. George Perkins Marsh," 192, 194.

31. Harris, *The Cultural Work of the Late Nineteenth-Century Hostess*, 2.

32. Harris, *The Cultural Work of the Late Nineteenth-Century Hostess*, 122.

33. Harris, *The Cultural Work of the Late Nineteenth-Century Hostess*, 122–123.

34. Daniels, "In Italy with Mr. and Mrs. George Perkins Marsh," 191.

35. Qtd. in Daniels, "In Italy with Mr. and Mrs. George Perkins Marsh," 192.

36. Daniels, "In Italy with Mr. and Mrs. George Perkins Marsh," 194.

37. Daniels, "In Italy with Mr. and Mrs. George Perkins Marsh," 194.

38. Corson, "An American Salon in Rome."

39. Stoddard, "Roman Receptions."

40. Hawthorne, *The Marble Faun*, 131.

41. Carson, *The Roman Years*, 47–48.

42. EBG to GPM, 7 February 1867. Special Collections include this letter in 1867 but it is clearly dated 1868.

43. EBG to GPM, 11 July 1869.

44. EBG to GPM, 7 February 1867.

45. AHB, Journal, 19 February, 19 March 1883.

46. Carson, *The Roman Years*, 57.

47. Carson, *The Roman Years*, 57.

48. AHB, "Autograph Album."

49. AHB, Journal, 26 January 1883.

50. AHB, Journal, [27 January], 7, 19 February 1883; Capel to AHB, 1883.

51. AHB, Journal, 19 February 1883; Stoddard, "Roman Receptions"; Moulton, "For Queen Anne."

52. Harris, *The Cultural Work of the Late Nineteenth-Century Hostess*, 3, 121.

Chapter 6

1. EBG to GPM, 7 August 1869, emphasis mine.

2. EBG to GPM, 10 August 1869. The second letter quoted is dated only 1869 but Gould refers to herself being in Kipingen and her husband having reached "home" in the US on the 27th. It likely was enclosed with the August 10 letter.

3. CCM to GPM, 19 August 1869.

4. EBG to GPM, 23 September 1869.

5. EBG to GPM, 20 August 1869.

6. Jackson, *The Business of Letters*, 38–40. For the discourse of gift exchange in modernist literary circles, see Colesworthy, *Returning the Gift*.

7. Lyons, "Love Letters and Writing Practices," 232–239, 235; Gaul, introduction, *To Marry an Indian*, 66, 42–44.

8. Qtd. in Madden, *Selections from Eliza Leslie*, 263.

9. Arbesser to GPM, 1 September [1869].

10. Lowenthal, *George Perkins Marsh: Prophet*, 248.

11. Moulton, "For Queen Anne." Title underlining on manuscript.

12. She traveled with author Sherwood Bonner (the pseudonym for Katherine McDowell), who was sending regular contributions to the *Boston Sunday Times*. Bonner, *The Radical Club*, 14.

13. Moulton, "For Queen Anne."

14. Cohen, *The Social Lives of Poems*, 1–2.

15. Bennett, *Nineteenth-Century American Women Poets*, xl.

16. Cohen, *The Social Lives of Poems*, 3, 4, 7, 9.

17. Henderson, "The Friendship Elegy," 110.

18. Henderson, "The Friendship Elegy," 110–117.

19. Trollope, *In Memoriam*, 205–220.

20. Henderson, "The Friendship Elegy," 116–117.

21. Trollope, *In Memoriam*, xix.

22. Henderson, "The Friendship Elegy," 117.

23. Henderson, "The Friendship Elegy," 117.

24. Trollope, *In Memoriam*, xi, xiv.

25. Trollope, *In Memoriam*, xxii–xxiii.

26. Trollope, *In Memoriam*, xxiii.

27. Trollope, *In Memoriam*, xxii–xxiii.

28. Migliorini, "Pasquale Villari."

29. Boase, "Hemans, Charles Isidore."

30. V. Eyre, Alfred Pearson, Howard M. Ticknor, N. Lawless, W. Davies (publisher of *History of the Decline and Fall of Roman Empire*), A. Y., Frances Mary Peard, E. T. H., and Elizabeth M. Farmar also contributed.

31. Cowden-Clarke to AHB; Mary Howitt to AHB. Four undated letters refer to shared books and a newspaper.

32. Mandler, "Howitt, William"; Drain, "Howitt, Mary."

33. William Howitt, "Progressive Steps of Popular Education," 55.

34. Howitt, "Progressive Steps of Popular Education," 55, 57, 68, 66.

35. Howitt, "Progressive Steps of Popular Education," 70.

36. Howitt, "Progressive Steps of Popular Education," 70–71.

37. Howitt, "Progressive Steps of Popular Education," 72.

38. Howitt, "Progressive Steps of Popular Education," 83–84.

39. Bacon, *A Life Worth Living*, 164, 166–167, and 123.

40. Pasquale Villari, "Un educatore italiano del secolo XV," in Trollope, *In Memoriam*, 179, 185, 186.

41. Migliorini, "Pasquale Villari."

42. Riall, *Risorgimento*, 150.

43. Pasquale Villari to AHB, 2 February 1875; Pasquale Villari to CCM, 3 April 1870; Pasquale Villari to GPM, 30 November 1872; Pasquale Villari to GPM,

3 March 1875; Pasquale Villari to CCM, 22 March 1875; Linda Villari to CCM, 26 July 1882.

44. *Rutland Daily Globe*, 29 December 1875; *Burlington Weekly Free Press*, 7 January 1876.

45. "La festa degli arcadi," *Il popolo romano*, 9 January 1874. Translations are mine. "Catalogo dei Pastori Arcadi 1870–1888," no. 201; Arcadia Certificate of Membership for Anne Hampton Brewster; "Venerdi Santo 11 Aprile 1873."

46. Lee, "The Arcadian Academy"; AHB wrote of the Arcadia in "Pope Leo's Household" and "A 'Clever' Abbe's Drama"; Dabakis, *A Sisterhood of Sculptors*, 28, refers to Corilla Olimpica of the Arcadia as a source for *Corinne* (220 n. 65–66); Dabakis, "Angelika Kauffmann, Goethe, and the Arcadian Academy in Rome."

47. Album: pubblicazioni periodiche.

48. Molinari, "Il popolo romano," 723–723.

49. "Adele Bergamini nell'ode Su Monte Mari," in Cantatore, Lanzetta, and Roscetti, *Carducci e Roma*, 5; Lee, "The Arcadian Academy," 56.

50. [Miss Jennison], "Longfellow Sonnet Miss Jennison for Arcadia 1883."

51. Brewster's membership had been sponsored by Agostino Bartolini the previous year. "Catalogo dei Pastori Arcadi 1870–1888," no. 201.

52. "Catalogo dei Pastori Arcadi 1870–1888."

53. "La scuola americana," *Il popolo romano*, 9 January 1874. Translations are mine. Ridolfi, "Pianciani, Luigi." Similar Christmas celebrations appear in annual reports Gould sent back to New York for fundraising purposes. *Italo-American Schools in Rome: First Annual Report, 1872*, 10–11; *Italo-American Schools in Rome: Second Annual Report, 1873*, 13.

54. Soper, *Building a Civil Society*, 45, 4–7, 223.

55. Soper, *Building a Civil Society*, 45, 46, 50; Lowenthal, *George Perkins Marsh: Prophet*, 249.

56. Soper, *Building a Civil Society*, 46–48, 143.

57. Soper, *Building a Civil Society*, 107, 110.

58. *Christian Work in Rome*, 6–9.

59. Carson *The Roman Years*, xxix.

60. Longfellow to George Washington Greene, 30 January 1869, in *Letters, Volume V*, 274. Hilen notes that the letter is dated 27 December 1868.

61. Soper, *Building a Civil Society*, 84–85.

62. Price, *Florence in the Nineteenth Century*, lists several family libraries in Florence, such as the Gabinetto Vieusseux. On Brewster's collections, see Stoddard, "Roman Receptions."

63. Balcony to AHB, permission to use the Corsini Library.

64. Harris, *The Cultural Work of the Late Nineteenth-Century Hostess*, 127, 125.

65. Soper, *Building a Civil Society*, 117–141, 223 n. 46.

66. Soper, *Building a Civil Society*, 121.

Chapter 7

1. Bonner, *The Radical Club*, 14. The copy also names others, including Col. T. W. Higginson, Mrs. Crane, Mrs. Ednah D. Cheney, and Louise Chandler Moulton. A 15 November 1890 article by "A Cambridge Girl" in the *Cambridge Tribune* acknowledges her copy is also inscribed with names, identified by a member of the club. Some names differ from those in Brewster's copy.

2. CCM to GPM, 5 August 1869; AHB to TD, 30 March 1879; Howe to AHB, 29 January 29 1871; AHB, "Autograph Album."

3. Elizabeth Palmer Peabody, "To Susan Cole."

4. On various approaches to social reform, apart from the literary, see Parker, *Articulating Rights*; Dowling, *Charles Eliot Norton*; Brown, *Dorothea Dix*; Hartley, *Evangelicals at a Crossroads*; Schreiber, *Modern Print Activism in the United States*.

5. Bonner, *The Radical Club*, 14.

6. Initially published anonymously in the Boston Sunday *Times*, 8 May 1875, the poem was republished soon after with the author's name affixed. McKee, "Writing Region from the Hub"; McAlexander, *The Prodigal Daughter*, 68, 70.

7. Good, "The Value of Thomas Davidson," 290; Howe, *Reminiscences*, 406, 408.

8. Sargent, "Origins of the Club," n.p.

9. Emerson, "Man the Reformer," 129–147.

10. Knight, *Memorials of Thomas Davidson*; Good, "The Value of Thomas Davidson"; Davidson, "Autobiographical Sketch," 531–536.

11. Good, "The Value of Thomas Davidson," 313 n. 5. Letters from AHB to TD at YUL are catalogued as beginning in 1876, likely a misreading of 1878. AHB to TD, May 28, 1878, refers to her having written to Goddard to thank him for introducing the two. She also requests a photo of Davidson and refers to a postcard she has received and is "enchanted with."

12. Qtd. in Good, "The Value of Thomas Davidson," 308.

13. AHB to TD, 30 March 1879, refers to Carson having taken over his apartment, above Brewster's. AHB to TD, 12 June 1878.

14. AHB to TD, 14 April 1883.

15. AHB, Journal, 7 April, 4 January 1880.

16. *Shakerism Unveiled* (1869) followed and excerpted from popular works such as Dyer, *A Portraiture of Shakerism* (1822), and Lamson, *Two Years' Experience among the Shakers* (1848). See also Ward and Ferris, *Female Life Among the Mormons* (1855).

17. AHB, Journal, 30 May 1880.

18. AHB, Journal, 6 June 1880.

19. AHB to TD, 11 October 1880.

20. Benjamin inscribed the gift volume to his sister on 25 December 1849. Brewster annotated the St. Leander entry in 1859.

21. AHB to TD, 11 October 1880. Brewster quoted a line from the letters of Mme. du Deffand, a leading salonnière of the late seventeenth century and a famous wit: "Ce n'est que le premier pas qui coûte." That is, it's the first step that matters most, and we don't really need to hear the rest. Thanks to Professor Carol E. Harrison (email to author), for this translation and explication: the Cardinal Polignac was discussing the story of St. Denis, his long walk and his terrible sufferings, and Mme. du Deffand shut him up.

22. AHB to TD, 18 January 1882.

23. AHB to TD, 21 September 1882.

24. AHB to TD, May 1883.

25. AHB to TD, 21 September 1882.

26. AHB, *St. Martin's Summer*, 154; AHB, Journal, 17 January, 27 April, 9 June 1869.

27. AHB, *PEB*, 9 December 1869.

28. Bailey, *American Travel Literature*, 172, cites Larry J. Reynolds.

29. McGreevy, *Catholicism and American Freedom*.

30. Vance, *America's Rome*, vol. 2, 94–95.

31. McGreevy, *Catholicism and American Freedom*, 11–15; Gemme, *Domesticating Foreign Struggles*, 131–155.

32. Gemme, *Domesticating Foreign Struggles*, 133.

33. See especially letters from Leonard Woolsey Bacon to J. Scudder, 7 September 1868; to S. W. Crittenden, 29 July 1871 and 26 April 1872; John R. McDougal, series of letters to S. W. Crittenden and Robert Baird, October 1872–February 1878; W. C. Van Meter, letter to S. W. Crittenden, 12 November 1872; A. R. Van Nest, Jr., report of September 1871 and series of letters to Joseph Scudder and S. W. Crittenden, 29 March 1865–4 January 1873; and Matteo Prochet to Howard Crosby, 13 July 1876.

34. McGreevy, *American Jesuits and the World*, 45, 45–46, 47.

35. "Death of Anson D. F. Randolph."

36. McGreevy, *American Jesuits and the World*, 49, cites "Dr. Bacon's Speech at the Annual Meeting of the Society."

37. McGreevy, *American Jesuits and the World*, 48–49.

38. McGreevy, *American Jesuits and the World*, 10, 21.

39. The undated gift inscription, difficult to read, begins "To Miss Brewster, from Charles T."

40. McGreevy, *American Jesuits and the World*, 11.

41. *Catalogue*, 278; Mortara, *Writing for Justice*, 57.

42. McGreevy, *American Jesuits and the World*, 37.

43. O'Shea, "Francis Patrick and Peter Richard Kenrick."

44. Griffin, *Anti-Catholicism and Nineteenth-Century Fiction*, 91–114.

45. Gemme, *Domesticating Foreign Struggles*, 146–147, called my attention to this cartoon.

46. Armellini, note, n.d. In Atkinson and Grippe, "Anne Hampton Brewster papers," Armellini's first initial is likely in error, as Torquatus Armellini seems the most likely correspondent; see "Armellini, Torquato."

47. Carlo, who had been one of Pope Pius IX's closest supporters in his early years, later would be responsible for an inventory of church property, a step that religious institutions rightly saw as a threat toward "confiscation of church holdings." Clergy who refused to participate were jailed. After the pope's flight from Rome, Carlo, at age 71, had been elected by the Roman citizens along with radicals Giuseppe Mazzini and Aurelio Saffi as a member of their new Constituent Assembly in January 1849. His opening address to the assembly asked them "to construct a building" to "rise from that rubble" lying between the Italy of the Caesars and the Italy of the Popes. Soon after, the Assembly voted that the pope would no longer have temporal power. Kertzer, *The Pope Who Would Be King*, 179, 190.

48. Armellini to AHB, 29 March 1870.

49. Armellini to AHB, n.d. Armellini referenced "the *Univers* (Sept. 22d & 23d 1854)." On the *Univers*, see McGreevy, *American Jesuits and the World*, 29.

50. From Fergola, *Teoria de' miracoli esposta.*

51. AHB, Journal, 17 January 1871.

52. AHB, Journal,19 January 1871.

53. "Francis Silas Marean Chatard"; AHB, Journal, 14 January 1870.

54. AHB, Journal, 18 September 1870, emphasis mine.

55. AHB, Journal, 27 December 1869.

56. Simon, *The Papers of Ulysses S. Grant*, 224–225, n. 1; Savidge, *Life of Benjamin Harris Brewster*, 101–105.

57. AHB, Journal, 5 August, 15 December 1870. Brewster attributed her illness to the excitement of Italian troops entering Rome on 20 September. She spent a month in Florence and did not pick up her journal again until mid-December.

58. AHB, Journal, 23 November 1869.

59. AHB, Journal, 23 November 1869.

60. AHB, Journal, 27 December 1869.

61. AHB, Journal, 1 January 1870.

62. AHB, Journal, 9 January 1870.

63. AHB, Journal, 16 January 1870.

64. AHB, Journal, 23, 30 January 1870.

65. Crane, *Caroline Crane Marsh*, 38; Browning, "To Miss I. Blagden."

66. *Catalogue*, 220, lists Michael Faraday, "Observations on the Education of the Judgment," and Tyndall, "Life and Letters of Faraday." Tyndall's volume also included the essay "Miracles and Special Providences" and his "Scope and Limit of Scientific Materialism." The Marsh library also contained several works by Tyndall on science and religion.

67. Browning, "To Miss I. Blagden"; Crane, *Caroline Crane Marsh*, 38, 41–42.

68. CCM, Journal, 27 March 1863; Lowenthal and Quartermaine, *Un'americana alla corte dei Savoia*, 164.

69. From "Saints and Miracles" (1867), qtd. in Lowenthal, *George Perkins Marsh: Prophet*, 347.

70. Lowenthal, *George Perkins Marsh: Versatile*, 302.

71. Lowenthal, *George Perkins Marsh: Prophet*, 346–347.

72. CCM, "Story, Italian Setting."

73. CCM, Journal, 19 October 1873.

74. Although the author is not given, the title and publication date adhere to the description in Bacon, *A Life Worth Living*, 39. American Tract Society publication seems to have played off the popular and longstanding monthly newspaper *The Little Pilgrim*, edited and published in Philadelphia by Grace Greenwood (Sara Jane Lippincott) and Leander K. Lippincott, from 1854 through 1868. Contributors included Mary Howitt and Mrs. S. C. Hall.

75. Martin, "Two Women," 114, describes Gould as having taught a class of forty "when herself little more than a child." [EBG], "Little Caroline," 5–6.

76. [EBG], "Little Caroline," 10–11.

77. [EBG], "Little Caroline," 15–16. The narrator explains to her "dear children" that although little Carrie was "lovely," she will become "a thousand times lovlier." She will not be "subject to sickness and decay," so when they see her again she "will have a form of heavenly beauty."

78. [Mitchell], "Miss Mitchell's Journal."

Chapter 8

1. EBG to Dr. Thompson, 22 December 1867.

2. Peabody, "To Susan Cole," 369–370.

3. Gaul, *To Marry an Indian*, 66, 42–44.

4. AHB, Journal, 7 July 1870 and 28 March 1872; Peabody, "To Susan Cole," 369–370; Martin, "Two Women," 115; Bacon, *A Life Worth Living*, 155–162; Trollope, *In Memoriam*; Pons, "Fuà Fusinato e Emilia Gould," 60–62; "Gould, Emily Bliss," 693–694; and "Memorials of Mrs. Gould of Rome," 723–724.

5. Sánchez-Eppler, *Dependent States*, 191, 189, 218.

6. Robbins, *Managing Literacy, Mothering America*, 206–207.

7. Bailey, *American Travel Literature*, 17, 72.

8. Bailey, *American Travel Literature*, 74–75, 165–169.

9. [EBG], "Rambles among the Italian Hills," 399, 403.

10. [EBG], "Rambles among the Italian Hills," 402, 401.

11. [EBG], "Rambles among the Italian Hills," 402.

12. [EBG], "Rambles among the Italian Hills," 402.

13. [EBG], "Rambles among the Italian Hills," 404.
14. [EBG], "Rambles among the Italian Hills," 406.
15. [EBG], "Rambles among the Italian Hills," 404.
16. [EBG], "Rambles among the Italian Hills. No. II," 325.
17. [EBG], "Rambles among the Italian Hills. No. III," 46–47.
18. [EBG], "Rambles among the Italian Hills. No. III," 33, 39–40.
19. [EBG], "Rambles among the Italian Hills. No. III," 41.
20. D. Reynolds, *Beneath the American Renaissance*, 64–65; McGreevy, *American Jesuits*, 20.
21. [EBG], "Rambles among the Italian Hills. No. II," 325.
22. [EBG], "Rambles among the Italian Hills. No. II," 320.
23. [EBG], "Rambles among the Italian Hills. No. II," 325.
24. [EBG], "Rambles among the Italian Hills. No. II," 321.
25. [EBG], "Rambles among the Italian Hills. No. II," 321.
26. [EBG], "Rambles among the Italian Hills. No. IV," 256.
27. Dennis, *The Cities and Cemeteries of Etruria.*
28. [EBG], "Rambles among the Italian Hills. No. IV," 259.
29. Acts 17:27–28.
30. Dennis, *The Cities and Cemeteries of Etruria*, 54.
31. [EBG], "Gossip Abroad," January 1869, 95.
32. [EBG], "Gossip Abroad," January 1869, 95.
33. [EBG], "Gossip Abroad," February 1869, 195.
34. [EBG], "Gossip Abroad," February 1869, 197.
35. [EBG], "Gossip Abroad," March 1869, 286.
36. [EBG], "Gossip Abroad," March 1869, 287.
37. [EBG], "Gossip Abroad," May 1869, 481.
38. *Italo-American Schools in Rome*, 15.
39. *Italo-American Schools in Rome: Mrs. Gould's Work and Wants* [187-], 13; EBG, *Italo-American Schools at Rome*, [1874].
40. Ditz, "Formative Ventures," qtd. in Gaul, *To Marry an Indian*, 42–43.
41. Gaul and Harris, *Letters and Transformations in the United States*, 9–10; Waggoner and Nemmers, *Yours in Filial Regard*, 2.
42. *Italo-American Schools in Rome*, 3. All quotes in this paragraph are from this page.
43. *Italo-American Schools in Rome: First Annual Report*, 13; Bacon, *A Life Worth Living*, 103; Romani, "Erminia Fuà Fusinato."
44. *Italo-American Schools in Rome: First Annual Report*, 4; *Italo-American Schools in Rome*, 7, 8, 10.
45. *Italo-American Schools in Rome: First Annual Report*, 15; Bacon, *A Life Worth Living*, 124; Volpicelli, "Un'americana a Roma," 637; *Italo-American Schools in Rome: Second Annual Report*, 9–10; EBG to Caetani, 187?; *Italo-American Schools in Rome*, 15.

46. *Italo-American Schools in Rome: First Annual Report*, 4; Bacon, *A Life Worth Living*, 114; Ellis to the Trustees of the Seminary, July 3, 1872.

47. *Italo-American Schools in Rome: Second Annual Report*, 7; *Italo-American Schools in Rome: First Annual Report*, 13; *Italo-American Schools in Rome: Second Annual Report*, 16–17.

48. *Italo-American Schools in Rome*, 13; *Italo-American Schools in Rome: First Annual Report*, 5–8.

49. D. Reynolds, *Beneath the American Renaissance*, 64–65; McGreevy, *American Jesuits and the World*, 20; Griffin, *Anti-Catholicism and Nineteenth-Century Fiction*, 91–114; Jacob Brinkerhof, for example, compelled to state he was not Jewish by blood or faith, wrote from the Supreme Court of Ohio inquiring about what would happen to Mortara: Brinkerhof to GPM, 29 September 1870; Kolich, "Miriam and the Conversion of the Jews"; Kertzer, *The Kidnapping of Edgardo Mortara*, 154–166.

50. *Italo-American Schools in Rome: First Annual Report*, 9; Bacon, *A Life Worth Living*, 162.

51. *Italo-American Schools in Rome: First Annual Report*, 12.

52. EBG, *Italo-American Schools at Rome*, 1.

53. EBG, *Italo-American Schools at Rome*, 7, 13.

54. EBG, *Italo-American Schools at Rome*, 13.

55. Porterfield, *Mary Lyon and the Mount Holyoke Missionaries*, 41.

56. Soper, *Building a Civil Society*, 4–7.

57. Gaul, *To Marry an Indian*, 64.

58. Copies of letters Prochet wrote to Gould exist in the Fondo Prochet, Waldensian Archives (ATV); the location of letters Gould wrote to Prochet is unknown.

59. Prochet to EBG, 28 April 1873.

60. EBG to GPM, 8 September 1869, emphasis mine.

61. EBG to GPM, 23 January 1869, emphasis mine.

62. GPM, to EBG, 3 August 1868. The letter concludes with personal details about travel: "If I had my way, we would go to Paris, but my wife won't. Well I wish you health & wealth."

63. Lowenthal, *George Perkins Marsh: Versatile*, 316.

64. Qtd. in Madden, *Selections from Eliza Leslie*, 263. Leslie explains, "Even if the wife sees and reads every letter, she will, in all probability, feel a touch of jealousy, (or more than a touch,) if she finds that they excite interest in her husband, or give him pleasure." The jealously "will inevitably be the case if the married lady is inferior in intellect to the single one, and has a lurking consciousness that she is so."

65. Santini, *Cento anni di vita dell'Istituto Gould*, 7; Volpicelli, "Un'americana a Roma," 633.

66. *Italo-American Schools in Rome: First Annual Report*, 12; *Italo-American Schools in Rome: Second Annual Report*, 9.

67. In addition, Prochet's four letters to Giovanni Paolo Buffa discuss specifically his teaching in Rome. Prochet wrote four letters to Enrico Bosio in 1874 to

address his being sent to Rome to teach and to work with the sick, by decision of the Evangelism Committee. The same year, Prochet wrote nearly a dozen letters to Carolina Dalgas, a hymnwriter and translator, author of Sunday school literature, and teacher in Livorno, who moved to Rome after having been offered a position to direct the superior school there.

68. Spoken communication with archivist Gabriella Ballesio, TP, September 2015.

69. *Christian Work in Rome*, 5–6.

70. *Christian Work in Rome*, 6–7, qtd. from the *Italian Daily News*.

71. Prochet to Garnier, 22 January 1874.

72. Prochet to Ribetti, 28 June, 7 July, 5, 7 August 1871. Prochet to Buffa, January, 8 October 1873, 6 February, 10 March 1874.

73. Prochet to Ribetti, 2 and 9 December 1873, January 1874. He asks advice on who should assume directorship (doubting Dalgas's ability to "perservere"), confirms that it is the "Signora" rather than the "Signorina" DeSanctis, and says that he has not extended a formal invitation but only raised a semi-official question of her interest. Of Arnoulet, he explains that he has high regard for her but some doubts of her capacity as a director. Having rarely left the region of Torre Pellice, she knows little of the world. Letters later in the spring refer to Dalgas's appointment as directress (March and May 1874). On August 8 of that year, he writes about a room having been found and that Mlle. Josephine Arnoulet has accepted the position to teach. He writes Dalgas five letters in this period: 4, 23 April, 19 May, 1 July, 15 August 1874, and six more before year's end.

74. Prochet to EBG, 24 April 1873.

75. Prochet to EBG, 28 April 1873.

76. Prochet to EBG, 24 November 1874.

77. Prochet to EBG, 1 December 1874.

Chapter 9

1. AHB, Journal, 12 January 1872.

2. AHB, Journal, 26 August 1876.

3. Lutes, *Front-Page Girls*; Edelstein, *Between the Novel and the News*; Fahs, *Out on Assignment*; and Beasley, *Women of the Washington Press*. Wright, *American Novelists in Italy*, 108–114, Larabee, *Anne Hampton Brewster*, 4, and "Brewster, Anne Hampton," 134, place Brewster among American women writers.

4. Fahs, *Out on Assignment*, 232–233.

5. Madden, "American Anne Hampton Brewster's Social Circles," 117–144.

6. Lanciani to AHB, n.d.; AHB, Journal, 17 May 1871 and November 1873. AHB, "In the Roman Campagna" and "Roman Archaeology," are her last references to Lanciani in news accounts.

7. AHB, "Italian Academies"; Lanciani, *Topografia di Roma antica.*

8. Palombi, *Rodolfo Lanciani*, 47, 51–52, 120.

9. AHB to Jackson, 5 July 1869.

10. AHB to Jackson, 5 July 1869, emphasis mine.

11. AHB, translations; Murray, *A Handbook of Rome*, 29; AHB, "Foreign Notes. Letter from Italy," *PEB*, 2 October 1873, 6. WorldCat lists copies in French of Visconti's and Lanciani's *Guide du Palatin* (1873).

12. AHB, Journal, 7 January 1876; Lanciani, "The Hidden Wealth of the Tiber." From 1876 to 1913, Lanciani regularly sent letters to the English *Athenaeum*, collected later in Cubberly, *Notes from Rome.* Murray, *A Handbook of Rome*, iii, 9, 29, 59, 67, 101, 273, 279, 337, 442, 472; Baedeker, *Italy*, 224; Lanciani, *A Handbook of Rome.*

13. Jackson, *The Business of Letters*, 38, 40.

14. AHB to TD, 27 January 1881.

15. AHB, Journal, August 1867–May 1871, p. 187.

16. AHB, Journal, August 1867–May 1871.

17. AHB, Journal, August 1855–April 1858. On this period of her life and its influence on her decade in the US, see Madden, "Anne Hampton Brewster's *St. Martin's Summer.*"

18. There's no evidence of this article having been published.

19. AHB, Journal, August 1867–May 1871, p. 187.

20. AHB, Journal, 7 November 1868.

21. AHB, Journal, 7 November 1868.

22. AHB, Journal, 2 January 1869.

23. Fisher, *A Gentle Journalist Abroad*, 18.

24. AHB, Journal, 17 January 1869; Kertzer, *Prisoner of the Vatican*, 127–128.

25. Lamberts, *The Black International*, 7–9.

26. AHB, Journal, 2 January 1869.

27. Ducci, *George P. Marsh Correspondence*, 10–11.

28. AHB, Journal, 2 January 1869.

29. Nardi to AHB, n.d. (with 2 calling cards).

30. Fisher, *A Gentle Journalist Abroad*, 16; Larabee, *Anne Hampton Brewster*, 24. Brewster explained that "Mr. Childs has sent three letters home for me to a New York journal which . . . he thinks will engage me to send letters twice a month." Later she recorded that she had been sending letters to the *Philadelphia Evening Bulletin* for two months and occasionally to other journals. AHB, Journal, January 2, and 27 April 1869.

31. AHB, 17 January 1869. See also Fisher, *A Gentle Journalist Abroad*, 18.

32. Vance, *America's Rome*, vol. 2, 95.

33. Beasley, *Women of the Washington Press*, 7, 17–18, 20–22.

34. AHB, Journal, 17 January 1869.

35. Lyons, "Love Letters and Writing Practices," 232–239, 235; Gaul, *To Marry an Indian*, 66, 42–44.

36. Nardi to AHB, n.d.

37. Fisher, *A Gentle Journalist Abroad*, 18. She cites Brewster's copybook entry of 21 September 1871.

38. AHB, "Letter from Rome," *PEB*, 9 December 1869.

39. AHB, "Letter from Rome," *PEB*, 9 December 1869.

40. Madden, "Reconfiguring the Margins" and "Woolson's Rome and Anne Hampton Brewster's American Newspaper Audiences, 1881." Graduate student assistants Natalie Whitaker and Gail Edie conducted this bibliographic research: At least 102 appeared in twenty-one different states, beginning in 1868 and continuing through 1886. To date, forty-seven distinct accounts with several reprints have been located. Sixty-six of these note where original publication locale, while thirty-seven provide no source. Most reprints appeared first in seven publications: *Blackwood's* (1), *BDA* (7), *Lippincott's Magazine* (3), *New York Evening Post* (1), *New York World* (15), *PEB* (32), and *Philadelphia Telegraph* (7). Reprints appeared most frequently in the *St. Louis Globe-Democrat* (11) and the Memphis *Public Ledger* (10). Reprints appeared in nineteen states, Washington, DC, and Hawaii, with the majority in the Midwest and upper South. Almost half appeared in Tennessee (19), Missouri (15), and Ohio (14). The *Public Ledger* may have published Brewster's work due to a relationship between *Ledger* owners the Whitmore brothers and Childs, publisher of the Philadelphia *Public Ledger* and Brewster's long-time friend and professional supporter. Reputedly, William Whitmore visited the *Philadelphia Public Ledger* and was so impressed with it that he adopted the name for his own newspaper. See "About Public Ledger."

41. Bailey, *American Travel Literature,* 172, quotes L. Reynolds, *European Revolutions*, 1988, 76; Putzi, introduction, *Two Men*, xviii; Amstutz, "Elizabeth Stoddard as Returned Californian," 74, qtd. in Putzi, xlix n. 10.

42. Edelstein, *Between the Novel and the News*, 89–92, 94, 108–109.

43. AHB, "Letter from Rome," 6, 10, 12, 13, 20, 23, 28, 30 April 1869. Letters on page 2 appeared 23 April, 7 July, 13 October 1869. Letters appeared in *PEB* (p. 2 except as indicated) on 4, 12, 22 August, 1, 8 (p. 1), 16, 21, 29 September, and 11, 20, 29 October 1870; in *BDA* (p. 2), 8 August, 10 October 1870; in the *Cincinnati Commercial*, 26 September 1870, p. 2, 24 October 1870, p. 1.

44. AHB, "Letter from Rome," *PEB*, 9 December 1869, p. 1; AHB, "Gossip from Rome Chat about the Infallibility Dogma," *BDA*, 8 August 1870; *OED Online*, 2018, s.v. "Jonathan, n."

45. The volume is one of two by Hemans in Brewster's library, which also contains a volume of Felicia Hemans's poems.

46. Fahs, *Out on Assignment*, 233. She cites Ardis and Collier, *Transatlantic Print Culture, 1880–1940*, 170.

47. AHB, "Letter from Rome (News)."

48. AHB, Journal, 12 January 1872.

49. Almost all of the approximately 50 letters from Brewster to Davidson, composed between May 1878 and February 1885, include such terms.

50. AHB to Jackson, 5 July 1869.

51. Larabee, *Anne Hampton Brewster*, 27, 29. Larabee draws from Brewster's journals to list 1871 as the first year and 1885 as the last, but a typo reads 1871–75.

52. AHB, Journal, 25 July 1875.

53. AHB, Journal, 14 March 1875.

54. AHB, Journal, 14 March 1875. She wrote similarly of Anna Vernon in 1890. Larabee, *Anne Hampton Brewster*, 30.

55. AHB, Journal, 4 [January] 1882 [mislabeled December].

56. Carson, *The Roman Years*, 27, 132, 140, 143–144, 155–156, 159, 167, 174–178, 188; AHB, Journal, 18 July, 7 December 1884, 26 February 1885.

57. AHB, Journal, 17 January 1869, 7 June, 13 August 1870, 18 April 1871, 17 May, 12 June 1874, 17 January, 29 June 1875.

58. Hosmer, *1975*.

59. AHB, Journal, 17 January 1875.

60. AHB, Journal, 6 June 1876.

61. Atkinson and Grippe, "Anne Hampton Brewster papers," 7, 37; AHB, Journal, 27 December 1869, 8 March 1876.

62. Edwards to AHB. The dated letters begin 31 December 1871 and continue through 15 November 1873. Edwards, *Ballads*, 71–72. The last letter refers to another gift book, *Untrodden Peaks* (Leipzig, Tauchnitz, 1873), in Brewster's library.

63. AHB, Journal, 29 December 1871, 12, 13, 14 January, 8 February [mislabeled 8 January], 26 February 1872.

64. AHB, Journal, 12 January 1872.

65. AHB, Journal, 12 January 1872.

66. AHB, Journal, 12 January 1872.

67. Corson, "An American Salon in Rome," 619.

68. Emerson, "Fate"; AHB, Journal, 12 January 1872.

69. Emerson, "Give all to Love," 688–689.

70. AHB, Journal, 12 January 1872.

71. AHB, Journal, 12 January 1872.

72. AHB, Journal, 13 January 1872.

73. AHB, Journal, [14 January 1872].

74. AHB, Journal, 8 [February, mislabeled] January 1872.

75. AHB, Journal, 26 February 1872.

76. Edwards, *Ballads*, 72.

77. AHB, Journal, 16 January 1870; Howe to AHB, 29 January 1871; AHB to TD, 3 June 1878; Larabee, *Anne Hampton Brewster*, 28–29.

Chapter 10

1. Haight to CCM, 1868.

2. Haight to CCM, 1868; "Luigi Vannuccini."

3. A lengthy testimony survives in the Crane Family Papers and vague discussions appear in correspondence among others in the Anglo community in Florence, such as Joanna Horner. Thanks to Lindsey Nichole Chappell for this information. San Clemente to CCM, 1 November 1875; Lindbert to CCM, 12 October 1877.

4. CCM to ABC, 19 December 1876.

5. CCM, "Family." See Guide to the Crane Family Papers, https://www.nypl.org/sites/default/files/archivalcollections/pdf/cranefamily.pdf. Carrie was the child of Caroline's brother Thomas of Indiana, who was widowed. His three children returned to Massachusetts to be raised by Caroline's mother.

6. Marsh wrote of visits by children of her sister Lucy: "Fred": "a brilliant young man, now practicing law in St. Louis . . . was with us in Europe one year" and "namesake . . . 'Carrie' who came to us in 1877 and spent one year." Also Mary, daughter of her brother, and nephew Alexander B. Crane and his family, including Laura Vernon, a relative of Alexander, who served as a governess to daughters Elizabeth Green, Caroline Emma, Helen Cornelia, Aurelia Blair, and Laura Vernon—named for the governess. CCM, "Family." Lowenthal, *George Perkins Marsh: Prophet*, 361, notes that the governess and "six children, ranging in age from twelve to two" began a long stay in 1881 and were joined by their father and mother sometime thereafter, remaining through George's death in 1882.

7. Daniels, "In Italy with Mr. and Mrs. George Perkins Marsh," 194.

8. CCM, Journal, 1 October–1 December 1873. Caroline refers four times in the fall of 1873 to their "wards": 9 October refers to "two photos of our blessed child" brought by Miss Bennett; 10 October says "The Wards come to-morrow"; 11 October says "Our little maid Filomena came to see us just returned from her long journey east, west, north & south with the Wards"; and 29 October says "My little protégé Cappelli is a nice looking boy of 3 or 4 very revolutionary apparently." On the Marshes' role with the orphanange and school, see Lowenthal, *George Perkins Marsh: Prophet*, 384, and *Report of the Executive Committee of the Protestant Orphanage for Girls*.

9. CCM to ABC, 19 December 1876.

10. Lowenthal, *George Perkins Marsh: Prophet*, 181, 315–317.

11. CCM, "Family"; Crane, *Caroline Crane Marsh*, 71. Letters documenting these losses include: on George Ozias, GPM to CCM, 26 January 1856; on Carrie's drowning, Fox to GPM, 1 June 1875; Mathews to Edmunds, 23 June 1875; Fox to GPM, 1 July 1875; Mathews to ABC, 7 July 1875; on Ellen's health and death, Briggs to CCM, 18 April 1873, and numerous family letters from 1868 through 1871.

12. Helen Crane to ABC, 30 October 1871.

13. Mario Gigliucci to Elena, 21 May 1869.

14. Cooper, "Novello, Clara Anastasia"; Brewster, "Autograph Album."

15. CCM to GPM, 19 August 1869.

16. Mario Gigliucci to Elena, 21 May 1869. The names Helen and Ellen are used almost interchangeably in Italian, which does not pronounce the letter "H."

17. CCM, Journal, 1 October–1 December 1873; Marsh wrote of plans for Ellen's voyage to New York and of Helen's arrival; she and George exchanged one niece for another, CCM to ABC, 16 September 1871, 3 and 5 October 1871; Clara Gigliucci to CCM, 31 August 1874. In the winter of 1875, Marsh wrote to Alick that it would be "best for Helen to go home in the spring" and for niece Carrie to replace her. Her stated concern was Alick's stress-induced ill-health and reasoning that Helen could be of assistance to their aging parents. Letter to ABC, 26 January 1875. Helen writes from Providence to Caroline in March of 1879, explaining that she has written to the Gigliuccis in Genoa and hoping that the address she has used is the correct one. When A. B. Crane's daughters Helen, Aurelia, and Eizabeth travel abroad between 1889 and 1900, they write of seeing the Gigliuccis.

18. CCM to GPM, 19 August 1869; EBG to GPM, 11 July 1869, 21 July 1869, 20 August 1869, 8 September 1869, 23 September 1869.

19. Lowenthal, *George Perkins Marsh: Prophet*, 361.

20. Lowenthal, *George Perkins Marsh: Prophet*, 361; CCM, Journal, 22 August 1880.

21. CCM to GPM, 15 August 1869.

22. Allen to CCM, 29 September 1869.

23. CCM, Journal, 6 November 1873.

24. Lowenthal, "The Marriage of Choice,"169; Lowenthal, *George Perkins Marsh: Prophet*, 384. His sources include Collegio Ferretti (Protestant Orphanage for Girls), *Report of the Executive Committee for the Year 1882* (Florence, 1883).

25. Astor to CCM, n.d.; Phillipson to CCM, 9 May 1868; Wurts to CCM, 13 July 1868; Ross to CCM, 20 December 1868; Forbes to CCM, 1868.

26. Cyrus Field to GPM, via ABC, 17 March 1871.

27. CCM to GPM, 5 August, 15 August 1869. See also CCM to GPM, 9 August 1869; Jeannie Field [Mrs. Dudley Field] to CCM, August 1869, and Jeannie Field [Miss] to CCM, August 4, 1869.

28. Wheeler to CCM, 22 September 1869; Allen to CCM, 29 September 1869; Mrs. Lyndon Marsh to CCM, 7 December [1870].

29. Graham to CCM, 1874; Gadda to CCM, n.d.; Limone to CCM, 8 March and 15 March 1874; Madame Hedwig de Kendell [1875], unable to attend a bazaar, sent "a gift"; E[lizabeth] Lawrence to CCM, [1875], enclosed 100 fr for poor Madame Biscaccianti (an Italian in Boston who was ill) and trusted that the subscription list was successful. Fonda Gadda in Gabinetto Vieusseux includes several

Luisa Gadda manuscripts connected to senator Giuseppe Gadda; see https://www.vieusseux.it/inventari/gadda_mittenti.pdf.

30. Elizabeth Crane to CCM, 8 July 1873.

31. Possibly a decimal is missing. CCM, Journal, 6 November, 9 November 1873. Conversions from https://www.historicalstatistics.org/Currencyconverter.html and https://www.in2013dollars.com/us/inflation/1873.

32. CCM, Journal, 6 November, 9 November 1873. *Catalogue*, 222, 570, includes "Remarks on the Character and Writings of Fénelon" in Channing's *Works* and De Ribbe's *Les familles et la société en France*. Froude's essay, "Philosophy of Catholicism," is not listed in the *Catalogue*.

33. GPM, "Translation."

34. CCM, Journal, 19 October 1873.

35. CCM, Journal, 19 October 1873. *Catalogue*, 35, lists Arnold's *Literature and Dogma*.

36. GPM, "Translation," 616, my emphasis.

37. Staël, *Politics, Literature, and National Character*, 301, 289. *Catalogue*, 642, includes Richter's Review of Madame de Staël's *Allemagne*, *Corinne*, and *Pensées et Lettres*.

38. Staël, "The Spirit of Translations," 1816, qtd. in Boggs, *Transnationalism and American Literature*, 95.

39. Boggs, *Transnationalism and American Literature*, 100.

40. Taylor to CCM, 10 April 1873; Mme. Katie de Saint Seigne to CCM, 29 March 1875. Later in the decade her literary connections would include Mrs. Mark H. Emilia Pattison and Mrs. William Grey, also known as Maria Emelia Sherriff.

41. Elizabeth Crane to CCM, 5 May 1873; CCM, "Life's Lesson," 29–34.

42. Bell, *The First Total War*, 54–65. Marsh likely accessed Fénelon's ideas through William Ellery Channing's comments on them and reprinted selections, translated by "A Lady" [Lydia Maria Child] and published in *The Christian Examiner* (Boston 1829). The Marsh library also included Fénelon's *Le siege de Metz par Charles-Quint en 1552*, in Michaud and Poujoulat, *Mémoires*, 1866, vol. 8. *Catalogue*, 222. CCM, Journal, 6 November, 9 November 1873.

43. Mortara, *Writing for Justice*, 57.

44. Gemme, *Domesticating Foreign Struggles*; Vance, *America's Rome*.

45. CCM, Journal, 9 November 1873.

46. Lowenthal, "The Marriage of Choice," 157–174; Quartermaine, "Views from Beyond the Alps," 61–77; Lowenthal and Quartermaine, *Un'americana alla corte dei Savoia*.

47. Lowenthal, "The Marriage of Choice," 157–158.

48. In Lowenthal and Quartermaine, *Un'americana alla corte dei Savoia*, 9 (Notebook I, 16 June 1861), 21 (Notebook I, 27 August 1861), 155 (Notebook VIII, 8 February 1863), 164 (Notebook VIII, 27 March 1863), 173 (Notebook

IX, 20 April 1863), 166 (Notebook VIII, 27 March 1863), 176 (Notebook IX, 26 April 1863).

49. In Lowenthal and Quartermaine, *Un'americana alla corte dei Savoia*, 174 (Notebook IX, 23 April 1863); *Catalogue*, 286. The anthology may have been Giuseppe Tigri's *Il montanino toscano volontario alla guerra della indipendenza italiana del 1859: racconto popolare*, which appeared in this period and includes tales of Siena. Tigri wrote from Pistoia, in Tuscany. One of Tigri's essays was bound in the volume in the Marsh library (Catalogue, 673). Another possibility is Pietro Thouar, *Racconti popolari*, which was also in the Marsh library (Catalogue, 671), but the contents do not align.

50. In Lowenthal and Quartermaine, *Un'americana alla corte dei Savoia*, 174 (Notebook IX, 23 April 1863); CCM, "Story, Italian Setting." The tale continues for forty-nine manuscript pages. Fifty draft pages exist as well. The tale also includes parental love and celebrates missionaries, goal-setting and achieving success—themes appearing in Marsh's later journal entries.

51. CCM, "Frustra Laboravi!"

52. *Catalogue*, 329, 422.

53. Bennett, *Nineteenth-Century American Women Poets*, xl.

54. CCM, Journal, 22 November, 1 December 1873.

55. Preminger and Brogan, *The New Princeton Encyclopedia of Poetry and Poetics*, 73.

56. ABC to CCM, 21 January 1870; CCM to ABC, 26 January 1875; CCM to ABC, 5 September 1875; CCM to Cornelia Crane, 11 November 1876; CCM to ABC, 19 December 1876. Lowenthal, *George Perkins Marsh: Prophet*, 361, refers to A. B. Crane in 1876 as a "half worn-out New York lawyer."

57. CCM to ABC, 22 May 1882. Alexander married Laura Cornelia Mitchell after the Civil War. *Guide to the Crane Family Papers*, 1–2. The May 22 letter from Rome predicts the entire family's journey from Florence to Vallombrosa in July 1882, where George died. According to Crane, *Caroline Crane Marsh*, 78, and Lowenthal, *George Perkins Marsh: Prophet*, 367–368, the family had been in Florence since winter, which explains why the Simboche photos are dated ca. 1881.

Coda

1. Eliot, *Middlemarch*, vol. 3–4, 371.

2. GPM, *Life and Letters of George Perkins Marsh*. The proposed second volume was never completed. However, UVM holds the manuscript.

3. Crane, *Caroline Crane Marsh*, 82.

Bibliography

Primary Sources

"About Women." *Sunday Morning Appeal*, 22 May 1870.

Album pubblicazioni periodiche stampate in Roma dal 20 settembre 1870 al 31 dicembre 1875. Archivio Storico Capitolino, Rome. www.archiviocapitolino risorsedigitali.it/index.php/esplora/albero/album-pubblicazioni-periodiche-stampate-in-roma-dal-20-settembre-1870-al-31-dicembre-1875/14141/14141.

Alison, Archibald. *History of Europe from the Commencement of the French Revolution in 1789 to the Restoration of the Bourbons in 1815*. Edinburgh: Blackwood Magazine, 1866.

Allen, Mrs. C. Letter to CCM, 29 September 1869. Box 19. CFP.

Arbesser, Rosa. Letter to GPM, 1 September [1869]. Carton 5, folder 48, item 313. UVM.

Arcadia Certificate of Membership for Anne Hampton Brewster (with envelope), 1873. Series VI, box 20, folder 8. AHBP.

Armellini, J. Note, n.d. Series I, box 1, folder 4. AHBP.

———. Letter to AHB, 29 March 29 1870. Series I, box 1, folder 3. AHBP.

Arnold, Matthew. *Literature and Dogma: An Essay Towards a Better Understanding of the Bible*. London: Smith Elder, 1873.

Astor, Mrs. J. J. Augusta. Letter to CCM, n.d. Box 19. CFP.

Bacci, Daniele. "Il Fondo Angelo Conti." *Il Vieusseux*, Gennaio-Aprile 1989, 79–91.

Bacon, Leonard Woolsey. Letter to S. W. Crittenden, 29 July 1871. Box 1, folder 21. AFCU.

———. Letter to S. W. Crittenden, 26 April 1872. Box 1, folder 21. AFCU.

———. Letter to J. Scudder, 7 September 1868. Box 1, folder 21. AFCU.

———. *A Life Worth Living: Memorials of Emily Bliss Gould of Rome*. New York: A. D. F. Randolph, 1879.

Baedeker, K. *Italy. Handbook for Travellers: Second Part: Central Italy and Rome*. Leipzig: Baedeker, 1879.

Balcony, San Andrea A.N. Letter to AHB. Series I, box 1, folder 59. AHBP.

Bonner, Sherwood [Katherine Sherwood Bonner McDowell]. "The Radical Club: A poem/respectfully dedicated to 'The Infinite' by 'An Atom.'" *Boston Times*, 8 June 1875.

————. *The Radical Club: A Poem*, Boston: Times Publishing, 1876.

Botta, Anne C. Lynch. *Memoirs of Anne C. L. Botta: Written by Her Friends. With Selections from Her Correspondence and from Her Writings in Prose and Poetry.* New York: J. Selwin Tait and Sons, 1894. name.umdl.umich.edu/ABX9247.0001.001.

Brewster, Anne Hampton. "Autograph Album," n.d. Series XI, box 26, folder 25. AHBP.

———. "A 'Clever' Abbe's Drama." *New York World*, 8 July 1878.

———. *Compensation; or, Always a Future*. Philadelphia, 1860.

———. "Foreign Notes. Letter from Italy." *PEB*, 2 October 1873.

———. "In the Roman Campagna." *Boston Sunday Herald*, 6 November 1887.

———. "Italian Academies." *BDA*, 19 January 1881.

———. Journal, August 1855–April 1858. Series II, box 2, folder 3. AHBP.

———. Journal, May 1865–July 1867. Series II, box 3, folder 4. AHBP.

———. Journal, August 1867–May 1871. Series II, box 4, folder 1. AHPB.

———. Journal, October 1871–April 1874. Series II, box 4, folder 4. AHBP.

———. Journal, April 1874–Feb. 1877. Series II, box 4, folder 5. AHBP.

———. Journal, February 1877–November 1877. Series II, box 5, folder 1. AHBP.

———. Journal, December 1877–October 1882. Series II, box 5, folder 2. AHBP.

———. Journal, October 1882–October 1885. Series II, box 5, folder 3. AHBP.

———. Journal, September 1886–September 1888. Series II, box 6, folder 1. AHBP.

———. "Letter from Italy." *PEB*, 1 July 1870.

———. "Letter from Rome." (Series of articles.) *PEB*, 4 April 1869–29 October 1870.

———. "Letter from Rome (News)." *BDA*, 6 October 1870.

———. Letter to Angelo Conti, 22 December 1886. Fondo Angelo Conti, Archivio Contemporaneo, Gabinetto Vieusseux, Florence, Italy.

———. Letter to TD, 28 May 1878. MS 169, series I, box 3, folder 77. YUL.

———. Letter to TD, 3 June 1878. MS 169, series I, box 3, folder 77. YUL.

———. Letter to TD, 12 June 1878. MS 169, series I, box 3, folder 77. YUL.

———. Letter to TD, 13 November 1878. MS 169, series I, box 3, folder 77. YUL.

———. Letter to TD, 30 March 1879. MS 169, series I, box 3, folder 77. YUL.

———. Letter to TD, 6 July 1879. MS 169, series I, box 3, folder 77. YUL.

———. Letter to TD, 11 October 1880. MS 169, series I, box 3, folder 77. YUL.

———. Letter to TD, 23 October 1880. MS 169, series I, box 3, folder 77. YUL.

———. Letter to TD, 27 January 1881. MS 169, series I, box 3, folder 77. YUL.

———. Letter to TD, 18 January 1882. MS 169, series I, box 3, folder 77. YUL.

———. Letter to TD, 21 September 1882. MS 169, series I, box 3, folder 77. YUL.

———. Letter to TD, 14 April 1883. MS 169, series I, box 3, folder 77. YUL.

———. Letter to TD, May 1883. MS 169, series I, box 3, folder 77. YUL.

———. Letter to Helen Hunt Jackson, 5 July 1869. Part 2, Ms0156, folder 23a, Helen Hunt Jackson Papers, Colorado College. libraryweb.coloradocollege.edu/library/specialcollections/Manuscript/HHJ2-2-23a.html.

———. "Miss Cushman." *Blackwoods Magazine*, August 1878.

———. "Pope Leo's Household." *New York World*, 5 April 1878.

———. "Roman Archaeology." *Boston Sunday Herald*, 19 December 1887.

———. *St. Martin's Summer*. Boston: Ticknor & Fields, 1866.

———. Translations: "Historical Compendium of the Palatine" by Lanciani and Visconti, n.d. Series V, box 20, folder 1. AHBP.

Briggs, Mrs. C. A. Letter to CCM, 18 April 1873. Box 19. CFP.

Brinkerhof, Jacob. Letter to GPM, 29 September 1870. Busta 723.12.8. Archivio del Museo Centrale del Risorgimento, Rome.

Browning, Elizabeth Barrett. "To Miss I. Blagden," 26 July 1853. In *The Letters of Elizabeth Barrett Browning*, edited by Frederic G. Kenyon, 125–126. New York: MacMillan, 1897.

Burlington Weekly Free Press (Burlington, VT), 7 January 1876. *Chronicling America: Historic American Newspapers*. Library of Congress. chroniclingamerica.loc.gov/lccn/sn86072143/1876-01-07/ed-1/seq-1/.

Butler, Alban. *The Lives of the Fathers, Martyrs, and Other Principal Saints*. Baltimore: Metropolitan Press, 1844–45.

Capel, Monsignor. Letter to AHB, 1883. Series I, box 1, folder 11. AHBP.

Carson, Caroline. *The Roman Years of a South Carolina Artist: Caroline Carson's Letters Home, 1872–1892*. Edited by William H. Pease and Jane H. Pease. Columbia: University of South Carolina Press, 2003.

"Catalogo dei Pastori Arcadi 1870–1880." No. 201. Archives of the Accademia dell'Arcadia, Biblioteca Angelica, Rome.

Catalogue of the Library of George Perkins Marsh. Burlington: University of Vermont, 1892. archive.org/details/librarygeorgeper00univ.

Channing, William Ellery. *Remarks on the Character and Writings of Fenelon*. London: Edward Rainford, 1830.

———. *The Works of William E. Channing, D.D.* 8th ed. Boston: J. Munroe; New York: C. S. Francis, 1848.

Christian Work in Rome, 1872–73. A Sketch of the Organization and Work of the American Union Church, the English and American Christian Association, the Italian Young Men's Christian Association, Church Among the Soldiers and Christian Training School for Young Men. Rome: Henry Sinimberghi, 1873.

Cowden-Clarke, Mary. Letter to AHB, n.d. Series I, box 1, folder 15. AHBP.

Corson, C. R. "An American Salon in Rome." *Lippincott's Magazine*, June 1881.

Crane, Alexander B. Letter to CCM, 21 January 1870. Box 19. CFP.

Crane, Edward A. Letter to CCM. 1 February 1870. Box 19. CFP.

Crane, Elizabeth Greene. *Caroline Crane Marsh. A Life Sketch*. [S.l.: s.m., 190?]. Available at the New York Public Library; see also Hathitrust, hdl.handle.net/2027/uc1.31175035250656.

———. Letter to CCM, 5 May 1873. Box 19. CFP.

———. Letter to CCM, 8 July 1873. Box 19. CFP.

Crane, Helen. Letter to ABC family, 30 October 1871. Box 19. CFP.

———. Letter to ABC, 3 December 1871. Box 19. CFP.

"Death of Anson D. F. Randolph." *New York Times*, 8 July 1896.

Dennis, George. *The Cities and Cemeteries of Etruria.* London: John Murray, 1848. penelope.uchicago.edu/Thayer/E/Gazetteer/Places/Europe/Italy/_Periods/Roman/Archaic/Etruscan/_Texts/DENETR*/1.html.

De Ribbe, Charles. *Les familles et la société en France avant la Révolution, d'après des documents originaux.* Paris: Albanel, 1873.

de Saint Seigne, Mme. Katie. Letter to CCM, 29 March 1875. Box 19. CFP.

"Dr. Bacon's Speech at the Annual Meeting of the Society." *Christian Union* 4 (July 1853): 311–313.

Ducci, Lucia, ed. *George P. Marsh Correspondence: Images of Italy, 1861–1881.* Madison, NJ: Fairleigh Dickinson University Press, 2012.

Dyer, Mary M. *A Portraiture of Shakerism: Exhibiting a General View of Their Character and Conduct, from the First Appearance of Ann Lee in New-England Down to the Present Time, and Certified by Many Respectable Authorities.* Concord, NH, 1822.

"The Ecumenical Council." *Daily Phoenix*, 8 August 1869.

Edwards, Amelia. *Ballads: By the Author of "Barbaras History."* London: Tinsley Bros., 1865.

———. Letters to AHB. Series I, box 1, folder 17. AHBP.

Eliot, George [Marianne Evans]. *Middlemarch: A Study of Provincial Life.* 4 vols. Berlin: A. Asher & Co.; Phil., J.B. Lippincott & co., 1872.

Ellis, Mary. Letter to the Trustees of the Seminary, 3 July 1872. LD 7092.8 Ellis. Mount Holyoke College Special Collections.

Emerson, Ralph Waldo. "The American Scholar." In *Selected Essays*, edited by Larzer Ziff, 83–105. New York: Penguin, 1985.

———. "Fate." Poetry Foundation. www.poetryfoundation.org/poems/45875/fate-56d22595a165d.

———. "Give All to Love." In *The Portable Emerson*, edited by Jeffrey S. Cramer, 688–689. New York: Penguin, 2014.

———. "Man the Reformer." In *Selected Essays*, edited by Larzer Ziff, 129–147. New York: Penguin, 1985.

———. "Self-Reliance." In *Selected Essays*, edited by Larzer Ziff, 175–203. New York: Penguin, 1985.

Emerson, Ralph Waldo, William Henry Channing, and James Freeman Clarke, eds. *Memoirs of Margaret Fuller Ossoli.* Boston: Phillips, Sampson, 1852.

Faraday, Michael. "Observations on the Education of the Judgment." In *Modern Culture: Addresses and Arguments on the Claims of Scientific Education*, edited by E. L. Youmans. London: Macmillan, 1867.

Fergola, Nicola. *Teoria de' miracoli esposta con metodo dimostrativo, seguita da un discorso apolotetico sul miracolo di S. Gennaro.* Napoli, 1839.

"La festa degli arcadi." *Il popolo romano*, 9 January 1874.

Field, Cyrus W. Letter to GPM via A. B. Crane, 17 March 1871. Box 2. CFP.

Field, Jeannie [Mrs. Dudley Field]. Letter to CCM, August 1869. Box 19. CFP.

Field, [Miss] Jeannie. Letter to CCM, 4 August 1869. Box 19. CFP.

Forbes, Miss. Letter to CCM, 1868. Box 19. CFP.

Fox, Henry. Letter to GPM, 1 June 1875. Box 19. CFP.

———. Letter to GPM, 1 July 1875. Box 19. CFP.

Friendly, Aunt. "Miss Jones." In *In Memoriam: A Wreath of Stray Leaves to the Memory of Emily Bliss Gould*, edited by Thomas Adolphus Trollope, et al., 205–220. Rome: Italo-American School, 1875.

Froude, James Anthony. "Philosophy of Catholicism." In *Short Studies on Great Subjects*, 124–132. London: Longman's, 1867. catalog.hathitrust.org/Record/101714555.

Fuller, Margaret. "Autobiographical Romance." In *The Essential Margaret Fuller*, edited by Jeffrey Steele, 24–43. New Brunswick, NJ: Rutgers University Press, 1995.

———. "Things and Thoughts in Europe." *New York Daily Tribune*, 1 January 1848. In *"These Sad but Glorious Days": Dispatches from Europe, 1846–1850*, edited by Larry J. Reynolds and Susan Belasco Smith, 161–166. New Haven, CT: Yale University Press, 1991.

Gadda, Luisa. Letter to CCM, 1874. Box 19. CFP.

Gigliucci, Clara. Letter to CCM, 31 August 1874. Box 19. CFP.

Gigliucci, Mario. Letter to Elena [Ellen Crane], 21 May 1869. Box 19. CFP.

———. *Reminiscenze d'un uomo inutile ovvero "Reminiscenze inutili d'un uomo più inutile."* Carate Brianza: Tipografia G. Moscatelli, 1937.

Goddard, D. A. Letter to AHB, 9 May 1870. Series I, box 1, folder 23. AHBP.

"Gould, Emily Bliss." In *Appleton's Cyclopaedia of American Biography*, vol. 2, edited by J. G. Wilson and J. Fiske, 693–694. New York: 1888.

Gould, Emily Bliss. "The Children's Manual for Speaking and Writing the English Language." Florence: Claudian Press, 1874.

[———.] "Gossip Abroad." (Series of articles.) *Overland Monthly*. January–May 1869.

———. *Italo-American Schools at Rome.* [1874.] NYHS.

———. Letter to Michelangelo Caetani, 187?. Fondo Caetani contemporanei, Archivio Caetani, Fondazione Camillo Caetani, Rome.

———. Letter to CCM, 12 September 1870. Carton 5, folder 61, item 312. UVM.

———. Letter to GPM, 7 February 1867. Carton 5, folder 15, item 38. UVM.

———. Letter to GPM, 23 January 1869. Carton 5, folder 40, item 21. UVM.

———. Letter to GPM, 2[?] February 1869. Carton 5, folder 41, item UVM.

———. Letter to GPM, 11 July 1869. Carton 5, folder 46, item 234. UVM.

———. Letter to GPM, 21 July 1869. Carton 5, folder 46, item 246. UVM.

———. Letter to GPM, 7 August 1869. Carton 5, folder 47, item 243. UVM.

———. Letter to GPM, 10 August 1869. Carton 5, folder 47, item 248. UVM.

———. Letter to GPM, 20 August 1869. Carton 5, folder 47, item 276. UVM.

———. Letter to GPM, 8 September 1869. Carton 5, folder 48, item 317. UVM.

———. Letter to GPM, 23 September 1869. Carton 5, folder 48, item 334. UVM.

———. Letter to GPM, 29 September 1870. Carton 5, folder 60, item 322. UVM.

———. Letter to Dr. Thompson, 22 December 1867. Box 5, folder 4. G-Miscellaneous 1865–1878. AFCU.

[———.] "Little Caroline." *Little Pilgrims*, 5–15. New York: American Tract Society, 1866.

[———.] "Rambles among the Italian Hills." *Hours at Home*, March 1866, 399–406.

[———.] "Rambles among the Italian Hills. No. II." *Hours at Home*, August 1866, 322–326.

[———.] "Rambles among the Italian Hills. No. III." *Hours at Home*, November 1866, 41–47.

[———.] "Rambles among the Italian Hills. No. IV." *Hours at Home*, January 1867, 255–259.

[———.] "Rambles among the Italian Hills. No. V. Tivoli." *Hours at Home*, May 1867, 36–43.

Gradi, Temistocle. *Racconti popolari; e Rispetti politici [di Giuseppe Tigri]*. Torino, 1862.

Graham, Mrs. Josephine. Letter to CCM, 1874. Box 19. CFP.

Greenwood, Grace [Sara Jane Lippincott]. *Haps and Mishaps of a Tour in Europe*. Boston: Ticknor, Reed, & Fields, 1854.

Guide to the Crane Family Papers. CFP. www.nypl.org/sites/default/files/archival-collections/pdf/cranefamily.pdf

Haight, Mrs. J. R. Letter to CCM, 1868. Box 19. CFP.

"Hans Andersen at a Child's Party." *Columbia Herald*, 5 November 1869.

Hare, Augustus John Cuthbert. *The Story of My Life*. New York: Dodd, Mead and Company, 1896.

Hawthorne, Julian. *Nathaniel Hawthorne and His Wife: A Biography*. 2 vols. Boston: Houghton Mifflin, 1884. catalog.hathitrust.org/Record/007472695.

Hawthorne, Nathaniel. *The French and Italian Notebooks*. Edited by Thomas Woodson. Columbus: Ohio State University Press, 1980.

———. *The Marble Faun*. Edited with introduction by Richard Brodhead. New York: Penguin, 1990.

———. *The Scarlet Letter*. New York: Penguin, 2016.

Heeren, Arnold Hermann Ludwig. *A Manual of the History of the Political System of Europe and Its Colonies*. London: Henry G. Bohn, 1857.

Hemans, Charles Isadore. *A History of Mediaeval Christianity and Sacred Art in Italy: A.D. 900–1350*. Florence: Goodban, 1869.

Hopkins, Louise. Letter to CCM, 18 February 1867. Box 18. CFP.

Hosmer, Harriet Goodhue. *1975*. [Rome]: Da Piale, [1875?].

———. Letter to GPM, 1872. Box 19. CFP.

"Housekeeping in Rome." *Charleston Daily News*, 25 December 1869.

Howe, Julia Ward. Letter to AHB, 29 January 1871. Series I, box 1, folder 31. AHBP.

———. *Reminiscences, 1819–1899*. Boston: Houghton Mifflin, 1899.

Howitt, Mary. Letter to AHB, n.d. Series I, box 1, folder 32. AHBP.

Howitt, William. "Progressive Steps of Popular Education." In *In Memoriam: A Wreath of Stray Leaves to the Memory of Emily Bliss Gould*, edited by Thomas Adolphus Trollope, et al., 55–84. Rome: Italo-American School, 1875.

Italo-American Schools in Rome: Mrs. Gould's Work and Wants. [New York? : s.n., 187-?]. NYHS.

Italo-American Schools in Rome. [1871.] NYHS.

Italo-American Schools in Rome: First Annual Report, 1872. New York: A. S. Barnes, 1872. NYHS.

Italo-American schools in Rome: Second Annual Report, 1873. NYHS.

James, Henry. *William Wetmore Story and His Friends*. 2 vols. New York: Houghton Mifflin, 1903.

[Jennison, Miss]. "Longfellow Sonnet Miss Jennison for Arcadia 1883." Series I, box 20, folder 36. AHBP.

"(Jesuits have nearly all left Rome)." *Home Journal*, 17 November 1870.

Knight, William Angus, ed. *Memorials of Thomas Davidson: A Wandering Scholar*. Boston: Ginn, 1907.

Lamson, David R. *Two Years' Experience Among the Shakers*. New York: AMS, 1972.

Lanciani, Rodolfo. *A Handbook of Rome and its Environs*. London: J. Murray, 1894.

———. "The Hidden Wealth of the Tiber." *New York Herald*, 29 March 1875.

———. Letter to AHB, 24 August 1869. Series I, box 1, folder 37. AHBP.

———. Letter to AHB, 26 August 1869. Series I, box 1, folder 37. AHBP.

———. Letter to AHB, n.d. Series I, box 1, folders 37, 38, 39. AHBP.

———. *Topografia di Roma antica*. Rome: Salviucci, 1880.

Lawrence, E[lizabeth]. Letter to CCM, [1875]. Box 19. CFP.

Lee, Vernon. "The Arcadian Academy." In *Studies of the Eighteenth Century in Italy*, 7–64. London: W. Satchell, 1880.

Leslie, Eliza. *The Ladies' Guide to True Politeness and Perfect Manners, or Miss Leslie's Behavior Book*. Philadelphia: T. B. Peterson & Brothers, 1864.

"Life in Boston." *Daily Inter-Ocean*, 2 February 1895.

Limone, Augusta. Letter to CCM, 8 March 1874. Box 19. CFP.

———. Letter to CCM, 15 March 1874. Box 19. CFP.

Lindbert, Mme. Letter to CCM, 12 October 1877. Box 19. CFP.

"Literary Folk Once Found Pleasure in a 'Botta Evening': Receptions of New York's Cultivated Instituted by Anne Charlotte Lynch, Brought Together Many of America's Brilliant Men and Women of Letters." *Christian Science Monitor*, 4 January 1914.

Longfellow, Henry Wadsworth. *The Letters of Henry Wadsworth Longfellow, Volume V, 1866–1874*. Edited by Andrew Hilen. Cambridge, MA: Harvard University Press, 1982.

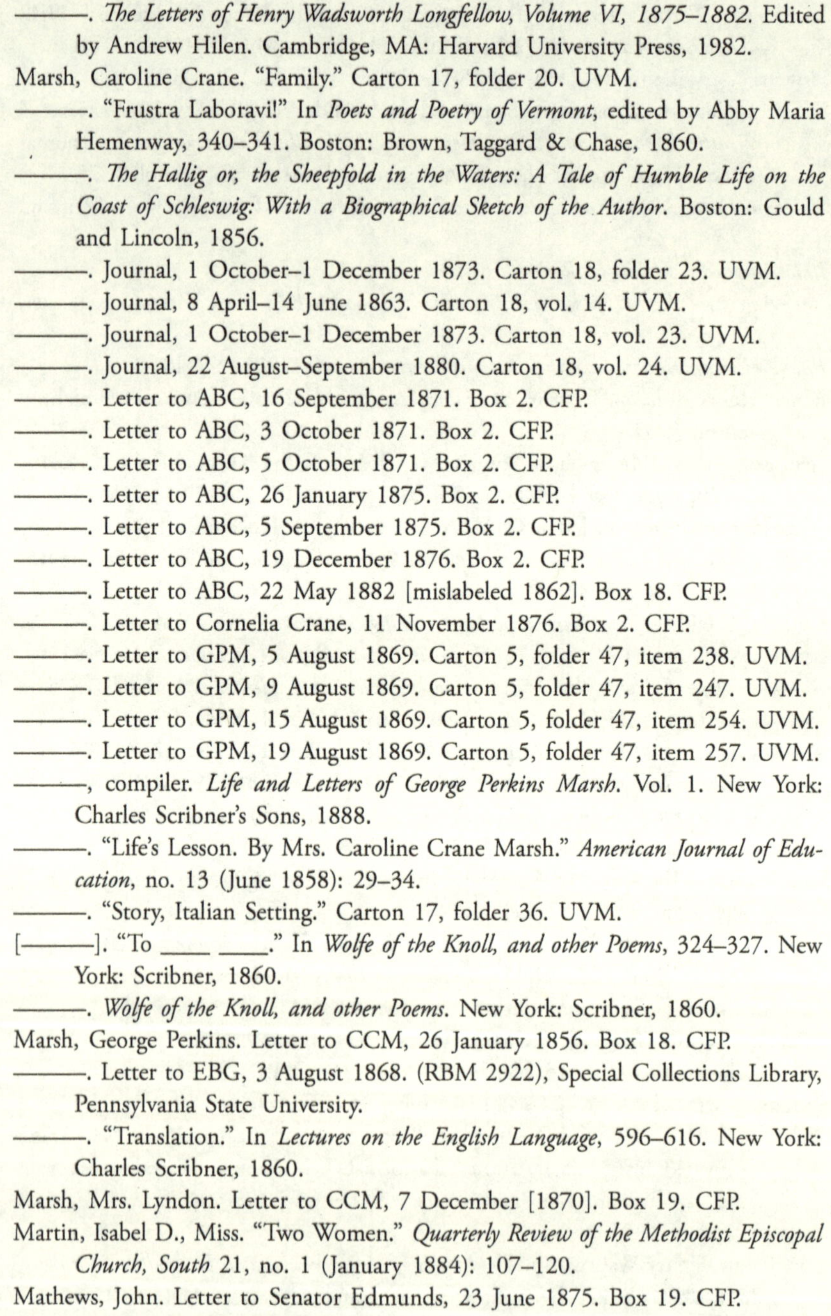

———. *The Letters of Henry Wadsworth Longfellow, Volume VI, 1875–1882.* Edited by Andrew Hilen. Cambridge, MA: Harvard University Press, 1982.

Marsh, Caroline Crane. "Family." Carton 17, folder 20. UVM.

———. "Frustra Laboravi!" In *Poets and Poetry of Vermont,* edited by Abby Maria Hemenway, 340–341. Boston: Brown, Taggard & Chase, 1860.

———. *The Hallig or, the Sheepfold in the Waters: A Tale of Humble Life on the Coast of Schleswig: With a Biographical Sketch of the Author.* Boston: Gould and Lincoln, 1856.

———. Journal, 1 October–1 December 1873. Carton 18, folder 23. UVM.

———. Journal, 8 April–14 June 1863. Carton 18, vol. 14. UVM.

———. Journal, 1 October–1 December 1873. Carton 18, vol. 23. UVM.

———. Journal, 22 August–September 1880. Carton 18, vol. 24. UVM.

———. Letter to ABC, 16 September 1871. Box 2. CFP.

———. Letter to ABC, 3 October 1871. Box 2. CFP.

———. Letter to ABC, 5 October 1871. Box 2. CFP.

———. Letter to ABC, 26 January 1875. Box 2. CFP.

———. Letter to ABC, 5 September 1875. Box 2. CFP.

———. Letter to ABC, 19 December 1876. Box 2. CFP.

———. Letter to ABC, 22 May 1882 [mislabeled 1862]. Box 18. CFP.

———. Letter to Cornelia Crane, 11 November 1876. Box 2. CFP.

———. Letter to GPM, 5 August 1869. Carton 5, folder 47, item 238. UVM.

———. Letter to GPM, 9 August 1869. Carton 5, folder 47, item 247. UVM.

———. Letter to GPM, 15 August 1869. Carton 5, folder 47, item 254. UVM.

———. Letter to GPM, 19 August 1869. Carton 5, folder 47, item 257. UVM.

———, compiler. *Life and Letters of George Perkins Marsh.* Vol. 1. New York: Charles Scribner's Sons, 1888.

———. "Life's Lesson. By Mrs. Caroline Crane Marsh." *American Journal of Education,* no. 13 (June 1858): 29–34.

———. "Story, Italian Setting." Carton 17, folder 36. UVM.

[———]. "To ____ ____." In *Wolfe of the Knoll, and other Poems,* 324–327. New York: Scribner, 1860.

———. *Wolfe of the Knoll, and other Poems.* New York: Scribner, 1860.

Marsh, George Perkins. Letter to CCM, 26 January 1856. Box 18. CFP.

———. Letter to EBG, 3 August 1868. (RBM 2922), Special Collections Library, Pennsylvania State University.

———. "Translation." In *Lectures on the English Language,* 596–616. New York: Charles Scribner, 1860.

Marsh, Mrs. Lyndon. Letter to CCM, 7 December [1870]. Box 19. CFP.

Martin, Isabel D., Miss. "Two Women." *Quarterly Review of the Methodist Episcopal Church, South* 21, no. 1 (January 1884): 107–120.

Mathews, John. Letter to Senator Edmunds, 23 June 1875. Box 19. CFP.

———. Letter to ABC, 7 July 1875. Box 19. CFP.

McDougal, John R. Letters to S. W. Crittenden and Robert Baird, October 1872–February 1878. Box 7, folder 9. AFCU.

Meehan, Thomas. "Bernard John McQuaid." In *The Catholic Encyclopedia*, vol. 9. New York: Robert Appleton, 1910. www.newadvent.org/cathen/09507b.htm.

"Memorials of Mrs. Gould of Rome." *New Englander and Yale Review* 38, no. 152 (September 1879): 723–724.

Ministero della Pubblica Istruzione. Letter to CCM, 17 February 1870. Carton 5, folder 54, item 55. UVM.

[Mitchell, Cornelia]. "Miss Mitchell's Journal," 1860. Box 12. CFP.

Moulton, Louise Chandler. "For Queen Anne." Series VIII, box 23, folder 11. AHBP.

Murray, J. *A Handbook of Rome and its Environs*. London: John Murry, 1875.

Nardi, Monsignor Francesco. Letters to AHB, n.d. (with 2 calling cards). Series I, box 1, folder 52. AHBP.

Norton, Charles Eliot. *Notes of Study and Travel in Italy*. Boston: Houghton Mifflin, 1859.

O'Shea, John J. "Francis Patrick and Peter Richard Kenrick." In *The Catholic Encyclopedia*, vol. 8. New York: Robert Appleton, 1910. www.newadvent.org/cathen/08618a.htm.

"An Outrage at Rome." *Reformed Church Monthly*, January 1869.

Peabody, Elizabeth Palmer. "To Susan Cole," July 10, 1872. In *Letters of Elizabeth Palmer Peabody: American Renaissance Woman,* edited by Bruce A. Ronda, 369–370. Middletown, CT: Wesleyan University Press, 1984.

Phillipson, Mrs. Caroline Jeffries. Letter to CCM, 9 May 1868. Box 19. CFP.

Pons, G. Pietro. "Fuà Fusinato e Emilia Gould." *La Rivista Cristiana*, Anno V, 60–62. Firenze: Tipografia Claudiana, 1877.

Price, Alyson. *Florence in the Nineteenth Century: A Guide to Original Sources in Florentine Archives and Libraries for Researchers into the English-Speaking Community*. Florence: Centro Di for the British Institute of Florence, 2011.

Prochet, Matteo. Letter to Enrico Bosio, 22 September 1874. ATV.

———. Letter to Enrico Bosio, 30 September 1874. ATV.

———. Letter to Enrico Bosio, 29 October 1874. ATV.

———. Letter to Giovanni Paolo Buffa, January 1873. ATV.

———. Letter to Giovanni Paolo Buffa, 8 October 1873. ATV.

———. Letter to Giovanni Paolo Buffa, 6 February 1874. ATV.

———. Letter to Giovanni Paolo Buffa, 10 March 1874. ATV.

———. Letter to Howard Crosby, 13 July 1876. Box 12, folder 7. AFCU.

———. Letters to Carolina Dalgas, 4 April–12 December 1874. ATV.

———. Letter to Signor G. Garnier, n.d. ATV.

———. Letter to Signor G. Garnier, n.d. ATV.

———. Letter to Signor G. Garnier, 22 January 1874. ATV.

———. Letter to Signor G. Garnier, 12 July 1874. ATV.

———. Letter to Signor G. Garnier, 22 September 1874. ATV.

———. Letter to EBG, 24 April 1873. ATV.
———. Letter to EBG, 28 April 1873. ATV.
———. Letter to EBG, 24 November 1874. ATV.
———. Letter to EBG, 1 December 1874. ATV.
———. Letter to Giovanni Ribetti, 28 June 1871. ATV.
———. Letter to Giovanni Ribetti, 7 July 1871. ATV.
———. Letter to Giovanni Ribetti, 5 August 1871. ATV.
———. Letter to Giovanni Ribetti, 7 August 1871. ATV.
———. Letter to Giovanni Ribetti, 2 December 1873. ATV.
———. Letter to Giovanni Ribetti, 9 December 1873. ATV.
———. Letter to Giovanni Ribetti, 2 January 1874. ATV.
———. Letter to Giovanni Ribetti, 30 March 1874. ATV.
———. Letter to Giovanni Ribetti, 19 May 1874. ATV.
———. Letter to Giovanni Ribetti, 8 August 1874. ATV.
———. Letter to Giovanni Ribetti, 14 August 1874. ATV.

Report of the Executive Committee of the Protestant Orphanage for Girls, Florence, Italy, for the Year 1882. Florence: Claudian, 1883.

"Roman Catholic or Infidel." *Pacific Commercial*, 27 May 1871.

Ross, Mrs. Janet. Letter to CCM, 20 December 1868. Box 19. CFP.

Rutland Daily Globe (Rutland, VT). 29 December 1875. *Chronicling America: Historic American Newspapers*. Library of Congress. chroniclingamerica.loc.gov/lccn/sn84022473/1875-12-29/ed-1/seq-3/.

Sabatier, Caroline. Letter to CCM, March 25, 1870. Box 19. CFP.
———. Letter to CCM, 9 April 1870. Box 19. CFP.

San Clemente, Duchess Mary. Letter to CCM, 1 November 1875. Box 19. CFP.

Sansay, Leonora. *Secret History: Or the Horrors of San Domingo*. 1808. Edited with introduction by Michael J. Drexler. Peterborough, ON: Broadview, 2008.

[Sargent, Mary Elizabeth Fiske]. "Origin of the Club." In *Sketches and Reminiscences of the Radical Club of Chestnut Street, Boston*, edited by Mrs. John T. Sargent, [vii]. Boston: James R. Osgood and Company, 1880.

Savidge, Eugene Coleman. *Life of Benjamin Harris Brewster: With Discourses and Addresses*. Philadelphia: J. B. Lippincott, 1891.

"La scuola americana." *Il popolo romano*, 9 January 1874, p. 3.

Second Annual Report of the Italo-American Schools in Rome, 1873. Florence: Claudian, 1873.

Sedgwick, Catharine Maria. *Clarence*. 1830. Edited with introduction by Melissa Homestead. Peterborough, ON: Broadview, 2011.
———. "An Incident in Rome." *Graham's American Monthly Magazine*, 1845, vol. 27, 104–108.

Shakerism Unveiled: A Truthful Sketch of Their History, Belief, Manner of Life, Cruel and Inhuman Treatment of Their Subjects, Especially the Women and Children from 1688 Down to the Present Time, with Extracts from the Holy Roll, or Shaker Bible and Mrs. Mary Dyer's Work, Who Was 18 Years Among Them. 1869.

Staël, Germaine de. *Politics, Literature, and National Character.* Translated and edited by Morroe Berger. New Brunswick, NJ: Transaction, 2000.

Stoddard, Charles Warren. "Roman Receptions." *San Francisco Chronicle,* 15 September 1878.

Taylor, Bayard. Letter to CCM, 10 April 1873. Box 19. CFP.

Thouar, Pietro. *Racconti popolari.* Firenze: Barbera, 1860.

Tigri, Giuseppe. *Il montanino toscano volontario alla guerra della indipendenza italiana del 1859: racconto popolare.* Torino: Sebastiano Franco e Figli, 1860.

Tincker, Mary Agnes. *By the Tiber.* Boston: Roberts Brothers, 1881.

———. *Signor Monaldini's Niece.* Boston: Roberts Brothers, 1879.

Trollope, Thomas Adolphus, et al. *In Memoriam: A Wreath of Stray Leaves to the Memory of Emily Bliss Gould.* Rome: Italo-American School, 1875.

Tyndall, J. "Life and Letters of Faraday." In *Fragments of Science for Unscientific People,* 3rd ed., 347–372. London: Longmas, Green, and Co., 1871.

Van Meter, W. C. Letter to S. W. Crittenden, 12 November 1872. Box 12, folder 2. AFCU.

Van Nest, A. R. Jr. Report of September 1871, included in papers of William Clark. Box 3, folder 3. AFCU.

———. Series of letters to Joseph Scudder and S. W. Crittenden, 29 March 1865–4 January 1873. Box 12, folder 2. AFCU.

"Venerdi Santo 11 Aprile 1873" (with envelope), 1873. Series VI, box 20, folder 23. AHBP.

Villari, Linda. Letter to CCM, 26 July 1882. Carton 7, folder 61, item 161. UVM.

Villari, Pasquale. Letter to AHB, 2 February 1875. Series I, box 1, folder 69. AHBP.

———. Letter to [Caroline Crane] Marsh, 3 April 1870. Busta 723.25.5. Archivio del Museo Centrale del Risorgimento, Rome.

———. Letter to GPM, 30 November 1872. Carton 6, folder 11, item 316. UVM.

———. Letter to GPM, 3 March 1875. Carton 6, folder 43, item 60. UVM.

———. Letter to CCM, 22 March 1875. Carton 6, folder 43, item 77. UVM.

———. "Sara Margaret Ossoli (Fuller)." In *Saggi di storia, di critica e di politica: nuovamente racconti,* 363–384. Florence: Tipografia Cavour, 1868.

Ward, Maria, and B. G. Ferris. *Female Life Among the Mormons; a Narrative of Many Years' Personal Experience.* New York: J. C. Derby, 1855.

Wheeler, Miss L. T. Letter to CCM, 22 September 1869. Box 19. CFP.

Whitman, Walt. "Europe." *New York Daily Tribune,* 21 June 1850. In *Heath Anthology of American Literature,* vol. B, 7th ed., edited by Paul Lauter et al., 3303–3304. Boston: Wadsworth, 2014.

Wislizenus, Mrs. L. C. Letter to CCM, 8 May 1870. Box 19. CFP.

Woolson, Constance Fenimore. *The Complete Letters of Constance Fenimore Woolson.* Edited by Sharon L. Dean. Gainesville: University Press of Florida, 2012.

Wordsworth, William. "The Excursion, Being a Portion of the Recluse, a Poem." London: Longman, Hurst, Rees, Orme, and Brown, 1814.

Wurts, Mrs. Martha P. Letter to CCM, 13 July 1868. Box 19. CFP.

Secondary Sources

"About Public Ledger." ChroniclingAmerica. Library of Congress, n.d. chroniclingamerica.loc.gov/lccn/sn85033673/.

Amstutz, Margaret A. "Elizabeth Stoddard as Returned Californian: A Reading of the *Daily Alta California* Columns." In *American Culture, Canons, and the Case of Elizabeth Stoddard*, edited by Robert McClure Smith and Ellen Weinauer, 65–82. Tuscaloosa: University of Alabama Press, 2003.

Ardis, Ann, and Patrick Collier, eds. *Transatlantic Print Culture, 1880–1940: Emerging Media, Emerging Modernisms.* London: Palgrave, 2008.

"Armellini, Torquato." *Manus OnLine,* Istituto Centrale per il Catalog Unico. manus.iccu.sbn.it//opac_SchedaAutore.php?ID=288582&lang=en.

Atkinson, Megan, and Christiana Dobrzynski Grippe. "Anne Hampton Brewster Papers." Library Company of Philadelphia, 2010.

Atwood, Margaret. "Dire Cartographies: The Roads to Ustopia." In *In Other Worlds: SF and the Human Imagination,* 66–96. Toronto: McClelland & Stewart, 2011.

Bailey, Brigitte. *American Travel Literature, Gendered Aesthetics, and the Italian Tour, 1824–1862.* Edinburgh: Edinburgh University Press, 2018.

———. "Fuller, Hawthorne, and Imagining Urban Spaces in Rome." In *Roman Holidays: American Writers in Nineteenth Century Italy*, edited by Robert K. Martin and Leland S. Person, 175–190. Iowa City: University of Iowa Press, 2002.

———. "Tourism and Visual Subjection in Letters from Abroad and 'An Incident in Rome.' " In *Catharine Maria Sedgwick: Critical Perspectives,* edited by Lucinda Daman Bach et al., 212–229. Boston: Northeastern University Press, 2003.

Barolini, Helen. *Their Other Side: Six American Women Writers and the Lure of Italy.* New York: Fordham University Press, 2006.

Beasley, Maurine H. *Women of the Washington Press: Politics, Prejudice and Persistence.* Evanston, IL: Northwestern University Press, 2012.

Becchetti, Piero. *Fotografi e fotografia in Italia, 1839–1880.* Rome: Edizioni Quasar, 1978.

Bell, David A. *The First Total War: Napoleon's Europe and the Birth of Warfare as We Know It.* New York: Houghton Mifflin, 2007.

Bennett, Paula Bernat, ed. *Nineteenth-Century American Women Poets: An Anthology.* Malden, Massachusetts: Blackwell, 1998.

Bergland, Renée. "Emily Dickinson's Italy." Paper presented at the conference *Transatlantic Women: Nineteenth-Century American Women Writers in Great Britain, Ireland, and Europe*, Oxford, England, 17 July 2008.

———. *Maria Mitchell and the Sexing of Science. An Astronomer among the American Romantics*. Boston: Beacon, 2008.

Berthold, Dennis. *American Risorgimento: Herman Melville and the Cultural Politics of Italy*. Columbus: Ohio State University Press, 2009.

Bischof, Libby. "A Summer in England: The Women's Rest Tour Association of Boston and the Encouragement of Independent Transatlantic Travel for American Women." In *Transatlantic Women: Nineteenth-Century American Women Writers and Great Britain*, edited by Beth L. Lueck, Bridgette Bailey, and Lucinda L. Damon-Bach, 152–171. Lebanon: New Hampshire University Press, 2012.

Boase, G. C. "Hemans, Charles Isidore (1817–1876)." In *Oxford Dictionary of National Biography*, online edition, edited by David Cannadine. Oxford: Oxford University Press, 2004. www.oxforddnb.com/view/article/12887.

Boggs, Colleen Glenney. *Transnationalism and American Literature: Literary Translation 1773–1892*. New York: Routledge, 2007.

Boyd, Anne E. *Writing for Immortality: Women and the Emergence of High Literary Culture in America*. Baltimore: Johns Hopkins University Press, 2004.

Brann, Henry. "The American College in Rome." In *The Catholic Encyclopedia*, vol. 1. New York: Robert Appleton, 1907. www.newadvent.org/cathen/01423a.htm.

Brown, Thomas J. *Dorothea Dix: New England Reformer*. Cambridge: Harvard University Press, 1998.

Bryant, John, et al., editors. *Facing Melville, Facing Italy: Democracy, Politics, Translation*. Rome: Sapienza Università Editrice, 2014.

Buick, Kirsten Pai. *Child of the Fire: Mary Edmonia Lewis and the Problem of Art History's Black and Indian Subject*. Durham, NC: Duke University Press, 2010.

Buzard, James. *The Beaten Track: European Tourism, Literature, and the Ways to Culture, 1800–1918*. Oxford: Clarendon Press, 1993.

Cahill, Susan, ed. *Desiring Italy: Women Writers Celebrate the Passions of a Country and Culture*. New York: Fawcett, 1997.

Cantatore, Lorenzo, Letizia Lanzetta, and Fernanda Roscetti. *Carducci e Roma: Atti del convegno, Roma, 18–19 novembre 1999*. Rome: Istituto Nazionale di Studi Romani, 2001.

"Centri Educativi Gould e Ferretti." Diaconia Valdese Fiorentina. www.istitutogould.it.

Ciampi, Paolo. *Miss Uragano: La donna che fece l'Italia*. Florence: Romano Editore, 2010.

Claeys, Gregory, and Lyman Tower Sargent, eds. *The Utopia Reader*. New York: New York University Press, 1999.

Cohen, Michael C. *The Social Lives of Poems in Nineteenth-Century America*. Philadelphia: University of Philadelphia Press, 2015.

Colesworthy, Rebecca. *Returning the Gift: Modernism and the Thought of Exchange*. Oxford University Press, 2018.

Cooper, Victoria L. "Novello, Clara Anastasia (1818–1908)." In *Oxford Dictionary of National Biography*, online edition, edited by David Cannadine. Oxford: Oxford University Press, 2004. www.oxforddnb.com/view/article/35263.

Cubberly, A., ed. *Notes from Rome.* London: British School at Rome, 1988.

Culkin, Kate. *Harriet Hosmer: A Cultural Biography.* Amherst: University of Massachusetts Press, 2010.

Dabakis, Melissa. *A Sisterhood of Sculptors: American Artists in Nineteenth-Century.* University Park: Pennsylvania State University Press, 2014.

———. "Angelika Kauffmann, Goethe, and the Arcadian Academy in Rome." In *The Enlightened Eye: Goethe and Visual Culture*, edited by Evelyn K. Moore and Patricia Anne Simpson, 25–41. Amsterdam: Rodopi, 2007.

Damon-Bach, Lucinda. "'My Readers Will Thank Me': J.-C. L. Simonde de Sismondi, Civil Liberty, and Transatlantic Sympathy in Catharine Sedgwick's *Letters from Abroad to Kindred at Home* (1841)." In *Transatlantic Conversations: Nineteenth-Century American Women's Encounters with Italy and the Atlantic World*, edited by Beth L. Lueck et al., 3–22. Lebanon: University of New Hampshire Press, 2016.

Daniels, Tom. "In Italy with Mr. and Mrs. George Perkins Marsh." *Vermont History* 47, no. 3 (Summer 1979): 191–195.

Davidson, Thomas. "Autobiographical Sketch." *Journal of the History of Ideas* 8 (1957): 531–536.

Dean, Sharon L., ed. *The Complete Letters of Constance Fenimore Woolson.* Gainesville: University Press of Florida, 2012.

Ditz, Toby. "Formative Ventures: Eighteenth-Century Commercial Letters and the Articulation of Experience." In *Epistolary Selves: Letters and Letter-Writers, 1600–1945*, edited by Rebecca Earle, 59–78. Farnham, UK: Ashgate, 1999.

Dowling, Linda. *Charles Eliot Norton: The Art of Reform in Nineteenth-Century America.* Durham, NH: University Press of New England, 2007.

Drain, Susan. "Howitt, Mary (1799–1888)." In *Oxford Dictionary of National Biography*, online edition, edited by David Cannadine. Oxford: Oxford University Press, 2004. www.oxforddnb.com/view/article/13995.

Dunlavy, Patricia Valenti. *Sophia Peabody Hawthorne: A Life, Vol. 2.* Columbia: University of Missouri Press, 2015.

Edelstein, Sari. *Between the Novel and the News: The Emergence of American Women's Writing.* Charlottesville: University of Virginia Press, 2014.

Elsden, Annamaria Formichella. *Roman Fever: Domesticity and Nationalism in Nineteenth Century American Women's Writing.* Columbus: Ohio State University Press, 2004.

Fahs, Alice. *Out on Assignment: Newspaper Women and the Making of Modern Public Space.* Chapel Hill: University of North Carolina Press, 2011.

Fisher, Estelle. *A Gentle Journalist Abroad: The Papers of Anne Hampton Brewster in the Library Company of Philadelphia.* Philadelphia: Free Library of Philadelphia, 1947.

"Francis Silas Marean Chatard." *Indiana Catholic History*. indianacatholic.mwweb.org/icath/?p=136.

Frapiselli, Luciana. "Harriet Hosmer, 'Testimone della Presa di Roma.'" *Strenna dei romanisti*, 2011, 313–323.

Gaul, Theresa Strouth, ed. *To Marry an Indian: The Marriage of Harriett Gold & Elias Boudinot in Letters, 1823–1839*. Chapel Hill: University of North Carolina Press, 2005.

Gaul, Theresa Strouth, and Sharon M. Harris, eds. *Letters and Cultural Transformations in the United States, 1760–1860*. New York: Routledge, 2009.

Gemme, Paola. *Domesticating Foreign Struggles: The Italian Risorgimento and Antebellum American Identity*. Athens: University of Georgia Press, 2005.

Good, James A. "The Value of Thomas Davidson." *Transactions of the Charles S. Peirce Society* 40, no. 2 (Spring 2004): 289–318.

Griffin, Susan M. *Anti-Catholicism and Nineteenth-Century Fiction*. New York: Cambridge University Press, 2004.

Harris, Susan K. *The Cultural Work of the Late Nineteenth-Century Hostess: Annie Adams Fields and Mary Gladstone Drew*. London: Palgrave Macmillan, 2002.

Hartley, Benjamin L. *Evangelicals at a Crossroads: Revivalism and Social Reform in Boston, 1860–1910*. Durham: University of New Hampshire Press, 2011.

Henderson, Desirée. "The Friendship Elegy." In *A History of Nineteenth-Century American Women's Poetry*, edited by Jennifer Putzi and Alexandra Socarides, 110–117. Cambridge: Cambridge University Press, 2017.

Herbert, T. Walter. *Dearest Beloved: The Hawthornes and the Making of the Middle-Class Family*. Berkeley: University of California Press, 1993.

Huemer, Christina. "To Be Remembered and to Please." In *Spellbound by Rome: The Anglo-American Community in Rome, 1890–1914, and the Founding of the Keats-Shelley House*, edited by Christina Huemer, 9–16. Rome: Palombi, 2005.

Jackson, Leon. *The Business of Letters: Authorial Economies in Antebellum America*. Stanford, CA: Stanford University Press, 2008.

Jenkins, Regina Randolph. "Mary Agnes Tincker." In *The Catholic Encyclopedia*. New York: Robert Appleton Company, 1912. www.newadvent.org/cathen/14735a.htm.

Johanningsmeier, Charles. *Fiction and the American Literary Marketplace: The Role of Newspaper Syndicates, 1860–1900*. Cambridge: Cambridge University Press, 1997.

Johnson, William S. *Nineteenth-Century Photography: An Annotated Bibliography, 1839–1879*. Boston: G. K. Hall, 1990.

Kaplan, Amy. "Manifest Domesticity." *American Literature* 70, no. 3 (1998): 581–606.

Kertzer, David I. *The Kidnapping of Edgardo Mortara*. New York: Random House, 1997.

———. *The Pope Who Would Be King: The Exile of Pius IX and the Emergence of Modern Europe*. New York: Random House, 2018.

———. *Prisoner of the Vatican: The Pope's Secret Plot to Capture Rome from the New Italian State*. Boston: Houghton Mifflin, 2004.

Kohn, Denise, et al. *Transatlantic Stowe: Harriet Beecher Stowe and European Culture.* Iowa City: University of Iowa Press, 2006.

Kolich, Augustus M. "Miriam and the Conversion of the Jews in Nathaniel Hawthorne's *The Marble Faun.*" *Studies in the Novel* 33, no. 4 (December 2001): 430–443.

Lamberts, Emiel, ed. *The Black International. L'Internationale noire. 1870–1878. The Holy See and Militant Catholicism in Europe. Le Saint-Siège et le Catholiscisme militant en Europe.* Rome: Institut Historique Belge de Rome, 2002.

Larabee, Denise M. *Anne Hampton Brewster: 19th-Century Author and "Social Outlaw."* Philadeplphia: Library Company of Philadelphia, 1992.

———. "Brewster, Anne Hampton." In *The Oxford Companion to Women's Writing in the U.S.*, edited by Cathy N. Davidson and Linda Wagner-Martin, 134. Oxford: Oxford University Press, 1995.

Lawson, Benamin S. "Miller, Joaquin [Cincinnatus Hiner]." In *Encyclopedia of American Literature*, edited by Stephen R. Seraphin, 771. New York: Continuum, 1999.

Liming, Sheila. *What a Library Means to a Woman: Edith Wharton and the Will to Collect Books.* Minneapolis: University of Minnesota Press, 2020.

Livorni, Ernesto. "American Writers in Rome during the Risorgimento." *Forum Italicum* 46, no. 2 (2013):, pp. 364–396.

Lowenthal, David. *George Perkins Marsh: Prophet of Conservation.* Seattle: University of Washington Press, 2003.

———. *George Perkins Marsh: Versatile Vermonter.* New York: Columbia University Press, 1958.

———. " 'The Marriage of Choice and the Marriage of Convenance': A New England Puritan Views Risorgimento Italy." *Journal of Social History* 42, no. 1 (Fall 2008): 157–174.

Lowenthal, David, and Luisa Quartermaine. Introduction to *Un'americana alla corte dei Savoia: Il diario dell'ambasciatrice degli Stati Uniti in Italia d'anno al 1861 al 1865*, by Caroline Crane Marsh, edited by David Lowenthal, translated by Luisa Quartermaine. Torino: University of Allemandi Press, 2004.

"Luigi Vannuccini." *Geni.* 13 November 2018. www.geni.com/people/Luigi-Vannuccini/6000000072104903257.

Lutes, Jean Marie. *Front-Page Girls: Women Journalists in American Culture and Fiction, 1880–1930.* Ithaca, NY: Cornell University Press, 2006.

Lyons, Martyn. "Love Letters and Writing Practices: On *Écritures Intimes* in the Nineteenth Century." *Journal of Family History* 24, no. 2 (1999): 232–239.

Madden, Etta M. "American Anne Hampton Brewster's Social Circles: Bagni di Lucca, 1873, and Roman Rodolfo Lanciani." In *Questioni di genere: Femminilità e effeminatezza nella cultura vittoriana*, edited by Roberta Ferrari and Laura Giovannelli, 117–144. Bologna: Bononia University Press, 2016.

———. "Anne Hampton Brewster's *St. Martin's Summer* and Utopian Literary Discourses." *Utopian Studies* 28, no. 2 (2017): 305–326.

———. "Reconfiguring the Margins: Mapping Anne Hampton Brewster's Letters from Rome, 1869–1890." Presentation at the Society for the Study of American Women Writers conference, Philadelphia, PA, 4–8 November 2015.

———. " 'To Make a Figure': Benjamin Rush and the Rhetoric of Self-Construction and Scientific Authorship." *Early American Literature* 41, no. 2 (2006): 241–272.

———. "Travels, Translations and Limitations: *Ambasciatrice* Caroline Crane Marsh." *Transatlantica: American Studies Journal* 2018, no. 1 (posted 16 September 2019). journals.openedition.org/transatlantica/12574

———. "Woolson's Rome and Anne Hampton Brewster's American Newspaper Audiences, 1881." Presentation at the Biennial Conference of the Constance Fenimore Woolson Society, Washington, DC, 19–21 February 2015.

———, ed. *Selections from Eliza Leslie.* Lincoln: University of Nebraska Press, 2011.

Mandler, Peter. "Howitt, William (1792–1879)." In *Oxford Dictionary of National Biography*, online edition, edited by David Cannadine. Oxford: Oxford University Press, 2004. www.oxforddnb.com/view/article/13998.

Markus, Julia. *Across an Untried Sea: Discovering Lives Hidden in the Shadow of Convention and Time.* New York: Alfred A. Knopf, 2000.

Marshall, Megan. *Margaret Fuller: A New American Life.* Boston: Houghton Mifflin Harcourt, 2013.

"Matteo Prochet." *Dizionario Biografico dei Protestanti in Italia.* Società di Studi Valdesi. www.studivaldesi.org/dizionario/evan_det.php?secolo=XIX&evan_id=121.

Martin, Robert K., and Leland S. Person, editors. *Roman Holidays: American Writers in Nineteenth Century Italy.* Iowa City: University of Iowa Press, 2002.

Matteson, John. *The Lives of Margaret Fuller.* New York: W. W. Norton, 2012.

Mazzoni, Guido. "Scifoni, Felice." In *Enciclopedia Italiana—I Appendice* (1938). Treccani. www.treccani.it/enciclopedia/felice-scifoni_%28Enciclopedia-Italiana%29/.

McAlexander, Hubert Horton. *The Prodigal Daughter: A Biography of Sherwood Bonner.* Knoxville: University of Tennessee Press, 1999.

McGreevy, John T. *American Jesuits and the World: How an Embattled Religious Order Made Modern Catholicism Global.* Princeton: Princeton University Press, 2016.

———. *Catholicism and American Freedom: A History.* New York: W. W. Norton, 2003.

McKee, Kathryn. "Writing Region from the Hub: Sherwood Bonner's Travel Letters and Questions of Postbellum U.S. Southern Identity." *Legacy* 22, no. 2 (2005): 126–143.

Merrill, Lisa. *When Romeo Was a Woman: Charlotte Cushman and Her Circle of Female Spectators.* Ann Arbor: University of Michigan Press, 1999.

Migliorini, Luigi Mascilli. "Pasquale Villari." In *Il Contributo Italiano alla storia del Pensiero: Storia e Politica* (2013). Treccani. www.treccani.it/enciclopedia/pasquale-villari_%28Il-Contributo-italiano-alla-storia-del-Pensiero:-Storia-e-Politica%29/.

Milder, Robert, and Randall Fuller, eds. *The Business of Reflection: Hawthorne and His Notebooks*. Columbus: Ohio State University Press, 2009.

Mitchell, Sally. *Frances Power Cobbe: Victorian Feminist, Journalist, Reformer*. Charlottesville: University of Virginia Press, 2004.

Molinari, Olga Majolo. "Il popolo romano." In *La stampa periodica romana dell'ottocento*, vol. 2, 763. Rome: Istituto di Studi Romani Editore, 1963.

Mortara, Elèna. *Writing for Justice: Victor Séjour, the Kidnapping of Edgardo Mortara, and the Age of Transatlantic Emancipations*. Hanover, NH: Dartmouth College Press; University Press of New England, 2015.

Moylan, Tom. *Demand the Impossible: Science Fiction and the Utopian Imagination*. 1986. Bern: Peter Lang, 2014.

Oliva, Justine. "The Circles of Anne C. Lynch Botta: Friendship and Power in the Nineteenth Century." PhD diss., University of New Hampshire, 2018.

"Online Books by Sarah S Baker (Baker, Sarah S (Sarah Schoonmaker), 1824–1906)." onlinebooks.library.upenn.edu/webbin/book/lookupname?key=Baker%2C%20 Sarah%20S%20%28Sarah%20Schoonmaker%29%2C%201824%2D1906.

Pacini, Monica. "Firenze Capitale d'Italia: scene da un cambiamento." *Annali di storia di Firenze* 10–11 (2015–2016): 65–84.

Palombi, Domenico. *Rodolfo Lanciani: L'archeologia a Roma tra ottocento e novecento*. Roma: L'Erma di Bretschneider, 2006.

Parker, Alison M. *Articulating Rights: Nineteenth-Century American Women on Race, Reform, and the State*. DeKalb: Northern Illinois University Press, 2010.

Porterfield, Amanda. *Mary Lyon and the Mount Holyoke Missionaries*. New York: Oxford University Press, 1997.

Preminger, Alex, and T. V. F. Brogan, eds. *The New Princeton Encyclopedia of Poetry and Poetics*, 3rd ed. Princeton, NJ: Princeton University Press, 1993.

Pritchard, Elizabeth A. "The Way Out West: Development and the Rhetoric of Mobility in Post-Modern Feminist Theory." *Hypatia* 15, no. 3 (2000): 45–72.

Putzi, Jennifer. Introduction to *Two Men*, by Elizabeth Stoddard, xi–lvii. Lincoln: University of Nebraska Press, 2008.

Quartermaine, Luisa. "Views from Beyond the Alps: An American in Turin: The Diary of Caroline Marsh, Wife of the First American Minister to Italy 1861–64." In *Marginal Voices, Marginal Forms; Diaries in European Literature and History*, edited by Rachel Langford and Russell West, 61–77. Amsterdam: Rodopi, 1999.

Rendina, Claudio. *I palazzi storici di Roma*. Rome: Newton & Compton Editori, 1993.

Reynolds, David S. *Beneath the American Renaissance: The Subversive Imagination in the Age of Emerson and Melville*. Cambridge, MA: Harvard University Press, 1989.

Reynolds, Larry J. *European Revolutions and the American Literary Renaissance*. New Haven, CT: Yale University Press, 1988.

Reynolds, Larry J., and Susan Belasco Smith, eds. *"These Sad but Glorious Days": Dispatches from Europe, 1846–1850*. New Haven, CT: Yale University Press, 1991.

Riall, Lucy. *Risorgimento: The History of Italy from Napoleon to the Nation State.* London: Palgrave Macmillan, 2009.

Ridolfi, Maurizio. "Pianciani, Luigi." In *Dizionario Biografico*, vol. 83 (2015). Treccani. www.treccani.it/enciclopedia/luigi-pianciani_%28Dizionario-Biografico%29/.

Rioux, Anne E. Boyd. *Constance Fenimore Woolson: Portrait of a Lady Novelist.* New York: W. W. Norton, 2016.

———. "Introduction" *Miss Grief and Other Stories*, by Constance Fenimore Woolson, xvii–xxxvi. New York: W. W. Norton, 2016.

Robbins, Sarah. *Managing Literacy, Mothering America: Women's Narratives on Reading and Writing in the Nineteenth Century.* Pittsburgh: University of Pittsburgh Press, 2004.

Rockwell, Peter. Preface to *Spellbound by Rome: The Anglo-American Community in Rome, 1890–1914, and the Founding of the Keats-Shelley House.* Edited by Christina Huemer. Rome: Palombi, 2005.

Romani, Gabriella. "Erminia Fuà Fusinato: A Jewish Patriot in Rome (1871–76)." *Annali d'Italianistica* vol. 36, 2018, 1–20.

Rome in Early Photographs: The Age of Pius IX, 1846–1878. Copenhagen: Thorvaldsens Museum, 1977.

Rush, Benjamin. *Letters of Benjamin Rush.* Edited by L. H. Butterfield. 2 vols. Princeton, NJ: Princeton University Press, 1951.

Salenius, Sirpa, ed. *American Authors Reinventing Italy: The Writings of Exceptional Nineteenth-Century Women.* Padua: Il Prato, 2009.

———. *An Abolitionist Abroad: Sarah Parker Remond in Cosmopolitan Europe.* Amherst: University of Massachusetts Press, 2016.

———. *Florence, Italy: Images of the City in Nineteenth-Century American Writing.* Joensuu, Finland: University of Joensuu, 2007.

———. *Set in Stone: 19th-century American Authors in Florence.* Padua: Il Prato, 2003.

"Salvatore Ferretti." *Dizionario Biografico dei Protestanti in Italia.* Società di Studi Valdesi. www.studivaldesi.org/dizionario/evan_det.php?evan_id=133.

Sánchez-Eppler, Karen. *Dependent States: The Child's Part in Nineteenth-Century American Culture.* Chicago: University of Chicago Press, 2005.

Santini, Luigi. *Cento anni di vita dell'Istituto Gould (1871–1971).* Torre Pellice, Italy: Tipografia Subalpina, 1971.

Sargent, Lyman Tower. *Utopianism: A Very Short Introduction.* New York: Oxford University Press, 2010.

Schreiber, Rachel, ed. *Modern Print Activism in the United States.* Burlington, VT: Ashgate, 2013.

Schriber, Mary Suzanne. *Writing Home: American Women Abroad, 1830–1920.* Charlottesville: University of Virginia Press, 1997.

Simon, John Y., ed. *The Papers of Ulysses S. Grant.* Volume 19, 1 July 1868–31 Oct. 1869. Carbondale: Southern Illinois University Press, 1995.

Smith, Bonnie G. *The Gender of History: Men, Women, and Historical Practice.* Cambridge, MA: Harvard University Press, 1998.

Snailham, Fiona. " 'The Reality Is Far Removed from the Ideal': Eliza Lynn Linton Discovers Italy." Presentation at the North American Victorian Studies Association Conference, Florence, Italy, 17–20 May 2017.

Soper, Steven C. *Building a Civil Society: Associations, Public Life, and the Origins of Modern Italy*. Toronto: University of Toronto Press, 2013.

Steele, Jeffrey. *Transfiguring America: Myth, Ideology, and Mourning in Margaret Fuller's Writing*. Columbia: University of Missouri Press, 2001.

———, ed. *The Essential Margaret Fuller*. New Brunswick, NJ: Rutgers University Press, 1995.

Sutcliffe, Marcella Pellegrino. *Victorian Radicals and Italian Democrats*. Woodbridge, UK: Boydell, 2014.

Urry, John. *The Tourist Gaze: Leisure and Travel in Contemporary Societies*. Thousand Oaks, CA: Sage, 1990.

Vance, William L. *America's Rome*. New Haven, CT: Yale University Press, 1989.

Vogelius, Christa Holm. "Fuller's Reproductive Originality." Presentation at the Society for the Study of American Women Writers conference, Bordeaux, France, 5–8 July 2017.

Volpicelli, Luigi. "Un'americana a Roma: Emily Bliss Gould." *Strenna dei romanisti*, 1979, 629–648. Rome: Gruppo dei Romanisti, 1979.

Waggoner, Kassia, and Adam Nemmers, eds. *Yours in Filial Regard: The Civil War Letters of a Texas Family*. Fort Worth: Texas Christian University Press, 2015.

Wagner-Lawlor, Jennifer A. *Postmodern Utopias and Feminist Fictions*. Cambridge: Cambridge University Press, 2013.

Wright, Nathalia. *American Novelists in Italy: The Discoverers: Allston to James*. Philadelphia: University of Pennsylvania Press, 1965.

Ziff, Larzer. *Return Passages: Great American Travel Writing, 1780–1910*. New Haven, CT: Yale University Press, 2000.

Index

1975 (Hosmer), 216–17

Accademia dell'Arcadia, 95–96, 124–28, *125*, 130
Adam Bede (Eliot), 252
Adams, John, 30
Advance (newspaper), 37
Agnes of Sorrento (Stowe), 147
Ajani, Giulio, 173
Alcott, Amos Bronson, 102, 135, 136, 137
Alcott, Louisa May, 62, 199, 210
Alison, Archibald, 9
Allen, Mrs. C., 239
Alta California (periodical), 1, 211. See also *Daily Alta California* (newspaper)
American and Foreign Christian Union (AFCU), 5, 41–44, 143–44, 159, 161
American Civil War: Brewster and, 5; A. B. Crane and, 68; Kendrick and, 146; Roman Catholic Church and, 21; Whitman and, 35–36; women as journalists and, 50, 62, 210
American College, 60–61
American exceptionalism: Brewster and, 8, 13, 130; E. B. Gould and, 8, 13, 130, 141, 174, 181–82; C. C. Marsh and, 8, 13, 130, 141, 242; utopianism and, 13, 22
"The American Scholar" (Emerson), 10
American Sunday School Union (ASSU), 9, 144
American Tract Society, 34, 157–58
American Union Church, 187
Ames, Mary Clemmer, 207
Anson D. F. Randolph & Company, 144
Antonelli, Giacomo, 66, 203
"Appeal to Womanhood Throughout the World" (Howe), 135–36, 226
Arbesser, Rosa, 114–15
d'Arcais, Guglielmo, 231–32
archaeological excavations, 92, 196–97, 198
Aristotle, 138
Armellini, Carlo, 148
Armellini, Torquatus, 148, 149–50
Arnold, Matthew, 5, 47, 102, 121, 156, 241–43
Arnoulet, Josephine, 189
associations, 128–31, 187–88
Astor, Augusta, 237
Astor, John Jacob III, 237
Athenaeum (periodical), 284n12
Atlantic Monthly (magazine), 40, 73–74, 167

Atlantic Telegraph Company, 238
Atwood, Margaret, 22
Augustine, St., 31
"Autobiographical Romance" (Fuller), 19
autograph albums, 107–8, 233–34
d'Azeglio, Massimo, 155, 245

Bacon, Francis, 154
Bacon, Leonard Woolsey, 33–34, 36, 37, 193. See also *A Life Worth Living* (Bacon)
Baedeker (publishing house), 198
Bailey, Brigitte, 35, 265n51
Baker, Sarah Schoonmaker, 74. *See also* "Miss Jones" (Aunt Friendly)
Ball, Percival, 219
Ballads (Edwards), 219, 225, *226*
Ballerini, Paolo Angelo, 152
Ballou, Adin, 136
Bapst, Johanne, 146
Barolini, Helen, 17
Barrett Browning, Elizabeth: Fuller and, 80; E. B. Gould and, 178; C. C. Marsh and, 31–32, 47, 104, 153–55; in Rome, 59
Barrett Browning, Elizabeth—works: *Casa Guidi Windows*, 31–32, 154; "The Cry of the Children," 31–32, 154, 178
Bartoli, Marietta and Pepino, *55*, 163, 179–81
Bartolini, Agostino, 276n51
Beasley, Maurine H., 207
Bedini, Gaetano, 143–44
Beers, Julia, 268n16
Belgiojoso, Cristina Trivulzio, 31, 182
Bell, Andrew, 122
Benedict, Clare, 76
Bennett, Paula Bernat, 117, 247
Bergamini, Adele, 126
Bergland, Renée, 17–18, 265n40
Bert, Mr., 244–45
Biernatzki, Johann C. See *The Hallig, or the Sheepfold in the Waters* (Biernatzki)
Billings, Frederick, 47
Birkbeck, George, 122
Biroccini, Maria Rosa Pieromaldi, 126
Blackwood's Magazine (periodical), 31–32, 39, 285n40
Blagsden, Isa, 113
Bly, Nellie (Elizabeth Cochraine Seaman), 199, 210, 253
Boggs, Colleen Glenney, 242
Bonaparte, Pauline, 56, *57*
Bonner, Sherwood (Katherine McDowell), 131, 135–38, 142, 275n12
Bosio, Enrico, 183–84, 282–83n67
Boston Daily Advertiser (newspaper): Brewster and, 3–4, 6–7, 39, 60, 62, 118, 195–96, 209, 285n40; Goddard and, 60; readership of, 209
Boston Sunday Times (newspaper), 136, 275n12
Botta, Anne Lynch, 102, 243
Botta, Vincenzo, 102, 155, 175–76, 245
Boudinot, Harriet Gold, 182, 266n61
Boyd, Anne E., 265n40
Brewer, Gardner, 238
Brewster, Anne Hampton: Accademia dei Lincei and, 130; Accademia dell'Arcadia and, 95–96, 124, *125*, 126–27, 130; American exceptionalism and, 8, 13–15, 130; backstory of, 38–40; Circolo Dante and, 129, 130, 178; Davidson and, 136–41, 149–50, 198–99, 214, 215–16, 226–27; death and grave of, 253; fictional "foreign correspondents" and, 48–50; Fuller and, 11–12, 211; E. B. Gould and, 85, 162; Harnisch and, 64, 77–78,

100, 107, 214, 216; Lanciani and, 63, 108, 196–99, 202, 206, 214, 222; language skills and, 95–96, 97–98, 196–97, 208; lodging and household management and, 59–60, 77–78, 98, 99–100, 107, 197, 202–3, 252; Nardi and, 3–4, 5, 196, 202, 203–8, 214; political views of, 5; portraits of, 50–51, 54–57, *56*; on private collections, 130; "For Queen Anne" (Moulton) and, 104, 108, 115–18, *116*; Read family and, 3, 59, 99–100, 199–201, 202–3; readings and library of, 8–10, 40, 145, 217–18, 252–53; receptions and, 2–4, 101–3, 104–6, 107–9, 135–36, 140, 206–8, 233–34; relationships with women, 78, 213–25; as reporter and correspondent, 2–4, 59–64, 70, 142–43, 171–72, 195–99, 200–13, 226–27; Roman Catholicism and, 5, 60–64, 87, 138–42, 145–46, 147–53, 209–10; Roman Question and, 60–64, 70; Tincker and, 48–50, 84–85, 146, 196, 216; translation and, 13; as translator, 197–98; travels, 76–78, 199–203; utopianism and, 12–15, 131, 135–42

Brewster, Anne Hampton—journals: on faith and religion, 148–53; on lodging and household management, 98, 100; on Nardi, 203–8; on receptions, 2–4, 107; on relationships, 199; on relationships with women, 14, 78, 215, 216, 217–24; on Roman Question, 59–64; on traveling, 76, 141; on work as correspondent, 195–96, 213; on young Americans in Italy, 85–88

Brewster, Anne Hampton—private correspondence: T. Davidson, 14, 84–85, 138–41, 142–43, 198–99, 214, 226–27; R. Lanciani, 196–97; Villari, 123

Brewster, Anne Hampton—writings: *Compensation; or, Always a Future*, 40; *Philadelphia Evening Bulletin* letters and, 142–43, 210–13; *Spirit Sculpture*, 38, 141; *St. Martin's Summer*, 40, 76–77, 147–49, 200

Brewster, Benjamin (AHB's brother), 14, 39–40, 86, 140, 150–52, 277n20

Brewster, Francis Enoch (AHB's father), 14

Brinkerhof, Jacob, 282n49

Bristed, Grace, 78, 214–15

Brook Farm, 11, 136

Browning, Robert, 31–32, 59, 80

Brownson, Orestes, 102, 143

Bruno, Giordano, 138

Bryant, William Cullen, 175–76

Buffa, Giovanni Paolo, 189, 190–91

Bull, Mrs., 238

Burlington Weekly Free Press (newspaper), 124

Burr, Aaron, 204

Butler, Alban, 140

By the Tiber (Tincker), 48–50, 83–84, 196

Byron, Lady, 122

Caetani, Michelangelo, 129–30, 178, 216

Caffarel, Milca, 186

Caffarel, Pier Paolo, 186

Calhoun, John C., 30, 216

Cambridge Tribune (newspaper), 277n1

Campbell, Mr., 173

Canori, Guglielmo, 126

Canova, Antonio, 56, 63

Capel, Thomas John, 61–62, 108, 152–53

Carson, Caroline: associations and, 129; Brewster and, 77, 136, 216; on receptions, 102–3, 105–6, 107; on Strong, 77
Casa Guidi Windows (Barrett Browning), 31–32, 154
Casa per Orfane (Florence), 33, 65, 229, 230, 237–40, 242–43
Cataldi, Monsignor, 142–43
Channing, William Ellery, 288n42
Channing, William Henry, 79
Chatard, Silas, 150
Cheever, John, 144
Cheney, Ednah D., 277n1
child labor, 31–32
Childs, George W., 2–4, 40, 204, 205–8, 285n40
The Christian Examiner (periodical), 288n42
Christian Training School for Young Men, 187
Christian Work in Rome (1873 report), 187
Church, Mrs., 202
Church Among the Soldiers, 187
The Churchman (newspaper), 37
Ciccolini, Stefano, 126, 127
Cincinnati Commercial (newspaper), 62, 209, 213
Circolo Dante, 129–30, 178
The Cities and Cemeteries of Etruria (Dennis), 170–71
Civil War. *See* American Civil War
Clarence (Sedgwick), 56
Clark, Emily, 76
Clarke, Charles Cowden, 121
Clarke, James Freeman, 79
Clarke, Mary Cowden, 121, 233
Clay, Henry, 30
Cobbe, Frances Power, 16
Cohen, Mathew C., 23
Cohen, Michael C., 117
Commercial (Hartford newspaper), 37
Compensation; or, Always a Future (Brewster), 40
Congregational (newspaper), 190
Constantinople, 31
Conti, Angelo, 96
Corinne (Staël), 8–9, 14, 73, 102, 104, 276n46
Corsani, Madame, 230
Corson, J. R., 222
Costa, Giovanni, 224
Crane, Abiathar (CCM's brother), 231
Crane, Alexander B. ("Alick") (CCM's nephew): Civil War and, 68; death and grave of, 252; marriage to Cornelia Mitchell, 5; C. C. Marsh and, 231–32, 238, 249, 250, 251, 287n10; portraits of, 52, *53*
Crane, Caroline Emma ("Lina") (CCM's great-niece), 52, *54*
Crane, Caroline Marsh ("Carrie") (CCM's niece): death of, 232, 237; C. C. Marsh and, 105, 231, 238–39, 246, 287n10
Crane, Elinor ("Ellen") (CCM's niece): death of, 232; Gigliucci and, 88, 112, 232–34, *233*; E. B. Gould and, 101, 111–14; C. C. Marsh and, 68–69, 88, 231, 235, 237
Crane, Elizabeth Green (CCM's niece), 252
Crane, Helen (CCM's niece), 231–32, 235
Crane, Lucy (later Wislizenus) (CCM's sister), 30, 51, *51*, 68, 146, 287n10
Crane, Mary (CCM's niece), 230, 287n10
Crane, Milton (CCM's nephew), 232
Crane, Mrs. E. (CCM's sister-in-law), 240, 243
Crane, Silas (CCM's brother), 29
Crawford, Annie, 238

Crawford, Francis Marion, 143
Crawford, Thomas, 202
Crosby, Howard, 175–76, 253
Cross, John Walter, 252
"The Cry of the Children" (Barrett Browning), 31–32, 154, 178
Cushman, Charles Augustus, 202
Cushman, Charlotte, 14, 39, 215, 218

Dabakis, Melissa, 265n40
Daily Alta California (newspaper), 210. See also *Alta California* (periodical)
Daily Graphic (newspaper), 118, 195–96
Daisy Miller (James), 73–74, 80–81, 91, 93, 200
Dalgas, Carolina, 186, 189, 282–83n67
Daniel Deronda (Eliot), 217–18
Dante Alighieri, 138
Davidson, Thomas: Accademia dell'Arcadia and, 127; Brewster and, 14, 84–85, 136–41, 142–43, 149–50, 198–99, 214, 215–16, 226–27; Roman Catholicism and, 138–41; utopianism and, 138–41
Davis, Rebecca Harding, 167
De Sanctis, Francesco, 42
Deffand, Mme. du, 278n21
Dennis, George, 170–71
Desanctis, Martha Sommerville, 189
Dickinson, Emily, 8–9
Ditz, Toby, 175
Dodge, Mary Abigail, 207
Doré, Gustave, 145
dreams and dream interpretation, 147–48, 149–50
Drew, Mary Gladstone, 108

Edelstein, Sari, 50, 210
Edie, Gail, 285n40
Edmunds, George F. (CCM's nephew), 46, 238–39
Edmunds, Mary (CCM's niece), 103, 231
education: Accademia dell'Arcadia and, 124–28, *125*; Fuà Fusinato and, 162, 177, 178; fundraising and, 44–45, 236–41; Mount Holyoke Female Seminary and, 162, 178, 181–82; Roman Catholic Church and, 144–45; Sunday schools and, 121, 162–63; women and, 229–30, 237–38, 243. *See also* Italo-American Schools (Rome)
Edwards, Amelia, 14, 78, 216, 219–21, 222–23, 224–25, *226*
Eliot, George, 217–18, 252–53
Ellis, Enrichetta, 129
Ellis, Mary, 178
Elmer, Charles, 108
Elsden, Annamaria Formichella, 265n43
Emerson, Ralph Waldo: Brewster and, 49, 199, 222, 225; Fuller and, 10–11, 15, 19, 79; Radical Club and, 137–38; salon culture and, 102
Emerson, Ralph Waldo—works: "The American Scholar," 10; "Fate," 222; "Give All to Love," 222; "Self-Reliance," 10, 222
"Emilie Wyndham" (Marsh-Caldwell), 243
English and American Christian Association, 187
English Archaeological Society, 121
eutopia, 13
Evangelist (periodical), 190, 192
The Evening Post (newspaper), 37
exemplary ownership, 129–30

Fahs, Alice, 196
Les familles et la société en France avant la révolution (Ribbe), 240–41
Faraday, Michael, 154

"Fate" (Emerson), 222
Fellenberg, Philipp Emanuel von, 122
female education, 229–30, 237–38, 243
female reporters and correspondents: L. M. Alcott as, 50, 62, 199, 210; Brewster as, 2–4, 59–64, 70, 142–43, 171–72, 195–99, 200–13, 226–27; Civil War and, 50, 62, 210; fictional accounts of, 48–50; Fuller as, 10–12, 15–16, 20–21, 31, 37, 63, 73–74, 142, 171–72, 199, 210; gender boundaries and, 198–99, 207; women abroad as, 196
Fénelon, François, 240–41, 243–44
Ferretti, Salvatore: Casa per Orfane (orphanage and school) and, 33, 65, 229, 230, 237–40, 242–43; Free Church and, 5, 182; E. B. Gould and, 184; C. C. Marsh and, 33, 237–40, 242–43
Field, Cyrus West, 238
Field, Dudley, 238
Field, Jeannie, 238
Fields, Annie Adams, 108, 215
Fields, Kate, 49
Filippini, Ernesto, 187
Florence Evangelical School, 42–44
"For Queen Anne" (Moulton), 104, 108, 115–18, *116*, 136, 259–60
Forbes, Miss, 238
Forster, E. M., 99
Fortis, Leone, 126
Fortnightly Review (periodical), 139
Fourier, Charles, 122
France, 204–5
Franco, Dr., 85
Franklin, Benjamin, 50
Free Church, 5, 65, 182
French (language): Brewster and, 95, 96, 196–97; E. B. Gould and, 96–97; C. C. Marsh and, 97, 240–41
friendship elegies, 118
Froebel, Friedrich, 177
"The Front Yard" (Woolson), 83, 165
Froude, James Anthony, 240–41
Fruitlands, 135, 136
"Frustra Laboravi!" (C. C. Marsh), 247–50
Fuà Fusinato, Erminia, 162, 177, 178
Fuller, Margaret: Brewster and, 11–12, 211; Emerson and, 10–11, 15, 19, 79; gender boundaries and, 14, 19; Ossoli and, 15–16, 79; Parker and, 144; political views of, 79, 182; Radical Club and, 137–38; receptions and, 102; as reporter and correspondent, 10–12, 15–16, 20–21, 31, 37, 63, 73–74, 142, 171–72, 199, 210; Spring family and, 76, 79–80; on translation, 242; travels, 8–9, 38
Fuller, Margaret—works: "Autobiographical Romance," 19; *Memoirs*, 73–74, 79
fundraising, 44–45, 236–41

Gadda, Giuseppe, 239
Gadda, Luisa, 239
Gaggiotti Richards, Emma, 221
Galvazzi, Alessandro, 65
Garfield, James, 143
Garibaldi, Giuseppe, 21, 148, 177–78
Garnieri, Giovanni (Jean Garnier), 183–84, 186, 187, 188
Gaul, Theresa Strouth, 182, 266n61
Gay, Olympe, 186
Geary, John W., 151
Geburt und Wiedergeburt (Hurter), 148
Gemme, Paola, 143–44, 209
German (language), 96–97
Il gesuita moderno (Gioberti), 145
gift exchanges, 113–14, 135–37, 198
Gigliucci, Giovan Battista, 88, 233–34

Gigliucci, Giovanni, 233–34
Gigliucci, Mario, 88, 232–35, *233*
Gigliucci, Porzia, 233–34
Gigliucci, Valeria, 233–34
Gigliucci family, 108, 112
Gilman, Charlotte Perkins, 84
Gioberti, Vincenzo, 145
"Give All to Love" (Emerson), 222
Goddard, Delano A., 60
Goethe, Johann Wolfgang von, 8–9
Gotelli family, 178
gothic novels, 168
Gould, Emily Bliss: American and Foreign Christian Union and, 41–44, 144, 159, 161; American exceptionalism and, 8, 13–15, 130, 141, 174, 181–82; backstory of, 33–38; Brewster and, 60, 85; death, memorial service, and grave of, 253, *254–55*; Fuller and, 11–12; health of, 33, 69, 162, 168; Italian Young Men's Christian Association and, 129; Italo-American Schools and, 4–5, 6, 106–7, 111, 124, 128, 161, 188–93. See also *In Memoriam* (Trollope et al.); language skills and, 96–98; lodging and household management and, 101, 229; marriage to James, 7, 14, 29, 65, 111–14, 253; G. P. Marsh and, 111–14, 161–62, 183–86; *In Memoriam* (Trollope et al.) and, 75–76, 119–24, 193; Peabody and, 135–36; portraits of, 50–51, 52–54, *55*, 57, 163, 179–81; readings, 8–9; receptions and, 101–3, 106–7, 108–9; Roman Catholicism and, 4–5, 36, 65–68, 165–70, 178–79; Roman Question and, 65–68, 70; utopianism and, 12–15, 131, 135–36, 141, 156–59. See also *A Life Worth Living* (Bacon)
Gould, Emily Bliss—journals, 34, 70
Gould, Emily Bliss—private correspondence: style of, 182; C. C. Marsh, 66–68; G. P. Marsh, 67–68, 96–97, 101, 106, 111–14, 161–62, 183–86, 193, 235; M. Prochet, 161–62, 183–84, 186; Dr. Thompson, 41–44, 161
Gould, Emily Bliss—writings: documents of the Italo-American Schools, 161, 174–82, *180*, 186–87; "Gossip Abroad" column in *Overland Monthly*, 1–2, 36–37, 66–67, 161, 171–74; "Little Caroline," 34, 36, 157–58, 159, 161, 181; sketches in *Hours at Home*, 36, 161, 164–71, 174, 250
Gould, James: marriage to Emily, 7, 14, 29, 65, 111–14, 253; Roman Catholic Church and, 4
Gradi, Temistocle, 245–46
Graham, Josephine, 239
Graham's American Monthly Magazine (periodical), 38
Grant, Ulysses, 143
Grant, Ulysses S., 100
Greeley, Horace, 10, 15–16
Greenough, Richard S., 127
Greenwood, Grace (Sara Jane Lippincott): *The Little Pilgrim* and, 267n19, 280n74; receptions and, 102; as reporter and correspondent, 37, 199, 207
Greenwood, Grace (Sara Jane Lippincott)—works: *Haps and Mishaps of a Tour in Europe*, 211; *Stories and Sights of France and Italy*, 73–74
Guida del Palatino (Lanciani), 197–98

Hacker, Ludwig, 121
Haight, Mrs. J., 229

Hall, Mrs. S. C., 267n19
The Hallig, or the Sheepfold in the Waters (Biernatzki), 32, 97
Hamilton, Mrs., 230
Handley, Mr., 108
Haps and Mishaps of a Tour in Europe (Greenwood), 211
Hare, Augustus John Cuthbert, 62
Harnisch, Albert, 64, 77–78, 100, 107, 214, 216
Harper, James, 145
Harper's Magazine (periodical), 40, 155
Harper's Weekly (periodical), 148
Harris, Susan K., 103, 108–9, 130, 182, 266n61
Harte, Bret, 1, 36–37, 171–74
Hawthorne, Nathaniel: Brewster and, 211; Brook Farm and, 11; on daughter Una, 78–79, 81–82; on filth and *mal aria*, 92; on Fuller, 80; on Powers, 97–98; Roman Catholicism and, 146; in Rome, 59; on salon culture and receptions, 102, 105
Hawthorne, Nathaniel—works: *The Marble Faun*, 4, 92, 105, 116–17, 179; "Rappaccini's Daughter," 8–9; *The Scarlet Letter*, 146
Hawthorne, Rose, 85
Hawthorne, Sophia, 59, 85
Hawthorne, Una, 78–79, 81–82, 85–86
Hayes, Matilda, 218
Hayes, Rutherford B., 143
Healy, Mary, 223
Hecker, Isaac Thomas, 61
Heeren, A. H. L., 9
Heine, Heinrich, 40
Hemans, Charles Isidore, 121, 142, 211–13, 214
Hemans, Felicia, 121, 211
Hemenway, Abby Maria, 247
Henderson, Desirée, 118, 119
Hicks, Mrs., 150–51, 152
Higginson, T. W., 277n1
History of Europe (Alison), 9
Hooker, James Clinton, 150
Hopedale, 136
Horace, 97, 247
Hosmer, Harriet: Brewster and, 62, 64, 78, 206, 216–18, 225; gender boundaries and, 14, 17; Hawthorne on, 79; James on, 80–81; lodging and household management and, 99; political views of, 16
Hospital Sketches (Alcott), 210
Hours at Home (magazine), 36, 161, 164–71, 174, 250
Howe, Julia Ward, 135–36, 137, 226, 238
Howell, Mary, 218–19
Howitt, Anna, 121
Howitt, Mary, 75, 119, 120–21, 223, 243, 267n19
Howitt, William, 121–23
Hughes, John Joseph, 61
Humboldt, Alexander von, 154
humility, 117–18
Hurter, Friedrich, 148

Illustrated London News (periodical), 148
Immaculate Conception, 60–61, 66–67
In Memoriam (Trollope et al.), 75–76, 119–24, 193. *See also* "Miss Jones" (Aunt Friendly)
"An Incident in Rome" (Sedgwick), 82–83
Innocents Abroad (Twain), 1, 211
Istituto Gould (Florence), 6
Italian (language): Brewster and, 95–96, 208; C. C. Marsh and, 245–46
Italian News (newspaper), 128
"Italian Scenery" (Longfellow), 8–9

"Italian Tale" (C. C. Marsh), 155–56
Italian Unification, 20–21, 34–36. *See also* Roman Question
Italian Young Men's Christian Association, 129, 187
L'Italie (newspaper), 178, 213
Italo-American Schools (Rome): documents of, 161, 174–82, *180*, 186–87; E. B. Gould and, 4–5, 6, 106–7, 111, 124, 128, 161, 188–93; *Il Popolo romano* on, 124, 128; Prochet and, 188–93. See also *In Memoriam* (Trollope et al.)

Jackson, Helen Hunt, 37, 78, 197, 214
Jackson, Leon, 113–14, 198
James, Henry, 11, 20, 143
James, Henry—works: *Daisy Miller*, 73–74, 80–81, 91, 93, 200; *Portrait of a Lady*, 49–50, 80–81; *William Wetmore Story and His Friends*, 121
Jameson, Anna, 146–47
Januarius, St., 147–49
Jennison, Lucy White, 126–27
Jesuits (Society of Jesus), 4–5, 144–46, 148, 152
John Murray (publishing house), 198
Jordan, Miss, 113
Juárez, Benito, 204–5
Le Juif errant (Sue), 145

Kaplan, Amy, 264n39
Keats, John, 59
Kenrick, Francis Patrick, 61
Kenrick, Peter, 146, 152
Kertzer, David, 3
Kingdom of Italy, 20–21. *See also* Roman Question
Kossuth, Louis, 31

Ladies' Guide to True Politeness (Leslie), 114
Lady Byron Vindicated (Stowe), 122
Lanciani, Rodolfo: archaeological excavations and, 196–97, 198; Brewster and, 14, 63, 64, 96, 108, 153, 196–99, 202, 205, 214, 222
Lander, Louisa, 14, 79, 85
Lane, Charles, 136
language skills: Brewster and, 95–96, 97–98, 196–97, 208; E. B. Gould and, 96–98; C. C. Marsh and, 97–98; as tool for women abroad, 95–96. *See also* translation; *specific languages*
"Lars" (Taylor), 243
Latin (language), 97
La legende du Juif errant (Doré), 145
Legends of the Madonna, as Represented in the Fine Arts (Jameson), 146–47
Lenox, Mrs., 158
Leslie, Eliza, 114, 186
Letters from Abroad to Kindred at Home (Sedgwick), 73–74, 82
Lewis, Edmonia, 16, 17, 148
Life Amongst the Modocs (Miller), 272n40
Life in the Iron Mills (Davis), 167
A Life Worth Living (Bacon), 52–54, *55*, 144, 193
"Life's Lesson" (C. C. Marsh), 243, 249
Limone, Augusta, 239
Linton, Eliza Lynn, 16
Lippincott, Leander K., 267n19, 280n74
Lippincott, Sara Jane. *See* Greenwood, Grace (Sara Jane Lippincott)
Lippincott's Magazine (periodical), 40, 222, 285n40
Literature and Dogma (Arnold), 156, 241–43
"Little Caroline" (Gould), 34, 36, 157–58, 159, 161, 181

The Little Pilgrim (monthly newspaper), 267n19, 280n74
Little Pilgrims (American Tract Society), 34, 157–58
The Lives of the Fathers, Martyrs, and Other Principal Saints (Butler), 140
Locke, John, 177
Lockhart, William, 139, 142–43
lodging and household management: Brewster and, 59–60, 77–78, 98, 99–100, 107, 197, 202–3, 252; E. B. Gould and, 101, 229; C. C. Marsh and, 100–1; women abroad and, 77–78, 98–101. *See also* receptions
Longfellow, Henry Wadsworth: Accademia dell'Arcadia and, 125, 126–27; Caetani and, 129–30; Circolo Dante and, 178; E. B. Gould and, 37, 173; receptions and, 1–4, *2*, 204, 207–8
Longfellow, Henry Wadsworth—works: "Italian Scenery," 8–9; "The Old Bridge at Florence," 8–9
Lowenthal, David, 155, 185, 287n10
Lunardi, Luigi, 95–96
Lutèce (Heine), 40
Lutes, Jean Marie, 49–50
Luzzi, Pietro, 173
Lynch, Dr., 61
Lyon, Mary, 162, 181–82

Macpherson, Mrs., 202
malaria, 59, 85
Manning, Henry Edward, 108, 152–53
A Manual of the History of the Political System of Europe and Its Colonies (Heeren), 9
The Marble Faun (Hawthorne), 4, 92, 105, 116–17, 179
Mario, Jessie White, 16, 182
Mariology, 155–56
Marsh, Carlo (CCM's adopted son), 236, 237
Marsh, Caroline Crane: American and Foreign Christian Union and, 144; American exceptionalism and, 8, 13–15, 130, 141, 242; Arbesser and, 115; backstory of, 29–33; death and grave of, 252; fundraising and, 44–45, 236–41; E. B. Gould and, 41–44, 66–68; health of, 30, 33, 68–69; Howe and, 135; language skills and, 97–98, 240–41, 251; library and, 44–48, *45*, 68–69, 145, 154, 230–31; lodging and household management and, 100–1; marriage to George, 14, 30, 44–48, 68, 69, 88, 111–14; political and religious views of, 5, 153–56; portraits of, 50–52, *51–53*, 57; readings, 8–9, 47, 145, 156, 240–44, 245–46; receptions and, 101–4, 106, 107, 108–9; Roman Catholicism and, 32, 33, 145–46, 242–43, 244–45; Roman Question and, 68–70; as translator, 13, 32, 97, 241, 242, 244, 245–49; utopianism and, 12–15, 131, 135–36, 141; as widow in United States, 251–52; as wife and surrogate mother, 68–69, 88, 105, 229–36
Marsh, Caroline Crane—journals, 88, 235, 236, 239–41, 243–46, 248–49
Marsh, Caroline Crane—private correspondence: E. Barrett Browning, 154; A. B. Crane, 68, 231–32, 250; E. B. Gould and, 69; G. P. Marsh, 44–48, 88, 231, 234, 235, 238; L. Wislizenus, 68, 146
Marsh, Caroline Crane—writings: "To ____ ____.," 32–33, 257–58; "Frustra Laboravi," 247–50; "Italian Tale," 155–56; "Life's Lesson," 243,

249; *The Wolfe of the Knoll, and other Poems*, 32–33, 97, 257–58
Marsh, Charles (CCM's brother-in-law), 46
Marsh, George Ozias (CCM's stepson), 30, 231, 232, 248
Marsh, George Perkins (CCM's husband): American newspapers and, 210; Arbesser and, 114–15; biography of, 230, 252–53; clubs and, 129; death and grave of, 33, 250, 252; diplomatic career of, 15, 29, 30, 33, 183, 204; Fuller and, 11–12; E. B. Gould and, 41–44, 67–68, 96–97, 101, 106, 109, 111–14, 161–62, 183–86, 193, 235; Hosmer and, 99; as lecturer, 32; lodging and household management and, 100–1; marriage to Caroline, 14, 30, 44–48, 68, 69, 88, 111–14; as member of Congress, 30; *In Memoriam* (Trollope et al.) and, 121; political and religious views of, 5, 154–55, 156; portraits of, *45*, 51, *51*; readings, 247; Roman Catholicism and, 155; on translation and languages, 97, 241–42; Villari and, 123
Marsh, Mrs. Lyndon, 239
Marsh-Caldwell, Anne, 243
Martineau, James, 155
Masonry, 182, 183
Maturin, Charles, 211
Maximilian of Hapsburg, 204–5
Mazzini, Giuseppe, 23, 63, 80, 279n47
McClellan, Mary Marcy, 49
McCloskey, John, 124–25, 127, 152
McDowell, Katherine (Sherwood Bonner), 131, 135–38, 142, 275n12
McGreevy, William, 143–44, 145
McNeiring, Father, 61
McQuaid, Bernard John, 61, 62, 152
Meille, Pastor, 189–90
Melmoth the Wanderer (Maturin), 211
Melville, Herman, 253
Memoirs (Fuller), 73–74, 79
Meurer, Dr., 247
Mexico, 204–5
Middlemarch (Eliot), 252–53
Miller, Joaquin, 87, 105–6
The Minister's Wooing (Stowe), 146
miracles, 147–49
"Miss Grief" (Woolson), 83
"Miss Jones" (Aunt Friendly), 70, 74–76, 88–93, 95, 98, 118–19
Mitchell, John W., 68
Mitchell, Laura Cornelia (later Crane) (CCM's niece-in-law), 5, 77, 159, 250, 288n57
Mitchell, Maria, 17–18
Mitchell, Martha, 29–30
Monroe Doctrine, 204
Il montanino toscano volontario alla guerra della indipendenza italiana del 1859 (Tigri), 288n49
Monti, Giuseppe, 173
Moore, Mrs., 108
More, Thomas, 13
Morelli, Maria Maddalena, 126
Mortara, Edgardo, 4, 179
Mortara, Elèna, 23
Moulton, Louise Chandler: Bonner and, 131, 136, 275n12, 277n1; Brewster and, 78, 104, 108, 215; receptions and, 105
Moulton, Louise Chandler—works: "For Queen Anne," 104, 108, 115–18, *116*, 136, 259–60
Mount Holyoke Female Seminary, 162, 178, 181–82
Mozier, Joseph, 3, 80
Murray, John Courtney, 143

Napoleon Bonaparte, 20, 67
Napoleon III, 204–5
Nardi, Ernesto Francesco, 3–4, 5, 196, 202, 203–8, 214
Nast, Thomas, 148
The Nation (periodical), 81, 155, 210
Neumann, John, 61
New York Evening Post (newspaper), 251, 285n40
New York Herald (newspaper), 198, 211
New York World (newspaper), 118, 195–96, 210, 285n40
Newark Courier (newspaper), 208
Newman, Cardinal, 108
Newton, Isaac, 154
New-York Tribune (newspaper): Fuller and, 10–11, 15–16, 20–21, 31, 73–74, 142, 210; as liberal newspaper, 210; Twain and, 211
Norton, Caroline, 86
Norton, Charles Eliot, 81–82, 143, 210
Norton, Jane, 3
Norton, Susan Sedgwick, 81–82
Notes of Study and Travel in Italy (Norton), 81–82
Novello, Clara, 88, 233–34, 235
La nuova Roma (newspaper), 126

obituary literature, 119. See also *In Memoriam* (Trollope et al.)
Observer (newspaper), 37, 190
O'Connor, Michael, 61
Odo, Russell, 9
Official Gazette (newspaper), 213
"The Old Bridge at Florence" (Longfellow), 8–9
On Germany (Staël), 97
L'Opinione (newspaper), 213
Osservatore Romano (newspaper), 107
Ossoli, Angelo, 80
Ossoli, Giovanni, 15–16, 63, 79
Ottoman Empire, 29, 31
Overland Monthly (periodical), 1–2, 36–37, 66–67, 161, 171–74
Owen, Robert Dale, 38, 76, 122, 200

Paine, Mrs., 238
papal infallibility. See *Syllabus of Errors* (1864)
Papal States, 20–21
Parker, Theodore, 144
Peabody, Elizabeth Palmer: Brewster and, 215; education and, 177; Fuller and, 11; E. B. Gould and, 162; on U. Hawthorne, 85–86; Radical Club and, 135–36, 137
Peabody, Sophia, 8–9
Peacock, Gibson, 60. See also *Philadelphia Evening Bulletin* (newspaper)
Pestalozzi, Johann Heinrich, 122
Peterson's (periodical), 40
Philadelphia Evening Bulletin (newspaper): Brewster and, 3–4, 6–7, 11, 39, 59–60, 118, 142–43, 195–96, 209, 210–13, 285n40; readership of, 142, 209
Philadelphia Telegraph (periodical), 285n40
"Philosophy of Catholicism" (Froude), 240–41
Pianciani, Luigi, 128
Il Piemonte 1850–52 (Gioberti), 145
Pius IX, Pope, 20–21, 64, 203. *See also* Roman Question; *Syllabus of Errors* (1864)
Poe, Edgar Allan, 102
Poets and Poetry of Vermont (Hemenway), 247
Pons, Giovanni Pietro, 186–87

Il popolo romano (newspaper), 118, 124–28
Porterfield, Amanda, 181–82
Portrait of a Lady (James), 49–50, 80–81
posthumous tribute volumes, 119. See also *In Memoriam* (Trollope et al.)
poverty, 30–31, 36, 165–70, 249
Powers, Hiram, 31–32, 97–98
Preston, Harriet Waters, 126–27, 215–16
Pritchard, Elizabeth A., 265n43
Prochet, Matteo, 161–62, 183–84, 186–87, 188–93
propriety, 176
Public Ledger (Memphis newspaper), 285n40
Public Ledger (Philadelphia newspaper), 3, 40, 205

Racconti popolari (Gradi), 245–46
Racconti popolari (Thouar), 288n49
Radical Club, 135–38
"The Radical Club" (Bonner), 131, 135–38, 142
Rambaldoni, Vittorino, 123
"Rappaccini's Daughter" (Hawthorne), 8–9
Ravenscliffe (Marsh-Caldwell), 243
Read, Hattie, 59
Read, Thomas Buchanan: Brewster and, 3, 59, 86, 99–100, 199–201, 202–3; receptions and, 1, *2*; Roman Question and, 62
receptions: Brewster and, 2–4, 101–3, 104–6, 107–9, 135–36, 140, 206–8, 233–34; E. B. Gould and, 101–3, 106–7, 108–9; Longfellow and, 1–4, *2*, 204, 207–8; C. C. Marsh and, 101–4, 106, 107, 108–9
Reggio, Mrs., 108
Religion and Dogma (Arnold), 5
Reminiscences (Howe), 137
Reminiscenze d'un uomo inutile ovvero "Reminiscenze inutili d'un uomo più inutile" (Gigliucci), 235
Remond, Sarah Parker, 16
Reni, Guido, 100–1
Riall, Lucy, 123
Ribbe, Charles de, 240–41
Ribetti, Giovanni, 183–84, 186, 188–90
Rioux, Anne E. Boyd. *See* Boyd, Anne E.
Ripley, George, 136
Risorgimento, 20–21
Ritchie, A. H., 54, *55*
Robbins, Sarah, 162, 163, 181
Roman Advertiser (newspaper), 121
Roman Catholic Church: American Civil War and, 21; Brewster and, 5, 60–64, 87, 138–42, 145–46, 147–53, 209–10; education and, 144–45; E. B. Gould and, 4–5, 36, 65–68, 165–70, 178–79; J. Gould and, 4; C. C. Marsh and, 32, 33, 145–46, 242–43, 244–45; G. P. Marsh and, 155; US views of, 4–5, 143–47. *See also* Nardi, Ernesto Francesco; Pius IX, Pope; Roman Question; *Syllabus of Errors* (1864)
Roman fever (malaria), 59
Roman Question: overview of, 5; Brewster and, 60–64, 70; E. B. Gould and, 65–68, 70; C. C. Marsh and, 68–70; Nardi and, 3–4; Radical Club and, 137; US views of, 21–22
Roman Republic, 20–21
Rome: archaeological excavations in, 92, 196–97, 198; as capital of Kingdom of Italy, 92; receptions in, 1–4. *See also* Roman Question

Rosmini Serbati, Antonio, 138–39, 140
Ross, Janet, 237
Rossetti, Dante Gabriel, 64
Rossi, Giovanni Battista de, 153
Rota (periodical), 203
Rousseau, Jean-Jacques, 138
Rush, Benjamin, 50
The Rutland Daily Globe (newspaper), 124

Saffi, Aurelio, 23, 279n47
Saints and Miracles (anon.), 155
Salenius, Sirpa, 17
Salis-Schwabe, Julie, 122
salon culture, 101–2. *See also* receptions
Salviato, Duchess, 108
San Francisco Chronicle (newspaper), 104–5
Sánchez-Eppler, Karen, 162–63, 181
Sand, George (Amantine Lucile Aurore Dudevant), 96, 102
Sansay, Leonora, 56
Sargent, Mary Elizabeth, 137
The Scarlet Letter (Hawthorne), 146
Schuyler, Eugene, 127, 139
Scifoni, Anatolia, 150
Seaman, Elizabeth Cochraine (Nellie Bly), 199, 210, 253
séances, 147–48, 149, 154
Sears, Edmund, 155
Secret History (Sansay), 56
Sedgwick, Catharine Maria, 17, 37, 76, 130
Sedgwick, Catharine Maria—works: *Clarence*, 56; "An Incident in Rome," 82–83; *Letters from Abroad to Kindred at Home*, 73–74, 82
Séjour, Victor, 23
"Self-Reliance" (Emerson), 10, 222
Seward, Olivia Rigby, 126–27
Shakerism Unveiled (Anon.), 277n16
Shakespeare, William, 204
Shelley, Mary Wollstonecraft, 59
Shelley, Percy Bysshe, 59
Shepard, Ada, 85
Sherwood, James M., 164
Shrubb, Mr., 128
Siena, 252
Signor Monaldini's Niece (Tincker), 268n16
Sismondi, J.-C.-L. Simonde de, 82
Sketches and Reminiscences (Sargent), 137
slavery, 31, 35–36, 144–45
Smith, Joseph, 87
social dreaming. *See* utopianism (social dreaming)
The Social Lives of Poems in Nineteenth-Century America (Cohen), 23
Società degli Acquarellisti, 129
Society for the Promotion of Catholic Interests, 179
Songs of the Sierras (Miller), 272n40
Soper, Stephen, 128, 130
Spalding, Martin John, 61–62
Spirit Sculpture (Brewster), 38, 141
Spring family, 76, 79–80
St. Louis Globe-Democrat (newspaper), 285n40
St. Martin's Summer (Brewster), 40, 76–77, 147–49, 200
St. Simon, Henri de, 122
Staël, Germaine de, 16, 97, 102, 242
Staël, Germaine de, works: *Corinne*, 8–9, 14, 73, 102, 104, 276n46; *On Germany*, 97
Stanton, Elizabeth Cady, 253
Stebbins, Emma, 218, 220
Stoddard, Charles Warren, 104–5, 108, 116, 117, 140
Stoddard, Elizabeth, 37, 210
Stories and Sights of France and Italy (Greenwood), 73–74

Story, William Wetmore, 86, 121, 216, 225
Story family, 102, 216
Stowe, Harriet Beecher, 17, 37, 122, 146–47
Strong, Eleanor Fearing, 77
Sue, Eugène, 145
Sunday schools, 121, 162–63
Suscipj, Lorenzo, 54, *55*
Sutcliffe, Marcella, 23
Swedish (language), 97
Swisshelm, Jane Gray, 207
Syllabus of Errors (1864), 3–4, 21, 155, 207–8

Taussig, Dr., 140–41
Taylor, Bayard, 243
Telemachus (Fénelon), 243–44
Terry, Louisa Ward, 202
Terry family, 102, 216
Thayer, Dr., 238
Thomas Aquinas, St., 138
Thompson, Dr., 41–44, 161
Thouar, Pietro, 288n49
Tigri, Giuseppe, 288n49
Tincker, Mary Agnes: Brewster and, 48–50, 84–85, 196, 216, 221–22; receptions and, 105; Roman Catholicism and, 146. See also *By the Tiber* (Tincker)
"To ____ ____." (C. C. Marsh), 32–33, 257–58
Tognetti, Gaetano, 173
Topografia di Roma antica (Lanciani), 197
Transcendentalism, 135–36
translation: Brewster and, 13, 197–98; Fuller on, 242; C. C. Marsh and, 13, 32, 97, 241, 242, 244, 245–49; G. P. Marsh on, 241–42; Staël on, 97, 242
"Translation" (G. Marsh), 241–42
"A Transplanted Boy" (Woolson), 83, 98–99
trasformismo, 23–24
travel diaries, 8. *See also specific authors*
Trollope, Theodosia, 121
Trollope, Thomas Adolphus, 75–76, 105, 119–24, 193
Tuckerman, Henry Theodore, 238
Turkish (language), 31
Twain, Mark, 1, 11, 20, 211
Twelfth Night (Shakespeare), 204
Tyndall, John, 279n66

Ultramontanism, 143
Underwood, Cornelia, 103, 104
Univers (periodical), 148
Upton, Sara Carr, 126–27
Utopia (More), 13
utopianism (social dreaming): concept of, 13, 22; American exceptionalism and, 13, 22; Bonner's satire of, 131, 135–38, 142; Brewster and, 12–15, 131, 135–42; Davidson and, 138–41; E. B. Gould and, 12–15, 131, 135–36, 141, 156–59; C. C. Marsh and, 12–15, 131, 135–36, 141

Vance, William, 143
Vannuccini, Dina, 229–30
Vannuccini, Luigi, 229–30
Venus Victrix (Canova), 56, *57*
Vernon, Anna, 78, 214–15
Vernon, Laura, 250, 287n10
Veuillot, Louis, 148
Victor Emmanuel II, 21, 34, 101
Villari, Pasquale, 121, 123
Vittorino Rambaldoni da Feltre, 123
La voce della verità (periodical), 203

Waldensian Church: education and, 182; E. B. Gould and, 42–44, 65, 158, 176, 253; C. C. Marsh and,

Waldensian Church *(continued)* 244–45. *See also* Ferretti, Salvatore; Prochet, Matteo
Wales, Mr. & Mrs., 238
Webster, Daniel, 30
Wheeler, L. T., 239
Wheelwright, Edward, 127
Whelan, Mrs., 61
Whitaker, Natalie, 285n40
Whitman, Walt, 35
Whitmore, William, 285n40
Wilhelm Meisters Wanderjahre (Goethe), 8–9
William Wetmore Story and His Friends (James), 121
Wislizenus, Lucy Crane (CCM's sister), 30, 51, *51*, 68, 146, 287n10
The Wolfe of the Knoll, and other Poems (C. C. Marsh), 32–33, 97, 257–58
women: education and, 229–30, 237–38, 243; Fuller on, 10–11; as poets, 247; propriety and, 176
women abroad: depictions of, 73–74, 78–88. See also *Daisy Miller* (James); "Miss Jones" (Aunt Friendly); language skills and, 95–96. *See also specific languages*; lodging and household management and, 77–78, 98–101; myths and realities of independence and, 76–78; types of travelers, 7–12. *See also* female reporters and correspondents; receptions
Women's Rest Tour Association, 76
women's rights, 50, 226
Woolf, Virginia, 99
Woolson, Clara, 76
Woolson, Constance Fenimore: Hawthorne and, 82; lodging and household management and, 98–99; as reporter and correspondent, 49; travels, 17, 19, 37, 76
Woolson, Constance Fenimore—works: "The Front Yard," 83, 165; "Miss Grief," 83; "A Transplanted Boy," 83, 98–99
Wordsworth, William, 83
Wurts, Martha P., 237–38

"The Yellow Wallpaper" (Gilman), 84

www.ingramcontent.com/pod-product-compliance
Lightning Source LLC
LaVergne TN
LVHW050148080826
844660LV00002B/115

* 9 7 8 1 4 3 8 4 8 8 4 3 1 *